THE THINGS WE CARRY

THE THINGS WE CARRY

Strategies for Recognizing and Negotiating Emotional Labor in Writing Program Administration

EDITED BY
COURTNEY ADAMS WOOTEN,
JACOB BABB, KRISTI MURRAY COSTELLO,
AND KATE NAVICKAS

UTAH STATE UNIVERSITY PRESS
Logan

© 2020 by University Press of Colorado

Published by Utah State University Press
An imprint of University Press of Colorado
245 Century Circle, Suite 202
Louisville, Colorado 80027

All rights reserved

 The University Press of Colorado is a proud member of the Association of University Presses.

The University Press of Colorado is a cooperative publishing enterprise supported, in part, by Adams State University, Colorado State University, Fort Lewis College, Metropolitan State University of Denver, Regis University, University of Colorado, University of Northern Colorado, University of Wyoming, Utah State University, and Western Colorado University.

ISBN: 978-1-60732-946-6 (paperback)
ISBN: 978-1-64642-000-1 (ebook)
https://doi.org/10.7330/9781646420001

Library of Congress Cataloging-in-Publication Data

Names: Wooten, Courtney Adams, editor. | Babb, Jacob, editor. | Costello, Kristi Murray, editor. | Navickas, Kate, editor.
Title: The things we carry : strategies for recognizing and negotiating emotional labor in writing program administration / edited by Courtney Adams Wooten, Jacob Babb, Kristi Murray Costello, and Kate Navickas.
Description: Logan : Utah State University Press, [2020]. | Includes bibliographical references and index.
Identifiers: LCCN 2020023993 (print) | LCCN 2020023994 (ebook) | ISBN 9781607329466 (paperback) | ISBN 9781646420001 (ebook)
Subjects: LCSH: Writing centers—Administration. | Writing centers—Psychological aspects. | Writing centers—Social aspects. | College adminstrators—Psychology.
Classification: LCC PE1404 .T479 2020 (print) | LCC PE1404 (ebook) | DDC 808/.0420711—dc23
LC record available at https://lccn.loc.gov/2020023993
LC ebook record available at https://lccn.loc.gov/2020023994

The University Press of Colorado gratefully acknowledges the generous support of the College of Humanities and Social Sciences at George Mason University toward the publication of this book.

Cover illustration © agsandrew/Shutterstock.

CONTENTS

Foreword
  Laura R. Micciche ix

Preface xiii

Acknowledgments xvii

Introduction: Emotional Labor, Writing Studies, and Writing Program Administration
  Kristi Murray Costello and Jacob Babb 3

SECTION I: PRESERVING WORK IDENTITIES

1. Don't Worry, Be Happy: How to Flourish as a WPA
   Carrie S. Leverenz 19

2. You Lost Me at "Administrator": Vulnerability and Transformation in WPA Work at the Two-Year College
   Anthony Warnke, Kirsten Higgins, Marcie Sims, and Ian Sherman 37

3. The Emotional Labor of Becoming: Lessons from the Exiting Writing Center Director
   Kate Navickas 56

4. Educating the Faculty Writer to "Dance with Resistance": Rethinking Faculty Development as Institutional Transformation
   Janelle Adsit and Sue Doe 75

5. Unleashed Emotion: Centering Emotional Labor in Our Professional Documents
   Amy Ferdinandt Stolley 96

SECTION II: PRESERVING COMMUNITIES

6. Handling Sexual Assault Reports as a WPA
   Kim Hensley Owens 115

7. And So I Respond: The Emotional Labor of Writing Program Administrators in Crisis Response
   Kaitlin Clinnin   129

8. Shelter in Place: Contingency and Affect in Graduate Teacher Training Courses
   Carl Schlachte   145

9. Making Visible the Emotional Labor of Writing Center Work
   Matthew T. Nelson, Sam Deges, and Kathleen F. Weaver   161

10. Emotional Labor and Writing Program Administration at Religiously Affiliated Institutions
    Elizabeth Imafuji   177

SECTION III: PRESERVING BALANCE

11. Administrating While Black: Negotiating the Emotional Labor of an African American Female WPA
    Sheila Carter-Tod   197

12. It Gets Bitter: Considering Andy Warhol and Harboring Anger as a Gay WPA
    Joseph Janangelo   215

13. From Great to Good Enough: Recalibrating Expectations as WPA
    Elizabeth Kleinfeld   237

14. Navigating WPA Emotional Labor with Mindfulness: Practical Strategies for Well-Being
    Christy I. Wenger   251

15. How to Be a Bad WPA
    Courtney Adams Wooten   270

    Conclusion: What Now and What Next? Strategy Sheets for Negotiating Emotional Labor
    Courtney Adams Wooten, Jacob Babb, Kristi Murray Costello, and Kate Navickas   285

STRATEGY SHEETS

How We Flourish as WPAs: Strategies from Positive Psychology
Carrie S. Leverenz   289

You Lost Me at "Administrator": Vulnerability and Transformation in WPA Work at the Two-Year College
Anthony Warnke, Kirsten Higgins, Marcie Sims, and Ian Sherman   291

Emotional Labor Interview
Kate Navickas   293

What We Take and What We Modify from NCFDD
Janelle Adsit and Sue Doe   295

Strategies for Discussing Emotional Labor in Your Professional WPA Documents
Amy Ferdinandt Stolley   297

Preparing for and Managing the Emotional Labor of Sexual Assault Reports
Kim Hensley Owens   299

Strategies for Managing the Emotional Labor of Crisis Response
Kaitlin Clinnin   301

A Heuristic for WPAs in Disaster Response
Carl Schlachte   303

Strategies for Making Writing Center Emotional Labor Visible
Matthew T. Nelson, Sam Deges, and Kathleen F. Weaver   305

Coping with the Emotional Labor of Writing Program Administration at Religiously Affiliated Institutions
Elizabeth Imafuji   307

Administrating While Black: Negotiating the Emotional Labor of an African American WPA
Sheila Carter-Tod   309

Things to Do and Remember: "It Gets Bitter: Considering Andy Warhol and Harboring Anger as a Gay WPA"
Joseph Janangelo   311

Strategies for a Sustainable, Equitable, and Humane WPA Practice
Elizabeth Kleinfeld   313

Mindfulness: A Valuable Emotion Practice for WPAs
Christy I. Wenger   315

How to Be a Bad WPA
Courtney Adams Wooten   317

Index   319

FOREWORD

Laura R. Micciche, University of Cincinnati

Reading this much-needed collection on emotional labor and WPA work made me very aware of how much energy and research have gone into making a case for the intellectual aspects of WPA-ing and how little into emotional aspects of the work. The CWPA's "Evaluating the Intellectual Work of Writing Administration" (1998), for example, "refigure[s] writing administration as scholarly and intellectual work" in order to "argue that it is worthy of tenure and promotion when it advances and enacts disciplinary knowledge within the field of Rhetoric and Composition." As any current or former WPA knows, affective knowledge is both required and produced through the position, though it is not the basis for promotions or reappointments, nor is it generally viewed as knowledge that "advances and enacts disciplinary knowledge."

Why not?

That legitimate question gains traction throughout this collection of essays, stitched together by story, experience, research, and strategy. The authors navigate the seemingly bottomless well of emotional labor extracted and expected from WPAs. Among the topics addressed are affective components of mentoring across status and identify differentials; racism experienced by African American female WPAs; efforts to lead programs in the midst of national, regional, and personal trauma; strategic uses of anger and resentment banked by a gay WPA; making space for personal grief; and the ongoing need for self-care among program participants. Binding these foci together is what WPAs and faculty can do with insights about emotional labor. I have a feeling I'm not the only one who will read this book and wish I'd read it sooner.

Had I read *The Things We Carry: Strategies for Recognizing and Negotiating Emotional Labor in Writing Program Administration* sooner, I might have done a better job addressing peer-to-peer gender-based harassment when it surfaced in my graduate seminar in fall 2018. For starters, I would have recognized my student's behavior for what it was—deliberate, repeated acts of intimidation directed against women—instead of explaining it to myself as familiar peacocking by a jerky student. Maybe, if I'd acted sooner, worse behaviors (offensive sexually oriented comments on and off campus, inappropriate touching, raging at a female student in another class) could have been thwarted. I might have initiated a dialogue or a writing activity with my class to address what we had all experienced but spoken of only individually and privately, in hushed spaces. I could have discussed issues addressed by these authors: self-care, the value of mindfulness meditation, and systemic inequities that often play out in academic spaces. Or I could have informed students about available counseling services on campus. I've been teaching for twenty years, four as WPA and three as assistant WPA, but I was unprepared and, if I'm being honest, scared to face directly the toxic presence in my class and in our teaching community. Doing so meant acknowledging that this place painstakingly made together by students, administrators, and faculty relied overly much on good intentions and markedly less on concrete guidelines, creating vulnerabilities when our tacit intentions were brazenly trespassed.

It's no small irony that my seminar was a *feminist* writing class. We were reading and discussing epistemic justice, social positionality, sexual and gender-based harassment, rhetorical listening, standpoint theory, and the power of feminist anger. Simultaneously, feminist knowledge, credibility, and voices were being hostilely undermined, resisted, and dismissed. Maybe the material sowed the seeds of resentment that played out in the classroom. I can't really know.

I asked the offending student to stop attending my class, filed Title IX reports when students confided in me about troubling encounters, met with the accused, and partnered with the head, WPA, and colleagues in my department to address the issue. None of that was as neat as it sounds. With a staff member and student who no longer felt safe attending class, I walked to the Title IX office to find out if action would be taken before the next class meeting in two days. We were told the case wasn't actionable; no "accommodations" could be made to stop the accused from attending class. The Office of Student Conduct and Community Standards similarly offered no recourse; we were referred back to the Title IX office. Students came to my office and cried; others were newly haunted by old memories of sexual manipulation and assault. I cried in a colleague's office. Faculty and students created backchannels for information sharing in closed offices and after-hours phone conversations. I thought I should have seen it coming; I thought my teaching methods over-assumed cooperation and respect; I felt myself betraying the very work I was teaching and supposed to be modeling.

Self-doubt and self-blame, constant emotional stress as students placed trust in faculty who felt both responsible and powerless, the weight of discreteness, seething anger—this and more swirled during what was a relatively short amount of time, about eight weeks before the accused student left the program voluntarily. All of this behind-the-scenes emotional and institutional labor needed a public-facing one in order to perform the care and program preservation work this volume advocates. The authors say that my unpreparedness is more normative than not; they seek to change that. Rather than treating a crisis in a community as a problem tied only to individual students, the authors help me understand the value of a systemic, public response. People need to hear faculty and administrators acknowledge conflicts and offer reparative and future-oriented strategies.

While individuals fail all the time at proactive community care, such failures are not limited to individuals but are emblematic of larger system failures. Maybe rhet-comp's focus on status has limited holistic approaches to administration, made us too inner-focused on the discipline itself. Or, to use the terms that organize this book, maybe we have undervalued what's required to preserve identity, community, and balance because we've been too busy making a case for what we know, our *intellectual* value. What's important to say is that we need to take better care of each other and of ourselves *when* (not *if*) something terrible happens. And we need to do so as a matter of course, through integrated training and professional development, which requires forethought, planning, and outreach, as goes the refrain across this collection.

In the "Preserving Communities" section of this book, where contributors describe administering during times of crisis and trauma (sexual assault cases, the Las Vegas shooting massacre, Hurricane Sandy devastation), the case is made powerfully for normalizing self-care plans, for developing coalitions that take responsibility for community preservation (not the WPA's job alone), and for creating graduate and professional training that acknowledges emotional labor inflected by status and identity differences. I think the process-based approach to emotional labor modeled throughout this book advances the discipline. In fact, the following pages offer a blueprint for a CWPA statement devoted to the affective circumstances, both ordinary and extraordinary, WPAs regularly find themselves navigating.

The strategy sheets at the end of the book, outlining a "range of ideas for negotiating the emotional labor of administration," could form the basis of a user-focused professional statement, one that would pair naturally with the existing Framework for Success in Postsecondary Writing (Council of Writing Program Administrators et al. 2011). The concept of "college readiness" described in the framework takes on new significance when we consider that "as many as 50 percent of college students are exposed to a PTE [potentially traumatizing event] in the first year of college" (Davidson 2017). How might habits of mind interface with emotional distress and conflict? Likewise, "The Portland Resolution's" focus on WPA labor and job descriptions should acknowledge that "counseling and advising" means more than "arbitrating grade disputes and resolving teacher and student complaints, such as placement, plagiarism, grade appeals, scheduling problems . . ." (Council of Writing Program Administrators 1991). This book demonstrates how to take emotional labor seriously by treating it not as a by-product of WPA work but as a central job requirement.

Why does a stamp of approval from the WPA organization matter? It matters in the same way it does when we try to persuade administrators of the value of small class sizes or WPA stipends for summer work. These statements (imperfectly) validate our labors while establishing professional guidelines. The contributors to this book make a clear and persuasive case for emotional labor as real labor that has significant consequences for both WPAs and the programs they serve. It's time our discipline and professional organizations caught up.

REFERENCES

Council of Writing Program Administrators. 1991. "'The Portland Resolution': Guidelines for Writing Program Administrator Positions." *WPA: Writing Program Administration* 16 (1–2): 88–94.

Council of Writing Program Administrators. 1998. "Evaluating the Intellectual Work of Writing Administration." http://wpacouncil.org/positions/intellectualwork.html.

Council of Writing Program Administrators, National Council of Teachers of English, and National Writing Project. 2011. "Framework for Success in Postsecondary Writing." https://www.nwp.org/cs/public/print/resource/3479.

Davidson, Shannon. 2017. "Trauma-Informed Practices for Postsecondary Education: A Guide." https://educationnorthwest.org/sites/default/files/resources/trauma-informed-practices-postsecondary-508.pdf.

PREFACE

Courtney Adams Wooten, Jacob Babb,
Kristi Murray Costello, and Kate Navickas

As we put the final touches on this collection in the summer of 2020, we have found ourselves in a crisis situation unlike anything any of us have had to contend with before. Due to the COVID-19 pandemic, universities are no longer able to engage in business as usual. Students, faculty, and staff are at risk of getting sick or are forced to watch loved ones struggle with this illness and its many complications, often from an agonizing distance. College classes and meetings across the world have quickly and often haphazardly been moved online, hiring freezes have become pervasive, and faculty and staff are being laid off or furloughed at an alarming rate. And we are still in the early stages of discovering the impact the pandemic will have on higher education specifically and on the world in general. Like just about everyone else, we sit in our homes and wait to learn how our work will be changed by this virus.

As our collection explores, the intellectual and emotional labor that results from university crises like the COVID-19 pandemic places writing program administrators (WPAs) in situations in which we are not only worrying about the health and safety of ourselves and our families while engaging in the labor of moving our own classes and meetings online but also worrying about the health, safety, and livelihoods of our colleagues, students, and programs. Crises like the global pandemic make it even more vital to think, talk, and write about emotional labor than it was when the four of us first started the conversations in Knoxville, Tennessee, in 2017 that led to the development of this collection.

As we write this preface, we are still recovering from the shockingly fast and seismic changes in our lives. Just three months ago, in the middle of the spring semester, we found ourselves developing triage training for faculty and graduate assistants with minimal online teaching and tutoring experience; finding and distributing access to technologies to students, faculty, and staff; and navigating the typical but now more complicated tasks of WPA work, such as placing students into writing courses; responding to increased class caps; creating course schedules for future, now-unknown, and dramatically reconfigured semesters; training teaching assistants and tutors; providing campus outreach; managing conflicts; revisiting, revising, and implementing new policies, such as grading and attendance in online writing courses; and consistently recalibrating and strategizing as plans and resources shift, sometimes almost daily.

Many of us have spent ample time listening to and supporting our colleagues and students during these transitions and advocating for the jobs of our part-time colleagues, office staff, and graduate assistants; working to recruit and retain students; and justifying our course releases. And we've done this all over Zoom while distracted by our children, pets, partners, and neighbors' weed eaters and without the hallway conversations, classroom interactions, professional development sessions, office drop-ins, and break room cookies and bagels that remind us why we do what we do. Work-life balance was a struggle before the pandemic. It has all but dissolved now, and none of us have yet had the chance to take a breath and to grieve for what we took for granted before—not to mention the need to mourn the vast and tragic loss of lives to COVID-19. With the ground continuing to shift under our feet, we certainly can't make plans for moving forward yet.

These have indeed been strange and unprecedented times, but as we and the authors in our collection argue, the ways in which labor—intellectual, physical, and, the focus of this collection, emotional—disproportionately falls on the shoulders of WPAs are likely only surprising to non-WPAs, which is why we expect that the chapters in this book, though written before the pandemic, will still be timely and useful. The collection includes several chapters on varying struggles and emotional labor faced by WPAs, as well as chapters that specifically discuss navigating emotional labor in crisis response (Kaitlin Clinnin), in disaster response (Carl Schlachte), for sustainable, equitable, and human WPA practice (Elizabeth Kleinfeld), and for mindfulness for WPAs (Christy I. Wenger). We highlight these chapters because they struck us as most immediately relevant in the midst of the pandemic, but we believe readers will discover value in all of our authors' contributions as we all move forward into whatever the new normal will be.

And now, beyond the initial shocks of COVID-19, as this book goes to press, we are in the midst of a heavy moment; we are grieving for Black lives threatened and killed by police, and white vigilante violence, and the injustices of our justice system. We find ourselves overwhelmed and unsure how best to help or address these tragic circumstances, but we do know that we—as a field and as a nation—need to move beyond statements to meaningfully transform our cultural practices. In this collection, we have one chapter, by Sheila Carter-Tod, that speaks to the emotional labor of women of color. While we know readers will benefit from her insightful analysis of racism, emotional labor, and WPA work, we also want to acknowledge that we need more work interrogating these intersections. As Carter-Tod's chapter in this collection suggests and has been likewise established by writing studies scholars (such as Craig and Perryman-Clark 2011; García de Müeller and Ruiz 2017; Inoue 2016; Perryman-Clark and Craig, 2019), writing program administration as a field of study and a community of scholar-teachers has been limited by a lack of representation of people of color and by a lack of serious engagement with antiracist work.

While we acknowledge these limitations, which have become more pronounced as we move to press and BLM protests are occurring around the country, we opted not to engage in quick rewrites that would do little to initiate meaningful change. We need more than token efforts aimed at making us as editors and scholars feel better. Instead, we pledge to support future work that takes these conversations forward and we promise to stand in solidarity with people of color and listen to their lived experiences, pursue antiracist pedagogies in our classrooms and in our administrative work, and be a part of the movement to call out and dismantle racism. We want to support all of our colleagues of color, who already carry so much of the emotional labor of antiracist work, in word and in action.

Our current moment is teaching us that there are no easy solutions to the ongoing devastation of systemic racism and a global pandemic. Indeed, we believe that, similarly, studying, engaging with, and taking seriously emotional labor is the hard work of *moving through*—acknowledging what's hard, sitting with it, and avoiding easy answers. With this collection, we hope the stories and strategies shared in *The Things We Carry: Strategies for Recognizing and Negotiating Emotional Labor in Writing Program Administration* are useful and motivational to fellow WPAs for navigating the emotional labor of our current and future shared social upheavals; we also hope that as a field, we will continue to add to these stories and strategies and continue to make our emotional labor visible, viable, and valued every day but especially in times of crisis. Last but not least, we hope that you and yours are happy and healthy despite the circumstances we all find ourselves in. We look forward to engaging with you in conversation about emotional labor in the future, when being in the company of our fellow WPAs is once again a possibility.

REFERENCES

Craig, Collin, and Staci Perryman-Clark. 2011. "Troubling the Boundaries: (De)Constructing WPA Identities at the Intersections of Race and Gender." *WPA: Writing Program Administration* 34 (2): 37–58.

García de Müeller, Genevieve, and Iris Ruiz. 2017. "Race, Silence, and Writing Program Administration: A Qualitative Study of US College Writing Programs." *WPA: Writing Program Administration* 40 (2): 19–39.

Inoue, Asao B. 2016. "Racism in Writing Programs and CWPA." *WPA: Writing Program Administration* 40 (1): 134–154.

Perryman-Clark, Staci, and Collin Craig, eds. 2019. *Black Perspectives in Writing Program Administration: From the Margins to the Center.* Urbana, IL: NCTE.

ACKNOWLEDGMENTS

The editors would like to thank and praise all of the contributors for their hard work on this collection. Without their willingness to be transparent and vulnerable about the emotional labor they experience as writing program administrators (WPAs) and to offer others their insights, this collection would not have been possible. The authors have shared stories of emotional hardships, traumas, and other difficult situations that we believe reaffirm to other WPAs that they are not alone in similar situations. We are deeply grateful for the authors' development of a diverse array of strategies, as we foresee that they will support other WPAs by providing practical advice, allyship, and hope—as they have already provided for us in our daily administrative duties. We would also like to thank Laura Micciche for her astute observations about the emotional labor WPAs perform and the need for more attention from our professional organizations to this aspect of WPA work. Indeed, we are further indebted to Laura's insights as they have motivated us to continue to make emotional labor a significant labor concern within the larger WPA community—work we hope others will also get involved in. Finally, we offer our wholehearted appreciation to the entire team at Utah State University Press, including Rachael Levay and Laura Furney, who encouraged us as we worked on this collection and enthusiastically offered support along the way.

Courtney Adams Wooten would like to thank her co-editors, Jacob, Kristi, and Kate, for allowing her to be part of this journey, especially Kristi, who was confident enough to come up to two strangers after a CWPA panel and ask them if they wanted to work on an edited collection together. She also offers her wholehearted thanks to all of those around her who provide the regular emotional support that makes her ability to handle the emotional labor of WPA-ing possible: Mikell Wooten, Alison Johnson, Megan Condis, Ansley Adams, her colleagues at GMU, and, of course, her miniature dachshund, Dottie (follow her on Instagram at @dottie.the.doxie).

Jacob Babb is grateful to his co-editors for being so generous with their time and their intellectual energy as we called this collection into being. He would especially like to thank his frequent coauthor Courtney, who keeps agreeing to take on new projects with him. He is also thankful for all the WPA mentors who have demonstrated how to engage in WPA work in sustainable, meaningful ways. In addition, Jacob would like to thank Indiana University Southeast for supporting and recognizing his research. As always, Jacob is grateful to his wife, Niki, and his kids, Annabelle and Oliver, for being patient, funny, and loving.

Kristi Murray Costello would like to thank her co-editors, Courtney, Jacob, and Kate, for their brilliance, kindness, and creativity without all of which this project would not have been possible. She would also like to extend her appreciation to her family: Kendra Eads, Airek Beauchamp, the Collins-Tribbetts, Sean Murray, her brilliant and brave nieces Lillian and Evelyn, and her parents whose awesomeness and unwavering support make dreaming possible. Kristi would like to give a well-deserved shout-out to her dear friends and frequent work-party companions: Katherine Baker, Lisa Bohn, Sarah Mayberry Scott, Ruth Osorio, Tabatha Simpson-Farrow, and Carmen Williams. In following with the theme, Kristi would like to recognize her dog, Rafa, whose cuddles and adorable little face (photos available upon request) make sitting on the couch for long periods of time writing and editing achievable. Last but not least, she would like to send a world record–worthy round of thanks and love to her partner, Liam, for his insights, patience, and support.

Kate Navickas echoes the above gratitude for her co-editors, Courtney, Jacob, and Kristi. In addition to what has already been appreciated, Kate is thankful for her co-editors' thoughtful insights, their friendly and easy Skype meetings, and everyone's determination and efforts to not be the person who's not doing enough for this project. Through working with Courtney, Jacob, and Kristi, Kate has found new friends and collaborators who inspire her thinking and research and motivate her continued work to make emotional labor visible and accountable in the work we do. She is especially grateful for Kristi, whose original inquiries into administrative transitions for a CCCC panel sparked Kate's chapter in this collection and have since led to a number of fruitful and fun collaborative projects. Further, Kate is indebted to her dear friends Nicole Gonzales Howell and Missy Watson, who regularly read her work, offer emotional support and warm critiques, and inspire her to continue trying to do the hard work of making invisible systems more transparent and just. Finally, Kate is forever grateful for her loving husband, Adam Williams, who is patient, kind, generally wonderful, and an excellent listener, as well as their dog, Olive, and cohort of three sometimes-supportive gray cats.

Collections are the work of a village, one that spans multiple states and includes the press and editors, authors and their various institutions, families and fur-families, and many others. We appreciate and acknowledge everyone's work, support and commitment to this project—those named here and likely others we've unintentionally forgotten to include. And finally, we are grateful to you, reader; we hope you will read this, teach and share it, critique our ideas, and continue the important work of interrogating and making visible emotional labor.

THE THINGS WE CARRY

INTRODUCTION
Emotional Labor, Writing Studies, and Writing Program Administration

Kristi Murray Costello
Old Dominion University

Jacob Babb
Indiana University Southeast

On June 19, 2018, something rare happened. "The AP has just broken some new news," Rachel Maddow explained on her MSNBC show as she was handed news in the middle of her broadcast.

She stopped, visibly flustered, and she tried again without looking at the camera.

"Um, this has just come out from the Associated Press. This is incredible. The Trump administration has been sending babies [her voice cracked] and other young children . . ." She paused, waving her finger at the screen. "Hmm, hold on . . . to at least three [waving her finger and shaking her head]. Put up the graphic of this," she directs, finally making eye contact with the camera. "I think I am going to have to hand this off."

In that unfiltered moment, we were reminded that a newscaster's job is not only to share the news but often to hear the news first and carry the weight of that news even as they are expected to appear emotionally detached, somehow untouched and unaffected by whatever news they are charged to relay. The incident was so shocking and so memorable because for a moment, we saw what Rachel Maddow carried and the effect it had on her.

Later that evening Maddow tweeted, "Ugh, I'm sorry. If nothing else, it is my job to actually be able to speak while I'm on TV."

The next day there were several news stories about Maddow's broadcast with headlines like "Rachel Maddow breaks down in tears on air while reading report on 'tender age' shelters" (Schmidt 2018).

Commentary from the press and the public ranged from praise for her bravery and compassion to conspiratorial theories and petty insults about her gender, sexuality, and acting skills, which were referred to by one commenter as worse than those displayed in *Sharknado*. The response to Maddow's broadcast illuminated, among so many other things, the typically tacit expectation that newscasters present the information in an appropriately stoic manner and do so without visible emotions or vulnerability. Suppression and emotion management are part of the job, and the constant negotiation of these prevailing dialectical tensions is emotional labor.

As writing program administrators (WPAs), we felt a deep resonance with Maddow's struggle to constrain her emotions. We recognized the powerful tension between how we are perceived separately as professionals and as people with emotions. We certainly know what it is like to apologize when our emotions and our work collide or cross trajectories.

If you ask a WPA to draft a brief list of their responsibilities, it would likely include scheduling classes, training teaching assistants, developing and assessing curriculum, observing and evaluating faculty, and maybe arbitrating student complaints about instructors and grades. It probably wouldn't include fielding aggressive responses and pointed questions about policies passed down by upper administration, helping homeless students find housing and helping adjunct colleagues obtain food stamps, or sharing with a classroom full of students that their teacher passed away suddenly the day before—concurrently aware that your next steps need to be getting the classes covered, compiling information for the new instructors, initiating compensation paperwork, and supporting colleagues and students through the mourning process even though you are likely also struggling with the loss. There is a weariness simply in reading that last sentence. Yet, many of us have lived it.

If you ask a WPA to describe their work, you will likely not get a sense of how rewarding that work can be even as they struggle with the constant effort to find balance in their working lives (How do you find time to conduct research and write? When do you have time to grade assignments and plan for class? How do you have the energy to plan professional development and assessment activities? Why haven't you answered my email? When will I know what courses I teach next semester? Why weren't you in your office when I came by this morning?) and their personal lives. Most WPAs have learned to present a persona rooted in professionalism and energetic commitment to improving student writing. But inevitably, many of those same WPAs struggle with burnout, depression, and a sense of powerlessness. Administering a writing program can be equally exhilarating and tumultuous. It can be easy to disregard, ignore, or minimize the emotional labor of writing program administrators, though as our experiences, the scholarship of our field, and the chapters in this collection illustrate, we carry plenty.

We put this collection together in a cultural moment that is saturated with traumatic events, such as mass shootings, sexual assaults, racial violence, and hate crimes; and we recognize that everyone involved in the work of writing programs—including WPAs, instructors, and students—carry things seen and unseen. Readers will doubtless recognize that we borrowed from Tim O'Brien's famous collection, *The Things They Carried*, for the title of this collection. In calling back to this book, we do not mean to suggest that the experiences of WPAs are somehow analogous to the horrors of war—although we may sometimes feel tempted to make such a suggestion. Nor do we mean to suggest that the things we carry are to be seen as inherently negative, as burdens we would prefer to put down when given the chance. Rather, like O'Brien, we believe we must examine the things we carry and think about the narratives attached to those things. As O'Brien (1990, 255) put it, "Stories can save us." We see this collection as an opportunity to embrace the power of storytelling as a means to build theoretical approaches to emotional labor. We see the stories that comprise the exigence of each chapter as the basis for reflection, for engagement with scholarship, for continuing the work of theorizing emotional labor in writing studies, and for seeking practical strategies for writing program administration.

The chapters in this collection in one form or another all find their origins in stories, and it is our hope in assembling these stories and building scholarship around them that we will provide a resource to help all WPAs, whether they're experienced first-year writing program coordinators, pre-tenured writing across the curriculum directors, or non-tenure-track writing center directors (WCDs). We use the term *WPA* as an inclusive term that encompasses the work of many kinds of faculty and staff at many kinds of institutions. As we selected and worked with the authors in this book, we kept as a central tenet the need to represent the diverse range of WPAs at work in higher education. We hope readers will find that representation both useful and welcoming as we seek to extend the conversation about emotional labor in writing program administration.

ORIGINS AND DEVELOPMENT OF THEORIES OF EMOTIONAL LABOR

Though we can date the concept of emotional labor back to Aristotle, it was sociologist Arlie Hochschild many years later in her book *The Managed Heart: Commercialization of Human Feeling* (2012), first published in 1983 and republished many times since, who coined the term *emotional labor*. Hochschild (2012, 7, 35) defines emotional labor as the "management of feeling to create a publicly observable facial and bodily display [that] is sold for a wage and therefore has exchange value" and differentiates between two different types of emotional labor: deep acting and surface acting. More broadly put, according to Hochschild's (2012, 7) framework, emotional labor calls for "a coordination of mind and feeling." As Ronnie J. Steinberg and Deborah H. Figart (1999, 9) explain, emotional labor is also "the relational rather than the task-based aspect of work." The scope of emotional labor is perhaps best illustrated through Hochschild's (2012) examples, which include the hospital coordinator who rallies the staff to tackle a shared goal set by the administration, the judge who returns home after having had to practice objectivity while observing evidence of monstrosity, and the Wall Street trader who works to manage the anxiety of their clients. Hochschild's study suggests that "one-half of women workers" and "one-third of all workers" experience emotional labor (Steinberg and Figart 1999, 24).

In the years since Hochschild's coining of the term *emotional labor*, several scholars across many different fields have built on the definition and added categorizations to help us better recognize it. In "Emotional Labor: Why and How to Teach It," Sharon H. Mastracci, Meredith A. Newman, and Mary E. Guy (2010, 125) take the definition beyond the outward display described by Hochschild, defining it as "the expression of one's capacity to manage personal emotions, sense others' emotions, and to respond appropriately, based on one's job." Some scholars have responded to these more capacious definitions of emotional labor by adapting Hochschild's initial heuristic to include different categorizations (Ashforth and Humphrey 1993; Morris and Feldman 1996; Glomb and Tews 2004). Guy, Newman, and Mastracci (2008, 5–6) provide perhaps the most detailed list of "dimensions to emotional labor," which includes, but is not limited to: Verbal Judo, Caritas (or caring labor), Gameface, Show Time, Compassion Fatigue, Emotion Management, Professional Face, Deep Acting, Emotional Suppression, Emotional Equilibrium, and Emotional Facade. Though they use different categories to describe emotional labor, the scholarship seems to agree with few exceptions that recognition of and research about emotional labor are important because "silence" about emotional labor "means avoidance: avoiding crucial conversations, mismanaged emotions, and mismanaged emotion regulation" (Mastracci, Guy, and Newman 2014, 19). Silence, dismissal, or minimization of emotional labor can also lead to burnout, decreased trust in people and institutions, anxiety, and anguish (Mastracci, Guy, and Newman 2014, 9). Though many scholars focus on what could be seen as the burdens of emotional labor, other scholars (Ashforth and Humphrey 1993; Wharton 1993; Constanti and Gibbs 2004) make a point of discussing the ways it can also be positive, though Panikkos Constanti and Paul Gibbs (2004) do still suggest that it often goes unrewarded.

Work in emotional labor studies takes place in numerous fields (criminal justice, economics, academic advising and education, hotel management and hospitality, industry and retail, linguistics, nursing, psychology, public service, sociology, and tourism) and spans multiple continents, including Asia, Europe, North America, and Australia. Scholars have also studied copious disparate populations, ranging from Hochschild's (2012) study of the service economy to Guy, Newman, and Mastracci's (2008) works relating to public service. The resulting insights, data, and heuristics aptly apply to the work of WPAs. Of particular interest to WPAs is the understanding that emotional labor is "part of an occupation, not just something that a person brings to the job" (Mastracci, Guy, and Newman 2014, xv) and the unfortunate reality that such labor "is seldom recognized, rarely honored, and almost never taken into account by employers as a source of on-the-job stress" (Hochschild 2012, 153).

EMOTIONAL LABOR IN WRITING STUDIES AND WRITING PROGRAM ADMINISTRATION

The rich history of WPA stories housed in iconic texts, such as Diana George's (1999) *Kitchen Cooks, Plate Twirlers, and Troubadours,* helps WPAs understand how our individual struggles connect to larger disciplinary and institutional issues, provide emotional connection, and illustrate that the struggles of the profession need not stay silent. In addition, recent work by affect scholars, such as Sara Ahmed, Brian Massumi, and Lauren Berlant, opens opportunities for scholars in rhetoric, composition, and writing studies to consider applications of affect theories to WPA work and complicates such theories by considering material conditions WPAs experience. Because of the important groundwork covered by colleagues, this more recent strain of scholarship exploring the relationship between work and emotion from scholars such as Laura

Micciche, Eve Kosofsky Sedgwick and Adam Frank, Nicole I. Caswell, Kelly Ritter, Elizabeth Saur and Jason Palmeri, Laura J. Davies, and others explores how emotions work and relate to different institutional contexts. This work has become so prevalent and been so transformative and empowering that in a recent review essay, Erin Rand (2015, 161) describes a contemporary "affective turn" in academic discourse.

Almost every treatment of emotion in writing studies refers back to Lynn Worsham's "Going Postal: Pedagogic Violence and the Schooling of Emotion" (1998), an article that takes the eponymous phrase; explores its adaptation to cover multiple forms of violence, such as what we now with far too much familiarity call mass shootings; and theorizes what she calls a rhetoric of pedagogic violence. Worsham (1998, 216) defines violence from a disciplinary (à la Foucault) perspective, asserting that a "rhetoric of pedagogic violence will focus specifically on the way violence address and educates emotion and inculcates an affective relation to the world," then defining emotion itself as "the tight braid of affect and judgment, socially and historically constructed and bodily lived, through which the symbolic takes hold of and binds the individual, in complex and contradictory ways, to the social order and its structure of meanings." Worsham's definition recalls Hochschild's (2012) explanation that emotional labor emphasizes the relational aspect of work.

Worsham's work was followed shortly thereafter by Dale Jacobs and Laura Micciche's (2003) collection *A Way to Move: Rhetorics of Emotion and Composition Studies*. Echoing Worsham's turn to violence, Jacobs and Micciche (2003, 1) write that their book was drafted "in the shadow of the terrorist attacks on September 11, 2001," noting that those attacks and their aftermath required "immediate response." As chapters in our collection also highlight, such massive events can make emotional labor more visible, but Jacobs and Micciche are careful to emphasize that emotional labor can also be seen in the extraordinary and the more mundane tasks of teaching and administering. Their collection offers ways to theorize emotion that build on the classical rhetoric concept of pathos, which historically has been denigrated as a lesser form of persuasion. The collection includes chapters by Alice Gillam, Brad Peters, and Mara Holt, Leon Anderson, and Albert Rouzie that specifically explore workplace emotions in writing program administration.

Laura Micciche's *Doing Emotion: Rhetoric, Writing, Teaching* extends the work of that collection. Micciche (2007, 7) asserts that we cannot dismiss emotion as "subjugated knowledge" that has functioned as "analog to women, opinion, the personal, and the body." Instead, rejecting that dismissal "is to take seriously the work that emotions do in the context of disciplinary formation, teaching, and administering writing" (7). Micciche includes a chapter specifically focused on WPAs called "Disappointment and WPA Work" in which she claims that disappointment and WPA work are often joined together. She calls for a resistance to this common narrative through the promotion of WPA work built on attention to the materialist conditions of emotional labor and the mentoring of graduate students in administrative work. This collection is in many ways a response to her call.

Scholarship on affect and emotion in writing studies has taken several directions in recent years. The *Composition Forum* 2016 special issue demonstrates the range of scholarly treatment of emotion in writing studies. Edited by Lance Langdon, the issue includes an author retrospective from Laura Micciche (2016), who advocates that we as a field need to "stay with emotion." Articles address student disposition and transfer (Driscoll and Powell 2016), empathy as pedagogy (Leake 2016), and emotion as critical inquiry in community-based writing courses (Prebel 2016). The issue also offers a section titled "Reflections on Emotional Labor," which includes brief articles on teaching in the aftermath of traumatic events (DeBacher and Harris-Moore 2016), writing center administration as emotional labor (Jackson, Grutsch McKinney, and Caswell 2016; see also Caswell, Grutsch McKinney, and Jackson 2016 for a book-length work on this topic), and training consultants to handle the inherently emotional labor of writing center work (Perry 2016). As a whole, Langdon's special issue illustrates that writing studies has accepted Micciche's call to stay with emotion.

While the *Composition Forum* 2016 special issue is a useful illustration of the range of issues within writing studies that scholars are using emotional labor as a lens to explore, scholars are also publishing on emotional labor elsewhere. Attention to emotional labor has proven productive in areas such as failure (Carr 2013), the academic job market (Sano-Franchini 2016), responding to student writing (Caswell 2014), plagiarism (Robillard 2007), TA training (Reid 2017; Saur and Palmeri 2017), and departmental politics (Schell 2006). The recent edited collection *Bad Ideas about Writing* (Ball and Loewe 2017) aims to dispel popular myths about writing, and implicit in that collection is the emotional labor of repeatedly responding to such myths. Cheryl E. Ball and Drew M. Loewe acknowledge the emotional work of the collection in the introduction: "The project has its genesis in frustration, but what emerges is hope" (2). Rand's description of an affective turn in writing studies is supported by the significant body of scholarship that continues to grow addressing emotional labor in writing studies.

Within writing program administration itself, scholars have approached transitions as important emotional moments. For example, Laura J. Davies (2017, 49) examines the sense of grief instructors experienced when she replaced a beloved WPA, noting that "we are called on to take care of the people within our program by attending to both their professional and emotional needs." Along another line of inquiry, Amy Rupiper Taggart (2018, 155) attributes a loss of professional identity to an unexpected disruption of her role as writing program administrator due to illness, writing that she "felt unseated and tetherless." Scholarship on the fluidity of WPA positions also draws attention to how our sometimes complex or unstable positions in hierarchy can affect our work. Referring to untenured or uncredentialed WPAs as "liminals," Talinn Phillips, Paul Shovlin, and Megan Titus (2014, 62) assert that the positions of WPAs are far from stable and that liminals "will continue to enact positive change at their institutions, even while simultaneously experiencing the anxiety, frustration, and exploitation that comes with liminality."[1]

WPAs must also consider establishing sustainable practices for the long term. Cindy Moore's (2018) "Mentoring WPAs for the Long Term: The Promise of Mindfulness" emphasizes the need for mentorship at multiple stages of a WPA's career and offers mindfulness as a framework for sustaining WPAs through their careers, whether they transition to other positions or not. Regardless of the roles they hold, WPAs routinely experience tumultuous emotional responses in their work. Kristi Costello (2018) captures this sentiment well in her article on listening to complaints about writing centers from faculty members: "During my first year as a WPA and WCA, I kept (outwardly) calm and diplomatic during these kinds of conversations though a stream of expletives was surely flowing through my mind." She ultimately suggests that "the best way to build this rapport and set the stage for real work, real improvement, and real talk is to begin with listening," an approach that may lead to progress but certainly is not without emotional labor.

While recent work to make emotional labor visible takes a more explicit and theoretical look at administrative affect, less attention has been paid to concrete strategies for negotiating the emotional labor inherent in these real-life work situations. How should a WPA or WCD respond to a traumatic massive local shooting, to their eighth sexual assault report of the year, or to the tragic and untimely death of a beloved tutor, research partner, and friend? *The Things We Carry: Strategies for Recognizing and Negotiating Emotional Labor in Writing Program Administration* offers scholarly interventions into such conversations and pushes the field forward by applying and re-theorizing work outside of rhetoric and composition in emotion and affect theory; offering concrete and practical strategies for a wide range of larger traumatic events faced by the administrator, students, teachers, and the community; and providing strategies aimed at preserving our senses of self and balance.

CONTENT AND STRUCTURE

We have arranged the collection in three sections: Preserving Work Identities, Preserving Communities, and Preserving Balance. Authors draw from fields such as positive psychology, sociology, and higher education broadly as well as from the interdisciplinary field of affect studies. While a number of potential themes run across these chapters, we have decided to highlight both the broad areas of the work that tend to require emotional labor—a WPA's own work identity, a WPA's fostering of community in writing programs, and a WPA's balance of the professional and the personal—and the larger hopeful theme of preserving. The three areas of WPA work these sections interrogate are represented in the chapters through very diverse WPA positions, identities, institutional contexts, and, thus, types of emotional labor. More than just covering a wide array of areas of WPA work that are influenced by emotional labor, we hope the sections' emphasis on preserving speaks to our goal for WPA negotiations of emotional labor. That is, we want to open up a conversation in this collection about what to do with emotional labor and offer options for how to respond, giving readers tools while also recognizing that the act of negotiating emotional labor is an ongoing process that is not intended to eliminate emotions. We believe that preserving acknowledges that emotional labor is neither good nor bad; it's necessary to feel and to reflect upon emotional states as opposed to the continual movement away from emotions.

Preserving Work Identities

The first section includes chapters that critically examine the emotional labor of different WPA contexts and discourses and offer strategies for making that emotional labor more visible and productive. The first three chapters of this section consider the specific emotional labor that different institutional contexts create throughout different points in WPA and WCD careers. Carrie S. Leverenz examines the emotional strain of reentering a WPA position mid-career and uses positive psychology to offer concrete strategies for working toward well-being. Anthony Warnke and his coauthors trace the creation and evolution of the WPA position at their two-year college (TYC) across four administrators who held it; they offer a TYC perspective on the emotional labor throughout this evolution as well as a nine-part heuristic mantra for persevering. Kate Navickas examines the emotional labor of both transitioning into a new WCD position and of influential field narratives around the work that constrained her happiness through an interview with the previous writing center director.

The last two chapters of this section consider the emotional influence of two related documents: professional documents and the National Center for Faculty Development and Diversity's (NCFDD) promotional materials that foster faculty writing for tenure and promotion and the kinds of documents we use to chronicle our professional lives. Janelle Adsit and Sue Doe look at the affective implications of the NCFDD's discourses that foster some of the very writing Amy Ferdinandt Stolley examines in the following chapter. Stolley offers survey data on the documentation of emotional labor of WPAs in professional documents (job materials, writing, and institutional documents) and a heuristic for accounting for emotional labor and including it in such professional documents.

Preserving Communities

The second section considers the emotional labor of the WPA as well as of the communities the WPA engages with and supports. Specifically, these chapters offer strategies for supporting first-year composition (FYC) teachers, students, and tutors in the face of traumatic events and the everyday emotional labor of composition. The first three chapters in this collection speak to the emotional labor a community struggles through in response to trauma. Kim Hensley Owens explores the logistics and effect of eight sexual assault reports for students in FYC courses—the logistical movement of students and confidential support of teachers, the programmatic decision for all FYC courses to teach students a consent activity, and the preservation of herself as well as student victims in the program. In response to the 2017 Las Vegas Strip shooting of fifty-eight people, Kaitlin Clinnin shares a strategy that emphasizes a larger process of prevention, response, and recovery as well as the ongoing work of identifying and understanding student and instructor needs. In the third crisis-response chapter in this section, Carl Schlachte analyzes interviews that question instructors and a WPA on the emotional labor of teaching after Hurricane Sandy in New York City in 2012. Similar to Clinnin, Schlachte argues for the need for programmatic preparedness strategies that are grounded in sensibility and casuistry.

The final two chapters in this section consider the emotional labor of communities of teachers, students, and tutors in specific, non-crisis situations. Such routine emotional labor is just as important to address as the kinds of labor we deal with in crisis situations because the day-to-day emotion work of WPAs can be equally as intense given that we handle such issues regularly. Matthew T. Nelson, Sam Deges, and Kathleen F. Weaver offer a quantitative understanding of "emotional contagion" in tutoring, when tutors empathetically take on the emotions of their tutee; they offer strategies for WCDs to support their tutoring community in tutor training. Elizabeth Imafuji considers emotional labor in the specific context of religious institutions, ultimately advocating for preemptive teacher training about how to handle student disclosures.

Preserving Balance

The third section of this collection asks WPAs to consider the personal dimensions of their professional emotional labor, including frameworks and strategies for thinking about how the personal and professional interact as they seek to achieve emotional balance. The first two chapters in this section draw attention to the additional difficulties WPAs may face because of the particular bodies they inhabit. Sheila Carter-Tod examines the intersectionality of black women WPAs through interviews, pinpointing additional sources of emotional labor they experience and the effects of such emotional labor. Turning attention to a different often-marginalized group, Joe Janangelo explores the emotions gay WPAs can experience. After presenting a variety of difficult situations he was placed in because of his identity as a gay WPA, Janangelo discusses some possible reactions WPAs in similar positions may have and how to work through and with the anger that can accompany clearly discriminatory and oppressive workplace environments.

Shifting attention from particular bodies to more general strategies, the last three chapters in this section interrogate what it means to be a WPA and how to create sustainable approaches to the workload, goals, and challenges of writing program administration. Elizabeth Kleinfeld explores how WPAs can experience emotional labor from grief (the simultaneous loss of a tutor and a friend) both inside and outside of their jobs, ultimately concluding that sometimes it is useful and even necessary to recalibrate programmatic and career goals to make such work and a personal life manageable. Christy I. Wenger offers a specific strategy—mindfulness—to help WPAs thrive as professionals and as individuals. Finally, Courtney Adams Wooten builds on such calls for greater attention to the personal, calling on WPAs to embrace the label of "bad" as they challenge common happiness scripts that often include overworking and as they seek to achieve a sustainable work-life balance.

CONCLUSION

We conclude the collection with a series of one-page handouts, what we are calling strategy sheets, that correlate to each chapter in the collection. When conceptualizing the collection, we realized that these brief, condensed handouts derived from the chapters would help emphasize the practical goals of the text. This collection aims to help WPAs navigate the emotional labor of their work, and we envision the conclusion as a means of offering readers vital (and quick-reference) resources for applying the fine scholarship of our authors.

Regardless of whether it is recognized, documented, or appreciated, emotional labor is part of the work of writing program administrators. We often carry emotional labor beyond events, into unrelated meetings or into our personal lives during evenings and holidays, and often we carry it for longer than we need to. Sometimes we emote more than we'd planned or hoped, and other times we may hide more than we need to or should. It's the experience and memories of negotiating these kinds of emotions—shame, guilt, suppression—that lead us to admire the visibility and vulnerability of Maddow's emotions and those expressed by the authors in this collection.

Together, we are working to make emotional labor more visible and more normalized. Through reading this collection, you, too, are a part of this effort. Though we recognize the contextuality of each instance, institution, and individual, we hope this collection offers strategies for acknowledging the emotions intertwined with and engendered by writing program administration while working to preserve and sustain ourselves. We hope you will find these chapters and the strategies therein helpful for discovering and negotiating the things we carry.

NOTE

1. See Adams Wooten, Babb, and Ray 2018 for more on the impact of transitions on WPAs.

REFERENCES

Adams Wooten, Courtney, Jacob Babb, and Brian Ray, eds. 2018. *WPAs in Transition: Navigating Educational Leadership Positions.* Logan: Utah State University Press.

Ashforth, Blake E., and Ronald H. Humphrey. 1993. "Emotional Labor in Service Roles: The Influence of Identity." *Academy of Management Review* 1: 88–115.

Ball, Cheryl E., and Drew M. Loewe, eds. 2017. *Bad Ideas about Writing*. Morgantown: West Virginia University Libraries.

Carr, Allison. 2013. "In Support of Failure." *Composition Forum* 27. http://compositionforum.com/issue/27/failure.php.

Caswell, Nicole I. 2014. "Dynamic Patterns: Emotional Episodes within Teachers' Response Practices." *Journal of Writing Assessment* 7 (1). http://journalofwritingassessment.org/article.php?article=76.

Caswell, Nicole I., Jackie Grutsch McKinney, and Rebecca Jackson. 2016. *The Working Lives of New Writing Center Directors*. Logan: Utah State University Press.

Constanti, Panikkos, and Paul Gibbs. 2004. "Higher Education Teachers and Emotional Labor." *International Journal of Educational Management* 18 (4): 243–249. doi:10.1108/09513540410538822.

Costello, Kristi Murray. 2018. "From Combat Zones to Contact Zones: The Value of Listening in Writing Center Administration." *Peer Review* 2. http://thepeerreview-iwca.org/issues/relationality-si/from-combat-zones-to-contact-zones-the-value-of-listening-in-writing-center-administration/.

Davies, Laura J. 2017. "Grief and the New WPA." *WPA: Writing Program Administration* 40 (2): 40–51.

DeBacher, Sarah, and Deborah Harris-Morris. 2016. "First, Do No Harm: Teaching Writing in the Wake of Traumatic Events." *Composition Forum* 34. https://compositionforum.com/issue/34/first-do-no-harm.php.

Driscoll, Dana Lynn, and Roger Powell. 2016. "States, Traits, and Dispositions: The Impact of Emotion on Writing Development and Writing Transfer across College Courses and Beyond." *Composition Forum* 34. https://compositionforum.com/issue/34/states-traits.php.

George, Diana, ed. 1999. *Kitchen Cooks, Plate Twirlers, and Troubadours: Writing Program Administrators Tell Their Stories*. Portsmouth, NH: Heinemann.

Glomb, Theresa M., and Michael J. Tews. 2004. "Emotional Labor: A Conceptualization and Scale Development." *Journal of Vocational Behavior* 64 (1): 1–23.

Guy, Mary E., Meredith A. Newman, and Sharon H. Mastracci. 2008. *Emotional Labor: Putting the Service in Public Service*. New York: Routledge.

Hochschild, Arlie Russell. 2012. *The Managed Heart: Commercialization of Human Feeling*. Berkeley: University of California Press.

Jackson, Rebecca, Jackie Grutsch McKinney, and Nicole I. Caswell. 2016. "Writing Center Administration and/as Emotional Labor." *Composition Forum* 34. http://compositionforum.com/issue/34/writing-center.php.

Jacobs, Dale, and Laura Micciche, eds. 2003. *A Way to Move: Rhetorics of Emotion and Composition Studies*. Portsmouth, NH: Heinemann.

Leake, Eric. 2016. "Writing Pedagogies of Empathy: As Rhetoric and Disposition." *Composition Forum* 34. https://compositionforum.com/issue/34/empathy.php.

Mastracci, Sharon H., Meredith A. Newman, and Mary E. Guy. 2010. "Emotional Labor: Why and How to Teach It." *Journal of Public Affairs Education* 16 (2): 123–141.

Mastracci, Sharon H., Mary E. Guy, and Meredith A. Newman. 2014. *Emotional Labor and Crisis Response: Working on the Razor's Edge*. New York: Routledge.

Micciche, Laura R. 2007. *Doing Emotion: Rhetoric, Writing, Teaching*. Portsmouth, NH: Boynton/Cook.

Micciche, Laura R. 2016. "Staying with Emotion." *Composition Forum* 34. https://compositionforum.com/issue/34/micciche-retrospective.php.

Moore, Cindy. 2018. "Mentoring WPAs for the Long Term: The Promise of Mindfulness." *WPA: Writing Program Administration* 42 (1): 89–106.

Morris, J. Andrew, and Daniel C. Feldman. 1996. "The Dimensions, Antecedents, and Consequences of Emotional Labor." *Academy of Management Review* 21 (4): 986–1010.

O'Brien, Tim. 1990. *The Things They Carried.* New York: Penguin.

Perry, Alison. 2016. "Training for Triggers: Helping Writing Center Consultants Navigate Emotional Sessions." *Composition Forum* 34. https://compositionforum.com/issue/34/training-triggers.php.

Phillips, Talinn, Paul Shovlin, and Megan Titus. 2014. "Thinking Liminally: Exploring the (com)Promising Positions of the Liminal WPA." *WPA: Writing Program Administration* 38 (1): 42–64.

Prebel, Julie. 2016. "Engaging a 'Pedagogy of Discomfort': Emotion as Critical Inquiry in Community-Based Writing Courses." *Composition Forum* 34. https://compositionforum.com/issue/34/discomfort.php.

Rand, Erin J. 2015. "Bad Feelings in Public: Rhetoric, Affect, and Emotion." *Rhetoric and Public Affairs* 18 (1): 161–176.

Reid, E. Shelley. 2017. "On Learning to Teach: Letter to a New TA." *WPA: Writing Program Administration* 40 (2): 129–145.

Robillard, Amy E. 2007. "We Won't Get Fooled Again: On the Absence of Angry Responses to Plagiarism in Composition Studies." *College English* 70 (1): 10–31.

Sano-Franchini, Jennifer. 2016. "'It's Like Writing Yourself into a Codependent Relationship with Someone Who Doesn't Even Want You': Emotional Labor, Intimacy, and the Academic Job Market in Rhetoric and Composition." *College Composition and Communication* 68 (1): 98–124.

Saur, Elizabeth, and Jason Palmeri. 2017. "Letter to a New TA: Affect Addendum." *WPA: Writing Program Administration* 40 (2): 146–153.

Schell, Eileen E. 2006. "Putting Our Affective House in Order: Toward Solidarity Rather than Shame in Departments of English." *JAC* 26 (1–2): 204–220.

Schmidt, Samantha. 2018. "Rachel Maddow Breaks Down in Tears on Air While Reading Report on 'Tender Age' Shelters." *Washington Post*, June 20. https://www.washingtonpost.com/news/morning-mix/wp/2018/06/20/rachel-maddow-breaks-down-in-tears-on-air-while-reading-report-on-tender-age-shelters/.

Steinberg, Ronnie J., and Deborah M. Figart. 1999. "Emotional Labor since the Managed Heart." *Annals of the American Academy of Political and Social Science* 561 (1): 8–26.

Taggart, Amy Rupiper. "Reseeing the WPA Skill Set: GenAdmins Transitioning from WPA to University Pedagogical Leadership." 2018. In *WPAs in Transition: Navigating Educational Leadership Positions,* edited by Courtney Adams Wooten, Jacob Babb, and Brian Ray, 151–167. Logan: Utah State University Press.

Wharton, Amy S. 1993. "The Affective Consequences of Service Work." *Work and Occupations* 20 (2): 205–232.

Worsham, Lynn. 1998. "Going Postal: Pedagogic Violence and the Schooling of Emotion." *JAC* 18 (2): 213–245.

SECTION I

Preserving Work Identities

1
DON'T WORRY, BE HAPPY
How to Flourish as a WPA

Carrie S. Leverenz
  Texas Christian University

When I recently returned to my former position as director of composition after a ten-year hiatus, a lot had changed. I had the security of a recent promotion to full professor, I no longer had children living at home, and on the advice of a counselor, I had achieved a better work-life balance by spending weekends volunteering at the Humane Society. Just as important, the composition program I had once been hired to develop was running like a well-oiled machine, thanks to the committed work of the director who had done the job for the previous decade. Why, then, in the middle of the pre-semester workshop for new graduate instructors, did I find myself not wanting to be there? This WPA job, unlike many others, was eminently doable. My primary responsibility was to train and supervise the twenty or so graduate instructors who taught first- and second-year writing courses. I had a 2–1 teaching load and a graduate assistant. I had a supportive department chair and dean. My labor conditions and those of the teaching staff were by all objective measures good. If I were unhappy as a writing program administrator (WPA)—a position and professional identity I had willingly embraced—then it was up to me to figure out why and to fix it. I learned that in counseling, too.

   In this chapter, I want to explore how therapeutic interventions from positive psychology can help WPAs achieve more personal and professional happiness, a state psychologist Martin E.P. Seligman (2011) terms "flourishing." Importantly, flourishing depends not on the absence of negative emotion but on the strengthening of positive emotions. As the basis of clinical practice, positive psychology works to increase clients' sense of well-being by focusing on five elements: positive emotion, engagement, meaning, positive relationships, and accomplishment. Increased attention to these elements can contribute to resilience—the ability to maintain a positive attitude and positive action in the face of adversity—a quality that is essential for success as a WPA.

Of course, the pursuit of happiness, whether personal or professional, is inevitably fraught. As Sara Ahmed (2010, 2) and other cultural critics have pointed out, too often "happiness is used to reinscribe social norms as social goods." Our ideas about what it means to be happy, to have a happy life or even just a happy work-life, are inevitably influenced by the norms of dominant culture. As Ahmed (2010, 11) puts it, the face of happiness can look "rather like the face of privilege." It is those in power who determine what it means to be happy, who construct ideals of happiness based on their interests and whose ideals come to be seen not as a choice but as the way things are supposed to be. Consequently, those who are unhappy often blame themselves rather than blaming the ideals of happiness they feel compelled to pursue. Ahmed's (2010, 13, 207) project is to suspend "belief that happiness is a good thing" and to instead see unhappiness not as the absence of an inherent good but "as a form of political action: the act of saying no or of pointing out injuries" that can make visible the problematic price of happiness. Happiness—contentment with the ways things are—does not in itself lead to long-term flourishing as a WPA, but neither does unhappiness. As I will explore below, positive psychology can help WPAs increase their individual well-being, thus providing the positive emotional resources needed to respond productively to the very real sources of unhappiness that plague many writing programs.

One ideal of academic happiness that can make being a WPA challenging is that our jobs are different from other faculty jobs, and yet we are often evaluated according to the same standards as other faculty. While institutions typically have explicit guidelines for assessing teaching, research, and service, they often lack clear policies for assessing administrative work. To compensate, WPAs try to fit ourselves into the happiness ideal of academic life that was not created with us in mind. For example, when I accepted my first tenure-track job directing a writing center and supervising computer classrooms, two areas I had not been trained for in graduate school, my research agenda took a quick detour into writing program administration. There simply wasn't time to run these programs and develop research building on my dissertation, as most tenure-track assistant professors are expected to do. Unfortunately, in reviewing my tenure case, the dean found my research profile unfocused. And he saw my administrative work merely as the reason I had less extensive evidence of teaching. In other words, the administrative work contributed nothing because it didn't "fit." Frankly, there can be good reasons for wanting to "fit" into the academic happiness ideal. In the years when I wasn't WPA, I had more intellectual energy to devote to exploring new research interests and teaching many elective writing courses (Cyberliteracy, Women's Rhetorics, Editing and Publishing, Rhetoric of Social Media). As WPA, my teaching is more circumscribed: I teach the practicum course for new graduate instructors and a section of first-year composition every fall and in the spring, one upper-division writing course or graduate course. Lack of time to pursue research and teaching interests outside of writing program administration can feel like a loss.

Of course, there are gains that offset the losses. The work of building and supporting a writing program, while sometimes all-consuming, can also be exhilarating and creatively rewarding. Many of us also enjoy writing program administration because of the relationships we can build, both with teachers in our program and with other constituents across the institution. Being good at building relationships requires what Mara Holt, Leon Anderson, and Albert Rouzie (2003, 147) call "emotion work," which they define as "responsive attention to the emotional aspects of social life, including attention to personal feelings, the emotional tenor of relationships, empathy and encouragement, mediation of disputes, building emotional solidarity in groups, and using one's own or others' outlaw emotions to interrogate structures." Unfortunately, being a WPA who is good at emotion work also brings challenges. For one, the pleasure a WPA may feel in fostering relationships can be thwarted by pressure to prioritize other demands of the job. (Do I take an adjunct to lunch or finish this assessment report?) There is also danger in not establishing limits on how much time and energy we invest in emotion work because such work is often invisible and cannot make up for the visible, countable work that institutions prefer we do. Emotion work is simply not part of the academic happiness ideal. Rebecca Jackson, Jackie Grutsch McKinney, and Nicole I. Caswell (2016), in their discussion of emotional labor in writing center administration, use case studies to demonstrate the challenge of managing many competing relationships: "Directors had to forge, maintain, and grow relationships with their staffs, administrative assistants, supervisors, faculty, administrators, students in their classes, and users of their centers. Writing center directors' labor often involved weighing which relationships to prioritize." In addition, too much emotional work, when it takes us away from research, teaching, and other program responsibilities, can lead to negative evaluations, even denials of tenure (as I experienced in that first tenure-track writing center–computer classroom job). This is one reason some WPA scholars warn against assuming WPA responsibilities prior to tenure. Without the protection of tenure, we take care of writing programs and the people in them at our own risk.

Although I was seemingly risking little when I resumed my role as director of composition, I did have my own work life to guard. In those ten years when I wasn't a WPA, I had achieved a happy balance of teaching, research, mentoring, and service. When I returned to being a WPA, I feared losing that balance as my morning writing time was interrupted by urgent emails and the part of me that used to thrive on problem solving was often exhausted instead. During my first fall semester back as WPA, three of twenty graduate instructors, including the assistant program director, had babies, all delivered by C-section and thus requiring more extensive recovery time; one graduate instructor needed surgery to remove a potentially cancerous tumor (benign, thank God); and another underwent gender confirmation surgery and was actively transitioning while teaching for the first time. I willingly extended myself to care, in Nel Noddings's (2013) terms, for these instructors—checking my phone hourly for birth news, covering classes, meeting with concerned students. Such emotion work is one part of being a WPA that I typically enjoy. But I would be lying to say there isn't a point at which emotional labor becomes laborious. Recognizing that point and knowing what to do about it is key to flourishing as a WPA. As we learn on every flight, you need to put the oxygen mask over your own face before assisting those near you.

The emotional work of caring for others is closely tied to what Arlie Hochschild (2012) calls "emotional labor," the added burden of needing to manage one's feeling on the job. Importantly, not all emotional labor is equally taxing. In their study of the emotional demands in five occupations involving "people work," psychologists Celeste M. Brotheridge and Alicia A. Grandey (2002, 32) found that "people work may have unusual work demands but . . . these act as both stressors and resources for the employees." Hochschild observed two forms of emotional labor: surface acting and deep acting. In surface acting, employees (Hochschild studied flight attendants) labor to express appropriate emotions such as cheerfulness, regardless of their actual feelings. In contrast, employees who engage in deep acting work to genuinely feel the emotion they are expected to express (Hochschild 2012, 2). As researchers have found, while surface acting can cause profound mental and physical stress, deep acting often correlates with career satisfaction and feelings of self-efficacy, especially when exhibited by those in caring careers such as nursing, social work, and teaching (Brotheridge and Grandey 2002). In my case, because being a good mentor is something I personally value as well as a requirement of the job of WPA, I work at feeling empathy (rather than annoyance) when new teachers struggle with what seem like simple teaching tasks or need to vent about students who challenge their authority. For me, such work involves identifying with their struggles, reminding them that I, too, doubt myself when I have a bad class or when my authority is questioned, as when an economics teacher who saw my students working in small groups asked me if they were playing "kindiegarten." While the "deep acting" that mentoring sometimes requires is personally satisfying, the work of caring in this way does not easily fit into the academic happiness ideal.

One reason emotion work isn't included in measures of academic success is that the caring careers normally associated with it, like nursing, teaching, and social work, are dominated by women while the academy is still dominated by men. Work in composition, including writing program administration, which continues to be tied to teaching beginning students and training inexperienced teachers, is also feminized (Barr-Ebest 1995; Schell 1998). In her study of emotion in composition studies, Laura Micciche (2007, 82) highlights the ways the emotion work performed by female WPAs benefits the academy by "reinscrib[ing] women as nurturers whose job involves the unpaid labor of nurturing others." As a feminist WPA, I want to break the cycle of expecting women to play this (uncompensated) nurturing role and to disrupt notions of composition teaching as academic childrearing. But I also want the university to recognize that the work of caring (for students, teachers, programs) is legitimate labor, necessary for the health of any institution. While I feel personally rewarded when I work to authentically care for those in the writing program I administer, I am also cautious about putting immediate personal rewards ahead of longer-term professional ones. If I am to flourish as a WPA, I need to do what makes me happy now and also what will give me the emotional resources to fight for fairer assessments of administrative work, including emotion work, in the future.

As I was reentering the fray of being a WPA, I was also directing a dissertation that, among other things, explored how positive psychology, especially the experience of "flow," impacts writers. Assuming that positive psychology was merely a popular self-help movement, I advised the graduate student to address (my) reader skepticism; she did so in the next draft, citing *The Oxford Handbook of Positive Psychology*, 2nd edition (Lopez and Snyder 2011). Curious, I checked out the source and realized that maybe I needed to play the believing game, at least for a while, and not just for my student's sake but also for my own. An important principle of positive psychology is that well-being is not something you have but something you work at. Well-being also involves more than removing the negativity in your life. In Seligman's (2011, 182) words, "The skills of enjoying positive emotion, being engaged with the people you care about, having meaning in life, achieving your work goals, and maintaining good relationships are entirely different from the skills of not being depressed, not being anxious, and not being angry." As a WPA, knowing how to increase our well-being in the face of negative experiences is key to being able to do the positive work we want to do. And as so much of the discourse around being a WPA attests, there *will* be negative experiences. Unfortunately, the flood of cautionary tales that surround WPA work can lead to a focus on surviving—doing the best you can with what you have—rather than thriving—making choices that yield maximum productivity and happiness. I had just spent the last ten years thriving as a non-WPA. I did not want to go back to the frenzied dissatisfaction that led me to therapy in the first place. Positive psychology, with its emphasis on actively pursuing well-being, seemed worth a try.

The premise behind Seligman's program is fairly simple: we first need to know what makes us happy and then find ways to do more of it. Seligman calls those aspects of our character that we most enjoy using our signature strengths. According to Seligman (2011, 39), a signature strength gives us "a sense of ownership and authenticity, a feeling of excitement while displaying it, a rapid learning curve as the strength is practiced, a sense of yearning to find new ways to use it, a feeling of inevitability in using the strength, invigoration rather than exhaustion while using the strength, the creation and pursuit of personal projects that revolve around it. Joy, zest, enthusiasm, even ecstasy while using it."

Using widely validated questionnaires, Seligman (2011, 243–265) identified twenty-four signature strengths, which he organized into six broad categories:

Wisdom and Knowledge
1. Curiosity/Interest in the World
2. Love of Learning
3. Judgment/Critical Thinking/Open-mindedness
4. Ingenuity/Originality/Practical Intelligence/Street Smarts
5. Social Intelligence/Personal Intelligence/Emotional Intelligence
6. Perspective

Courage
7. Valor and Bravery
8. Perseverance/Industry/Diligence
9. Integrity/Genuineness/Honesty

Humanity and Love
10. Kindness and Generosity
11. Loving and Allowing Oneself to be Loved

Justice
12. Citizenship/Duty/Teamwork/Loyalty
13. Fairness and Equity
14. Leadership

Temperance
15. Self-control
16. Prudence/Discretion/Caution
17. Humility and Modesty

Transcendence
18. Appreciation of Beauty and Excellence
19. Gratitude
20. Hope/Optimism/Future-mindedness
21. Spirituality/Sense of Purpose/Faith/Religiousness
22. Forgiveness and Mercy
23. Playfulness and Humor
24. Zest/Passion/Enthusiasm

> (The Values in Action [VIA] Signature Strength questionnaire and many other questionnaires developed by the Authentic Happiness Program at the University of Pennsylvania can be found at https://www.authentichappiness.sas.upenn.edu/home).

According to Seligman (2011, 24), "Deploying your highest strengths leads to more positive emotion, to more meaning, to more accomplishment, and to better relationships." While it seems obvious that doing more of what we're good at will make us happier, Seligman's emphasis on intentionally cultivating opportunities to use our strengths can be an important reminder during those times when WPA work seems especially burdensome. As I sat in that pre-semester workshop for new graduate instructors, not wanting to be there, I was thinking about the job and why it was making me unhappy (the emails, the emotional demands); I was not thinking about what I needed in my work life to make me happier. By identifying my strengths and finding more ways to use them, I have increased the positive aspects of my job. The negative aspects have not gone away, but now I approach my work with a clearer understanding of how to maximize my happiness as I do it, leaving me in a better position to engage in the hard work of changing what makes me unhappy.

According to the VIA survey of character strengths, my top five signature strengths include (1) capacity to love and be loved, (2) love of learning, (3) curiosity and interest in the world, (4) fairness, equity, and justice, and (5) leadership. These findings are not a surprise for a feminist (#4) woman (#1) academic (#2 and #3) who is also a WPA (#5). Still, it was good to confirm that I am in the right profession. It was also not a surprise that my "capacity to love and be loved" is my greatest strength. (I have an Andy Warhol poster in my office with the caption "I think everybody should like everybody.") Interestingly, that finding did help explain the anxiety I felt during the training workshop, when my relationships with the new graduate instructors were as yet unknown. In Seligman's scheme, because I feel happiest when engaged in positive relationships, I should find ways to care (and be cared about) even more. But caring can come at a cost of time and energy that ultimately limits my ability to use my other character strengths such as "love of learning" and "curiosity and interest in the world." I need to recognize that I need the positive energy that comes from intellectual pursuits. This is not merely a concession to a normative ideal of academic happiness but actually makes me happier. To flourish as a WPA, I need to maximize the use of all of my character strengths toward increasing positive emotion, engagement, meaning, positive relationships, and achievement. Below I will describe some of the ways I have worked to do that in the last year.

Shifting to a focus on building positive emotion can be hard for WPAs since, as academics, we have been trained to see the world, our work, and ourselves critically. (As Peter Elbow pointed out long ago, academics are much better at doubting than believing.) WPAs are especially driven not just to identify problems but to try to solve them, often without the power or resources to do so. This may be why, in her analysis of WPA narratives, Micciche (2007) identifies disappointment as the prevailing emotion expressed by WPAs. Here she summarizes Richard Miller's description of the job: "The WPA must navigate the murky waters of institutional hierarchy where decisions to create any sort of change are seriously constrained; where daily existence requires pragmatic, sometimes morally problematic decisions, and where one's ability to act on one's conscience or political ideas is seriously compromised" (2007, 84). While acknowledging the many reasons why WPAs might feel justifiably disappointed, Micciche also notes that particular emotions can "function as the adhesive that aligns certain bodies together and binds a person/position/role to an affective state" (75). Specifically, reading WPA discourse and being in the company of other WPAs can lead one to believe that disappointment simply marks one as a member of the WPA community. As a result, negative states can "become naturalized . . . not framed as problems but . . . viewed as inevitable and unchangeable" (75). Although Micciche acknowledges that some WPA narratives do describe pleasurable parts of the job— "teacher training, collaborative work, and other aspects of the job that create a community of teachers committed to providing quality writing instruction"—she concludes that emotional ambivalence is perhaps the most WPAs can hope for (81).

The title of Theresa Enos and Shane Borrowman's (2008) *The Promise and Perils of Writing Program Administration* makes clear the emotional ambivalence of much WPA work. Perhaps not surprisingly, the graduate students who read the book in my WPA seminar found the stories collected there to be far more perilous than promising. As a result, even before becoming WPAs, these students were being socialized to accept peril and the negative emotions that come with it as a normal part of being a WPA. Ultimately, Micciche (2007, 85) argues that owning up to our (sometimes) negative feelings about our jobs is essential: "To deny the negative emotional realities of the academy does a disservice to faculty and the graduate students we train, for it leaves all of us unprepared to navigate our way through the material, including the affective realities of academic life." It was exactly for this reason that I framed my WPA graduate course as an exploration of writing program administration as a critical problem, encouraging students to consider whether the challenges WPAs face are inherent in the role. But I also wanted them to see that by accepting as normal the emotional ambivalence that often comes with WPA work, we reify the ideal of academic happiness that intentionally excludes what WPAs do. Ambivalence about our work is not a state that can or should be maintained long-term. And for those WPAs like me who want to feel not ambivalence about but happiness in our jobs, even while knowing there are problems we need to address, positive psychology offers strategies for working toward that goal.

POSITIVE EMOTION

The most obvious component of well-being is positive emotion—feeling happy. A widely advocated strategy for increasing positive emotion is the expression of gratitude. Seligman (2011) recommends an exercise known as the Gratitude Letter, which involves identifying an important person in your life, writing them a letter describing what you are grateful to them for, hand delivering the letter, and then reading it out loud to them. In another gratitude activity called the Three Blessings Exercise, you are charged with writing down at the end of each day three things that happened that made you happy and why they happened. Seligman (2010) argues that "becoming more conscious of good events reliably increases your happiness and decreases depression" by building the skill of savoring positive experience. As Seligman (2010) explains, doing so is necessary to overcome our Negativity Bias: the tendency for negative experiences "to exert greater psychological impact on us than positive experiences of the same magnitude." As I highlighted above, this bias toward the negative is especially keen in academe. While I did not complete the specific exercises Seligman describes, I have made a conscious effort to acknowledge and express gratitude for the positive people and events in my work life. For example, although I normally eat lunch at my desk, I've made an effort to take writing teachers for coffee or lunch or to visit with them in their offices. I also make sure I thank them every time I send them an announcement or ask them to do something like submit their syllabi. Saying "thank you" is a reminder to them and to me that I am grateful for their service to the program. And Seligman is right—feeling grateful does bring joy. Making it a habit to acknowledge and savor the positive in our work lives does not mean we are ignoring or denying the real problems we may face. It means we are taking steps to actively build up the store of positive emotion we'll need to deal with those problems.

ENGAGEMENT

Another crucial element of well-being is engagement. Positive psychologist Mihaly Csikzentmihaly (2004) refers to especially high levels of engagement as "flow," a mental state characterized by "being completely involved in an activity for its own sake. The ego falls away. Time flies. Every action, movement, and thought follows inevitably from the previous one, like playing jazz. Your whole being is involved, and you're using your skills to the utmost." Just as knowing our strengths and using them often can increase our reserve of positive emotion, so, too, can finding more ways to experience flow.

Based on hundreds of interviews, first with artists and scientists and then with people in many different occupations and cultures, from figure skating to business to sheep herding, Csikzentmihaly (2004) identified seven characteristics of a flow experience: (1) complete involvement with the task, (2) a sense of being outside everyday reality, (3) great inner clarity, (4) knowing that the activity is doable, (5) a sense of serenity—no worries about oneself, (6) timelessness—totally focused on the present, and (7) intrinsic motivation—whatever produces flow becomes its own reward. He then theorized how we might increase our experience of flow by charting various levels of engagement in relation to both challenge and skill. What he found is that people experience flow when the challenge they face is higher than average and their skill is also higher than average. But flow need not be triggered by a random lining up of the stars. The flow experience can be orchestrated. For example, in the state Csikzentmihaly calls Arousal, we experience a high level of challenge, but to move into flow we need to develop higher skills. Similarly, in the state Csikzentmihaly calls Control, we have high skill but to achieve flow we need to increase the challenge so as to create excitement. As WPAs we might ask, in what areas of our work do we experience flow and how can we find ways to do more of that kind of work? We might also ask in what areas we feel arousal—challenged but not yet with high skill. Or in what areas do we feel control—confident in our skill but not yet sufficiently challenged.

When I agreed to resume the role of director of composition, I knew I wanted to do more than be a caretaker for a program that was already running well. The fact that the program didn't *need* me may have been one reason for my initial discontent—how would I make my mark? Here again, as WPAs we are so attuned to the dominant narrative in which the heroic WPA sweeps in to save a program from its myriad problems that it can be hard to imagine a role for the WPA that doesn't require playing the fixer. When I first came to this program, it had been without a director for two years and had no required graduate instructor training, course outcomes, or common syllabus. Under these circumstances, it was easy to earn praise for "bringing sanity to the composition program," as a literature colleague described it. In Csikzentmihaly's terms, every day involved a high level of challenge for which I, as an experienced WPA, had a high level of skill. Where would I find those challenges now? Luckily, the composition program was due for its university-required assessment during my first year back as WPA, so I had an opportunity to identify where I could most beneficially invest my time. In deciding which of the assessment recommendations to prioritize, I considered not just what the program needed but also what I needed. Which projects represented the perfect intersection of high challenge and high skill that would facilitate flow? For me, that is curriculum design. When I am imagining how to put a course together, drafting assignments, looking for supporting materials, I experience flow: I am completely immersed in the activity and lose any sense of time; I believe the task is doable while also being challenged by it. I am intensely focused, with one idea leading to the next. I lose awareness of myself and become consumed by the task. The completion of the task is its own reward. Others with different signature strengths or flow experiences might choose different activities to invest in. The point is that to thrive as a WPA, we need to spend some part of our week deeply engaged in the most stimulating, satisfying parts of our work.

RELATIONSHIPS

It is well documented that positive relationships contribute significantly to both physical and mental well-being. Being connected to a network of support has been shown to yield not only increased happiness but also longevity. This is good news for me, whose highest signature strength is building and sustaining relationships (loving and being loved). Nevertheless, it can be dangerous to invest so heavily in one strength that we underutilize the others. Relationships, even good ones, can become too much of a good thing when they exhaust rather than replenish us. And nothing drains our store of well-being faster than overinvestment in relationships that yield a negative rather than a positive return.

Knowing how to respond to a difficult relationship can be hard for WPAs who often feel responsible for making everyone happy. Although as WPAs we advise new teachers not to dwell on that one negative student evaluation, it can sometimes be difficult to take our own advice, finding it personally painful when an instructor ignores or resists our guidance or when a new graduate instructor complains that the training we provide is a waste of time. While it is important for WPAs to attend to instructor morale, we also need to accept that not everyone will like us or want a relationship with us. After we have made a good faith effort to keep communication open and to invite and respond to instructors' concerns, we need to shift our attention to helping those teachers who want our help and focus on working with those who want to build relationships with us and the composition program.

For example, after some interpersonal conflicts my first semester back as WPA that exacerbated my unhappiness in the position, I was able to increase my happiness the following spring by strengthening positive relationships with graduate instructors who were interested in participating in curriculum revision with me. More specifically, a voluntary team of graduate instructors and I met every two weeks to brainstorm possible inquiry questions for the revised course, draft assignment sequences, and identify open online resources. We also set up focus groups so other composition instructors could share their perspectives on our tentative plans. Though adding more meetings to my schedule might seem a sure way to deplete whatever positive emotion I had accumulated, in fact, after each of the curriculum revision meetings, I felt buoyed by the thoughtfulness and creativity of these graduate instructors whose ideas for the new syllabus greatly enriched my own thinking.

MEANING

Meaning—belonging to and serving something you believe is bigger than yourself—is another key component of well-being (Seligman 2011). While many people find meaning primarily outside of work, academics who often spend years earning their PhDs, incur student debt, put off childbearing, and move to undesirable locations away from family do so because they expect the work to be worth it. The graduate students I know aspire to be WPAs because they care deeply about the teaching of writing. Unfortunately, many will find their desire to do meaningful work thwarted by institutional constraints—a punishing workload, no budget, unsupportive colleagues, lack of tenure protection. No WPA can be happy doing what we do without a sense that our work is important, and not just to us. At a recent meeting of the Conference on College Composition and Commnunication (CCCC), I was in a discussion group with a young WPA who was lamenting the lack of interest in her work at her small school. I gave her the obvious advice to attend a WPA conference so she could widen her circle, but I also suggested that she look for other groups on campus that she could affiliate with or start a reading or writing group that would help her feel valued and provide a sense of community. While it is possible to see writing program administration as a service position we simply move through, it is easier to do the mundane work of staffing courses, making schedules, and adjudicating plagiarism cases if we find meaning in the larger goals of developing teachers and delivering effective writing instruction, as well as improving the status of writing on our campuses.

Thankfully, in spite of the malaise I initially felt after returning to being a WPA, I have never doubted that writing program work is meaningful. If I did, I don't think I could do it; I don't think I *should* do it. As we deal with the daily frustrations of being a WPA, we need to remind ourselves—and others—of what is meaningful about what we do. Beyond the intrinsic meaning we find in being committed to writing, we can also find meaning by connecting with other projects and programs on our campuses, in our communities, and beyond. In my case, I have made a commitment to connect the composition program with the diversity, equity, and inclusiveness initiative now under way at TCU by drafting a diversity statement for the common syllabus, adding a diversity, equity, and inclusiveness representative to the Composition Committee, and taking concrete steps to more explicitly address diversity, equity, and inclusion in our curriculum and professional development.

ACHIEVEMENT

Seligman (2011, 18) admits that in his earliest conceptualization of positive psychology, he overlooked the important element of accomplishment: "success, winning, achievement, mastery, pursued for their own sake." But once prompted by a colleague, it was not hard for him to find confirmation of the value of accomplishment in his own life. As a competitive bridge player, Seligman realized that spending hours improving his game makes him happy for no other reason than that he enjoys being good at bridge. Even losing can be valuable for him if he sees it as an opportunity to get better.

How can we increase our sense of achievement as WPAs? As with the other elements of positive psychology, we need to assess what we're good at that we would like to do even better. This goal is fundamentally different from trying to get better at something we're *not good* at. Seligman breaks down the requirements for increased success into several components. Most obvious is effort, the product of self-discipline and grit, which Seligman (2011, 124) defines as "high persistence and high passion for an objective." If you've finished a PhD and landed a job as a WPA, you likely have plenty of self-discipline and grit. But achievement also depends on both speed and the ability to slow down. Speed comes as the result of having a lot of knowledge and skill on automatic pilot. Being fast at some parts of a task, Seligman (2011, 124) finds, gives us more time to be slow at the parts that require executive functions such as "planning, checking your work, calling up memories, and creativity." To be a high-achieving WPA, we need to ask which parts of the job we can learn to do quickly, thus enabling us to slow down for work that deserves more time. Dragging out or procrastinating about the boring or unpleasant parts of our job can cheat us out of time to do the work we find most satisfying. So can failing to delegate tasks that can be done by others (because we feel guilty asking or insist on micromanaging). We can also improve our sense of achievement by spending our most productive hours of the day doing what we're good at and want to get better at rather than what seems most pressing, that is, solving other people's problems. For me, spending a few hours writing (as I am doing right now) or meeting colleagues for lunch to work on a program initiative creates a greater sense of achievement than having an empty inbox.

SOME NEGATIVES OF POSITIVE PSYCHOLOGY

In spite of the academic credentials of many of the foundational figures in positive psychology (the Positive Psychology Center is affiliated with the University of Pennsylvania, where Martin Seligman is the Zellerbach Family Professor of Psychology, and a course on positive psychology at Harvard is the most popular course of all time), the movement has been criticized by some for a perceived lack of academic rigor and by others for an oversimplification of human experience. Given the scholarly predisposition toward the negative, it isn't surprising that popular psychology's "don't worry, be happy" message has been held up by scholars for special scrutiny. For example, in 2013, the journal *American Psychologist* was forced to retract a widely cited 2005 article by positive psychologists Barbara Fredrickson and Marcial Losada after the math they used to determine the exact ratio of positive to negative affect (identified as 2.9013) needed to flourish was shown to be faulty. Similarly, in *Bright-Sided*, Barbara Ehrenreich's (2009, 156) critique of positive thinking in America, she attacks what she calls the "pseudoscientific assertions" of positive psychology and accuses Seligman of being unwilling to address criticism. She is especially critical of claims that positive psychology can lead to improved health and longevity, pointing out that although studies on that question are, in fact, mixed, the results "tend to be spun toward the positive effects of positive emotions on health" (2009, 163).

While these academic critiques of positive psychology deserve consideration, we might also ask, how can a focus on increasing well-being be a bad thing? There are two potential dangers in what might otherwise seem like an innocuous theory. One is the underlying message that we alone are responsible for our happiness. Indeed, Seligman (2011, 105) acknowledges that "responsibility and free will are necessary processes within positive psychology." While it is good to be reminded that we have the agency to change our work lives in positive ways, it can be problematic to blame ourselves when we react negatively to circumstances that warrant a negative reaction. Women especially are socialized to think that our problems are of our own making and that if we are unhappy, it is we rather than our circumstances that need to be fixed (see my admission to that effect at the start of this chapter). We do not need the added burden of feeling guilty about legitimate unhappiness.

A second related problem, as noted above by Sara Ahmed (2010) and also pointed out by Ehrenreich (2009, 170), is that by encouraging people to focus on what's good rather than what's troubling, positive psychology reifies the status quo, "with all its inequalities and abuses of power." There may, in fact, be very good reasons to feel angry or dismayed rather than happy about the way things are, and it is these negative feelings that can motivate change, not just in oneself but in the world. In "Frameworks for Failure," Daniel M. Gross and Jonathan Alexander (2016, 282) make similar claims for the value of negative experience, calling into question "positive rhetorics linking happiness to success." Gross and Alexander (2016, 288) argue that for people positioned on the margins, negative emotions can serve as "entry points to critique the power structures and normalizing discourses that direct our lives and efforts along certain lines." In this, Gross and Alexander echo Ahmed's (2010, 20) contention that "to kill joy . . . is to open a life, to make room for life, to make room for possibility, for chance."

Positive psychologists themselves have begun to address the limitations of a theory of well-being focused exclusively on the positive. Tim Lomas and Itai Ivtzan (2016) acknowledge the criticism of positive psychology for lacking cultural nuance and for not adequately accounting for the complexity of human emotion. Specifically, they highlight the degree to which well-being depends on a dialectic between positive and negative experience. Our feelings of achievement are heightened in light of previous failures; love is intensified by past experience of loss. Ultimately, Lomas and Ivtzan (2016, 1756) argue for a Second Wave Positive Psychology that advances a theory of well-being characterized not by an elevation of positive over negative emotion but by "appreciating and even embracing the complex and ambivalent nature of life."

Which brings us back to Laura Micciche's contention that the feeling that best characterizes WPA experience is ambivalence. We feel ambivalent about being WPAs when the good work we want to do in our programs is thwarted or even crushed by institutional circumstance; we also feel ambivalent when our work as a WPA crushes us. As much of our WPA scholarship makes clear, too many WPA jobs are difficult to do at all, let alone do well and happily. Simply desiring to be happier in our jobs can't change that fact. But positive emotion, increased engagement, productive relationships, a sense of meaning, and feelings of achievement can help us be ready to do the work we want to do, including changing the negative narrative of writing program administration and the institutional conditions that feed that narrative. We also need to work—every day—to change our own identification with it.

Now in my second full year back as director of composition, I still have moments of not wanting to do this job. Just this week, I lost most of my Sunday afternoon after receiving an email from a graduate instructor notifying me that in the sixth week of the semester, he was withdrawing from the program due to a family emergency. In response, I spent several hours scrambling to find a teacher to take over his class *the next day*, pushing my own lesson planning into the evening and my overdue grading into another day. But rather than let these moments of frustration (disappointment, ambivalence) dominate the story I tell myself and the field about what it means to do writing program administration, I was able to counter the negative with more positive feelings because I had spent my Sunday morning writing and because my positive relationships with the other new instructors (and their positive relationships with each other) led one to offer to take over her colleague's course. In addition, my assistant director, who felt guilty that she had to say no to teaching the course for her own family reasons, told me she had learned a lesson about the importance of making choices that would enable her to stay happy in the job. To flourish as a WPA, you have to work at it. Being happy, thus, is its own form of emotional labor, but it is also its own reward.

REFERENCES

Ahmed, Sara. 2010. *The Promise of Happiness*. Durham, NC: Duke University Press.
Barr-Ebest, Sally. 1995. "Gender Differences in Writing Program Administration." *WPA: Writing Program Administration* 18 (Spring): 53–73.
Brotheridge, Celeste M., and Alicia A. Grandey. 2002. "Emotional Labor and Burnout: Comparing Two Perspectives of 'People Work.'" *Journal of Vocational Behavior* 60 (1): 17–39.
Csikzentmihaly, Mihaly. 2004. "Flow: The Secret to Happiness." TED Ideas Worth Spreading. https://www.ted.com/talks/mihaly_csikszentmihalyi_on_flow#t-1119503.
Ehrenreich, Barbara. 2009. *Bright-Sided: How Positive Thinking Is Undermining America*. New York: Picador.
Enos, Theresa, and Shane Borrowman. 2008. *The Promise and Perils of Writing Program Administration*. West Lafayette, IN: Parlor.
Fredrickson, Barbara, and Marcial Losada. 2005. "Positive Affect and the Complex Dynamics of Human Flourishing." *American Psychologist* 60 (7): 678–686.

Gross, Daniel M., and Jonathan Alexander. 2016. "Frameworks for Failure." *Pedagogy* 16 (2): 273–295.

Hochschild, Arlie. 2012. *The Managed Heart: Commercialization of Feeling.* Berkeley: University of California Press.

Holt, Mara, Leon Anderson, and Albert Rouzie. 2003. "Making Emotion Work Visible in Writing Program Administration." In *A Way to Move: Rhetorics of Emotion and Composition Studies,* edited by Dale Jacobs and Laura Micciche, 147–160. Portsmouth, NH: Boynton/Cook.

Jackson, Rebecca, Jackie Grutsch McKinney, and Nicole I. Caswell. 2016. "Writing Center Administration and/as Emotional Labor." *Composition Forum* 34. http://compositionforum.com/issue/34/writing-center.php.

Lomas, Tim, and Itai Ivtzan. 2016. "Second Wave Positive Psychology: Exploring the Positive Negative Dialectics of Wellbeing." *Journal of Happiness Studies* 17: 1753–1768.

Lopez, Shane J., and C. R. Snyder, eds. 2011. *The Oxford Handbook of Positive Psychology,* 2nd ed. Oxford: Oxford University Press.

Micciche, Laura R. 2007. *Doing Emotion: Rhetoric, Writing, Teaching.* Portsmouth, NH: Heineman.

Noddings, Nel. 2013. *Caring: A Relational Approach to Ethics and Moral Education,* 2nd ed. Berkeley: University of California Press.

Schell, Eileen E. 1998. *Gypsy Academics and Mother-Teachers: Gender, Contingent Labor, and Writing Instruction.* Portsmouth, NH: Boynton/Cook.

Seligman, Martin E.P. 2010. "The Three Blessings Exercise." *Building Personal Strength.* http://www.buildingpersonalstrength.com/2010/09/dr-martin-seligman-three-blessings.html.

Seligman, Martin E.P. 2011. *Flourish: A Visionary New Understanding of Happiness and Well-Being.* New York: Free Press.

2
YOU LOST ME AT "ADMINISTRATOR"
Vulnerability and Transformation in WPA Work at the Two-Year College

Anthony Warnke
Green River College

Kirsten Higgins
Green River College

Marcie Sims
Green River College

Ian Sherman
Green River College

A CHARGED LANDSCAPE: THE TWO-YEAR COLLEGE PROFESSIONAL IDENTITY AND WRITING PROGRAM ADMINISTRATION

In the two-year college (TYC), writing program administrators (WPAs) must navigate a uniquely challenging and fraught context. Historically framed as "the contradictory college" (Dougherty 1994), two-year colleges are sites of competing agendas and missions. The complicated status of two-year colleges reflects on the identity of the two-year college instructor—a position expected to be "teacher-scholar-activist" in the current disciplinary conception (Sullivan 2015), overworked literacy laborer (sometimes teaching more than 100 students per term), underpaid member of the proletariat as adjunct faculty, underpaid member of the middle class as full-time faculty, committee member and participant in shared governance, unofficial counselor to students, and grateful recipient of philanthropic organizations' and research universities' wisdom. Although at least half of first-year composition courses are taught at the two-year college (Raines 1990; Taylor 2009), the two-year college is rarely recognized as a site for producing authoritative, generalizable knowledge about these institutions generally and first-year composition in particular (Rodrigo and Miller-Cochran 2018). This is in spite of the fact that TYC scholars produce valuable knowledge and scholarship. Yet in our experience, many faculty members feel they must abide by knowledge created about them without being afforded the agency reflexively extended to university professors, foundation-funded researchers, and policymakers. In such charged contexts, a major hurdle to establishing a WPA may come from faculty members resisting the external actors that ostensibly undermine their autonomy and replicate the subordinated status of the two-year college professoriate as a whole. As Joseph Janangelo and Jeffrey Klausman (2012, 141) suggest, "The idea of a writing program [challenges] two-year college English departments that support pedagogical and curricular autonomy over coherent curricula and pedagogy." Our experience suggests that navigating the affective terrain of two-year college writing programs presents under-explored complexities as well as opportunities to negotiate the emotional labor of the TYC WPA.

Our three narrative case studies in this chapter demonstrate that even wanting to conceive of a "writing program" may cause umbrage, as it suggests absence or deficiency in outcomes and pedagogies that already exist. As pioneering two-year college WPA scholars (Klausman 2008; Janangelo and Klausman 2012; Raines 1990; Calhoon-Dillahunt 2011) have detailed, establishing a writing program at these institutions requires English faculty to uncomfortably question whether their first-year composition courses offer students experiences steeped in best practices in composition, such as those outlined in the "WPA Outcomes Statement" (Harrington et al. 2001). Undertaking such work requires that departments admit that their first-year composition courses may not consistently prepare students adequately or justly and that the composition structures—such as developmental composition sequences—fail to promote equitable access and knowledge transfer. Yet many two-year college English faculty regard the type of reform work taken up to remedy these conditions with suspicion at best. In the current moment, outside research casting community colleges as riddled with equity gaps and work attempting to "reform" two-year colleges—typified by initiatives such as the Bill and Melinda Gates Foundation's Achieving the Dream—often center on first-year and developmental composition courses. Reform work positions writing programs as key sites for fostering student success and completion. Such work frequently collides with faculty perceptions that powerful foundation funders such as Lumina and Gates seek to uproot long-standing, serviceable structures, thereby disrupting the emotional and identity landscapes faculty members have cultivated. These nonprofits' interventions may suggest that who you are and what you've done is insufficient for serving students and society. Two-year college WPAs, in taking up reform initiatives related to those catalyzed by these foundation funders, are in danger of being perceived as fully aligned with those forces of disruption.

Specifically, the role of the WPA ostensibly threatens classroom autonomy by managing classroom practices and dictating writing pedagogies. For many faculty members, the classroom represents the last open space for freedom, creativity, and authority that resists top-down initiatives. Writing program work threatens our colleagues' emotional attachments to what they love to do and must perpetually protect; therefore, WPAs at two-year colleges should begin their work by recognizing the attachments and emotions of their colleagues and attempting to understand the contexts in which they have developed. This chapter argues that we should resist regarding emotions as marginal concerns to ignore or manage. Sara Ahmed (2004, 119) argues that "emotions do things, and they align individuals with communities—or bodily space with social space—through the very intensity of their attachments." Ahmed (2004, 122) explains that emotions dictate and sanction identity positions, constructing what it takes to pass as an acceptable subject within a given space. It is at this intersection that we situate our own work, attempting to make visible a space for WPAs to be acceptable subjects within a two-year college writing program's social and emotional landscape while achieving key reforms that promote student success, especially for underserved students.

At the time of this writing, our WPA position has gone from being a glimmer in our eyes to an annual budget item at our college. The following narratives explore the difficult four-year process it took to institutionalize this position at a diverse, suburban two-year college outside Seattle. This position began with two newly tenured faculty members shaping, proposing, and assuming the co-WPA role. The following year, a well-established, highly esteemed faculty member took over the role. In the third year, a faculty member in his final year of the tenure process took on the position and currently occupies it. Our sequential case studies reflect the experiences of four WPAs and describe some major achievements as well as setbacks we encountered in navigating the emotional landscape of our writing program. From our narratives, we extrapolate a heuristic that lays out strategies for those undertaking WPA work at two-year colleges. We hope our work supports their successful engagement within the affective ecologies of their institutions.

Narrative 1: Startup Costs

Kirsten and Anthony: We began engaging writing program work before we ever considered establishing what was at first a co-WPA position. Our research and professional activities led us to first question the validity of our English course placement mechanisms. Findings suggested that our college's lengthy developmental sequence disproportionately discouraged students of color from continuing on to college-level courses. This initial WPA work pushed forward initiatives to reshape placement and to begin redesigning developmental English through an equity lens. As we saw ourselves taking on larger structural questions that our department had often neglected, we began researching how to create a WPA position that could formally undertake this work. The WPA charge took two years, including a year's worth of uncompensated research and advocacy, to create the position.

We wanted to establish a dynamic, conceptually sound WPA position; however, we had to somehow make this work compelling to colleagues whose identities and emotional attachments were not necessarily based on an affiliation with writing studies scholarship (for a deeper discussion of two-year college faculty's level of disciplinary engagement, see Toth, Griffiths, and Thirolf 2013). Implicitly, we were upstart crows working to systematically and logically question some of the long-accepted, settled structures of our department. In doing this, we were unearthing and activating many tensions. We saw the WPA as a role that could critically negotiate and refashion top-down mandates that prioritize efficiency and austerity, in effect employing a responsibility model over an accountability model (Stenberg 2015). However, most faculty members in our department were not familiar with the WPA as a role that could undertake these critical negotiations. Instead, many associated the WPA with the worst tendencies of neo-liberal management practices. The word *administrator* in the title was particularly unnerving because the faculty were embroiled in a contentious labor dispute with our college administration. As Michalinos Zembylas, (2005a, 26) argues, "Emotions are constituted through language and refer to a wider social life." In the two-year college social sphere, few words engender as much resistance as the word *administrator*, as we often see administrator roles proliferate and salaries rise while faculty are lectured about budget crises and urged to embrace austerity measures (Stolley, this volume). While we wanted to hang on to the "A" in WPA for its disciplinary resonance, we could understand how for some the WPA position triggered images of a bloated administrative bureaucracy seeking to dictate faculty work.

As newer, as yet untenured full-time faculty members, we struggled to figure out how to enact our disciplinary identities and values while negotiating the communities and hierarchies of our institution. We commiserated (usually at conferences) with other faculty members doing unofficial and official WPA work at peer colleges about the toll this work took on us. As we stepped into the role of co-WPA and began to define the parameters of this new position, we were overwhelmed with the emotional labor spent advocating for the position and its concomitant projects. But we were slower to empathize with the emotional labor that preceded us—that is, our fellow faculty members' struggle to establish their individual and group identities. Yes, these identities were sometimes fashioned from savior-model approaches to student abilities as well as a Wild West autonomy in terms of teaching. However, the resistance we faced was about more than knee-jerk turf protection or regressive ideology. For example, reading program faculty feared that reforming our department's labyrinthine developmental reading and writing pipeline would, in fact, eliminate the invisible labor they did with students in their reading courses. Especially since we approached this work as WPAs, with an emphasis on writing in the title, some faculty perceived our efforts as seeking to erase their professional identities. Their fears were existential and based in a lifetime's investment in student success. Reading instructors advocated for the preservation of the reading courses as a separate program and offered dire warnings of the impending loss of institutional history.

We initially thought of ourselves as the first to be liberated from the cave, blinking in the sunlight and eager to bring our light to those still shackled and gazing upon shadows. For example, we struggled with how to serve our linguistically diverse student population and critiqued our department's antiquated practices and attitudes toward multilingual writers. To better serve these students, we wanted our department to become conversant in translingual theories that questioned rigid, Standard English conceptions of composition courses. However, most English faculty members had long gauged their success with multilingual students in terms of how well the program had helped them acculturate into monolithic linguistic norms. Faculty members' lived experiences stood at odds with our vision for a program steeped in practices that translingual scholars like Min-Zhan Lu and Bruce Horner (2013), Suresh Canagarajah (2011), and others advocate. While our work extrapolated from cutting-edge scholarship (that, admittedly, rarely recognized two-year college contexts), faculty members' years of positive attachments and micro-interactions with multilingual students informed their perspectives. Our mistake, to be frank, was to assume that our scholarship was more significant than their affect. For community college faculty, research often oversimplified the diverse goals and backgrounds of students themselves (Adsit and Doe, this volume). Though our colleagues couldn't always couch their fears in terms of recent scholarship or evidence-based practice, their affective responses spoke to how university-generated research often repressed TYC faculty experiences with underserved students.

As Rochelle Rodrigo and Susan Miller-Cochran (2018) argue, the invisibility of composition in writing studies at two-year colleges—despite the large share of the first-year composition courses represented at those institutions—leaves out many important contributions two-year college faculty make to knowledge about teaching composition. The professional identities of two-year college faculty, often unconsciously, are not prominent in the scholarly imagination of writing studies, and the TYC faculty themselves often eschew a connection to scholarship. We might term this a kind of return of the repressed, caused by overlapping and little-recognized mechanisms, including the "socializing out" of scholarly impulses among new TYC faculty, the lack of awareness in four-year institutions—including grad programs—of TYC teacher-scholars, and the brutal workloads entailed in tenure-track positions at the TYC. As noted in 2016's "TYCA Guidelines for Preparing Teachers of English in the Two-Year College" (Two-Year College English Association 2016, 11): "Since many two-year colleges do not allocate resources toward or reward publication, two-year college faculty may lack the support or incentive to participate in national disciplinary dialogues; simultaneously, institutions that reward and support research may fail to include two-year college students and their learning spaces in their research projects on teaching and learning." As Sara Z. Johnson (2017) notes in her account of the shaping of the TYCA statement, there isn't much for us—as leaders among TYC faculty—to do but continue to grow the availability of the teacher-scholar-activist subject position and continue to deepen our values-driven commitments.

Ultimately, following our extensive, vulnerable process of negotiation, we secured the backing of our department and brought our initiative to establish a WPA position to the vice president of instruction. Over the next year, we worked on a variety of key initiatives: designing an equity-centered Accelerated Learning Program, further integrating adjuncts into our program, and spearheading a disparate impact study. As we reflect on establishing the WPA position, we have come to appreciate that forming a writing program at a two-year college is not inventing something out of nothing, breathing life into clay. Initiatives for change challenge "old ways of thinking," but, more significant, they alter existing affective landscapes—they reshape, displace, even replace deeply held attachments, practices, and identity positions that many faculty members have spent their working lives cultivating. And these ways of feeling, while not necessarily extrapolated from scholarship, aren't fundamentally illogical or immaterial.

WPAs have the potential to destabilize or realign the practices, discourses, and emotional habits of their departments; and their colleagues correctly sense the potential for disruption in that work. While the emotional labor it takes to establish a WPA is sensitive and perhaps destabilizing, it also opens up space for transformation. As Michalinos Boler points out, "Vulnerability provides the turbulent ground on which to negotiate truths (e.g., new emotional rules that are less oppressive) that is a necessary foundation of transformation" (quoted in Zembylas 2005b, 946). Vulnerability and transformation run hand in hand. WPAs must build an atmosphere of trust and support even as we shake the foundations that reproduce hierarchical inequities. We hoped that, as Shari J. Stenberg (2015, 11) has suggested, we were engaging in a "feminist repurposing" to locate and enact "new possibilities for teaching and learning, for relating to one another, and for enacting cultural change. It creates something new out of existing conditions." Our initial appointment as co-WPAs was for a one-year term, and, as Stenberg (2005) suggests, prioritizing collaboration within institutional power structures is a potentially system-disrupting move. We advocated for a rotating WPA position as a method of further distributing institutional power and prioritizing a long-term building of a dialogic community of teacher-scholar-activists invested in WPA work.

Narrative 2: Embracing Change and Emotions

Marcie. As I became the second WPA, following the good work of Kirsten and Anthony and continuing the fight to save the established position and the work accomplished through it, my priority tasks were to broaden the reach of the WPA in the division and to get more people involved in the ongoing work. We found out just weeks before my tenure as WPA that the position had been funded for another year, even though we had proven its value with national research and strong local examples and data as well as our own department-level data showing how the equity gap was already reduced and student success increased by the projects we were piloting. So, as I began my year as WPA, I prioritized informing my work with data and research, fighting for adjuncts' equity and offering meaningful professional development workshops for them, and being an advocate for and coordinator of the various pilot projects and accelerated models we were creating as we revamped our pre-college writing pipeline to try to reduce equity gaps and reduce the amount of time it took students to get to college-level writing classes.

Pretty quickly into the position, I found that much of the emotional labor that was woven into the WPA job had to do with navigating change and finding the fine balance between respecting and hearing feelings and concerns related to change and sometimes fixed mind-sets against change while still moving toward innovation and evolving student and program needs. So in addition to dealing with others' emotions, fears, and reactions to the research and proposed deep delve into our writing program and work for change that empowered students, as WPA I had to navigate my own emotional responses to the work and gracefully approach working with my colleagues—other faculty members, both full-time and adjunct—while also working against the institutional barriers to get positive outcomes and implement change.

The biggest ongoing challenge was the lack of time to get everything I wanted to get done accomplished with such a small part of my workload dedicated to being WPA (Adams Wooten, this volume). Other barriers included department and institutional barriers: a culture of initiative fatigue and resistance to change, as well as financial, logistical, and political barriers. At times, I found myself working with frustrated, overworked colleagues as we battled against a student-deficit mind-set that would shut down our progress. Once, for example, at a Problematizing English 101 workshop, the conversation quickly turned into a gripe session about students' deficits. One colleague asked, "How I am I supposed to help students if they don't read?" Another chimed in, "Yeah, and their language barriers make it impossible for me to teach them the material." I had to hone my skills in finding the right balance between letting colleagues air frustrations and commiserating with them versus navigating the conversation back to focusing on meeting students where they are, working with their strengths, and figuring out how best to be proactive in our program, curriculum, and classes to help students succeed. Therefore, respecting colleagues' emotional responses to the challenges of teaching reading and writing in the two-year college system while at the same time moving everyone forward in a positive, constructive way to accomplish those goals is one of the most essential and, at the same time, most draining tasks for two-year college WPAs.

So as WPAs, to succeed in affecting change, we have to learn how to channel the emotions of others as well as our own emotions as we work for program improvement (Wenger, this volume). Mary E. Guy, Meredith A. Newman, and Sharon H. Mastracci (2008, 8) explain that if we do not develop the skills to balance logic, communication, and emotions and to analyze both our own and others' emotional reactions and interactions, then we will not be successful in the work we set out to do: "To ignore this combination of analysis, affect, judgment, and communication is to ignore the 'social lube' that enables rapport, elicits desired responses, and ensures that interpersonal transactions are constructive." In addition to juggling several tasks and projects at once in our roles as WPA, we also have to juggle the emotions of others as well as our own: emotional labor is inevitable to affect genuine change. Donna Strickland (2001, 121) suggests that we must "notice and investigate our emotional stances towards our work, our beliefs about what constitutes a successful program, our beliefs even about the very values we see in the teaching of writing"; and she equates the emotional labor of the WPA to the investment it shows, both for the person doing the work and for the department supporting the work.

WPAs in a two-year college system are constantly battling the injustices of the system for our adjunct faculty members (and trying to get them paid for their time spent on projects, professional development, and curriculum input and thereby the ownership and quality of our program) (Kleinfeld, this volume). For example, my entire division agreed that our WPA should work to help adjunct faculty in an effort to right an ongoing wrong and because of the negative consequences that injustice has for both students and our program. As a result, I sometimes had to take the emotional hit for the inevitable frustration our adjunct faculty were feeling: sometimes it was tough being the WPA working so hard for equity and justice for adjunct faculty while being the emotional target of those frustrations or even anger because of how awful their situation was. That element of the position created one of the hardest tolls emotionally. I listened and fought even harder to get adjunct faculty paid for professional development and for participation in the program outcomes and curriculum, knowing how valuable their participation is not just for the writing program but also for our students, as adjunct teach the majority of our composition courses and are greatly underpaid.

On the positive side, the work I accomplished as WPA has been some of the most transformative and rewarding of my career because we have been able to affect positive change and make long-term improvements in our program for faculty and students. However, like most WPAs, I worked way beyond what the compensation/stipend was for this position, which I had to juggle in addition to my teaching load as well as other department committees, tenure committees, student advising, and other demands required of full-time faculty members. I couldn't anticipate the emotional labor involved in the position and the personal, emotional, intellectual, and philosophical investment I would have to make to succeed in my goals (Leverenz, this volume).

Two-year college WPAs must be strong communicators, sharing information and data but also listening to concerns and genuinely acknowledging and working them out. They must do the heavy lifting needed to achieve change, including holding several meetings, managing ongoing "ambassador" work among various departmental groups, and sharing research, data, and successful models to assuage doubts. In the end, everyone will see how that investment makes a difference.

Essentially, the position itself demands that our own emotional navigation skills grow. Thankfully, there are ways to grow one's skills at dealing with the emotions of others as well as those of oneself in the work required for affecting change as a WPA. Guy, Newman, and Mastracci (2008, 5) explore several aspects of the emotional tasks that come with such a position, such as developing a "spider sense" to be able to read other people's emotions; becoming an "emotional chameleon"; engaging "emotional mirrors" to reflect back other people's feelings in an effort to get the job done; sometimes using "emotional suppression," which entails disregarding one's own feelings to get the job done; and finally, building "emotional armor: the ability to gird oneself against one's own emotional response." WPAs must fight to keep up the level of drive and optimism needed for the position while constantly facing seemingly insurmountable barriers and exhaustion from the emotional labor getting things done as a WPA demands.

Therefore, the essential truth of a WPA affecting positive change in a two-year college writing program is that we have to learn to work effectively and gracefully both with and against the emotions evoked by change in our colleagues and ourselves. We must acknowledge, respect, and channel the inevitable emotional labor aspect of change. The skill of navigating emotional labor grows in this position, and it is a skill that doesn't get acknowledged as it should, for several reasons. One factor is the long tradition of seeing emotional labor as "feminine" and therefore "weak" when it is, in fact, an essential and refined strength (Guy, Newman, and Mastracci 2008, xii). This emotional work and developing the skills to navigate it are essential for achieving change and growth in a department, for both male and female leaders. We all experience the same pressures and emotions that come with a genuine campaign for change. Furthermore, "Emotional labor is taken for granted, not paid for" (xiii); basically, emotional labor has been ignored or devalued for many reasons, including a reliance on work that is physical or cognitive work that can be measured by clear outcomes. Without the emotional labor that goes into getting real change to happen, however, nothing really will happen: emotional labor is an "invisible, but necessary element in person-to-person transactions" (12).

Perhaps WPA position descriptions at two-year colleges should include the following qualification: "Must have skills at navigating one's own as well as others' emotional responses to change and growth." To use a cliché that is apropos for this discussion: being a WPA is (an emotional) labor of love.

Narrative 3: Listening as Leadership

Ian: One expression of the emotional labor of love is to take up the task of mediating. I have been asked at various points in my career to act as mediator between clashing groups—instructor versus student as well as instructor versus instructor. One of the latter disputes centered on outcomes assessment, which should come as no surprise to anyone who has discussed the issue with colleagues for ten minutes. In this case, the younger, female professor heading up a larger push toward outcomes assessment—mandated first by an accreditation report, then by higher administration, and finally by an all-faculty committee founded to implement a larger outcomes structure—was butting heads with an older, male colleague who had no desire to map or document the outcomes for his courses according to the language the committee had demanded. The main issue, it appeared, was verbs. The former, calling upon her work in outcomes assessment, was demanding more active verbs in the senior colleague's course outcomes. She issued the instructions kindly but directly. She even provided a handout from Quality Matters, a nonprofit organization that promotes well-designed online teaching materials, suggesting different verbs for each level of Bloom's Taxonomy. He balked, and suddenly we had a situation. I had nothing to do with the dispute. Our programs shared a dean but nothing else. However, because of my position as WPA in English inside a small community college system, both peers and upper-level administrators have sometimes tasked me (not by policy but by unspoken mandate) with work outside of my assigned duties and sometimes even outside of my department. In this case, the work was listening and translating across a deep rift in academic leadership culture between the world of administration, sometimes couched in an aspirational language of corporatism and management, and the world of faculty members, which often reacts to such language with visceral disgust.

As I talked to the senior faculty member, I could tell he was aware of the problematic power dynamic in his interactions with his colleague, but the anger he felt at her was still palpable. He was offended by the verb chart she emailed him. He didn't want to use his institutional privilege to resist her, but he was doing it anyway, in essence (Carter-Tod, this volume).

"You've got to understand," he told me. "I'm part of the old guard. When this job started, community colleges were basically the Wild West." He meant that at the beginning of his career, there was little to no mandate for assessment or evaluation of the effectiveness of teaching—community college faculty were doing good things merely by taking on their job. His colleague's call for measurement and tracking felt to him like a terrible, deeply administrative imposition on his own freedoms belied by an implicit distrust of his motives and competence. The power disparity between them added to the resentment he felt in a way he'd only admit begrudgingly.

The clash highlights a central tension of writing program administration within the community college system: bridging the cultures of administration and faculty. This common rift in the community college brings challenges and burdens that frequently encumber our work and have little to do with our actual charges. In the story above, I sided neither with the outcomes proponent nor with the outcomes resistor. It would have been wonderful to engage at the level of discourse and argumentation on the actual issues of outcomes assessment and academic freedom; however, the heart of the issue—and the reason I was pulled over—was anger, resentment, and resistance. The conflict stemmed less from a consideration of these pedagogical and professional questions than it did from a deep cultural, affective rift, which pits the values of the administration against the values of the faculty (Stolley, this volume). The WPA often stands right in the middle of that battlefield as each side digs its trench. The strong emotions accompanying this rift are unavoidable. Our job, positioned as we are, is neither to suppress nor justify them. I will suggest another tactic instead: that of compassionate listener.

James Papp reminds us that because higher education administrators may have little formal training in their fields, they may look to the jargon of management with an aspirational eye, belying a deeper anxiety. "University managers," he suggests, "tend to borrow management theory (or management catchphrases) as literature professors lift bits of psychoanalysis, cultural anthropology, and chaos theory for their work" (Papp 2002, 67). He suggests that the rift between administration and faculty is partly sociolinguistic and, as such, should be viewed in appropriate context. "The first condition of speaking to people who see themselves as managers is not to assume that management speak is always misleading," he says, anticipating the charges of corporate soullessness likely to echo back from any faculty member confronted with excessive corporate lingo (67).

However, it's inappropriate to minimize the rift as one of mere semantic difference. Management discourse signifies neo-liberal ideological underpinnings, and many academics have actively resisted this discourse in their own classes and research. Christopher Newfield (2011) analyzes the managerial ideology as he charts the complex movement of the public image of the University of California from evident public good, seen as a clear connection to values of democracy and capitalist self-betterment (especially as a tool for the ascendance of the middle class), to antagonist against capitalist and neo-liberal ideals, especially with the rise of affirmative action. Notions of "meritocracy" were used to mask a white-supremacist anxiety about the growing access of people of color to higher education and thus the middle class (Newfield 2011, 92–106). Accompanying this and the large public war against "political correctness" and multiculturalism of the 1990s were the slow, steady waves of de-funding of higher education leading up to the age of austerity.

Couched in terms of market logic, de-funding public higher education was explained in terms of poor internal management. As Newfield (2011, 127) documents, "University leaders were trying harder than ever to march in step with leaders in business." Thus, the strong reaction many academics have to the sometimes corporatist language of administration has roots in the neo-liberal turn. This reaction can further extend to new initiatives, mandates, or even well-researched academic reforms. In the "Wild West" of the community college world, the last thing you want to do is bring the law into town. To return to the story of the sparring colleagues, the senior professor could have easily created a narrative in which the junior professor was an unwitting tool of a neo-liberal machine that sought to penetrate and permeate higher education, and this narrative carried an emotional appeal too strong to resist.

Part of my emotional work as WPA, then, has required a very careful, open, and delicate form of compassionate listening (Wenger, this volume). In fact, while I spoke to the senior faculty member, I did very little actual speaking. Most of what I did was acknowledge what he was feeling, say that I saw the frustration and anger he felt, and frame these emotions as acceptable and natural. I did not tell him he was right—I took no side at all in the dispute, in fact, except to make sure the privileges of gender and seniority were not being used to stifle disagreement. Rather, I just gave him a space to feel frustrated and angry without judgment. I didn't try to explain the junior professor's position, though I did mention how she was feeling.

I also spoke with that junior faculty member. Here, too, most of my work was listening. I heard her talk about the offense she took to a man with greater institutional power treating her with such disrespect, and I told her what I truly believed: that his use of power (to use extreme vernacular) was fucked up. I listened as she spoke of her own ideological framing, of the institutional mandate she was following, and of her frustration at meeting resistance she did not understand. I didn't try to explain the senior faculty member's position, though I did mention how he was feeling.

I first learned some of these techniques while volunteering for the Shanti Project, a group that provides simple, compassionate listening to those suffering from terminal or life-threatening diseases. Shanti, founded by a clinical psychologist named Charles Garfield in the mid-1970s, bases its compassionate listening service on "mutual respect, positive regard, [and] empowerment"—that is, a belief that we need not always give advice or direction to those we are listening to; rather, that others often have "the solutions to [their] own problems" ("The Shanti Model" 2018). In their trainings, they're very clear on what compassionate listening should and should not provide. One strong admonition is against trying to either dismiss or help justify strong emotions. The job of the compassionate listener is simply to acknowledge the emotion's presence and allow it to exist. Both resisting the emotion and working to justify it with discourse can serve to entrench it more deeply.

As my colleagues have discussed above, the placement of the word *administrator* in our title already speaks to our strange hybrid identities. We carry the ideology of faculty and the expectations of administrators. In so doing, we are often distrusted by both sides. We have a job to do, and we have two very different populations to speak to. These disputes run deep, and it is expected that emotion should accompany them. Both administrators and faculty see their positions as necessary to resist fundamental, existential threats. Both are fighting for the lives of something they love. In such a situation, of course, the fighters will arm themselves with anger and resistance; they will use whatever powers they have in their arsenals. Our job is not to win such fights; if we approach conflict as a combatant, we risk at times strengthening the role emotion plays in these disputes.

I don't wish to suggest that all WPAs should receive training in compassionate listening (though I'm not saying they *shouldn't*, either). Instead, I suggest this: approach emotion, even difficult emotion, as an investigator. Do not seek to eliminate it, and do not seek to justify it. Rather, note its presence, be curious about it, and allow it be part of the work. Don't take it personally, and remember that your colleagues all approach their disputes from their own histories, their own ideologies, their own models. To them, their emotions and positions are clear and rational, even if they are not to you. Believe that their emotions stem from a consistent and coherent identity, and allow them to speak from it.

REPURPOSING STORIES, REMAKING PROGRAMS

Linda Adler-Kassner (2008) emphasizes the need for nimbly framing and shaping narratives of WPA work in ways that are palatable to, and correspond to the values of, institutional stakeholders. Framing her work as an extension of James Hertog and Douglas McLeod, Adler-Kassner (2008, 12) writes that "activating a narrative will in turn trigger connections to others, and the 'meaning' comes from the 'pattern of relations' among the nodes and issues." Indeed, to institutionalize and develop our WPA position, we attempted to deploy and activate narratives that would trigger connections and deepen relations with others, especially by increasing the possibilities of an acceptable WPA subject position and creating a dialogic community.

We would reorient Adler-Kassner's advocacy for storymaking *inward* as well. In our experience, effective narratives—narratives of productive struggle, of progressive change—must be framed and activated for oneself as much as for others. Even as we sat down to write this chapter, our stories continued to grow, and they continually refine our subject positions. Stories do not simply record reality; they construct reality as well, providing a retrospective framework for making meaning that perhaps wasn't coherently available at the time. In fact, the concept of "emotional labor" the CFP for this collection offered allowed us to narrativize and synthesize our individual experiences: to piece together and give form to our individual efforts as well as validate our decision to distribute the role of the WPA across several faculty members. This collection has helped us make sense of the questions: Why did we do this work? Why at times did it seem so difficult, not only from our perspective but also from the perspective of those we engaged? Making sense of our experiences through the frame of emotional labor has allowed us to transform our work and strategies into durable stories that we hope will sustain both us and others, even as the work and our relationship to it is constantly in flux.

In fact, it's partially through our storytelling that we engaged what Stenberg (2005, xxiii) has termed "critical processes." We recommend that affectively engaged WPAs shift their focus from "critical answers" to "critical processes: teaching, learning, questioning, collaborating, reflecting, revising" (Stenberg 2005, xxiii). WPAs who engage story and process, who continually make and remake their own internal narrative architecture as they cultivate their dialogic community within the TYC, are engaging in an ongoing critical process. Deep engagement can help them repurpose their writing programs' existing landscapes, narratives, and resources in compelling ways.

As we argued in our introduction, situating the two-year college WPA within a fragile and complex emotional landscape allows for the successful acceptance of the position. As our narratives demonstrate, attending to the concerns, identities, and entrenched ideologies of those in the ecosystem required deeply understanding and deftly navigating the attachments and commitments of many stakeholders. This would not have been possible without the strategies and trial and error we describe above. Yet we also emphasize self-compassion and storymaking as a mutually informing process for giving to others. The very process of doing stories displaces and disturbs others. Storymaking is always already prioritized as a piece of the work, as the work for cultivating our communities. As Jeffrey Klausman (2018, 400) notes, "To accept the moment and to make conscious the previously unconscious discourse is the compassionate thing to do. We can then accept that this new reality exists and ask, 'What, then, must we do together?'"

On our final note, we'd like to synthesize our experiences into a heuristic for those seeking to establish a WPA position at their own institutions. In our informal conversations with faculty at other two-year colleges, we know that every English/writing department has its own delicate ecosystem. We hope that other ambitious faculty will find our experiences and lessons adaptable and applicable to their own work.

The following strategy sheet offers suggestions for WPAs on how to navigate the contextual, political, and logistical landscape of two-year colleges. Because WPA positions are rare and novel at these institutions, this strategy sheet helps with establishing and implementing a WPA position as well as ensuring its sustainability.

1. Remember that change is inherently, not lamentably, emotional. Vulnerability and even some contention are essential for change and

progress. Listen and move forward in positive ways. See emotion as generative for progress.

2. Center your calls for change on repurposing (Stenberg 2015) the shared vision and preexisting structures. If at all possible, articulate the ways your ethos and your work as WPA align with or extend the already existing values and structures of your department. You're not remaking the department out of whole cloth; you're making a quilt from existing pieces.

3. Defensiveness is not always personal. Community colleges are contested territories that often devalue the professional identities of faculty. WPAs should read defensiveness as representative of tensions within a larger context.

5. On a related note, the epistemologies that drive reform exalt what is empirical and data-driven. However, faculty narratives are valuable, and it's in narrative where the emotions attach and circulate. Faculty stories of success can valuably add nuance to generalized, quantitative data. Remember that in both the disciplinary and larger research contexts, the lived experiences and professional identities of two-year college faculty are often left out or dismissed as "anecdotal" and "lore."

6. Community colleges often value more horizontal and autonomous structures. Introducing structures at a community college can feel like surveillance or intrusion. See Carolyn Calhoon-Dillahunt (2011) regarding how to do WPA work without the formal WPA role.

7. Make negotiating a new position within a history possible without obliterating that history. Rather than clinging to old stories or complete detachment from hard situations, stay close to difficulty with mindful presence. This is especially necessary in the face of deeply entrenched histories and narratives. Instead of allowing the status quo to control the narrative, recast the history to weave its narrative into the efforts of change. Innovation does not eclipse the battles of the past; they are fundamental to it.

8. Gain strength from the scholarly community. Immerse yourself in the rich subset of WPA scholarship concerning the two-year college as well as WPA and assessment scholarship more generally. Study the published work of Klausman, Ostman, Calhoon-Dillahunt, Raines, Hassel and Giordano, Adler-Kassner, Gallagher, Stenberg, Toth, and others. Reach out on the TYCA and WPA listservs. Create bonds with WPAs and others at two-year colleges in your state, region, and beyond. When you see a CFP that promises you an opportunity to further explore and reflect on your narrative, seize that opportunity and join the scholarly dialogue.

9. Work on multiple dimensions of equity. In our experience, for example, administration gave us permanent funding for the WPA position but cut the funding for adjuncts to attend events. The WPA must not accept that they are managing an unjust labor system that is out of their control but can be advocates for more equitable labor systems through WPA work.

REFERENCES

Adler-Kassner, Linda. 2008. *The Activist WPA: Changing Stories about Writing and Writers.* Logan: Utah State University Press.

Ahmed, Sara. 2004. "Affective Economies." *Social Text* 22 (2): 117–139.

Calhoon-Dillahunt, Carolyn. 2011. "Writing Programs without Administrators: Frameworks for Successful Writing Programs in the Two-Year College." *WPA: Writing Program Administration* 31 (1): 118–134.

Canagarajah, Suresh. 2011. "Codemeshing in Academic Writing: Identifying Teachable Strategies of Translanguaging." *Modern Language Journal* 95 (3): 401–417.

Dougherty, Kevin. 1994. *The Contradictory College: The Conflict Origins, Impacts, and Futures of the Community College.* Albany: State University of New York Press.

Guy, Mary E., Meredith A. Newman, and Sharon H. Mastracci. 2008. *Emotional Labor: Putting the Service in Public Service.* Armonk, NY: M. E. Sharpe.

Harrington, Susanmarie, Rita Malencyzk, Irv Peckham, Keith Rhodes, and Kathleen Blake Yancey. 2001. "WPA Outcomes Statement for First-Year Composition." *College English* 63 (3): 321–325.

Janangelo, Joseph, and Jeffrey Klausman. 2012. "Rendering the Idea of a Writing Program: A Look at Six Two-Year Colleges." *Teaching English in the Two-Year College* 40 (2): 131–144.

Johnson, Sarah Z. 2017. "A Tale of Two Statements." *Teaching English in the Two-Year College* 45 (1): 20–28.

Klausman, Jeffrey. 2008. "Mapping the Terrain: The Two-Year College Writing Program Administrator." *Teaching English in the Two-Year College* 35 (3): 238–251.

Klausman, Jeffrey. 2018. "The Two-Year College Writing Program and Academic Freedom: Labor, Scholarship, and Compassion." *Teaching English in the Two-Year College* 45 (4): 385–405.

Lu, Min-Zhan, and Bruce Horner. 2013. "Translingual Literacy, Language Difference, and Matters of Agency." *College English* 75 (6): 582–607.

Newfield, Christopher. 2011. *Unmaking the Public University: The Forty-Year Assault on the Middle Class.* Cambridge, MA: Harvard University Press.

Papp, James. 2002. "University Administration and the Language of Management: Seven Types of Ambiguity." *ADE Bulletin* 130: 66–72. doi: 10.1632/ade.130.66.

Raines, Helon Howell. 1990. "Is There a Writing Program in This College? Two Hundred and Thirty-Six Two-Year Schools Respond." *College Composition and Communication* 41 (2): 151–165.

Rodrigo, Rochelle, and Susan Miller-Cochran. 2018. "Acknowledging Disciplinary Contributions: On the Importance of Community College Scholarship to Rhetoric and Composition." In *Composition, Rhetoric, and Disciplinarity*, edited by Rita Malenczyk, Susan Miller-Cochran, Elizabeth Wardle, and Kathleen Yancey, 53–69. Logan: Utah State University Press.

"The Shanti Model." 2018. The Shanti Project. http://www.shanti.org/pages/shanti-model.html.

Stenberg, Shari J. 2005. "Introduction." *Professing and Pedagogy: Learning the Teaching of English.* Urbana, IL: National Council of Teachers of English.

Stenberg, Shari J. 2015. "Introduction." *Repurposing Composition: Feminist Interventions for a Neoliberal Age.* Logan: Utah State University Press.

Strickland, Donna. 2011. *The Managerial Unconsciousness in the History of Composition Studies.* Carbondale: Southern Illinois University Press.

Sullivan, Patrick. 2015. "The Teacher-Scholar-Activist." *Teaching English in the Two-Year College* 42 (4): 327–350.

Taylor, Tim. 2009. "Writing Program Administration at the Two-Year College: Ghosts in the Machine." *WPA: Writing Program Administration* 32 (3): 120–139.

Toth, Christina M., Brett M. Griffiths, and Kathryn Thirolf. 2013. "'Distinct and Significant': Professional Identities of Two-Year College English Faculty." *College Composition and Communication* 65 (1): 90–116.

Two-Year College English Association. 2016. "TYCA Guidelines for Preparing Teachers of English in the Two-Year College." National Council of Teachers of English. http://www.ncte.org/library/NCTEFiles/Groups/TYCA/GuidelinesPrep2YCEngFac_ REVISED.pdf.

Zembylas, Michalinos, 2005a. *Teaching with Emotion: A Postmodern Enactment*. Charlotte, NC: Information Age Publishing Incorporated.

Zembylas, Michalinos. 2005b. "Discursive Practices, Genealogies, and Emotional Rules: A Poststructuralist View on Emotion and Identity in Teaching." *Teaching and Teacher Education* 21 (8): 935–948.

3
THE EMOTIONAL LABOR OF BECOMING
Lessons from the Exiting Writing Center Director

Kate Navickas
Cornell University

Emotional labor is often thought of in the context of our *labors*—the stress and emotions required to *enact and do* our everyday work. My own experience transitioning into a position as a writing center (WC) director, however, has further revealed that the "internal struggle" that occurs whenever we transition into new positions (Caswell, Grutsch McKinney, and Jackson 2016b, 56)—indeed, into new "identities"—is another significant and particular kind of emotional labor. In accepting a new administrative position at a new institution, there is emotional labor in the inevitable process of *becoming* that professional identity. As the saying goes, you are what you do, and professional identities can cause emotional labor and struggle—especially if the identity conflicts with previous internal narratives, disciplinary narratives, or conceptualizations of one's sense of self and one's imagined professional identity. As the narratives in composition and rhetoric typically go, newly minted PhDs ought to be aiming for tenure-track positions, and they should be mindful of taking on administrative positions, especially during their first year or before obtaining tenure. But what do we do when we find ourselves at odds with this narrative? What are the challenges facing new administrators who fail to follow such well-worn advice?

In this chapter, I offer an intentionally vulnerable account of my own transitions into WC administrative work, especially my difficulties grappling with disciplinary narratives of "who and what we should become" versus my own sense of professional identity and becoming. I share the challenges of filling some very big shoes, and I advocate for and analyze the benefits of conducting *emotional labor interviews* with our administrative predecessors. Through conducting such an interview and reflecting on it alongside my own emotions during my first year in this position,

I have come to understand my greatest emotional labor as the institutional and professional identification transition—what Nicole Caswell, Jackie Grutsch McKinney, and Rebecca Jackson (2016b, 56) describe for one writing center director (WCD), Anthony, as the "internal struggle to figure out who he is, who he is in this place, and what the answers mean for his disciplinary labor." As my study helps to illustrate, this type of identity-based emotional labor is ongoing, consistent, and often the result of the conflict between previous values and narratives coming into conflict with new institutional context, narratives, and roles. That is, in my own case, identity-based emotional labor resulted from a conflict between the disciplinary narratives I previously associated with my identity and a new institutional context in which these disciplinary narratives no longer worked.

THE EMOTIONAL LABOR OF BECOMING A NEW WCD

As I transitioned into my first post-grad school position, as a non-tenure-track writing center director at an Ivy League university, I was overcome with a range of emotions. Naturally, I was nervous about stepping into an administrative position straight out of graduate school, knowing that I would need to be making serious decisions and engaging in high-stakes conversations without adequate institutional knowledge. Compounding these emotions, I was thrilled, on the one hand, to have landed a good position in a location that allowed me to live with my geographically bound husband, and, simultaneously, I felt defeated and guilty for having accepted a non-tenured job against the wishes of my adviser, against my own sense of the field's expectations, and after declining a tenure-track job 200 miles away. I was also uneasy about working at an Ivy League school that hosts a writing in the disciplines program but generally fails, at the larger institutional level, to recognize or value rhetoric and composition as a legitimate field of study.

Further, in becoming the new WCD, I was attempting to fill some very big shoes. The previous and highly celebrated WCD, Tracy Hamler Carrick,[1] moved into a position where she oversaw my labors; that is, Tracy, the "exiting" WCD, remains in the department and directs the program in which I also teach. Describing the collective grief a program experiences when a WPA leaves, Laura J. Davies (2017, 43) explains, "When a person leaves a writing program, especially a person who has an influential and highly visible position, an undercurrent of grief pervades the program and can surface in unexpected ways . . . Ideas, insights, initiatives, procedures, possibilities—all are lost, and this change and loss is deeply felt." Thus I anticipated a lot of emotional weight affecting all parties involved during this transition, including a sense of change and loss felt by Tracy as well as the tutors who worked for her. Entering this position, I was aware that not only was Tracy a particularly kind, fun, and wonderful WCD, beloved by tutors, but that the writing center was what she considered to be at the heart of all of her work—as she describes it, "the place where I heal. It's like my comfort food . . . my home." The emotional labors of tutors and Tracy, I realized, would impact how I made decisions and enacted changes in policies and procedures, writing center promotional materials and logos, and even a much-needed name change (the writing centers were called the Writing Walk-In Services when I became the WCD). Transitioning into new administrative positions can be contentious and emotional work; we stand to face tension as we "engage with ideas from the past" (Huber 2018, 127), even when our new practices are pedagogically sound (Smith and Morris 2018, 266).

To begin facing these emotions, indeed to actively embrace "staying with emotions" (Micciche 2016), I set out to interview Tracy during the winter break after my first semester about her sense of the position's emotional labor. Although the interview felt vulnerable, it was a strategy for digging into the uncomfortable and difficult emotional labor of the work and the professional identity we both were facing. I hoped to gain a better sense of how to acknowledge the loss for her and the tutors while also finding ways to honor her legacy that were appropriate for her. I came prepared to share my own emotional labor as an act of reciprocity. While the process required my careful negotiation so as to not force a discomforting situation, the act of centering the interview on emotional labor invited us both to confront emotions we might naturally have ignored and certainly never discussed. Even though an interview with an exiting administrator after one semester is not necessarily a strategy everyone can or should enact, I'm arguing for it as an ideal administrative practice when the circumstances and context make it an appropriate option. Indeed, the interview with Tracy further provided me with institutional history and context as well as mentorship and a greater bond with the previous administrator. In these ways, interviewing a former administrator about the emotional labors involved in the job functions both as self-reflective action-research that resulted in institutional data as well as a method for working through my own emotional labor.

In what follows, I use Caswell, Grutsch McKinney, and Jackson's (2016b) interviews with WCDs to help define and explain what I mean by the *emotional labor of becoming*, and I advocate for emotional labor interviews as ideal strategies for negotiating emotional labor during a transition into a new position and institution. To exemplify the power of emotional labor interviews, I share some insightful moments from my interview with Tracy, followed by a discussion of what I learned from consciously studying our conversation about emotional labor.

DEFINING THE EMOTIONAL LABOR OF BECOMING

Emotional labor of becoming arises when we must make decisions based on values that might conflict with our sense of identity. This conflict is echoed in WPA scholarship on transitioning into new positions, as with Smith's (Smith and Morris 2018, 264–266) aforementioned guilt at deciding to use a grading contract despite programmatic emphasis on weighted grades—his sense of pedagogical identity is in conflict with programmatic values. Several areas of rhetoric and composition, including rhetorical genre studies and work on discourse communities and literacies, have established how graduate school and becoming an academic *discipline* (in a Foucauldian way) identities. Even in this collection, Courtney Adams Wooten provides a quick example, referencing "happiness scripts [she] intuited as a graduate student" that helped normalize particular kinds of emotional labor for WPAs. As Adams Wooten's and Smith's (Smith and Morris 2018) examples hint, there is evidence that such disciplining requires emotional labor. Although there is likely precedence for stories of becoming that note emotional labor across stories of disciplinarity, within recent writing center scholarship, Caswell, Grutsch McKinney, and Jackson's recent work on WCDs (2016a, 2016b, 2018) takes a more explicit look at emotional labor. While Caswell, Grutsch McKinney, and Jackson's (2016b, 187) main finding about emotional labor is their surprise at the extent to which it was necessary for completing all of the WCDs' daily tasks and to-dos, reviewing their interview case studies also supports my claim—that the specific *emotional labor of becoming* can be a significant aspect of emotional labor. Thus I will review three of their interviews to extend the definition of emotional labor and to establish a snapshot of the precedence for the emotional labor of becoming.

Caswell, Grutsch McKinney, and Jackson (2016b, 27) define emotions explicitly in terms of labor—applying Sara Ahmed's (2004) explanation of the work of emotions to the specific context of administrative work, defining emotional labor as "work that involves care, mentoring, or nurturing of others; work of building and sustaining relationships; work to resolve conflicts; managing our display of emotion; usually an unstated requirement of the job." While the act of becoming and the emotions attached to it aren't necessarily emotional *labor* in the ways Caswell,

Grutsch McKinney, and Jackson define it in relation to "corresponding action" (26), it is if we broaden emotional labor to include internal struggles about the work. The act of becoming is emotional labor precisely because *becoming* is always a negotiation between who you understand yourself to be (often understood in terms of the values we hold) and the realities we come in contact with (here, a professional position).

In Caswell, Grutsch McKinney, and Jackson's (2016b) fourth chapter, they share Anthony's interview and experiences negotiating the divide between staff and faculty in a non-tenure-track WCD position in a small professional school (in which there are no tenure-track positions). Anthony reflects on "the internal struggle he has throughout the year to figure out who he is, who he is in this place, and what the answers mean for his disciplinary labor. He tells us flat out that one of his biggest internal challenges has been 'fostering some sense of identity—whether it's the identity of *who is this guy as a director?* Or *who am I as far as what my interests are?*'" (56, original emphasis). Anthony's identity-based "internal struggle" is an important example to dig into precisely because it highlights the emotions, often very conflicted and concealed ones, associated with the process of becoming that can occur during the first year as an administrator. In Anthony's case, this emotional labor (what the authors call "metalabor," 61) comes from the tensions around negotiating different types of labor (emotional, disciplinary and everyday) and "what they each mean for him as someone who started out in creative writing and ended up in rhetoric and composition and as someone who prepared for a scholarly life and ended up with an administrative one" (57). I suggest that this tension is likely the result of the conflict between Anthony's original vision for his future work and the reality of his job. While Caswell, Grutsch McKinney, and Jackson (2016b, 61) claim that "metalabor" is different from emotional labor, they admit that "worrying about identification has the same drag on his everyday and disciplinary labor that emotional labor (sometimes) has for other participants." I would argue that "worrying about identification" is, in fact, a specific type of emotional labor that happens in cases where the professional identity of the position (or aspects of the position) conflicts with a person's previous sense of identity or of the future work they hope or plan to do.

While we often talk about emotional labor in terms of struggle and negative experiences, the more joyful relational work many administrators enjoy is also an aspect of the emotional labor of becoming. Of Caswell, Grutsch McKinney, and Jackson's (2016b) nine case studies of new WCDs, Anthony's is the only one that explicitly notes "internal struggle" around identity. However, the chapters on Allison and Joe offer stories of people for whom writing center work was their "calling" (for Allison in particular, 30); thus, their professional identity aligns with their individual understanding of who they want to be and the work they want to do. For instance, the authors interview Joe during his first year in a tenure-track WCD position. He was in the corporate world prior to getting his PhD in rhetoric and composition (109). They describe the alignment between who he was before graduate school and his new position as a WCD: "[Tutoring] mimicked . . . the very same work he'd done in the corporate world . . . : working with writers and building relationships with them through conversations about writing" (109). Although they don't talk about Joe in terms of identity, his happiness and pleasure in the work and the lack of difficult emotions around identification might be the result of this alignment between his sense of self and the WCD position. That is, becoming a WCD aligned with not only who he was previously in the corporate world but also with who he wanted to become. Kevin Roozen (2015, 51) explains this alignment as a central threshold concept of writing studies, noting that "the extent to which we align ourselves with a particular community . . . can be gauged by the extent to which we are able and willing to use that community's language, make its rhetorical moves, act with its privileged texts, and participate in its writing processes and practices."

While both Allison and Joe easily identify as writing center directors, they both have smaller identity conflicts about who they want to be as WCDs. Despite being in a tenure-track WCD position with a rhetoric and composition PhD, Allison struggles to make time for or find interest in pursuing disciplinary research that will be required for tenure. Caswell, Grutsch McKinney, and Jackson (2016b, 35) describe the "happy outcome of emotional investment" she places in mentoring students and tutors—an overvaluing of relational work that may lead to potential emotional labor regarding who she is and who she needs to be as a WCD in this position. Joe articulates a similar conflict over the nature of his position, specifically how to divide his labor among being the WCD, the WAC director, and his teaching (120); while Joe's conflict is more about divisions of labor, it's also about who he wants to be as a professional versus what the position requires of him. These smaller identity conflicts faced by Allison and Joe are about what they value and how those values come in conflict with the expectations of their specific positions. I would argue that they also represent a form of emotional labor that comes from our sense of identity (which gets played out in our values) coming into conflict with position expectations. As Caswell, Grutsch McKinney, and Jackson confirm (2018, 111), "One of the biggest challenges new

WPAs face is reconciling their expectations about who they will be and the roles and labor they will take up in their new positions with the identities, roles, and labor these new positions demand."

As these few examples suggest, emotional labor of becoming is contingent on the varying relationships between individual values and identities and the contextual demands of different administrative positions. *Becoming* a new WPA or WCD involves the process of moving from the periphery of a community of practice to the center (Lave and Wenger 1991) in a very specific institutional context and requires learning and enacting the community's shared "genres, language, values, concepts and 'ways of being' (Geertz 1983)" (Johns 2010 [1997], 500). These few examples of WCD stories of becoming suggest a potentially larger trend of the emotional labor involved with negotiating who one is going to be in a position in relation to what is expected of them.

METHODS FOR CONDUCTING "EMOTIONAL LABOR INTERVIEWS"

My study utilizes interviewing as a method, which has proven valuable in much WPA and WCD scholarship. There are numerous generative and insightful arguments for the WPA as a researcher (Rose and Weiser 1999), for the action-research administration requires, and for the value of researching your institutional histories, contexts, and places using a variety of methods (see Anson and Brown 1999; Harris 1999; L'Eplattenier 1999; Mirtz 1999; Rose 1999; DeGenaro 2006; Roach 2008). To add to these conversations, I'm advocating for *centering* interviews on emotional labor, when possible and appropriate, as a strategy for interrogating that labor and for better understanding what to do with it.

In terms of interview methods, I used a semi-structured interview that was informed by feminist methodologies and interview methods. As Cynthia Selfe and Gail Hawisher (2012, 36–37) explain, feminist approaches to interviews are "a process not of extracting information but of sharing knowledge (Olesen; Reinharz; Visweswaran; Neilson; Oakley). Within such exchanges, we believe researchers and participants engage in a reciprocal, and often intimate, shaping of information, one fundamentally influenced by the material realities and situated perspectives of multiple partners (Ritchie and Lewis)." I used a semi-structured interview (see appendix for questions) to maintain the focus on emotions and emotional labor. When interviewing on a subject like emotional labor that is both sensitive and vulnerable for the interviewee as well as a less researched area, having a set of questions that act as a guide functions as a checklist and a reminder to focus the conversation.

Typically, in interviews, we think about the researcher as having more power in the researcher/subject dichotomy. However, this particular interview offers a more complicated interaction. As Tracy is the director of the program and one of the people who hired me, even as the questioner, I was conscious of my vulnerability in the conversation. That is not to say that Tracy has ever treated me as anything other than an equal and a peer; however, while I was consciously sharing my own emotional labor that first semester as an act of reciprocity, I was simultaneously trying to be cautious. This power dynamic is complex and functions as a caveat to my entire argument: the act of interviewing a superior or even a new colleague about emotional labor as a new administrator is risky and will involve varying layers of power based on institutional context, individual personalities and prior relations, individual identities and disciplinary alliances, and so on. In many ways, I actually felt overly familiar with Tracy: we are both cisgender white females in rhetoric and composition who graduated from the same alma mater and have complicated feelings regarding our relationship to our current university; indeed, our shared identities and similarities made the institutional power dynamic feel slightly less risky for me.

After transcribing the interview, I analyzed it with an eye toward an aerial view of the conversation—what Jacqueline Jones Royster and Gesa Kirsch (2012, 72), using Clifford Geertz, have methodologically called "tacking out," what they explain as similar to "the technologically enhanced ability to view the Earth from satellites in outer space in order to gain the capacity to see." Without the analysis and deeper knowledge about where the emotional labor was coming from, the emotional labor would have remained private and individual and been assumed to simply be a normal part of the work.

TRACY'S STORY

Tracy revealed to me that when she took the job eight years ago, she was told, only half-jokingly, that "there's no place for rhet-comp at Cornell." She heard this just as she was accepting a position in an independent writing program. She told me she would walk to her car—about a mile from the building—and cry about the vastness of the campus, of the job, of the writing center that didn't look or feel like a writing center, and about what this job might mean for her relationship with her community in rhetoric and composition. As she put it, "Cornell was a really, really big place. It felt large and overwhelming and the scale of what I had just signed on for at times was terrifying . . . How long I had to walk to get to places . . .

and the distance . . . that I perceived between me and all of the people and all of the buildings on campus just seemed kind of big." We talked about Cornell's unique institutional context and history—especially the relationship between an Ivy League school and the field; as she noted, "Cornell's story, like other Ivy Plus institutions, isn't really a part of the narrative that we see often in comp-rhet . . . and yet, here we are." And we talked about her transition to the writing center at Cornell. She described her previous two centers as "a real writing *center*," noting both her excitement and fear in discovering that "there's nothing like that at Cornell. We don't have that touch-point at all. There's no home base, really." These moments were our starting points to talk about things that are stressful, difficult, and emotionally challenging.

Of course, in her responses, Tracy shared her story as starting with challenges and then evolving, in ways that responded to and negotiated the emotional weight of the institutional history, the students, and eventually a developed sense of trust in herself. Thus these conversational trends move from negative emotional labor and struggles to how she's negotiated those struggles—and these are the positive emotions, the joy she's found, the ways she's built community despite everything that initially seemed against her. Although the arch of the conversation suggests a progress narrative, I have found that *negotiating* emotional labor is not equivalent to *eliminating* it. Throughout her responses, there is never evidence that her initial emotional labor is gone; more so that it is understood differently and negotiated.

While we covered a lot of ground in the interview, three larger conversational focal points emerged: status, the writing center, and administrative agency. These three focal points represent the disciplinary narratives we've bound ourselves to emotionally—through scholarship and research, graduate school, and professionalization—and how those narratives work or fail to work in particular institutional contexts. Precisely because, in Ahmed's (2004) terms, emotions have stuck to these narratives about what counts as status, a writing center, and administrative agency, as new WCDs our emotional labor involved negotiating the discrepancy between disciplinary narratives we believed in and vastly different institutional contexts.

Status Narratives: What Counts as a "Good Job"

One of the obvious focal points that emerged in our discussion was status. Both of our positions are non-tenure-track administrative jobs in an independent writing program that does not have any tenure-track positions, for the sake of equality (she was once offered such a position, but as there were not enough lines for everyone in the program, she declined). It's not uncommon for writing positions in Ivy League schools or even in writing centers to be non-tenure track. In regard to the status of WCD positions, reviewing the scholarship, Caswell, Grutsch McKinney, and Jackson (2016b, 171) refer to Emily Isaacs and Melinda Knight's 2014 study that cites only 29 percent of WCD positions as tenure track, while their own small 2016 study found that 33 percent of their participants held tenure-track positions. Anne Ellen Geller and Harry Denny (2013, 100) claim that a 2009 analysis of the International Writing Centers Association membership showed that 53 percent of WCDs "occupy administrative positions," while 47 percent "hold faculty lines";[2] they further note that in their study of fourteen writing center professionals, "research-intensive universities were more likely to have staff WCPs, [Writing Center Professionals],"[3] while other schools "suggest no clear trend" (100). While the numbers vary slightly here, the point is that many WCDs hold non-tenure-track positions of varying types.

While these numbers as well as contemporary job market trends toward more non-tenure-track positions in rhetoric and composition normalize the existence of those positions, it's also important to consider the emotional labor of transitioning into such positions with a PhD. Geller and Denny (2013, 108) describe the emotional impact of accepting a staff position, claiming their participants in staff positions "felt the varied ways a WCP's position did or didn't have cachet. Most appeared to have made conscious choices to bracket the 'bad rep' given to such positions in disciplinary discourse." They share the story of one participant in particular who was reprimanded by an adviser for not taking a tenure-track position: "Such positions, she was warned, were low status, even from the perspective of the seemingly self-aware, low-status composition world. Her goal ought to be a 'gold standard' tenure-track position or nothing. But she took a non-tenure-track job, and she reported a great deal of professional satisfaction and few regrets, although she did imagine her advisor's advice would be 'you've been there for a little while, you have some publications, now it's time to move on.' From this WCP, we had the sense that hearing her advisor's voice in her head sometimes interrupted an otherwise satisfying professional life" (108–109). Here, Geller and Denny note the power of the disciplinary narrative of the tenure-track versus non-tenure-track position, especially for the rhetoric and composition newly minted PhD student. While this particular participant seemed happy with her decision, there's still a clear sense of emotional weight the discourse around what counts as a "good job" holds in her mind—a feeling Geller and Denny suggest repeatedly causes her internal struggle.

In my interview, this topic came up for the same reasons as those for Denny and Geller's participant. Not unlike Tracy's story of walking to the car and crying, I had found myself walking to the car and holding defensive conversations in my head about why accepting this position was fine—imagined conversations I held with my advisers, my graduate student friends who've taken tenure-track jobs, random colleagues at conferences, and others. I imagined speaking back to colleagues in moments like the one Molly Tetreault (2018, 272–273) shares, when a 4Cs colleague walks away after hearing about her non-tenure-track status. Although I've never faced a situation in which I've actually had to defend my academic position, the idea of *becoming* a *lecturer* as a new PhD carried a lot of guilt, shame, and sadness. For me, this emotional labor was about how the position I had accepted reflected my identity in the discipline: it was about who I was becoming—or not becoming—as a professional. A lot of the emotional labor went into fighting the disciplinary narratives I had come to believe, support, and attach comfort and joy in.

Following suit, some of our conversation also involved working through this larger narrative about what a "good job" in rhetoric and composition looks like—or the tension between having a "good job" that doesn't fit the accepted disciplinary narrative of a "good job." Specifically in regard to taking a non-tenure-track position, Tracy said it "felt like a big, overwhelming deal. That seemed, in some ways, to pull me further away from my community . . . And in my case, I left a tenure-track position. I was like . . . why would you do that?" Here, she's referring to taking a non-tenure-track position as distancing her from her community within rhetoric and composition. She elaborates on this, making an important distinction between how we intellectually understand status, specifically a secure non-tenure-track position, and its emotional baggage. She says, "Intellectually, I think this is absurd, right? I would think that we have worked so hard as a community to create opportunities for people like us and for our work that you would think we would be supportive of all of the choices that people make. I haven't felt that. And I knew that making that decision was going to make things harder for me to connect to the community that I knew. So that was a big deal. I still cry about that." If we *know better but something still causes us a sense of loss, how do we account for that feeling?* Ahmed's (2004) understanding of the non-residence and stickiness of emotions is clarifying here. She explains, "While emotions do not positively reside in a subject or figure, they still work to bind subjects together. Indeed, to put it more strongly, the nonresidence of emotions is what makes them 'binding'" (119). Here, Tracy shares dismay at the felt social and professional consequences of being disconnected from her sense of community in the field. What is implied is a generally accepted belief not only in the value of a tenure-track position but also the belief that taking a non-tenure-track position is reproachable and marks one as unworthy. Her sense of loss seems to be from both the felt disconnect from her community and being bound to these field beliefs about status. Regardless of how true these status beliefs are, we hear them echoed as emotional struggles in Tracy's comments, through Geller and Denny's (2013) participants, Tetreault's (2018) exchange with a colleague, and likely other WPA and WCD stories and scholarship that include status issues.

While Tracy and I didn't talk explicitly about disciplinary narratives throughout the interview, they were a looming, ever-present force—the disciplinary narratives and our identities in relationship to them were the *thing* our emotions were bound up in. They present an imagined, invisible, and moving object that we are attaching emotions to, that constrains how we engage with new institutional contexts, and that limits our sense of what is possible and desired. While the interview didn't solve the difficult emotions I had in accepting this position, studying our conversation on emotional labor has helped me to see these emotions as not an individual problem I was having but rather the result of the circulation of disciplinary narratives in relation to a position that conflicted with those narratives.

Writing Center Narratives: Disciplinary Visions versus Institutional Realities

In addition, our conversation circled around our disciplinary stories about what a writing center should look like and be and how Tracy had negotiated administering a center that doesn't look or feel this way. She shared her history with writing centers, which started in 1993 at San Francisco State and continued at Colby College. While her first two writing centers were very different (one large and central to campus, one more "intimate"), they both offered a "very tight-knit, close community of students. A real writing *center*." She continued, "And so, writing center to me—what does it mean—it means a cozy space." While Tracy understands that there are multiple possible writing center configurations, this is still a disciplinary narrative that is so commonly valued and enacted that it's hard to imagine a writing center functioning successfully without the couches, community, and sense of coziness. Indeed, Jackie Grutsch McKinney (2013, 28, 20) argues that the cozy home view of writing centers is a "writing center grand narrative" and that "many stories could be told of our spaces, yet predominately, one story is told." Caswell and coauthors (2016b, 177–178) confirm the power of such narratives, reflecting that "the directors had an idea about what directing a writing center would look like. This idea often motivated the directors to pursue particular tasks . . . Nonetheless, the directors in our study . . . did not abandon their internalized narratives altogether when they found them difficult to enact. Instead, the directors often revised their goals in scope or time to completion." Their discussion focuses on narratives as an influence that motivated and constrained *what* WCDs do in the work. While these narratives do influence decisions, there is also an emotional aspect for WCDs who must work (because of context and similar factors) against this "one story" of what a writing center should look like and be, in part because a writing center configuration affects how it works, which likewise affects who the WCD is as a WCD. That is, there is emotional labor around the identity of the WCD when the job doesn't align with disciplinary narratives of the work and one's sense of what it should involve (as shown earlier with Caswell and colleagues' interviews with Allison and Joe).

At Cornell, because of the vast geography of the campus, we have five different writing center locations without the central hub, and this is an institutional challenge that has been hard for both us. The five locations mean that tutors are extremely autonomous and there isn't much direct oversight of tutoring. On a day-to-day basis, as the WCD, I might not see any tutors. Tracy explains, "It didn't hit until I started the job—that this was going to have to be a writing center that was different from anything I had ever known before." She emphasizes her feelings, noting "that was super overwhelming. Exciting and thrilling and awesome—you know, this is the language that we're supposed to attach to this. *What a great professional opportunity! And oh my gosh, I'm so looking forward to this challenge! And this is what I've been waiting for!* And all of that is true . . . but it's also terrifying!" Even in her emotional reactions to a challenging new context, there is a tension between what she actually feels versus her sense of what she is supposed to feel, the real versus the circling narratives.

However, Tracy also revealed how she came to better appreciate tutor-agency in tutors' pedagogical growth and reflection and the ways they self-select to get involved with the community or not. Specifically, she said, "I've . . . had to trust that what I have always seen as being necessarily collaborative can also happen more privately. That there are certainly some students, some tutors, who have all of these wonderful conversations with themselves over time as they tutor more and different kinds of people, as they develop more as tutors, as they become more experienced. And that I can be more someone who sets certain habits of mind and reflective practices in motion and have fewer points of contact and opportunities to reflect . . . And that has been hard for me." Here, Tracy is sharing her internal struggle and development regarding how tutors learn and develop pedagogically. Writing center and even pedagogical disciplinary narratives simultaneously value tutor/student agency and the role of the WCD/teacher in fostering learning. The emphasis of field narratives and stories on the WCD's or teacher's role in fostering learning leads to conflicted feelings around one's identity and role when one is less involved in this learning process. Indeed, Tracy reflects, "And I hear the ways [tutors] talk about their experiences in the writing center and with students, and I think: wow, they did all of this stuff. They didn't necessarily need me in the ways I thought they needed me. It's humbling, it's reassuring, it shows me a different way."

For me, one of the interesting parts of our discussion about the emotional labor of the writing center is that the sense of loss and upset over the Cornell Writing Center's formation is entirely based on our emotional attachment to the disciplinary narrative of WCs. Tracy noted how the tutors themselves offered her a new perspective on pedagogical growth, and I shared with her my own interest and joy in hosting regular tutor staff meetings on pedagogical topics, meetings that would be less necessary if our WC had a central hub. Meaning, our emotional loss is purely over the imagined idea of a writing center we both share, not over the reality of the actual writing center at Cornell. Through naming both the influence of the disciplinary narrative and our real joy in our actual writing center, I was able to let go of the power the narrative held over my understanding of my own identity as WCD—the feeling that real WCDs have traditional writing center spaces. The act of naming here also fostered a greater appreciation for the diversity of different writing center models and our own version.

Administrative Agency: Negotiating Conflicting Narratives

Throughout my conversation with Tracy, she shared her early stories of struggle and difficulty and how she negotiated these situations. We reflected collaboratively on my first year. Some of the most useful moments for me were when Tracy reflected on the process of becoming herself in the position—becoming an administrator with agency. While these moments are less about naming negative emotional labor, her reflections on administrative agency highlight how she negotiated conflicting narratives, identities, and emotions that were tied to both. That is, Tracy offered up her growth process as an administrator as a way of negotiating the emotional labor of the work. She said:

> I think in the beginning, I was so emotionally preoccupied by—"am I doing things right? Am I pleasing everyone?" And so all of the decisions that you're making, all of the things that you're doing, they're outside of you. I wasn't really thinking about what felt good and right to me. I was trying to channel other voices. Some at Cornell, some my mentors from institutions past. It's hard emotionally when things feel so external. A big transition for me, of course, was when I was able to trust myself... Part of what makes me better able to express myself and be myself is that I have other women who are, you know, a decade and two decades older than me, having lived a slightly different version of our reality in their own unique ways, reminding me that it's ok to figure out what it means for me to be Tracy-as-an-administrator and to be a woman-administrator today. And so that's a huge deal for me. The way that I'm being mentored helps me to be a truer and more sincere and authentic mentor.

These last thoughts are less rooted in reactions to particular disciplinary narratives; however, there is still a clear articulation that for her, the formation of an administrative-self requires locating agency independent of the swirling narratives, whether those are disciplinary, institutional, or otherwise. Tracy reflected on the importance of mentors who encouraged her to become herself—despite the felt pressure of such narratives. This is, of course, good advice—but good advice that bears repeating. Indeed, several authors in this collection highlight specific strategies for making administrative choices based on one's own values, identities, and sense of best practices (see Sheila Carter Tod's discussion of integrity as a strategy for WPAs of color, Elizabeth Imafuji's advice for faculty to reflect on their individual relationship to faith and their professional identities, and Christy Wenger's explanation of emotional mindfulness as "ecological agency" for WPAs). In many ways, the interview with Tracy functioned as a strategy for me that offered mentorship that encouraged me to have confidence in locating my own administrative identity.

CONCLUSION

As the above quotes and stories suggest, this interview is more than just data. It was a moment of dual reflection and mentorship. It was everything I needed to hear and talk about after my first semester on the job. Tracy's stories of struggle reminded me that I'm not alone, that challenges are to be expected, and that she's been through many of the emotions I'm going through this year, too.

More than just the personal value of this interview, however, I want to advocate for this type of self-reflective action-research. I reflected on my own experiences and emotional labor, interviewed the previous writing center director, and then analyzed these experiences. Each of these activities offered me a wealth of knowledge, specifically by:

- Providing more institutional history and context
- Offering a new perspective on the emotional labor of a position—creating understanding about where our specific work emotions come from and why
- Exposing the structures (here, disciplinary discourses and institutional realities) that cause emotional labor in ways that can remove the sense that emotional labor is the individual's problem
- Fostering empathy and sensitivity toward colleagues
- Affording the opportunity to reflect on what administrative agency means.

While my strategy for negotiating this emotional labor has provided a lot of unforeseen growth and insight, emotional labor is not eliminated. In a *WPA* article that also explores the significant influence of disciplinary narratives, Amy Ferdinandt Stolley (2015) argues against Laura Micciche's (more precisely, against Sara Ahmed's) understanding of emotions as "sticky." She says, "Micciche claims that narratives can function like a sticky adhesive, but I would argue that when an early career WPA reads a narrative that has an emotional tenor that does not match her own experiences, that narrative functions more like a solvent, unsticking her from the narrative, the rhetorical commonplace it reifies, and the field itself" (23). Stolley's point is echoed in Tracy's comments above. Specifically, Tracy talked about her sense of being disconnected from the community of rhetoric and composition by taking a non-tenure-track WCD position, and there is an implied disconnect from the writing center community that happens when the writing center feels un-disciplinary. I would argue that both Micciche (and Ahmed) and Stolley are correct here. Precisely because emotions stick to disciplinary discourses and voices (advisers, teachers, peers), when we are in situations that conflict with or challenge the values of those disciplinary discourses, there are felt and even real consequences (the disconnect from our communities). As Stolley and Tracy illustrate, those real consequences are feelings of isolation, disconnection, and, as I'm suggesting, an identity-conflict between a person's imagined professional identity and the necessary recalibrations of those identity-expectations based on institutional context and position. Locating strategies for better understanding and then negotiating emotional labor is important because this type of self-care research helps us move beyond an understanding of emotions as private, individual burdens.

Although this interview, focused on emotional labor, doesn't eliminate the negative feelings that are bound up with taking a non-tenure-track position or administering a writing center that doesn't match disciplinary visions of a writing center, I now see the *emotional labor of becoming* a WCD in these contexts as the result of the conflict between disciplinary discourses and institutional realities. That is, a better understanding of where this emotional labor has originated from has helped me feel less controlled by these feelings and by these narratives of imagined ideal jobs and writing centers. And this leads me to conclude by wondering about how we can better prepare graduate students and early-career WPAs and WCDs for not only emotional labor but also a more conscious consideration of the tension between disciplinary narratives and the reality of our diverse institutions and the diversity of the work.

APPENDIX 3.A: INTERVIEW QUESTIONS

1. What would you say was some of the emotional work or the emotional components of your work as WCD? And, if possible, could you also map out different emotions you attached to different parts of the work?
2. As you've transitioned to your new role as director of the writing workshop, what emotions have you experienced? How would you describe transitioning out of the WCD role in terms of emotional labor?
3. What do you feel is your most important work for the WWIS (Writing Walk-In Services, the original Writing Centers name)? What would you want your legacy to be? And what emotions do you attach to that work?
4. You've told me before a little bit about walking out to your car in tears your first semester . . . I've found this story to be reassuring, as I'm facing similar struggles, fears, and worries. Can you retell that story? What do you remember your first semester and/or first year here as the WWIS director being like, especially emotionally?
5. In what ways has the emotional labor of the job changed for you? Throughout your eight years as WWIS director and/or as you've transitioned to the official workshop director?
6. How have you negotiated the emotional labor of your work in relation to what is expected of you from others—deans, previous Knight Institute directors, your mentors, and so on?
7. What advice do you have for me as I enter my second semester, especially in terms of emotional labor?
8. What does it mean to acknowledge emotional labor for you? What does it mean to share the emotional labor of your work with me? With others publicly?

NOTES

1. Tracy has graciously allowed me to use her name and share her stories. Indeed, her support of this project suggests her generosity and kindness as a mentor and colleague.
2. Geller and Denny (2013, 100) clarify that the split is between "administrative professionals and tenure-track faculty"; thus "faculty lines" here implies tenure track.
3. Geller and Denny (2013, 98) explain their choice to use "WCP" to stand for writing center professional as a move to be more "inclusive of all individuals working in a professional capacity." I maintain their word choice, though I've continued to use WCD throughout the chapter.

REFERENCES

Ahmed, Sara. 2004. "Affective Economies." *Social Text* 79.22 (2): 117–139.

Anson, Chris, and Robert L. Brown. 1999. "Subject to Interpretation: The Role of Research in Writing Programs and Its Relationship to the Politics of Administration in Higher Education." In *The Writing Program Administrator as Researcher*, edited by Shirley K. Rose and Irwin Weiser, 141–152. Portsmouth, NH: Boynton/Cook.

Caswell, Nicole, Jackie Grutsch McKinney, and Rebecca Jackson. 2016a. "Writing Center Administration and/as Emotional Labor." *Composition Forum* 34 (Summer). http://compositionforum.com/issue/34/writing-center.php.

Caswell, Nicole, Jackie Grutsch McKinney, and Rebecca Jackson. 2016b. *The Working Lives of New Writing Center Directors*. Logan: Utah State University Press.

Caswell, Nicole, Jackie Grutsch McKinney, and Rebecca Jackson. 2018. "Metaphors We Work By: New Writing Center Directors' Labor and Identities." In *WPAs in Transition: Navigating Educational Leadership Positions*, edited by Courtney Adams Wooten, Jacob Babb, and Brian Ray, 111–125. Logan: Utah State University Press.

Davies, Laura J. 2017. "Grief and the New WPA." *WPA: Writing Program Administration* 40 (2): 40–51.

DeGenaro, William. 2006. "Why Basic Writing Professionals on Regional Campuses Need to Know Their Histories." *Open Words: Access and English Studies* 1 (1): 54–68.

Geertz, Clifford. 1983. *Local Knowledge: Further Essays in Interpretive Anthropology*. New York: Basic Books.

Geller, Anne Ellen, and Harry Denny. 2013. "Of Ladybugs, Low Status, and Loving the Job: Writing Center Professionals Navigating Their Careers." *Writing Center Journal* 33 (1): 96–129.

Grutsch McKinney, Jackie. 2013. *Peripheral Visions for Writing Centers*. Logan: Utah State University Press.

Harris, Muriel. 1999. "Diverse Research Methodologies at Work for Diverse Audiences: Shaping the Writing Center to the Institution." In *The Writing Program Administrator as Researcher*, edited by Shirley K. Rose and Irwin Weiser, 1–17. Portsmouth, NH: Boynton/Cook.

Huber, Beth. 2018. "Get Offa My Lawn! Generational Challenges of WPAs in Transition." In *WPAs in Transition: Navigating Educational Leadership Positions*, edited by Courtney Adams Wooten, Jacob Babb, and Brian Ray, 126–138. Logan: Utah State University Press.

Isaacs, Emily, and Melinda Knight. 2014. "A Bird's Eye View of Writing Centers: Institutional Infrastructure, Scope and Programmatic Issues, Reported Practices." *Writing Program Administration* 37 (2): 36–67.

Johns, Anne. 2010 [1997]. "Discourse Communities and Communities of Practice: Membership, Conflict, and Diversity." In *Writing about Writing*, edited by Elizabeth Wardle and Doug Downs, 498–519. Boston: Bedford/St. Martin's.

L'Eplattenier, Barbara. 1999. "Finding Ourselves in the Past: An Argument for Historical Work on WPAs." In *The Writing Program Administrator as Researcher*, edited by Shirley K. Rose and Irwin Weiser, 131–140. Portsmouth: Boynton/Cook.

Lave, Jean, and Etienne Wenger. 1991. *Situated Learning: Legitimate Peripheral Participation*. New York: Cambridge University Press.

Micciche, Laura. 2016. "Staying with Emotion." *Composition Forum* 34 (Summer). http://compositionforum.com/issue/34/micciche-retrospective.php.

Mirtz, Ruth M. 1999. "WPAs as Historians: Discovering a First-Year Writing Program by Researching Its Past." In *The Writing Program Administrator as Researcher*, edited by Shirley K. Rose and Irwin Weiser, 119–130. Portsmouth, NH: Boynton/Cook.

Roach, Stephanie. 2008. "Why I Won't Keep My Head Down or Follow Other Bad Advice for the Junior Faculty WPA." In *The Promise and Perils of Writing Program Administration*, edited by Theresa Enos and Shane Borrowman, 109–116. West Lafayette, IN: Parlor.

Roozen, Kevin. 2015. "Writing Is Linked to Identity." In *Naming What We Know: Threshold Concepts of Writing Studies*, edited by Linda Adler-Kassner and Elizabeth Wardle, 50–52. Logan: Utah State University Press.

Rose, Shirley K. 1999. "Preserving Our Histories of Institutional Change: Enabling Research in the Writing Program Archives." In *The Writing Program Administrator as Researcher*, edited by Shirley K. Rose and Irwin Weiser, 107–118. Portsmouth, NH: Boynton/Cook.

Rose, Shirley K., and Irwin Weiser. 1999. "WPA Inquiry in Action and Reflection." In *The Writing Program Administrator as Researcher*, edited by Shirley K. Rose and Irwin Weiser, v–xi. Portsmouth, NH: Boynton/Cook.

Royster, Jacqueline Jones, and Gesa Kirsch. 2012. *Feminist Rhetorical Practices: New Horizons for Rhetoric, Composition, and Literacy Studies*. Carbondale: Southern Illinois University Press.

Selfe, Cynthia, and Gail Hawisher. 2012. "Exceeding the Bounds of the Interview: Feminism, Mediation, Narrative, and Conversations about Digital Literacy." In *Writing Studies Research in Practice: Methods and Methodologies*, edited by Lee Nickoson and Mary Sheridan, 36–50. Carbondale: Southern Illinois University Press.

Smith, Bradley, and Kerri K. Morris. 2018. In *WPAs in Transition: Navigating Educational Leadership Positions*, edited by Courtney Adams Wooten, Jacob Babb, and Brian Ray, 260–271. Logan: Utah State University Press.

Stolley, Amy Ferdinandt. 2015. "Narratives, Administrative Identity, and the Early Career WPA." *WPA: Writing Program Administration* 39 (1): 18–31.

Tetreault, Molly. 2018. "Writing Center Professionals, Marginalization, and the Faculty/Administration Divide." In *WPAs in Transition: Navigating Educational Leadership Positions*, edited by Courtney Adams Wooten, Jacob Babb, and Brian Ray, 272–283. Logan: Utah State University Press.

4

EDUCATING THE FACULTY WRITER TO "DANCE WITH RESISTANCE"
Rethinking Faculty Development as Institutional Transformation

Janelle Adsit
Humboldt State University

Sue Doe
Colorado State University

$480 per year. For most of us in this profession, $480 is a significant sum of money. Yet that is what the more than 71,000 individual faculty members who subscribe to the National Center for Faculty Development and Diversity (NCFDD) may pay for a yearly individual membership. Providing the "on-demand access to the mentoring, tools, and support you need to be successful in the Academy," as advertised on the organization's homepage, the NCFDD exists as an independent nonprofit that offers a suite of professional development resources for faculty from graduate work through retirement.

    The NCFDD was founded in 2010 when Kerry Ann Rockquemore, a tenured faculty member, created "an independent professional development, training, and mentoring community for faculty members, postdocs, and graduate students," as the organization is described on the website. Today, over 230 universities and colleges hold institutional membership in the NCFDD, including wide participation from R1 universities. A quick Google search demonstrates that universities use their membership in NCFDD to signal their commitment to the retention of diverse faculty. While these universities' participation may be critiqued as a tokenistic institutional Band-Aid for an inequitable campus climate, their membership indicates that NCFDD has broad reach and direct influence on faculty lives, shaping the conversation about what faculty life is and should be. Given that NCFDD helps set a definition of faculty success that is subscribed to by the institutions that have paid for membership, it is important to interrogate that definition of success and how it foregrounds faculty members' writing lives, scholarly productivity, and emotional orientation to their work. For the writing program administrator (WPA), the definition of what counts as scholarly productivity and what does not is a matter of both theoretical interest and everyday practice, affecting not only oneself but the many others who look to the WPA for guidance, such as graduate teaching assistants, non-tenure-track faculty, and junior tenure-line faculty.

We came to NCFDD—as the subject of our study and as members (in Janelle's case) or would-be members (in Sue's)—with an interest in campus equity: how the organization's messages of faculty success might also challenge the systemic inequities built into the institutional structures of higher education, how NCFDD might be changing campus climates across the country while also supporting the individuals who persist within those climates. We come to our questions about NCFDD as two white women working at state institutions in the western part of the United States. One of us, Janelle, is in her tenure year at a unionized campus. Sue is a full professor and is director of composition in a state where no faculty are unionized. Both of us approach questions of campus equity with the objective of improving labor conditions for all faculty and staff and fostering antiracism on campus.

Because the NCFDD is rarely discussed in WPA scholarship, we seek to bring this organization to the attention of scholars in writing studies and especially WPAs so they can consider how this organization may reveal differently the rhetorics and theories of writing our institutions call upon to develop faculty through productivity measures associated particularly with scholarly writing. In our analysis, we argue that WPAs, whether tenured or not, must advocate for more varied forms of scholarship than NCFDD promotes, adding to the challenges facing WPAs in ways not accounted for by this professional development service and shining a bright light on why untenured WPAs are in a position shared by few other faculty in higher education.

This chapter also offers an opportunity to consider the affective constructions of the successful faculty member that may emerge in our own faculty mentoring discourse as we work with teachers of writing and with graduate students. Our analysis traces the contours of the "good faculty member" as this ideal subject-position is drawn in NCFDD communications to find what ideal of the "good faculty member" might lurk in our own rhetorics of faculty development—and what messages about emotion are constellated around this ideal. An analysis of NCFDD enables us to ask how we can shift discourses that "work on" the individual faculty member and neglect the work of systemic change.

We argue that to be an effective WPA or faculty developer, a WPA should be engaged in critical university studies to push back on the institutions in which we work. It is with this idea that we chose to include in our title the phrase "dancing with resistance," which is NCFDD language—although we use it here to mean differently. When NCFDD invokes this phrase, the words are used to recommend a level of acceptance of an individual's personal resistance to writing. For NCFDD, to dance with resistance is to fall into a mirroring step with the conscious and subconscious defenses that prevent us from *doing writing*; these defenses are posited as an explanation for our failures in new knowledge creation as they are understood, endorsed, and prioritized by our institutions. We take up the phrase to pursue a different kind of dance—one that resists the forces that create inequity on our campuses in their limited definitions of productivity. These limited definitions diminish or even invalidate the importance of the vast majority of productive work done by both teaching faculty and administrators of writing programs. The WPA who does not struggle to find time for writing is the exception, and not because of any shortcomings on her part; similarly, the non-tenure-track teaching faculty member who does not struggle to find time to write is truly anomalous. Yet if productivity is sanctioned and measured only in terms of scholarly writing, then the vast majority of the work of both WPAs and the people we supervise is invalidated institutionally and structurally, and groups like NCFDD participate in the construction of these flawed systems. In terms of emotion and the WPA, if we internalize the metrics of productivity forwarded by groups like the NCFDD, as they reflect problematic institutional values, we diminish ourselves and those who work with us; in contrast, pushing back against rhetorics of success such as those forwarded by the NCFDD is one place to begin.

In our analysis, we foreground the material realities of faculty life, which include the affective and embodied experiences of academic laborers. Our research questions are grounded in theories of affect, as they also emerge from the central concerns of academic labor studies (Bousquet, Scott, and Parascondola 2003; Kahn, Lalicker, and Lynch-Biniek 2017; Schell and Stock 2001; Strickland 2011) and critical university studies (Chatterjee and Maira 2014; Ferguson 2012; Giroux 2014; Newfield 2016; Subbaraman 2002)—attending to naturalized and often invisible forms of exploitation that characterize the contemporary university.

We understand NCFDD communications to be forms of rhetorical action that make sense of the traditional academic circumstance in which faculty reward follows faculty productivity and where productivity is defined as the production and circulation of new knowledge. However, the NCFDD's campaign to help faculty make time for research and writing has a politics that fails to account for the complex working lives of WPAs, whose personal concerns must be balanced alongside concerns about program and people, and teaching faculty, whose teaching loads rarely allow time for the heady work of writing for publication. In fact, NCFDD communications reveal a construct of the ideal academic whose circumstances bear little in common with the current reality of the majority of faculty whose workload does not build in the expectation for new knowledge construction in the form of publishing. The Coalition on the Academic Workforce (2012) established in its report on a 2010 study that fully 75 percent of faculty today are working off the tenure track, and as Kate Navickas points out in this collection, only between 29 percent and 47 percent of writing center directors (a subset of writing program administration) hold tenure-track lines. We can surmise that off the tenure track, these faculty are not rewarded for doing scholarly writing. As such, NCFDD is only narrowly conducive to equity in that it reflects a master narrative about who the academic is or should be. While it is crucial for WPAs to carve out space for writing in order to advance within university systems of tenure and promotion, the WPA must do more, carving out space for both their programs within institutions and their teachers as valued scholars in their own right.

The normative productivity model advanced by the NCFDD also calls attention to the double bind of the WPA, whose service load renders scholarly productivity more difficult to achieve than implied by the mere habit of self-disciplined writing, as advanced by NCFDD. For the WPA, the question is not only how do we construct a writing and scholarship life for ourselves, as NCFDD recommends, but also, how do we counter the dominant narrative that advances only one definition of productivity? For the WPA, equity demands the exertion of many forms of "dancing with resistance," both for the self and for those teaching in writing programs. As Navickas (this volume) points out, while WPA studies "has worked for decades to legitimize writing program administration as scholarly," we owe it to ourselves to add an additional layer, making "emotional labor count, too." Failing to do so reinforces hegemonic, institutional standards, "cutting ourselves off from a more generative, whole understanding of WPA work, which, at its core, is a human activity performed by, with, and for emotional, feeling humans." Navickas's illustration of the frequency of documents reporting measures of productivity—traditional articles and program reports versus documents where emotional labor is discussed (e.g., teaching philosophies, professional presentations)—reveals that as WPAs, we have internalized the normative measures just as NCFDD has. We join Navickas in calling for an accounting of how our (emotional) labor aligns with the outcomes valued by external audiences. Such labor will include not only an accounting for routine instances of emotional labor in writing classrooms and administration but also those not infrequent times when writing program administration comes in contact with the traumatic and catastrophic, as Kim Hensley Owens, Kaitlin Clinnin, Carl Schlachte, and Elizabeth Imafuji point out in their chapters in this collection on the WPA's handling of personal trauma, crisis, and disaster. The accounting must also take into account the WPA's ongoing and too little taken up responsibility for addressing racism, sexism, classism, ableism, and other forms of oppression as they occur in writing classrooms, in writing programs, and in institutional culture, as pointed out in this collection by Sheila Carter-Tod and Joseph Janangelo.

Our chapter consists of four sections in which we examine components of the narrative exhibited in the NCFDD materials. We begin by briefly explaining our methodology, which utilizes rhetorical analysis and affect theory. We then situate our analysis within theorizations of self-help literature. Next we move into the central discussion of the rhetorical moves we find throughout NCFDD discourse, and finally, we explain our conclusions. We posit that NCFDD's discourse of self-help and career coaching participates in three broad rhetorical strategies: these strategies affirm that (1) academic success requires a particular emotional configuration; (2) balance, health, and well-being are ultimately about scholarly productivity, or getting writing done, and, in turn, the academic's relationship to their writing is an indicator of their emotional health in the academic context; (3) since work-life balance/healthy emotion flows from being productive in ways predicated by university systems, marginalized scholars on the tenure track must self-regulate, conserving and dedicating their best energy toward the kinds of work that are likely to ensure success—in order to resist and persist in the university. This theory of equity focuses on the individual who achieves despite conditions, with success attributed to personal choices that are symptomatic of the health of the self-advocating academic. Such a theory extinguishes from the record the prevalent circumstance in which most writing teachers work, which is in contingent, non-tenurable positions, while also failing to acknowledge, much less argue for, the administrative effort of WPAs and other academics who manage programs. While we remain sympathetic to the need of all scholars, including WPAs who are tenurable, to care for the self as scholar-writers so they can survive the tenure process, we believe the online academic career-support/coaching service represented by NCFDD participates in corporate ideologies of success that privatize effort and advocacy and forget the circumstances under which three-quarters of today's academics labor—that is, circumstances of contingency. NCFDD locates the means to full success in the individual rather than within institutional structures, arguing for a form of protective self-advocacy that urges tenure-line faculty toward disciplined productivity while remaining for the most part silent in regard to the equity concerns of the many others with whom the WPA and other academics situate their work. However this, which perhaps could be considered a unseen area in NCFDD's orientation, is not our focus. Our project is to find, through an analysis of NCFDD as one organization that shapes and manifests institutional orientations, the affective messages that commonly circulate in higher education and that shape understandings of faculty development and faculty labor. We read NCFDD discourse as representative of dominant narratives that are presently circulating, as evidenced by the continually growing engagement with NCFDD from institutional partners. NCFDD writing provides a means for us to analyze these present messages in order to think about how we, as WPAs, might interrupt their circulation in our work as faculty/ student advocates and "faculty developers."

METHODOLOGY

As coauthors, we became aware of NCFDD after learning from tenure-track friends that they were finding daily information and inspiration from their online subscriptions. Subsequently, Janelle became a subscriber and gained direct experience with the NCFDD. Sue served as inter-rater to documents Janelle shared with her for purposes of this research. We gathered eight newsletters dating from June through December 2017, twenty-six Monday Motivator emails from throughout 2017, and nine Post-Tenure Pathways series documents that date from September and October 2017. As this informal collection method suggests, ours was a convenience sampling of a portion of one year's output from NCFDD. We confined our analysis to 2017 and have not updated our findings with more recent communications from the organization, and it should be noted that some of our findings may not represent the current orientations and communication strategies of the NCFDD. For the texts we analyzed we chose to focus on what was delivered to Janelle's email inbox to emphasize the communications that are passively received by members rather than sought out through webinar enrollment, for example. With a larger, more representative corpus, we could no doubt make firmer claims about the intentions and effects of the communication approaches represented by the organization, and we might more systematically study the range of genre types by carefully examining the conventions associated with each genre. Instead, in our analysis we explored the broad moves and larger patterns occurring across individual statements, following principles of qualitative textual analysis laid out by Johnny Saldana (2012) and conducting first-cycle and second-cycle coding. Our analysis yielded five rhetorical moves, which we eventually collapsed into three.

THEORETICAL FRAME

NCFDD discourse is legible in the self-help genre, as the organization's model relies on rhetorics of self-improvement and efficacy. We locate our analysis in methodological discussions from Tamika Carey regarding the rhetorics of self-help. As Carey shows in her book *Rhetorical Healing* (2016), self-help discourse can at once provide the grounds for collective transformation while remaining conservative or essentializing in its assumptions. Carey's (2016, 152) work prompts us to ask whether the "learning cures" the NCFDD suggests—in its recommendations about what faculty can learn to *do* in order to *do better*—are "essentially a form of deficit pedagogy" that blames the learner (the faculty member in this case) for the systemic problems they face.

In our analysis, we draw on theories of affect emerging from feminist scholars and theorists of the relationship between language and emotion. From Geoffrey M. White (1990, 47) we are prompted to ask: "'What are people doing with talk of emotion in this context?' and 'What are the presuppositions and social conditions necessary for the rhetoric of disentangling to have the pragmatic effects it does?'" These are questions White poses, as he notes (in a way that represents a broad range of constructivist theories of emotion) that "emotion talk . . . not only represents but creates social reality." White calls upon rhetorical analysis to identify the "specific rhetorical moves that work to transform socioemotional reality" (46–47). What socioemotional realities does NCFDD promote? What is the role of emotion in defining what counts as good academic practice?

We take seriously Sara Ahmed's (2004, 13) call that "we need to consider the circulation of words for emotion." And in this analysis, we are not asking "what are emotions" but rather "what do emotions do" (4). From Ahmed, Lauren Berlant (2008), Alison M. Jaggar (1992), and Lisa Langstraat (2002), we learn to be skeptical of rhetorical gestures that privatize emotion. To make emotion only individual and internal is to ignore the ways lived experience is conditioned by material and historical circumstance. As Langstraat notes, emotions are always "imbricated in power relations" (306). In our analysis, we seek to expose how power relations may be obfuscated in NCFDD discourse about emotion. In doing so, we seek to identify the mind-sets, values, and frameworks represented in that discourse. One of these frameworks is a prioritization of a particular definition of "productivity" in the academic context. NCFDD discourse works to persuade faculty members to construct a lifestyle that supports a writing life of "productivity." Writing is the way productivity is operationalized in the NCFDD context.

RHETORICAL MOVES IN NCFDD DISCOURSE

We observed several rhetorical moves in the examples of NCFDD discourse we analyzed. We think of these claims as three pillars of NCFDD's theory of academic labor. We read these claims as a rhetoric because they are identifiable and strategic ways of working upon an audience of faculty members.

Across the three rhetorical moves, we find the following formulation: particular affective dispositions lead to writing that leads to productivity that produces a notion of equity that argues everyone is able to access a notion of "success" when NCFDD recommendations are followed. When the individual self-advocates, their persistence in the professoriate contributes to equity, as the faculty member is able to continue being represented. As we show in what follows, this conception of equity falls neatly within a neo-liberal model and requires nothing from the institution, besides, perhaps, an NCFDD membership. Below, we elaborate each of the claims at work in this formulation.

Rhetorical Move 1: "Academic success requires a particular emotional configuration."

A theory of affect—and what constitutes "good" or "productive" feeling—undergirds much of what is written and distributed in the NCFDD Monday Motivator missives, delivered in members' emails each week. Efficiency is the priority in these theories of affect—how do we cultivate an academic self that has the emotional configurations conducive to the demands of the institution?

Cultivating a sense of *enjoyment* of one's writing life is an explicit goal of NCFDD's communications. At the same time, NCFDD seeks to dispel the counterproductive notion that one needs to feel a certain way "(inspired, excited, energized, confident, clear, etc.)" in order to write. Reflective of the research by Robert Boice and others, the NCFDD actively promotes a daily writing practice; to sustain this habit, writers need to attend to their affective relationship to writing and what is happening to them internally when they sit down to write. Rockquemore, who writes the Monday Motivators, offers common therapeutic techniques such as a daily self-observation log to "identify your [inner] critic's patterns and question the messages" discussed in the August 7 edition. The goal here is to uncover the limiting set of beliefs one may hold, whether consciously or unconsciously, in relation to writing. Characterizing the limiting set of beliefs as emanating from a self-conjured "bodyguard" that is about self-protection, Rockquemore writes in the August 7 Monday Motivator with the hope that her readers will deepen a "positive relationship with your bodyguard . . . If you can shift your perspective from one of trying to permanently banish your bodyguard to one where you love, accept, and appreciate him, your daily encounter with resistance will slowly change from an agonizing struggle to a sweet little dance." This dancing with resistance metaphor, discussed above, recurs throughout our corpus.

The resistance to writing—and the shame associated with this resistance—is read by NCFDD as a set of beliefs that limit the academic writer: a set of beliefs that are self-imposed. Across the corpus, the point is reaffirmed that academic success comes only through the self-excavation and subsequent reorientation of emotion. This aspect of NCFDD discourse might be instructive for writing teachers and WPAs who may neglect the realm of emotion in their own or their students' writing lives. However, this premise of NCFDD discourse is problematic in that it neglects to excavate the material and systemic forces that may produce a resistance to writing. If one's workweek consists of well over fifty hours of administrative, service, and teaching labors that involve many dimensions of affective output, one's relationship to writing may be complicated by exhaustion, a need for activity that is not tied to the institution, caretaking responsibilities, and many other factors that exceed a simple suggestion to just "shift your perspective." For some, the realities of the academic job relentlessly generate material barriers to writing. To call upon the individual to find a particular emotional configuration to overcome these barriers obfuscates the bind many faculty members find themselves in—and leaves the institution to continue its operations of relying on an inequitable labor system.

Rhetorical Move 2: "Balance, health, and well-being are ultimately about scholarly productivity, or getting writing done. In turn, the academic's relationship to their writing is an indicator of one's emotional and productive success."

NCFDD expressly states that its goal is to promote both well-being and productivity, at once and in conjunction. This goal guides the organization's self-assessment. In a September 2017 newsletter that advertises the Faculty Fellows program, the data are reported: "Among this summer's cohort, 92% increase[d] their productivity and 93% reported improved work-life balance as a result of participating in the program." Productivity and work-life balance are posited as complementary, rather than competitive, aims.

NCFDD considers multiple aspects of one's work-life balance—interpersonal relationships, conflict management, physical well-being, and even the interior design of one's home—as contributing to success in writing. For example, the July 3 Monday Motivator points to the importance of finding "a sense of comfort and home" in one's life. If "your constant work has left your living space bland and anonymous," Rockquemore suggests, "then buy a bucket of paint, hang something on the walls, or take an evening to cook a special dinner that will fill your home with comforting smells." The idea of balance, health, and well-being involves one's lifestyle and a manicured sense of place that betrays a relatively high level of affluence and exaggerated personal choice. This motivational language also reminds the subscriber to take breaks from work. The December newsletter advocates that we "let go and unplug from work" in approaching the holiday break. However, taking this break is ultimately about the productivity that is anticipated in the upcoming year. The next sentence in this newsletter advertises the faculty success program that is to start up in January, designed to enable faculty to get writing done. It is ultimately one's productivity in publishable writing that indicates one has achieved balance.

Writing and research become, in NCFDD discourse, a synecdoche for claiming a space for oneself. Sitting down to write is regularly described as "paying oneself first." In the November 20, 2017, Monday Motivator, Rockquemore observes the common circumstance that one's "daily routine is spent serving everyone else." She posits that this lifestyle of being "in service of" (our students, our departments, our institutions) is what prompts the need for "binge writing"—because writing only happens when one has a break from this day-to-day life of academic service. "A 'break,'" then, "means a break from meeting the needs of my students and colleagues and a time in which I can finally attend to my own needs." NCFDD discourse focuses on developing a relationship to one's writing—which is also, in this formulation, a relationship to one's own needs.

For NCFDD, productivity and well-being are conjoined and come in the form of writing for publication. This emphasis on research and publication does not account for the forms of scholarly productivity that may be most present in the WPA's academic life, much less the life of the adjunct cobbling together sections to eke out a living. Ironically, such awareness gap were addressed by the Boyer Commission (1998) when redefining best practices in regard to faculty work in the early 1990s. The commission called for research universities in particular to more fully address student learning as an obligatory part of university work, and the Boyer report emphasized scholarship on teaching, engagement, and service. This redefining of faculty work was reinforced by the development of the literature on universities as learning communities (Barr and Tagg 1995), faculty learning communities (Cox and Richlin 2004; Petrone and Ortquist-Ahrens 2004), and graduate student learning communities (Nyquist, Woodford, and Rogers 2004, as well as Richlin and Essington 2004)—all of which elevate the importance of the instructional mission and the professional development that sustains it. More recently, scholars such as Casie Fedukovich and Megan Hall (2016) have recommended the development of a new college teacher who is a critical pedagogue seeking to deepen student learning while interrogating university objectives. Neglecting scholarship like Fedukovich and Hall's, NCFDD takes a decidedly traditional approach to defining faculty productivity. Both before and after tenure, NCFDD urges self-regulation, with the burden of staying on track a matter of self-control and good habits.

NCFDD creates forms of accountability for research, built on the premise—articulated in the November 27, 2017, Monday Motivator—that "the core challenge of academic work is that the things that matter the most to your long-term success (writing and research) have the least built-in accountability while other activities (service and teaching) have high built-in accountability on a daily basis." What day-to-day institutional life lacks in accountability for research, NCFDD provides.

However, the double-valenced nature of scholarship, wherein what serves the institution also serves the self, is not noted, much less rectified, in the corpus we analyzed—not even in the post-tenure advice. Read optimistically, the Boyer model is a way of reclaiming the "self-directed" and "self-serving" side of scholarship that promotes creativity and critique over the confines of the institution that wants high cultural-capital scholarship for its own purposes. Yet NCFDD discourse does little to advocate for an expansion or problematization of traditional definitions of faculty success.

Rhetorical Move 3: "Individual success ultimately leads to equity. Equity mandates that individuals achieve within the system in traditionally prescribed ways."

Implicit in NCFDD discourse is a theory of equity that is formulated as follows: equitable access to success flows from the individual disciplining the self to be productive in ways predicated by university systems. The NCFDD's equity project involves coaching the individual who is pursuing tenure toward the accomplishment of scholarly productivity, with the warrant being that traditional modes of productivity are not equally available to all members of the professoriate. While not discussed explicitly in the corpus we analyzed, NCFDD recommendations seem to carry awareness that some faculty are more susceptible to having their labor co-opted than are others with service, teaching, and other low-value activities. These other activities are posited as seductive distractions that exploit the vulnerabilities of tenure-track faculty at the very time they can least afford it. Tenure-track faculty, NCFDD suggests, dare not become too involved in these areas but must instead stay vigilantly resistant to them to maintain a record of publication and gain tenure. These constructions risk reinforcing a hierarchy of types of work—with teaching, running programs, and mentoring students considered a lower or lesser form of labor. This hierarchy is untenable when the university needs to rectify the equity gaps students of color and marginalized groups experience as a result of institutional failures.

The ramifications of such stratification constitute a topic the NCFDD leaves unexamined. The NCFDD forwards a narrowly defined politic of self-care. Even the NCFDD's post-tenure advice is focused on taking a more deliberate approach to self-advocacy by pursuing passion projects rather than addressing a tenured faculty member's newly situated power and freedom to directly address campus politics, particularly with regard to equity. Arguably, this centers and affirms the faculty member who is least likely to be granted an institutional space for passion projects, but the question of how equity is defined by NCFDD remains ambiguous. The unstated conception of equity we find in NCFDD discourse focuses on the individual's access to the rights and privileges of tenure, or ever fuller participation in the enterprise associated with the individual intellectual entrepreneur. This view of equity is largely to the exclusion of broader concerns around inclusive and antiracist practices and policies in the higher education setting, as well as issues of academic labor disparities across faculty ranks and opportunity gaps experienced by the students we enroll. The leadership potential of the tenured faculty member is couched as a still internal, still individual, still quasi-psychological mind-set that is ever more fully a matter of personal choice. Even once tenured, the faculty member is not encouraged to consider the structural binds of the institution, much less speak back to them for purposes of institutional transformation—transformation that might change the circumstances of faculty on and off the tenure track, as well as those of their students. Instead of including systemic change in its project, the focus of NCFDD seems to be to teach the individual faculty member how to win at a system that is determined to undermine many, if not most, people—which subsequently has the effect of, in turn, perpetuating a system that justifies the coaching that NCFDD itself provides. NCFDD acknowledges that faculty are overburdened with institutional demands and that these demands are not evenly distributed among faculty members, but its primary gesture is to tell the individual faculty member to "do better" in vigilantly guarding their time and staying disciplined, regardless of the odds stacked against them. The implication, then, is that marginalized scholars must self-regulate even more fully than others, conserving and dedicating their best energy toward the kinds of work that are likely to produce tenure.

Among the 2017 Monday Motivators, the May 20 installment admonishes: "You have a vague sense that you SHOULD be writing and you NEED [all caps theirs] to write (in order to finish your dissertation, get a job, win tenure and promotion, etc.) but you're not putting conscious, direct, and intense energy into the actual act of writing." Similarly, on July 3 comes this advice, which starts off suggesting the value of collaboration but winds up with the reader reminded once again of her obligations and shortcomings: "Reconnecting with project participants, sharing work with the community, meeting with people on the ground to discuss research collaborations, ideas, and connections can remind you why it's so important for you to complete your writing projects and publish your work." This particular Motivator questions the reader's commitment: "When I have tried everything I know to break through resistance, I typically end by asking: Do you REALLY want to be a professor?" The reader is urged to consider whether escape fantasies are a matter of stress or "the genuine, gut-level resistance that occurs when you REALLY know you're on the wrong path." While this can be read as authorizing the junior academic to make the best decisions for themselves, it can also be read as a type of shaming disguised as coaching—testing the reader's commitment to the profession and perhaps exacerbating what one might already experience as legitimate exhaustion, including the racial battle fatigue of daily surviving a racist institution. This Motivator offers no discussion of how the message that "you're on the wrong path" may be something a faculty member has heard before—micro-aggressively stated in faculty meetings or hallway exchanges—and that this message is tied to prejudice and exclusion in the academy. Faculty work, as described, thus belongs to a system with a continually moving target and an upping of the requirements. Faculty work amid the impossibility of being as productive or available or willing as they are told they need to be. They work in a system that relentlessly seeks to extract more and more labor from its workers and that will continue to tax some more than others as it plays out the gross inequities that are so ubiquitous in US and global society. It is in this context that the question "do you really want to be a professor" is particularly fraught.

WHAT ABOUT AFTER TENURE?

Most of the discussion above is focused on the materials that are intended for the pre-tenure faculty member. In the tenure-track years, it is perhaps somewhat understandable that the individual's steady focus on tenure is given primacy. But even in the advice given in the post-tenure column (Post-Tenure Pathways), the guidance changes only slightly. On September 20, newly tenured members are urged to consider how to create a life that is "driven by authentic purpose, where your work has significant impact and influence, where you experience a deep sense of belonging, and that provides you with true joy." The tenured faculty member is also told in an entry focused on why it is important to "Interview Role Models" that "a prerequisite for post-tenure success is the mindset that you live in a friendly universe that is organized to support your highest good—that you can ask for what you need and the right people will respond and provide you with it." Such guidance fails to account for the fundamentally inequitable climate that prevails even after tenure is granted by a chosen few. When urged, as readers are again on October 18, to consider why some might be "reactive to any of this [guidance]," it is suggested that readers "gently ask yourself: Why?"—with that "why" pointing to an internal, privatized examination of one's individual psychology. There is no acknowledgment of the justifiable reasons why a reactive mind-set may endure, no awareness shown of the social stratifications of universities where those who have a sense of being untouchable are the few who have exceptional access to privilege. "Asking for what you need" has the potential for disparate repercussions for faculty, given the racist, sexist, xenophobic, homophobic, and ableist climates of our institutions. This unmentioned complexity is perhaps most evident in the November 1 installment titled "Finding Your Post-Tenure Pathway," in which members are told, following a convention of the self-help genre, "you will create your new pathway by speaking it into reality." The post-tenure part of what the NCFDD considers to be the "academic life-cycle" is the most likely space for campus activism, but we find little to no encouragement of this work in the NCFDD discourse we studied. Even with the supposed freedom and security that comes with tenure, the NCFDD academic is not focused on actual resistance or systemic change. The focus remains on the individual's self-optimization within the system.

DISCUSSION

NCFDD is inscribed within a self-help discourse. Undergirding this self-help orientation is a political fantasy that individuals have control over their own lives—that when therapized sufficiently in a discourse of academic self-help, the faculty member can control their "peace and productivity," the words Rockquemore uses when she signs off on her Monday Motivator missives. Present in the NCFDD discourse is an assumption of an academic self who might, without the NCFDD's intervention, undermine herself by teaching and serving too much. It is almost as if the imagined subject of the NCFDD intervention is understood as prone to self-sabotage due to a tendency toward caring for everything and everyone except herself. We read this as gendered and racialized—as non-cismale faculty and faculty of color are continually taxed with various forms of hidden labor as they are systematically asked to take on more of the emotional and cultural labor necessary for the institution to uphold its self-presentation as a welcoming space of learning for a diverse student body. It is these discriminatory institutional circumstances—and not a self-sabotaging deficiency within the individual—that account for disparities. University awareness of these disparities is one factor that sustains the NCFDD as an organization with a growing stable of institutional members. The university outsources a salve for the conditions students and faculty experience on the campus grounds—a mechanism that keeps the individual's focus on the individual. Lacking an interrogation of the state of affairs in higher education, NCFDD becomes a complicit partner in neoliberal market-based depictions of productivity and individual responsibility, even as it also affirms the traditional research university model, which attaches highest value to research and publication.

And yet we cannot neglect the important role the NCFDD may play in individual faculty members' lives. So ultimately, we offer a "both and" perspective here, in acknowledging that the NCFDD may be a source of comfort, sustenance, community, and sound advice for diverse faculty members at multiple stages in their careers. We note the risk of unfairly pigeonholing Rockquemore and her organization in our expectation that the organization participate in activism to address inequities. We acknowledge the role positionality plays in our analysis: the forms of privilege we access as white faculty in PWIs (predominantly white institutions) enable us to question the formulation "health = productivity = success = equity" we find in NCFDD discourse. To be clear, our critique is on the institutional narratives about faculty life and faculty work that NCFDD discourse may reproduce; these narratives do not originate with NCFDD. We read NCFDD discourse as encapsulating more diffuse messages that faculty may hear as subtext in their daily conversations and as tacit in institutional messaging. We chose the organization as a site of research because of the multivalenced and complex nature of what it offers, because of what its existence and its messaging reveal about academe—a system that produces the demand for an organization that can sustain faculty well-being and career continuity because universities cannot. We were motivated to study the NCFDD from our own personal (in Janelle's case) and observed (in Sue's case) sense that the NCFDD offers something important to the faculty members who make up its membership. Janelle can no longer afford a subscription, but she misses the sense the NCFDD provided her that she is not alone in experiencing challenges to getting her scholarly writing done and surviving academic life. Struggles to write, to find balance, to keep healthy boundaries are shared struggles, and the NCFDD offers the space to make this known. Our call is primarily to go one step further in translating shared struggles to activism within the academy; and NCFDD could be a well-equipped platform for such work, although our focus here is on the steps WPAs can take as we work toward systemic change and repair, and as we become ever more self-reflexive about the insidious messages that we may be, however unconsciously, reproducing. Our focus is not on the NCFDD as an organization; our focus is instead on how an analysis of NCFDD discourse can highlight narratives that we too may be mobilizing as WPAs, given how prevalent these narratives are in institutional spaces.

NCFDD AND WPA WORK

The assumptions represented in NCFDD discourse are in us, as WPAs, and call upon us to track the privatizing tendencies of the genres of academic self-help and faculty development that we've inherited. How can we attend to the emotional lives of faculty members in a way that is critical of the institutional structures that condition them? How can we uphold the value of faculty writing development—and the role of emotion in getting writing done—without reducing an image of the "good faculty" to an easy "health = productivity = success = equity" equation?

If a version of "success" prioritizes only one aspect of the professorial life for all faculty members, what may be lost? For example, do we sufficiently value forms of success that include participation in faculty governance, activism regarding academic labor, advocacy for antiracist and inclusive practices to change campus climate? Or do we prioritize research, teaching, or both to the exclusion of the other forms of work in which faculty members engage? Do we create two-tier environments within our own rhetoric and composition programs, where those with rhetorical leanings gain access to opportunity while those in composition and writing program administration do grunt work? Our values are maintained in how we train our graduate students: for example, how many MA and PhD programs in our field include courses that take faculty governance or union literacy as a focus to equip students with tools for fuller participation in institutional leadership in their careers? How many programs provide graduate students with the tools for community organizing and activism and the lenses with which to see the many layers and dimensions of inequity within educational systems? Do our programs today directly address the labor conditions our graduate students will soon find themselves in, such as the difficulty of scaling up from a GTA teaching load to a full-time teaching load in order to (minimally) put bread on the table or the emotional labor of teaching writing to first-year students for decades on end?

We seek a rhetoric that works toward change, that interrogates the emotional constructs that circulate in academic discourse as it also brings to light the affective experiences of those who populate our campuses. Our call is not so much to ask for more from NCFDD as it is to ask for something different from ourselves—without falling into the trap of the individualized "do better" model we critique here and without failing to account for the institutional changes that need to be made and that we can demand to see and help to construct.

What this looks like in practice is manifold, and it is an orientation that shows up in our daily work, in the decisions we make on and off of our campuses. As a way of translating this orientation into concrete practice, we've taken each of the rhetorical moves analyzed above and matched them with some counter-practices (see table 4.1). We offer affective strategies to address those constructions of academic labor that we find written out in NCFDD discourse and mobilized in our daily lives as academics. Many of these strategies have emerged in our conversations with colleagues, and we hope the following will be read in full

Table 4.1. Rhetorical moves and affective strategies

NCFDD Rhetorical Move	Alternative Affective Strategies We Propose
Academic success requires a particular emotional configuration.	The emotions that "show up" in our work tell us something about the institutional situations we are in. Rather than train ourselves to perform a particular emotional configuration for the sake of productivity, we pay attention to the emotions that arrive in our work, and we use these emotions to push back on the oppressive and inequitable forces of the university. Strategic and practical implications of this approach include: • Identifying, documenting, and talking back to statements we hear in meetings, hallways, and other settings that assume a shared definition of productivity, especially in terms of how such statements valorize certain forms of productivity (publication) while marginalizing other forms of productivity (e.g., teaching, mentoring, advising, service). • Addressing and revising formal definitions of productivity in policies, codes, and manuals relating to faculty reward, including tenure and promotion and merit pay raises. On this point, see also Amy Ferdinandt Stolley's suggestions in this book regarding strategies for articulating emotional labor in our professional documents. • Creating a work log that documents the emotional realities of the day-to-day experience of a WPA as a complement to an hourly work log designed to identify work speedups and "responsibility creep" for those tasks that are least valued in the university. This includes tracking the specific forms of emotional labor that occur in our workdays—as Stolley's chapter suggests, "count the hours." • Conducting regular "emotional labor interviews" (see Kate Navickas's chapter in this volume) that can provide similar data and an ongoing temperature-taking mechanism for the emotional climate of academic laborers. • Generating messaging campaigns that raise awareness about the emotional realities of university work, including WPA work.

continued on next page

Table 4.1—*continued*

NCFDD Rhetorical Move	Alternative Affective Strategies We Propose
Balance, health, and well-being are ultimately about scholarly productivity, or getting writing done. In turn, the academic's relationship to their writing is an indicator of one's emotional and productive success.	We pursue balance, health, and well-being despite, and in the face of, neoliberal institutional conditions. Balance, health, and well-being are "goods" for their own sake—not for the sake of productivity. Strategic and practical implications of this approach include: • Hosting workshops on "saying no" and "taking back our time and well-being" that explicitly identify structural and systemic forces that jeopardize emotional health and balance. • Re-storying and counternarrating common ideas about emotional labor in the university—to reject notions that emotional struggle is the fault of an individual rather than a material by-product of institutional conditions. • Bringing to light in faculty discussions the range of material hardship experienced by faculty off the tenure track, especially but not limited to those non-tenure-track faculty who teach writing. • Addressing pay inequities experienced by various marginalized groups, including writing instructors and those laboring in the arts and humanities, and focusing on the relationship between compensation and well-being. • Creating structures in which faculty will be supported and protected for refusing to do more than they are compensated for. Part of this work includes creating the conditions through which faculty can come to see that each sacrifice and donation of time has systemic ramifications. On every occasion where we work for no compensation, we create a precedent the university system can exploit. Refusing to volunteer one's labor is in the best interest of those who share our work now and in the future, and we need to be deliberate in making this understood. What may look to be the generous thing in the here and now (e.g., volunteering to teach a course with no compensation to address an emergent exigency) may have damaging effects later (e.g., the university comes to expect that compensation is no longer necessary for this labor).
Individual success ultimately leads to equity. Equity mandates that individuals achieve within the system in traditionally prescribed ways.	Equity will not be achieved through individual success alone. A de-privatized understanding of emotion can be a ground for coming together as a collective to transform campus climate and institutional conditions. Strategic and practical implications of this approach include: • Creating affiliate groups and faculty learning communities based on shared emotional experiences, as spaces for collaboratively initiated action. For example, a support group for dealing with "burnout" in the workplace can transform into a space for organizing and collective action (e.g., preventing exhaustion through structural transformation and addressing burnout itself as a cultural construct that blames the victim rather than targeting structural causes). • Maintaining ongoing agenda items and check-ins regarding emotional labor in trusted department- and university-level faculty committees to maintain the visibility of these issues. This should be done with critical attention to what may be at stake for faculty of diverse positionalities in voicing concerns in different spaces. • Surveying what faculty really need by way of support, and providing means for anonymously reporting ways exploitation is occurring on our campuses. • Creating mechanisms by which universities will be held accountable for exploitive and inequitable practices (e.g., through the mandatory publishing of reports on the topic; through alternative accreditation processes that prioritize equity).

continued on next page

Table 4.1—continued

NCFDD Rhetorical Move	Alternative Affective Strategies We Propose

Individual success ultimately leads to equity. Equity mandates that individuals achieve within the system in traditionally prescribed ways (continued)	• Making legible and visible the range of work faculty members, including WPAs, do to create change on campus and to sustain their own, their colleagues', and their students' persistence on campus, despite unjust conditions. This includes:
	  • Prioritizing the skill set needed for advocacy work in campus change and campus equity as a key part of graduate training.
	  • Arguing in faculty governance arenas and other spaces for expanded notions of what counts as productivity in the university so the work of transforming the university is unmistakably valued in material and symbolic ways.
	  • Generating funding sources to compensate faculty for cultural taxation and campus equity work. Borrowing from the model of the California State University system and the California Faculty Association, such funding could be named for forms of "extraordinary service."

acknowledgment of the collective, coalitional work that is involved in strategic activism within the academy.

The suggestions provided in this table offer a small sampling of action points and steps we can take to speak back to constructs of the academic who simply needs to "do better." We must keep our attention on the structural forces at work upon us, even as we fight to preserve a sense of self and sense of choice within such a system. This is itself a form of emotional labor. We take from NCFDD the importance of giving language to the emotional labors of our work, even as we seek to reconfigure how that emotional labor is thought of and enacted on our campuses.

REFERENCES

Ahmed, Sara. 2004. *The Cultural Politics of Emotion*. Edinburgh: Edinburgh University Press.

Barr, Robert B., and John Tagg. 1995. "From Teaching to Learning—a New Paradigm for Undergraduate Education." *Change: The Magazine of Higher Learning* 27 (6): 12–26.

Berlant, Lauren. 2008. *The Female Complaint: The Unfinished Business of Sentimentality in American Culture*. Durham, NC: Duke University Press.

Bousquet, Marc, Tony Scott, and Leo Parascondola. 2003. *Tenured Bosses and Disposable Teachers: Writing Instruction in the Managed University*. Carbondale: Southern Illinois University Press.

Boyer, Ernest. 1998. *Reinventing Undergraduate Education: A Blueprint for America's Research Universities*. Boyer Commission on Educating Undergraduates in the Research University. Stony Brook: State University of New York at Stony Brook for the Carnegie Foundation for the Advancement of Teaching.

Carey, Tamika. 2016. *Rhetorical Healing: The Reeducation of Contemporary Black Womanhood*. Albany: State University of New York Press.

Chatterjee, Piya, and Sunaina Maira, eds. 2014. *The Imperial University: Academic Repression and Scholarly Dissent.* Minneapolis: University of Minnesota Press.

Coalition on the Academic Workforce. 2012. "A Portrait of Part-Time Faculty Members: A Summary of Findings on Part-Time Faculty Respondents to the Coalition on the Academic Workforce Survey of Contingent Faculty Members and Instructors." http://www.academicworkforce.org/survey.html.

Cox, Milton D., and Laurie Richlin. 2004. *Building Faculty Learning Communities: New Directions for Teaching and Learning.* Jossey-Bass Series 97. San Francisco: Jossey-Bass.

Fedukovich, Casie, and Megan Hall. 2016. "GTA Preparation as a Model for Cross-Tier Collaboration: A Program Profile." *Composition Forum* 33. http://compositionforum.com/issue/33/ncsu.php.

Ferguson, Roderick A. 2012. *The Reorder of Things: The University and Its Pedagogies of Minority Difference.* Minneapolis: University of Minnesota Press.

Giroux, Henry A. 2014. *Neoliberalism's War on Higher Education.* Chicago: Haymarket.

Jaggar, Alison M. 1992. "Love and Knowledge: Emotion in Feminist Epistemology." In *Women and Reason*, edited by Elizabeth D. Harvey and Kathleen Okruhlik, 115–142. Ann Arbor: University of Michigan Press.

Kahn, Seth, William B. Lalicker, and Amy Lynch-Biniek, eds. 2017. *Contingency, Exploitation, and Solidarity: Labor and Action in English Composition.* Fort Collins: Colorado State University Open Press.

Langstraat, Lisa. 2002. "The Point Is There Is No Point: Miasmic Cynicism and Cultural Studies Composition." *JAC: A Journal of Composition Theory* 22 (2): 293–325.

Micciche, Laura R., and Allison D. Carr. 2011. "Toward Graduate-Level Writing Instruction." *College Composition and Communication* 62 (3): 477–501.

National Center for Faculty Development and Diversity (NCFDD) website. N.d. www.facultydiversity.org.

Newfield, Christopher. 2016. *The Great Mistake: How We Wrecked Public Universities and How We Can Fix Them.* Baltimore: Johns Hopkins University Press.

Nyquist, Jody D., Bettina J. Woodford, and Diane L. Rogers. 2004. "Re-envisioning the Ph.D." In *Paths to the Professoriate: Strategies for Enriching the Preparation of Future Faculty*, edited by Donald H. Wulff and Ann E. Austin, 194–216. San Francisco: Jossey-Bass.

Petrone, Martha C., and Leslie Ortquist-Ahrens. 2004. "Facilitating Faculty Learning Communities: A Compact Guide to Creating Change and Inspiring Community." *Building Faculty Learning Communities.* New Directions for Teaching and Learning. Jossey-Bass series 97. https://doi.org/10.1002/tl.133.

Richlin, Laurie, and Amy Essington. 2004. "Overview of Faculty Learning Communities." *Building Faculty Learning Communities.* New Directions for Teaching and Learning. Jossey-Bass Series 97. https://doi.org/10.1002/tl.130.

Saldana, Johnny. 2012. *The Coding Manual for Qualitative Researchers.* Thousand Oaks, CA: Sage.

Schell, Eileen E., and Patricia Lambert Stock. 2001. *Moving a Mountain: Transforming the Role of Contingent Faculty in Composition Studies and Higher Education.* Urbana, IL: National Council of Teachers of English.

Strickland, Donna. 2011. *The Managerial Unconscious in the History of Composition Studies.* Carbondale: Southern Illinois University Press.

Subbaraman, Sivagami. 2002. "(In)Different Spaces: Feminist Journeys from the Academy to the Mall." In *Women's Studies on Its Own: A Next Wave Reader in Institutional Change*, edited by Robyn Wiegman, 258–266. Durham, NC: Duke University Press.

White, Geoffrey M. 1990. "Moral Discourse and the Rhetoric of Emotions." In *Language and Politics of Emotion*, edited by L. Abu-Lughod and Catherine A. Lutz, 46–68. Cambridge: Cambridge University Press.

5
UNLEASHED EMOTION
Centering Emotional Labor in Our Professional Documents

Amy Ferdinandt Stolley
Grand Valley State University

In her recently published post-mortem of the 2016 presidential election, Jennifer Palmieri (2018, 8), Hillary Rodham Clinton's former communications director, claims that a contributing factor to Clinton's electoral college loss was her staff's decision to run a campaign that had "half of [Clinton's] humanity tied behind her back." She explains that the campaign believed that Clinton had to adopt the masculine mantle of a traditional presidential candidate to gain the trust of voters; as a result, Clinton downplayed her (presumably feminine) characteristics that might have been attractive to voters. Palmieri argues that because of this, voters didn't have a clear picture of Clinton as a whole person and were unable to see the full potential of her presidency. Clinton's staffers understood her to be compassionate, kind, and smart, but because they believed those qualities wouldn't be valued by voters, they advised her to downplay them.

The notion of not being seen as a whole person—one whose intellect *and* emotion drive her decision-making and interactions with colleagues—is an idea that resonates for many writing program administrators (WPAs). We've been trained, either in graduate school or on the job, to make our work understandable to those whose concerns are driven by full-time equivalencies (FTEs), retention rates, and student evaluations of instruction. While those data-driven arguments are an important part of WPA work, they don't often represent what it's really like to be a WPA because they render invisible the emotional work we do to keep the programs we direct running. We keep our emotional labor tied behind our backs because we believe others don't value it as much as they value direct measures of teaching effectiveness, scholarly production, or academic administration.

A few years ago, in the midst of my post-tenure sabbatical, I unexpectedly found myself in the mid-career slump so many had warned me of. I had spent the first seven years of my faculty life working to rebuild a first-year writing program from the ground up, and while the work had been engaging and ultimately successful, the path ahead was unclear—made more uncertain by the financial trouble my institution had found itself in. I tentatively went on the job market that fall, applying to three open WPA positions at schools whose programs I admired. I got an interview at one of them. At each stage of the interview process, I considered bowing out. As slumpy as I felt, I was still committed and connected to my university, my colleagues, and our students; I couldn't imagine leaving, so I wasn't sure why I agreed to the interview or the campus visit invitation that soon followed.

Perhaps because I didn't really think I'd take the job even if it was offered to me, I decided to be wholly myself on my campus visit. I'd be open and honest about how I approach teaching writing and program administration, focusing more on my beliefs and practices as a WPA rather than trying to suss out and mirror what my would-be colleagues wanted to hear. As part of the campus visit, I was asked to give a presentation to faculty about my administrative philosophy. So I shared with them the quotes, poems, and images I tape to the back of my office door that are reminders of the importance of emotional labor in my work and my desire to build a program rooted in empathy toward students and colleagues. One of the quotes I shared was from Donald Hall (2007, 86, original emphasis), who wrote of academics, "*We always bear responsibilities* for the communities of which we are a part," and I explained how I work to claim my responsibility for my community by enacting an empathetic stance toward those around me, particularly those who feel marginalized by the university system we call home. And I shared the last lines from Marge Piercy's poem "To Be of Use"—"The pitcher cries for water to carry / and a person for work that is real"—to illustrate that I actively choose WPA work because it feels practical and human to me in ways more traditional academic research often doesn't feel. It was the first time I've shared with others these very personal elements of my WPA work; after all, I put those quotes on the *back* of my door for a reason. It felt risky, a little touchy-feely, but also authentic.

I got the job, and to my surprise, I accepted it. My early days on campus felt different to me; I was confident my new colleagues had a fuller understanding of me as an administrator *and* a person. In this new environment, I've felt more comfortable discussing the emotional work I do with first-year writing instructors and students, and it has created opportunities for me to talk with my colleagues and unpack the negative emotions I experience as a WPA. Part of this is because I joined a well-established writing department with a culture of collaboration, innovation, and experimentation—one much different than the English department I left. But I am convinced that my relatively smooth transition also occurred because I was honest during my campus visit about who I am and how I do the work of a WPA. I can't say if my openness during the campus visit has had an influence on my colleagues, but it changed something in me, creating a space for me to be a more authentic WPA and feel for the first time in my career like I'm inhabiting my real professional, embodied, emotional self.[1]

When talking with other WPAs and reading narratives of their work, it's clear that many haven't had the same experience I had. Instead, WPAs struggle to find ways to make their emotional labor visible. As Mara Holt, Leon Anderson, and Albert Rouzie (2003, 152) note, WPAs believe "emotion work is crucially important, often fulfilling, but not officially recognized" as valid work. Even though most WPAs believe emotional labor is a central part of our jobs, it is often undervalued or worse, dismissed as un-intellectual or meaningless by our colleagues, remaining invisible to those who haven't done the work of a WPA. Part of this is due to what Sara Ahmed (2004, 9) refers to as the "inside out model of emotions." For Ahmed, this model is based on our assumption that emotion is centered internally within a person until it is expressed to others through facial expressions, physical reactions, or language (8). Although Ahmed ultimately rejects this model in favor of one that understands emotion as a cultural and social practice that occurs outside an individual, the assumption of and preference for emotion's interiority drives much of our social and professional interactions. When a colleague tells you to get a handle on your facial expression in meetings, she is telling you that she believes your emotion is inappropriate and needs to stay visible only to you. When a WPA tells an instructor that she shouldn't get angry when a student deliberately plagiarizes an essay in her class, the colleague hears that her emotion is best kept inside.

If we believe emotions are meant to be private and internal, it stands to reason that the work we do dealing with our own and others' emotions remains invisible as well, in part because of the nature of our professional communities. Many of us work in university communities that prioritize the rational over the emotional, or what Tom Kerr (2003, 24) refers to as the "academic suppression of pathos." In an environment where pathos or emotion is tamped down, we see our colleagues listen to and heed the rational voice more readily than the emotional, feeling voice. On the other hand, psychologists have found that expressions of emotion in the workplace are not always suppressed but are instead interpreted by others based on the type of emotion being expressed and the gender of the speaker. For example, Victoria L. Brescoll and Eric Luis Uhlmann's (2008, 268) study found that "men who expressed anger in a professional context were conferred higher status than men who expressed sadness," but women who expressed anger in the workplace were deemed "lower status" by their male and female colleagues alike. This study, which likely confirms the experience of many academics, suggests that it's not *all* pathos that is suppressed in the academic workplace but rather certain kinds of pathos (anger, sadness) from certain kinds of people.

For those who value the emotional nature of administrative work, the dismissal of emotion is particularly frustrating. Not talking about emotional labor doesn't make it go away; it just relegates it to areas where it is not as easy to identify, interpret, or measure. The emotional work WPAs do with students and colleagues requires tremendous personal investment and energy. Emotional labor is something we work hard at and try to improve on, but when it goes unnoticed or unvalued, it's difficult to know how to make it count. More important, when WPAs are socialized into academic communities that do not value or make space for emotion and the labor it generates, the costs are heavy and widely distributed. We bury our emotions and develop (often unhealthy) coping mechanisms to contain them (Janangelo, this volume). We get stuck in a disappointment loop and lose our sense of optimism (Micciche 2002). We harbor resentment that impedes communication, we argue unproductively with colleagues, or we check out and isolate ourselves (George 1999). Sometimes we quit altogether (Bishop and Crossley 1996).

As we are socialized into academic communities, we are either taught explicitly as graduate students or learn from experience on the job that WPA scholarship and WPAs are not always held in high esteem. The field of WPA studies has worked for decades to legitimize writing program administration as scholarly; when we still have to make those arguments, why would we want to add another layer of complexity to try to make our emotional labor count too? It makes sense that many of us choose not to. But the costs of suppressed emotion and unrecognized emotional labor extend beyond ourselves or our departments and into the discipline. If we aren't articulating the emotional labor of WPA work accurately and honestly, if we aren't exploring how emotion might help us do our work better, how are we mentoring early-career WPAs to work through and with workplace emotion more productively than we've been able to? And how are we, as a field, cutting ourselves off from a more generative, total understanding of WPA work, which, at its core, is a human activity performed by, with, and for emotional, feeling humans?

Despite how many reasons there are to ignore our emotional labor, more scholars are working to make their efforts visible in their work, and my experience on the job market has led me to seek more concrete ways I could make my emotional labor visible to myself and others. Before my last round on the job market, I hadn't explicitly addressed emotional labor in my CV, my administrative philosophy statement, or my tenure and promotion documents. How could colleagues see and value this work that I find so central to my responsibilities as a WPA if I don't talk about it? Do others talk about their emotional labor as WPAs in their professional documents? If so, how do they do it?

HOW AND WHY WE TALK ABOUT EMOTIONAL LABOR (OR NOT)

To find answers to these questions, I conducted a small survey that invited participants to reflect on their experiences with emotional labor and how—if at all—they discussed emotional labor in their professional personnel or program documents.[2] Invitations to the twenty-three–question survey were sent through the WPA-L listserv and the Council of Writing Program Administrators (CWPA) Facebook group, which reaches a broad audience of those involved with writing administration work. When participants completed the survey, they were also invited to submit examples of their professional documents that discussed emotional labor for further study. A total of fifty-one current and former WPAs responded to the survey, and three agreed to share their documents.

I asked respondents to report demographic information to offer a snapshot of who opted to participate in the study, and these questions were modeled on the large-scale study conducted by Jonikka Charlton and Shirley K Rose (2009) that they described in "Twenty More Years in the WPA's Progress." My survey response data indicate a general alignment with the data collected by Charlton and Rose in 2007, although a vast majority (92%) of the respondents to my survey identified as female compared to their figure of 64 percent (118). At least 42 percent of Charlton and Rose's respondents were non-tenure track or not yet tenured (124); 50 percent of my survey's respondents were untenured WPAs. Charlton and Rose's respondents had an average number of around 8 years as a WPA (129), whereas 70 percent of my respondents had served as a WPA for between 0 and 6 years in their careers.

Most of the demographic data I collected reflects similar figures to those collected by Charlton and Rose over 10 years ago, but my survey had a particular purpose of collecting data about experiences with emotional labor, whereas Charlton and Rose aimed to update 20-year-old data about the membership of the Council of Writing Program Administrators as a whole. As a result, I expect that respondents who completed the survey were particularly motivated by and interested in the issue of emotional labor, either because it is an area they study themselves or because it is an issue they consider in their own professional work life. Therefore, it is reasonable to consider that there are certain populations within the CWPA membership who are concerned about or interested in issues related to emotional labor: women, non-tenured WPAs, and those new to WPA work. All of these groups are arguably in liminal positions within the academy and thus perhaps more sensitive to how their work is perceived by colleagues.

WHAT TYPES OF EMOTIONAL LABOR DO WPAS PERFORM?

Survey respondents were asked to identify if they believe emotional labor is a part of WPA work; unsurprisingly, 100 percent of respondents affirmed that they see emotional labor and WPA work as inextricably linked. As one respondent put it, WPA work is "peopled, and attention to people is essential." Participants were asked to identify the types of emotional work they perform as a WPA, but because emotional labor has different connotations for different people, I asked respondents to identify the specific types of emotional labor they do using Holt, Anderson, and Rouzie's (2003, 147) definition of emotional work: "attention to personal feelings, the emotional tenor of relationships, empathy and encouragement, mediation of disputes, building emotional solidarity in groups, and using one's own or others' outlaw emotions to interrogate structures." The top three emotional labor activities WPAs identified were attending or responding to others' emotions, building relationships, and sustaining relationships, while the three least frequently identified activities were repairing damaged relationships, using personal emotions to interrogate structures, and using others' emotions to interrogate structures (see table 5.1).

External sources of emotional labor—those that come from others' need for support or solutions—rank highest on this list, which makes sense in terms of the day-to-day responsibilities of the WPA. In many departments, the WPA is seen as a faculty mentor and problem solver, so when classroom or departmental issues arise, they are often brought to the WPA's door. These external sources of emotional labor (the anxious student, the disgruntled colleague) are difficult to ignore and make up a good portion of the WPA's workday. However, the internal sources of

Table 5.1. Types of emotional labor identified as part of WPA work

Attending or responding to others' emotions	96%
Building relationships	96%
Sustaining relationships	94%
Encouraging colleagues	94%
Empathizing with others	92%
Considering others' emotions, subject positions, and identities when making programmatic decisions	92%
Encouraging students	89%
Considering others' emotions, subject positions, and identities when communicating programmatic information	89%
Attending or responding to your emotions	85%
Mediating disputes	74%
Repairing damaged relationships	68%
Using your emotions to interrogate structures	60%
Using others' emotions to interrogate structures	51%

emotional labor—our own reflective practices or the emotional work we do when we place ourselves in our colleagues' or students' shoes to discover how they experience the programs we administer—are, frankly, more difficult, requiring introspection, reflection, and time. With so many other pressing issues to address, it can often seem easier to avoid (or at least give lower priority to) those internal sources of emotional labor.

DO YOU WRITE ABOUT EMOTIONAL LABOR?

To determine whether faculty discussed emotional labor in their professional documents, I asked survey participants to indicate whether they had written or revised documents in the last five years that fell into one of two categories: personnel (e.g., CV, job application letter, teaching philosophy) or professional/programmatic (e.g., article or presentation, annual program report, curriculum proposal). Using the same list of document types, I asked participants to identify which of those documents included discussion of emotional labor. The results show little correlation between the documents that were written most frequently and those that discussed emotional labor (see table 5.2).

The only document type that appeared in the top five items on both lists was the teaching philosophy, but 66 percent of respondents who

Table 5.2. Frequency of documents written compared to documents discussing emotional labor

Rank	Documents Written (frequency)	Documents That Discussed Emotional Labor (frequency)
1	Curriculum vita (53)	Professional presentation (22)
2	Faculty activity report (45)	Publication or research (18)
3	Teaching philosophy (44)	Administrative philosophy (15)
4	Publication or research (44)	Teaching philosophy (15)
5	Annual program report (42)	Tenure and/or promotion materials (14)

wrote or revised their teaching philosophy did so without discussing emotional labor. The top two types of documents WPAs wrote that discussed emotional labor were professional presentations and scholarly publications, which indicate WPAs' sensitivity to genre, audience, or both. For example, survey participants might be actively researching and studying emotional labor and disseminating it through traditionally accepted genres of academic scholarship, or they might be writing for a sympathetic audience of WPAs who acknowledge emotional labor as both a legitimate type of labor and a significant factor in their day-to-day work. In addition, none of the top five documents in which WPAs wrote about emotional labor were specifically program-related (e.g., program reports, budget requests), indicating their belief that those genres are less appropriate for discussions of emotional labor.

WHAT ARE THE RISKS AND BENEFITS OF WRITING ABOUT EMOTIONAL LABOR?

Seventy percent of the survey respondents discussed emotional labor in at least one of the document types identified, and they did so in an effort to educate their colleagues: 63 percent of these respondents claimed they wanted their colleagues to understand the emotional labor WPAs do, while 55 percent wrote about emotional labor because they want it to count as legitimate WPA work. One respondent explained, "By sharing the true weight of the work we bear, colleagues who have never (and will never) hold this position can begin to understand it from an insider perspective instead of just a job description they read in these documents . . . If they can understand the emotional labor, they can begin to understand the work itself . . . and the underlying challenges of doing it well." These respondents understood their own professional documents as tools that might influence others' understanding of emotional labor, the roles that demand such labor, and the professionals who occupy those roles and do emotion work.

Among those who discussed emotional labor in their professional documents, 64 percent believed there was a moderate to a great deal of risk involved in doing so. When describing the perceived risks in more detail, respondents reported fears of being seen as "weak" or "vulnerable," and several explained that their female gender influenced their decision. The response of one non-tenure-track WPA who chose not to address emotional labor in her professional documents seemed to encapsulate the sentiments of women who viewed doing so as risky: "As a woman in a professional setting, it is always dangerous to discuss the emotional labor that I undertake . . . I do not want to be seen as less rigorous in my scholarship, less demanding of my students/employees, or less serious in my dedication to the institution. There is always a greater demand for emotional labor from faculty who are women, and in explicitly addressing that, I run the risk of seeming to complain or, ironically, to brag about all the extra work I do." This respondent tapped into the ongoing discussion of the feminization of WPA labor (Bloom 1992; George 1999) and the particular challenges women feel when the emotional labor they perform is dismissed as "women's work." At the same time that women are expected to perform emotional labor, they are often "held to a higher standard than is men's emotion work, and women are sanctioned more severely when they don't meet those gendered expectations," so it makes sense that female WPAs might perceive making their emotional labor visible as risky (Holt, Anderson, and Rouzie 2003, 150).

Perhaps because of the perceived risks in discussing emotional labor, 28 percent of respondents reported that they did not discuss emotional labor in any of their professional documents; 33 percent of these WPAs said they didn't do so because they were concerned about how they would be perceived, while 53 percent believed discussion of emotional labor did not seem appropriate for the audience or purpose of the document. When asked to provide further explanation for their choice not to discuss emotional labor, respondents' reasons centered around audience and the fear that their readers would not value discussions of emotional labor. One participant explained, "The gold of my university's realm is publication—so there's no interest in measuring emotional labor," while another echoed Kerr's statement about pathos in the university: "The academic environment values 'I know' over 'I feel.'"

STRATEGIES FOR ARTICULATING EMOTIONAL LABOR IN OUR PROFESSIONAL DOCUMENTS

As WPAs, we know we need—and want—to make our emotional labor visible because it accounts for so much of the work we do. But we worry that doing so will make us more vulnerable, either because it will cause others to perceive us negatively or the work won't be valued. Understandably, we think about our emotional labor emotionally; because we value it and believe it's important, we want to protect it, but we want to protect ourselves, too. It's difficult to find ways to discuss emotional labor in genres of professional documents that have historically been driven by observable, countable data. In the words of one survey respondent, it is "almost impossible" to discuss emotional labor using "'describe your administrative accomplishments' language."

How might we frame emotional labor in our professional documents in a manner that keeps it—and us—safe? Laura R. Micciche (2007, 104, original emphasis) claims that her book *Doing Emotion: Rhetoric, Writing, Teaching* was a project focused on "rendering emotion in more explicitly rhetorical terms by foregrounding what emotions *do*." I would argue that one strategy we might employ for making our emotional work visible in our professional documents would be to take Micciche's idea one step further. What if, after understanding what emotions do, we then articulate what *we* do when we pay attention to emotions? As the results from my small survey show, when we are attentive to our own and others' emotions, we listen to ourselves and others, incorporate reflection into our daily practices, ask for help, collaborate, and work to solve problems through creative, empathic solutions. If we can point to specific outcomes of the writing program that result from these activities, we can then articulate how the programs we direct change and become stronger, more collaborative, and more resilient as a result of our attention to emotion.

To illustrate how we might work to make our emotional labor count, I offer the following model (figure 5.1), which outlines specific strategies and heuristics that might create space for discussing emotional labor in our professional personnel documents. The strategies I offer here propose concrete ways WPAs might make their emotional labor visible in their professional personnel documents (job application materials, administrative philosophies, activity reports, and tenure and promotion documents in particular) in an effort to build colleagues' understanding of and respect for the work and those who perform it. These strategies might not erase the risks some may feel in articulating their emotional labor, however. Academic rank or tenure status certainly influences a

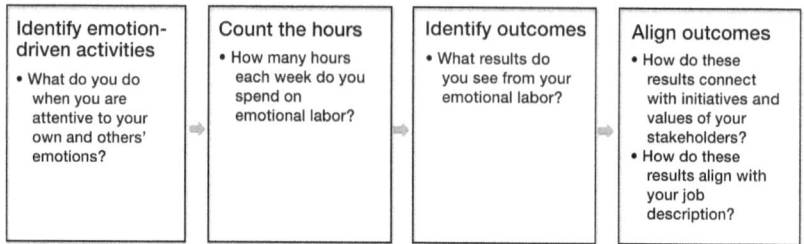

Figure 5.1. Illustration of the emotional labor heuristic.

WPA's willingness to take these risks, as do other identity markers such as gender, race, and sexual orientation (to name a few) that might place the WPA in a vulnerable position and lead the WPA to decide that discussing emotional labor would be unsafe, such as the difficulties explored in Sheila Carter-Tod's and Joe Janangelo's contributions to this collection. However, these strategies articulate a way to tie emotional labor to more quantifiable and universally valued outcomes a range of audiences would understand and appreciate when evaluating our faculty activity and the work we're doing in the programs we lead, which might minimize the risk some WPAs feel.

STEP ONE: IDENTIFY YOUR EMOTION-DRIVEN ACTIVITIES.

What are the things you do when you are attentive to your own and others' emotions?

The answer to this question will be different for different WPAs. My emotion-driven activities include a lot of listening, hearing what people say, and also listening for the values and concerns that undergird what they say. Being a new WPA in a well-established first-year writing program has created many opportunities for listening: When instructors talk about the program, I hear how much they value our group portfolio grading and the weekly meetings that bring faculty together to discuss teaching strategies and student writing, but I also hear their concerns about how group grading limits the types of assignments they give students or overemphasizes product over process. This listening has helped me learn more about the people I work with, but it has also taught me about the program I am responsible for leading.

Others might incorporate reflection into their administrative work. I started journaling again this year after a long hiatus, and I've used that reflective practice to become more intentional about writing down the thoughts I have on the drive home after a tough meeting or the pre-semester professional development workshop. Rigorous reflection has helped me become more attentive to my own emotions and leadership style and also to identify areas where I can improve to better support the instructors I work with and the students we all teach.

STEP TWO: COUNT THE HOURS.
How much time do you spend performing emotional labor?

Heeding the advice of more experienced WPAs, a few years ago I began carefully logging my work time each week in a spreadsheet, counting the hours I spend on different faculty tasks (e.g., teaching, grading, attending meetings). Recently, I added a column to my spreadsheet to include emotional labor. Any time I met with a student, instructor, or colleague to discuss concerns, complaints, anxieties, or worries, I counted it. At first, it felt strange to count the hours I spent listening to a colleague vent (or venting myself) over coffee, but if I felt the labor in my body after I was back in my office—if I was tired, distracted, or managing my own emotions—I counted it.

I averaged about five hours a week of emotional labor that semester; during midterms and finals week, I was at eight hours. But that term was a relatively quiet semester with no major illness or trauma in the department (such as those described by Kaitlin Clinnin, Carl Schlachte, and Kim Hensley Owens, this volume), which would have certainly changed the emotional workload. Several years ago, I had to take over a creative nonfiction course after spring break because the instructor became gravely ill. In my activity report that year, I described the additional teaching and course preparation I did for that class to justify the overload pay I received, which added up to about fifty additional hours of work. That number paled in comparison to the emotional labor I did as both the WPA and the substitute instructor—supporting colleagues and students concerned about the instructor, reassuring justifiably worried students about their status in the class, and positioning myself as an empathetic but fair instructor to students whose work I would be evaluating. At that point in my career, I wasn't paying much attention to emotional labor; had I been counting it, I'm sure the number I reported in my annual report would have been doubled.

Counting the hours spent performing emotional labor has helped me in a couple of ways: first, I can say more concretely that I spent 15 percent of my work week during midterms on emotional labor, which explains for myself why little of my own writing got done that week. It helps me understand the day to day of the job and find patterns in the semester for external sources of emotional labor so I might be (a little) more prepared next semester. Moreover, it's a number I can incorporate into my annual report if I know my audience is particularly numbers-oriented or if they need a specific accounting of how I spent my time.

STEP THREE: IDENTIFY OUTCOMES.
What are the outcomes of your emotional labor? Put another way, how does your emotional labor make itself visible (perhaps indirectly) within the program you direct?

To identify the outcomes of our emotional labor, we could articulate what our attentiveness to emotion allows us to accomplish. When we coach colleagues through frustration or anger, their concerns might highlight specific elements of the program we direct that might need attention and revision. In the last several months, for example, I've strategized with four different instructors as they've navigated challenging situations with students who have accrued more absences than the four permitted by our department policy. The students were missing class because they were struggling with health issues, mental illness, or sexual assault; and the faculty questioned if it was fair to enforce a policy that had been treated as an ironclad rule. These situations have highlighted to me the need to have conversations with the entire faculty about dealing with these types of student issues, so I planned a professional development meeting with staff from the university counseling center to help us learn strategies for better supporting our students. In the conversations that have ensued since that session, we've decided that we need to reevaluate our attendance policy and create some room for instructor discretion to offer fair accommodations for students and build environments in which they can be successful. Had we been guided by the policy alone rather than by our attention to our students' physical and emotional health, we likely would have come to a different decision about the students' status in the class; but because we were attentive to our own emotions and those of our students, we are working toward a flexible policy that creates some space for students.

While WPAs can use emotion to help us understand points of friction in the programs we lead, we might also look at the things that are working that are a result in part of our attention to others' emotions. For example, do you have a good retention of adjunct or non-tenure-track faculty? If so, it would be reasonable to assume that these colleagues' personal and professional satisfaction is due in part to the program's working conditions, which are likely shaped by your (and others') emotional labor. Do you have a large number of volunteers for department initiatives or projects? Do you have good attendance at professional development workshops? Do faculty seek you out to troubleshoot problematic classroom situations or to find university resources for themselves or students? All of these outcomes are signs of an emotionally healthy program, and while that emotional health doesn't depend only on the WPA, it is likely that the WPA's emotional labor contributes to these outcomes. As Donald Hall (2002, 39) notes, "Administration that is devoted to creating an environment of intellectual vitality in a department or university has an impact that is stunningly exponential, for the professional lives of numerous faculty are enhanced and invigorated. Individual successes are often dependent upon the successful working together of a group, in which successful administration plays a vital role." Although Hall is referring specifically to academics' intellectual labor and scholarship, his argument holds true if we were to replace "intellectual" with "emotional." Administrators who create room for emotion foster environments in which individuals can thrive, collaborate, and flourish; and it's important to identify the visible outcomes of the programs we direct as due in part to our emotional labor.

STEP FOUR: ALIGN OUTCOMES.
How do the outcomes of your emotional labor align with the outcomes external audiences value?

As WPAs, we're accustomed to tying our activities and efforts to outcomes. We develop learning objectives aligned with the guidelines of general education learning objectives, and we articulate how the curricular revision we propose or the budget requests we make align with the university's strategic initiatives. If we want our emotional labor to count, we must tie that work—and the outcomes it produces—to the values of the external audiences who are evaluating our labor in performance reviews or tenure and promotion processes. One of the survey respondents, Danielle,[3] who shared her writing made such a move in the first paragraph of her administrative philosophy. She explained that her work as a WPA is driven by the belief that WPAs "lead by critically understanding the individuals and units they work with, communicating in an open and transparent manner" with writing stakeholders across campus because "all of these people, and the individuals they work with, impact the Writing Program's ability to support undergraduate student writing instruction." Danielle chose to explain her ability to build and maintain relationships—a key component of emotional labor—as intrinsically linked to the success of the writing program's mission, and she provided concrete examples of that work and the outcomes it produced throughout her administrative philosophy statement.

Another survey respondent who shared her teaching philosophy centered her discussion about her role as a teacher around mentorship. Julie explained: "I frequently meet with students to chat about how they are doing, to help them with the college transition, or simply to listen. For me, teaching is about more than passing on information, it is a way of establishing intellectual communities and making sure that students feel like a part of that community." Julie's attention to mentoring illustrates the emotional labor she does with students; for those of us who have had those conversations, we know they require a good deal of listening, empathy, and energy. If Julie wanted to tie this form of her emotional labor to outcomes more explicitly in her annual report, she could explain how she spent an average of, say, three hours of office hours per week in these mentoring conversations. She could then articulate how they align with university initiatives to support first-year students in the transition to college or National Survey of Student Engagement (2017, 16) data that indicate that student-faculty interactions are a key marker in student engagement and retention. If Julie chose to address her emotional labor in this way, she would be framing the emotional labor she values within the outcomes her readers value, working to elevate both the visibility and perceived value of her efforts.

Those of us who hold tenured or more secure positions would do well to adopt these practices in our own professional documents to normalize the discussion of emotional labor and provide models for how early-career WPAs might do the same. Likewise, the Council of Writing Program Administrators could do more to publicly highlight the role emotional labor plays in writing administration by addressing emotional labor in the organization's position statement, "Evaluating the Intellectual Work of Writing Administration." WPAs' emotional labor often overlaps with the areas of curriculum, labor practices, professional development, and the politics of academic administration—issues that are more readily understood as "intellectual"—so framing emotional labor for audiences of WPAs and other academics alike as legitimate, crucial work would be powerful. Many WPAs rely on the "Intellectual Work" document to frame their work for a range of disciplinary audiences who review their job performance and tenure and promotion applications, so WPAs who elect to discuss emotional labor in their professional documents might feel more secure if our professional organization validated emotional work alongside the intellectual work we do.

Although she is writing about politics, Jennifer Palmieri's (2018) call to re-imagine our understanding of presidential leadership holds true for WPA work as well. She argues, "We have no idea what beneficial qualities we might be stifling in ourselves as long as we continue to follow an outdated set of behavioral rules" that no longer fit candidates or voters (80). If we allow ourselves to re-imagine the behavioral rules and values that drive our professional personnel documents, we might afford ourselves the opportunity to untie emotion from behind our backs. Once we no longer hide our emotional labor, we can begin to name it. We can watch what our emotions do, observe what they allow *us* to do, and see how they help us accomplish the outcomes that we and others prioritize. Doing so will help us understand that our emotions are valued, that the work we do attending to emotions is valued, and, ultimately, that we are valued.

NOTES

1. The centered agency I felt in the new job wasn't because of tenure; I was hired at the associate level without tenure because of the dean's policy to require all new faculty to go through the tenure process. Instead, the "realness" I felt came from my choice to take emotional risks during the interview and being rewarded with a job offer nonetheless.
2. The research protocol for this study (No. 18–140-H) was reviewed and approved by the Human Research Review Committee at Grand Valley State University.
3. Names changed to preserve respondent anonymity.

REFERENCES

Ahmed, Sara. 2004. *The Cultural Politics of Emotion*. New York: Routledge.

Bishop, Wendy, and Gay Lynn Crossley. "How to Tell a Story of Stopping: The Complexities of Narrating a WPA's Experience." *WPA: Writing Program Administration* 19 (3): 70–79.

Bloom, Lynn Z. 1992. "I Want a Writing Director." *College Composition and Communication* 43 (2): 176–178.

Brescoll, Victoria L., and Eric Luis Uhlmann. 2008. "Can an Angry Woman Get Ahead? Status Conferral, Gender, and the Expression of Emotion in the Workplace." *Psychological Science* 19 (3): 268–275.

Charlton, Jonikka, and Shirley K Rose. 2009. "Twenty More Years in the WPA's Progress." *WPA: Writing Program Administration* 33 (1–2): 114–145.

Council of Writing Program Administrators. 1998. "Evaluating the Intellectual Work of Writing Administration." Last modified 1998. http://wpacouncil.org/positions/intellectualwork.html.

George, Diana, ed. 1999. *Kitchen Cooks, Plate Twirlers, and Troubadours: Writing Program Administrators Tell Their Stories*. Portsmouth, NH: Heineman.

Hall, Donald. 2002. *The Academic Self: An Owner's Manual.* Columbus: Ohio State University Press.

Hall, Donald. 2007. *The Academic Community: A Manual for Change.* Columbus: Ohio State University Press.

Holt, Mara, Leon Anderson, and Albert Rouzie. 2003. "Making Emotion Work Visible in Writing Program Administration." In *A Way to Move: Rhetorics of Emotion and Composition Studies,* edited by Dale Jacobs and Laura R. Micciche, 147–160. Portsmouth, NH: Boynton/Cook.

Kerr, Tom. 2003. "The Feeling of What Happens in Departments of English." In *A Way to Move: Rhetorics of Emotion and Composition Studies,* edited by Dale Jacobs and Laura R. Micciche, 23–32. Portsmouth, NH: Boynton/Cook.

Micciche, Laura R. 2002. "More Than a Feeling: Disappointment and WPA Work." *College English* 64 (4): 432–458.

Micciche, Laura R. 2007. *Doing Emotion: Rhetoric, Writing, Teaching.* Portsmouth, NH: Boynton/Cook.

National Survey of Student Engagement. 2017. "Engagement Insights: Survey Findings on the Quality of Undergraduate Education." Last modified 2018. http://nsse.indiana.edu/NSSE_2017_Results/pdf/NSSE_2017_Annual_Results.pdf.

Palmieri, Jennifer. 2018. *Dear Madam President: An Open Letter to the Women Who Will Run the World.* New York: Grand Central Publishing.

Piercy, Marge. 1982. "To Be of Use." Last modified 2018. https://www.poetryfoundation.org/poems/57673/to-be-of-use.

SECTION II

Preserving Communities

6
HANDLING SEXUAL ASSAULT REPORTS AS A WPA

Kim Hensley Owens
Northern Arizona University

> *To make emotion's role explicit in pedagogical settings means attending to how cultural and social contexts and expectations shape both expressions of emotion and our subsequent readings of them: It allows us to imagine emotion—our emotional responses and our reactions on them—as resources for new knowledge.*
> —Shari Stenberg 2011, 367

Writing program administrator (WPA) may not sound like a position that has much, if anything, to do with sexual assault reports, but in my role as WPA at a mid-size southwestern university, dealing with sexual assault—usually with the teachers of student victims—has become an all-too-regular aspect of what I do. Because writing classes tend to be the smallest classes our students take in their first year and because writing teachers make a special effort to connect with students, our teachers are often among the first people students tell about an assault. And once the teachers know, they come to me.

This collection of chapters brings scholarly attention to the emotions experienced by and emotional labor done by the bodies who do WPA work. Emotions have a place in WPA work, whether hidden or visible, and, as Shari Stenberg (2011, 350, 367) notes, "while emotions are clearly a site of oppression, they are also, as feminists have long argued, a source for political resistance" and a resource for "new knowledge." My contribution to this collection details my emotional labor as a WPA handling a series of sexual assault reports during one school year at my university and how that emotional labor sparked if not political resistance, new knowledge as well as preventive and empathetic action. I describe how the sexual assault cases I dealt with that year affected me emotionally, affected my work logistically, and affected what I recommend pedagogically. Beyond examining the effects of sexual assault reports on me as a WPA and on the teachers I work with, I offer suggestions to help teachers implement activities that might help to prevent sexual assault. I also encourage WPAs and teachers toward trauma-informed practices and provide guidance for WPAs to intellectually understand and cope with the emotional labor involved in handling sexual assault reports of students in our programs.

SEXUAL ASSAULT CONTEXT

According to the National Sexual Violence Resource Center, about one in five women and one in sixteen men are sexually assaulted during college. A report from the US Department of Justice states that "during any given academic year, 2.8 percent of [college] women will experience a completed and/or attempted rape" (Fisher, Cullen, and Turner 2000, 32). Although teachers may not always get reports of these assaults, more victims are coming forward rather than staying silent as the culture surrounding such reports changes. Combined with increased reporting to authorities, federal enforcement of the Clery Act[1] has increased the number of sexual assault reports made public (Kingkade 2014). These cultural changes make sexual assaults more visible and more knowable than they had been in the past. The recent #MeToo movement, which invites victims of sexual assault and harassment to share their stories using that hashtag, further normalizes victims sharing such stories rather than hiding them.

My first year as WPA, when graduate teaching assistants (GTAs) came to me about two students who had been assaulted, I was deeply underprepared. At that point, I knew that university employees were required to report such assault disclosures, but I didn't know that the victim was not entitled to remain anonymous in those cases. Although I was in a mandated reporting situation—unlike that of Elizabeth Imafuji, who writes in this volume that she wasn't sure which office to turn to that would both support her pregnant student and maintain that student's confidentiality—I, too, felt I didn't know what the best support to offer would be beyond the reports I knew we had to make, and I wasn't prepared for the ways those reports would be handled. I also didn't know then that a very common response college students have to sexual assaults is not to report or to go to counseling but to stop going to classes and eventually drop out. Using what I did know, I worked with the teachers of these two victims to help them. We talked about ways to suggest counseling to the students and to encourage them to report the crimes themselves. We worked to make some exceptions to standard class policies, particularly surrounding absences, for these traumatized students. Although I muddled through and provided concrete help to the teachers and their victimized students, for weeks I couldn't shake the feeling that I should have been able to do more somehow; a lingering guilt became my second shadow. In part to assuage that guilt with better preparation, I organized a Title IX presentation to give all of our instructors and GTAs more context for and information about assault reports. I also asked the Title IX coordinator to present at the GTA orientation each year, added mandated reporting information to our standard policies, and thought that was enough.

THAT WAS NOT ENOUGH: THE FALL WITH EIGHT SEXUAL ASSAULT REPORTS

Over the course of a few weeks the following fall, I received eight explicit reports of sexual assault, one after another. It felt like an epidemic. When the first GTA came, she cried and shook with anger on the student's behalf. We discussed various supports and counseling for the student—and for her. In an attempt to spare the GTA further trauma, I reported the incident, sharing the details I'd learned third-hand. The second incident went much the same, as did the third. Then I got a pointed email from the Title IX investigator asking that I have teachers report directly rather than doing it for them—apparently, my attempt to take on some of the burden for the teachers was not helping the investigation process. In addition to carrying more of the reporting load than I needed to, I was taking on an emotional load by supporting the teachers. As Carrie S. Leverenz writes in this volume, "Being a WPA who is good at emotion work can bring challenges"; I was good at supporting others but less good at supporting myself. When a fourth teacher came in to report a student's assault, I began to feel a vicarious victimhood and took to wearing all black the day after such a report—my own silent protest and acknowledgment of these assaults.

At that point I reached out to my retired predecessor and a few other WPAs and former WPAs to ask if they'd experienced assault reports or assaults in first-year composition (FYC) classes. None had. None had had even a single report. Similarly, in my nineteen years of teaching prior to my WPA position at this university and in various WPA-like administrative roles at two previous universities, I had never received one either. One might suspect from these details that my university has a particular problem with sexual assault or that that semester was anomalous, but national statistics suggest that the assaults have been happening everywhere and are simply reported more regularly now. In addition, in terms of WPAs receiving those reports, gender may be a factor. Many of the WPAs and former WPAs I reached out to were male, and at least one suggested his gender was a likely reason he had not been consulted about any assault reports during his tenure. As with much emotional labor, handling sexual assault reports may be something more women than men, broadly speaking, are confronted with in their roles as WPAs.

I wore all black four more times that semester, eliciting some perplexed looks but no outright questions from colleagues who typically see me in brightly colored skirts and know my penchant for peacock-blue tops. Wearing something akin to mourning clothes provided me with a small sense of action and protest, although I knew drowning myself privately in black wasn't accomplishing anything—and unlike actual mourning clothes, the palette of my outfit wasn't communicating anything to others.[2] I learned from the first WPA I worked for that being able to calmly offer resources and information was a critical element of the gig, and I strove to prepare in the only way I knew how. I researched additional resources for victims of sexual assault, both locally and nationwide, gathering information to offer when another report came.[3] I knew another report would come.

While every sexual assault case involved emotional challenges for the reporting teachers and myself, two of the cases were particularly draining for me as WPA, in both emotional and logistical terms. In those two cases, not only the victims but also their accused assailants were enrolled in our FYC classes. The first such report came to me not from a teacher but from a representative of a campus office, and it left me gutted. Logically, of course, since the vast majority of students pass through FYC and some percentage of students commit crimes, it makes sense that some of our students perpetrate crimes. But the idea that a rapist could be lurking among the sea of twenty-four seemingly sweet faces in each FYC class was not something I had previously considered. Further, the realization that both perpetrator and victim could be in the same small class was heartbreaking. Suddenly, I saw the classroom we teachers think of as a safe space transformed into the place "where I met my assailant" for the victim; I saw the work we teachers do to help students connect with one another as people and to break down communication barriers transformed into an outrageous abuse of trust; I saw the kind of "matchmaking" we teachers do when setting up groups for peer review and collaboration transformed into a devastating question: Did the pedagogical practices I explicitly recommend to teachers contribute to this assault?

After that report, which came on a Friday, I had what might be described as a mini-breakdown. The week leading up to that Friday had been fraught with other WPA-related challenges in the extreme (counterintuitive and complicated new scheduling mandates, the staffing challenges all WPAs face, GTAs needing to talk about how various medical and mental health issues were affecting their work, and others), and that report felt like the proverbial last straw. I was depleted to an almost indescribable degree. When my husband picked me up from work, I burst into tears and told him I couldn't be a parent that night—I simply didn't have the energy to be present for a single other human. I was overwhelmed by the assault reports and oppressed by all of the requests for favors that were lighting up my email and Messenger accounts even more than usual that day. He got me home and sent me upstairs to take a bath, ordered Indian food and brought it up to our room, told the kids I'd gone to bed—and somehow kept them quiet all evening—and posted on Facebook that I was not available to anyone for any reason for the rest of the weekend. After that rejuvenating solitary night and a family-only home weekend with lots of alone time and no phone, email, texts, or Facebook (I had my husband confiscate my phone for the weekend), I was able to face work and people again on Monday.

Beyond the emotional fallout and pedagogical questioning this intraclass report sparked, it also presented significant logistical problems. It necessitated class changes against all usual policies. Despite our common refrain of "never" moving students from class to class after the first week of a semester, federal law and ethical imperatives superseded both writing program and university policies: we had to move the victim to a new class long after add deadlines had passed. The registrar balked at my request, citing the add/drop dates and insisting they'd have to record an F for the original class. Getting the registrar to process the required change without negatively affecting the victim and without breaking the law by revealing anything about the victim's case was a rhetorical, emotional, and logistical challenge requiring coordination with several campus entities through a variety of phone calls, emails, and laments to the universe.[4] I can't even recall which entities I enlisted in which order or which got me the necessary results, but I did eventually succeed in getting the registrar to process the move. Once the move was completed in the system, I emailed the affected teachers about the switch—being at once as vague and as clear as possible. Moments later, the victim's original teacher showed up in my office, distraught, thinking she must have done something wrong to prompt the student's abrupt and decidedly unusual departure from her class. I had to console the teacher with the reassurance that the move had nothing to do with her. I had to bite my tongue about the fact that a person accused of rape was in her class. I didn't know his name and I wasn't allowed to say anything, but that didn't stop my mind from churning with possibilities, usually at 3 a.m., over the next several days.

By that point, I'd bookmarked the campus assault–report page and had my set of links and resources to offer to both GTAs and their student victims. I thought I was prepared. The eighth report, though, a second intra-class incident, demonstrated the extent to which I was not. This time, the teacher came to me, and this time, the class itself was involved in the victim's story. Her classmate had invited her to his apartment *so they could review one another's drafts*—pedagogically, the kind of outside-of-class request we all dream might happen. At the apartment, though, the classmate gave her a drink that left her foggy, sleepy, unable to move. After she was incapacitated, he raped her. The student stumbled to her dorm the next morning and told her roommate everything that had happened. At her roommate's insistence and with her help, the victimized student had immediately gone to campus police. While police can notoriously ignore or downplay reports of sexual assault (Yung 2013) and while campuses typically aren't as compliant about reporting sexual assaults as they should be, unless they're in an audit year (Yung 2015), in this case both the police and the university acted lawfully. Police took her statement, gave her a physical exam, and had her blood tested—yes, positive for a substance commonly known as a "date-rape drug." The university documented the report, and the case of a composition student who, under the pretense of peer review, was accused of drugging and raping his classmate came to me through the victim's teacher the following week.

It was November, about a month after the previous intra-class case. This student victim didn't want to change classes to get away from her accused assailant. Instead, she wanted to keep her class, her life, as much the same as possible. She wanted him moved—and move him we did, with a still fumbling repeat of all the attendant bureaucratic and personnel complications from the previous case. As I looked at the sections of the class that would match his schedule, I couldn't help but think I was potentially putting additional students in harm's way. But I had to do so. I called the registrar—I'd landed on the language "due to an active legal and university investigation involving this student, federal law requires that we move him to a different class," which worked a lot faster than my previous attempt—and the switch was made.[5]

Although I could not share details with the teacher who was absorbing an extra student—over the normally nonnegotiable cap of twenty-four students no less—at that very late point in the semester, I did make a plea: I asked her to ensure that the student be grouped only with other male students for an upcoming collaborative project and for all peer review activities (to be clear: male students can be and are sexually assaulted, and I know it's possible that the same male student might assault both a female and a male student, but that likelihood seemed slim). I told her I couldn't explain why but that I thought it was in everyone's best interest. The teacher assured me she'd group accordingly, and for the rest of the semester she stopped by with weekly updates. She was concerned about the transferred student: he attended sporadically, had left class possibly crying one day, wasn't turning in assignments. I recommended the same kinds of support and interventions I would for any student. I suggested that she meet with him, encourage him to visit the counseling center, and help him create a calendar to track assignments. What I was thinking, though, I couldn't say, which was along the lines of *your new student has been accused of drugging and raping another student, and the police have medical evidence supporting the victim's claims, so there's bound to be some emotional impact affecting his ability to function as a student.*

EMOTIONAL IMPACT AND "SURFACE ACTING"

To say that this case, more than any other, affected my emotions would be a dramatic understatement. Lynn Worsham (1998, 216) describes emotion as a "tight braid of affect and judgment, socially and historically constructed and bodily lived, through which the symbolic takes hold of and binds the individual, in complex and contradictory ways, to the social order and its structure of meaning." If my pedagogical beliefs and choices—a social order shared with the entire FYC program—paved the way for a rapist, what was the appropriate action in response? Suggesting that teachers abandon peer review and collaborative work was impractical and practically impossible, but continuing to support a pedagogy that seemed to have contributed to such an egregious outcome also felt irresponsible. I spent nearly an hour the morning after that assault report swimming laps, turning these thoughts over and over with each stroke, working through the anger and betrayal I felt within my body, trying to flatten my feelings of frustration and helplessness with each slap and kick.

As a teacher and a WPA, I am usually careful not to show much emotion, in keeping with what Shari Stenberg (2011, 350) describes as the historical norm for "women teachers," who have "foster[ed] self-regulation by removing or controlling . . . emotion." I have sat with countless students crying in my office about all manner of sad things, from death to plagiarism confessions to abusive partners to homelessness to overwhelming roommate issues, and I have preferred and been able to keep my own emotions in check. I take deep breaths; I let the student know it's okay to cry; I offer Kleenex; I empathize; I wait for them to calm down; I work with them to brainstorm solutions and next steps—students crying in my office for one reason or another is a common-enough event that I can think of the process in clear, predictable steps. But when confronted with teachers bringing me case after case of sexual assault in one year and often crying on behalf of their students, I more than once found myself sitting in my office crying alongside them—and I firmly believe that was the right response for me and with those teachers. Ignoring or controlling my own emotions in those moments may have done a disservice to the emotion teachers were feeling on behalf of their students. Instead, together we let ourselves feel the rippling impacts of the assaults; we let ourselves process the shock and anger before we shifted to developing empathetic and productive responses to each student's situation.

For teachers as well as administrators, expressing emotion is tricky. Worsham (1998, 224), drawing on the work of Catherine Lutz, writes that "the pedagogy of emotion . . . teaches us to define and value the concept of emotion in a contradictory way—negatively, in terms of its opposition to reason and rationality (as the core of the true self); and positively, in terms of its opposition to estrangement and disengagement from the world." My crying with a couple of the teachers who shared with me their students' sexual assault reports seemed to bridge that divide; it felt simultaneously rational and opposed to disengagement from the world. Crying wasn't necessarily a conscious choice, but psychological research suggests it might sometimes be wise to consciously choose to cry and visibly express emotional overload rather than hide the emotion. The "surface acting" people do when trying to convey one emotional state while feeling another typically results in increased fatigue, as psychological researchers Daniel J. Beal, John P. Trougakos, Howard M. Weiss, and Reeshad S. Dalal (2013) write. Further, as they explain, "surface acting," or "emotion regulation, like any form of effortful regulation, leads directly to the exhaustion of resources needed to continue behavior regulation" (594). Choosing not to proffer an affect-less facade in the face of traumatic news, then, reduces the fatigue that can come from doing so and saves energy, which increases one's ability to successfully regulate emotions on the many other occasions when WPA surface acting may be both prudent and necessary.

By contrast, it is possible that allowing oneself to feel and express emotion during a short meeting behind a closed door may also require a greater amount of surface acting later, when the office door has to be reopened. Thoughts and feelings about the assaulted student may still be weighing on one's mind and heart, but if there's a line of teachers and students out the door with a series of mundane but pressing needs, that may require some surface acting: a pasted-on smile, a falsely bright greeting, and the best semi-divided attention one can offer. WPAs may benefit from an awareness of the effects of "effortful regulation" like surface acting, the consequences of which for most people continue to "produce fatigue hours later" (Beal et al. 2013, 601). It should not be surprising, then, that no matter how a WPA handles a report of an assault in the moment, it will likely affect the WPA's emotional state after the fact.

I don't want to suggest that every emotional disclosure invites or requires an explicit or similar emotional response from a WPA but rather that such responses with teacher colleagues can be valuable and are not a sign of weakness. Fellow teachers may need the connection of a shared release of emotion and lowering of emotional walls. While students in crisis need the institutional representative they're telling about an assault to be unflappable and capable, teachers subsequently reporting to their supervisor may need something different to help them release the emotions they held in check with their student-victims.

BEFORE EMOTION: SEXUAL ASSAULT PREVENTION AND TRAUMA-INFORMED TEACHER PREPARATION

I wanted to do something beyond crying with a teacher, suggesting counseling, biting my tongue, and wearing black. I wanted to make the reports stop, to make the assaults stop. I remembered the *Tea Consent (Clean)* (2015) video the Title IX coordinator had shown us. *Tea Consent (Clean)* explains the concept of sexual consent through a stick figure, a drawing of a cup of tea, and a voiceover, offering the following scenario: "If you're still struggling with consent, just imagine instead of initiating sex, you're making them a cup of tea." Through its comparisons to the innocuous act of making someone tea, the video makes clear that just because you've "made someone tea in the past," it doesn't mean they'll want tea again at any point in the future. The narrator calmly explains that if someone is unconscious, they don't want you to make them tea. The video takes the concept of consent as simple—as simple as whether you'd offer someone tea or force them to drink it. The angle and humor are innovative and rhetorically effective. I immediately wrote to all our teachers to remind them of it. I sent them the link and asked them all to show it in class as soon as possible—to incorporate it into their FYC classes any way they could. I suggested they examine its rhetorical effectiveness and its ethos, have students practice writing rhetorical analyses of it, and the like. It was the only thing I could think of to *do* that might possibly prevent more assaults and that also fit within the parameters of what we are charged with teaching students.

Implementing the *Tea Consent (Clean)* video across several dozen sections of FYC went very smoothly except in one instance. One GTA came to my office to let me know he'd used the video but would never do so again. Surprised, I asked why. The GTA told me one of his female students felt traumatized by the video. I have no way to determine whether the GTA was faithfully reporting the student's response or whether his report to me was embellished or over-dramatized, but I took the concern at face value. I tried to understand how a person could feel traumatized by a video about tea and consent, one that didn't use any nudity or profanity[6] or sexual detail or anything else that might typically seem triggering or traumatizing. Although I wasn't able to fully understand that response, the attempt did allow me to see how a student could, absent a clear framing and solid follow-up discussion guided by their teacher, feel the video trivializes the issue of sexual assault. In fact, in a way, the point of the video is to trivialize consent in an attempt to make obtaining consent for sex seem obvious and clear and unambiguous. To me, the risk of the video being interpreted as trivializing an important topic is worth the potential payoff, in terms of both rhetorical awareness and the possibility of assault prevention. The fact that not all students will agree with the video's methods seems an excellent exigence to explore rhetorical concepts like audience, reception, and ethos—these are opportunities to enrich the discussions of the many choices made by authors/creators and their effects on various audiences.

Other teachers shared various kinds of successes with using the video to teach various skills, and although there isn't a way to test whether the video explicitly prevented any sexual assaults, I did not get any more reports the rest of that year. Of course, not getting reports doesn't necessarily mean assaults weren't happening, given that 90 percent of the college students who experience sexual assault do not report it ("Statistics" 2015). If that statistic holds for my university, there were likely 63 more assaults of FYC students that year than the 8 I learned about. While that number is appalling on its own, a look at the overall statistical likelihoods—20 percent of female and 6 percent of male college students are sexually assaulted, many in their first year on campus—suggests that around 619 (516 female and 103 male) students on my university's campus alone could be sexually assaulted in a given year. Whether it's 619 or 63 or 8 or even just 1, I feel as though I have to try to do something to prevent it.

Sexual assault prevention is not an official component of my position as an English professor and director of a writing program. Nevertheless, working to prevent the ricocheting trauma of sexual assault has become a component of the work I do and encourage others to do. I don't know if asking our teachers to incorporate the consent video or something like it into their classes prevents sexual assaults. What I do know is that since that's the only element of this issue that I can control, I can't *not* do at least that.

I do not think first-year composition can (or should be asked to) solve the world's problems, and I don't believe any FYC curriculum change could erase sexual assault on this or any other college campus. Rape culture is too pervasive and deeply embedded to allow for that outcome, even in the wake of the #MeToo and #WhyIDidntReport movements. That said, I do believe FYC can contribute to writing growth and other forms of positive change, and where I can find ready overlap between teaching about rhetoric and teaching about sexual assault prevention, I'm more than willing to request that teachers incorporate it, as I did with the *Tea Consent (Clean)* video. I would say I'm willing to require teachers to incorporate it and to some degree I've tried, but I also know some teachers love to defy requirements or present "required" material in a way that would thwart the goals, so instead I frame it as a request, provide teachers with the rationale and a chance to discuss the material with other teachers, and hope for the best—always.

Another intervention my writing program is working toward focuses on helping teachers become better prepared to teach students who have experienced trauma—not just sexual assault but any trauma. The majority of college students—65 percent–85 percent—report having experienced trauma, and many report having experienced multiple traumatic events (Davidson 2017, 5), a range that dwarfs even the nation's very high sexual assault statistics. Education Northwest's guide, *Trauma-Informed Practices for Postsecondary Education* (Davidson 2017), is a critical resource to help teachers avoid compounding the effects of trauma on students through uninformed practices in the classroom. Shared with all teachers this year by email, the guide will be a core text we discuss in our August orientation next fall. The guide helps teachers recognize that high absenteeism, acting out, anxiety, and withdrawal can all be effects of trauma and offers suggestions for helping students feel safe, de-escalating classroom disruptions, and finding ways to promote resilience through pedagogy. The suggestions in this guide will help all teachers and students, especially those students who have experienced sexual assault, regardless of whether they've reported those assaults to anyone at the school.

STRATEGIES FOR HANDLING EMOTIONAL LABOR

Given the commonality of sexual assault on college campuses, the likelihood of having a victim (or perpetrator) in any class is extremely high. The likelihood of those assaults being reported to teachers or to WPAs is lower, but that likelihood is increasing. While increased reporting evidences a culture shift from the shame that has for too long kept many victims quiet, it also presents new challenges for teachers and WPAs who have to handle various forms of fallout, from institutional challenges to legal entanglements to emotional repercussions. I've shared the ins and outs of my first forays into this issue in hopes that my experiences might help prepare other WPAs for similar challenges.

The emotional labor required to handle sexual assault reports is far from trivial, and although I have come to see such reports as "normal" to some degree, they never fail to affect me. As I was completing the draft of this chapter, I was called in to my chair's office to hear firsthand my first such report directly from a student. This report came with yet another obvious yet somehow startling discovery: sometimes alleged assailants are teachers[7]—maybe a teacher you know, a teacher you've mentored, a teacher you've had to your home with your children. Details about this case can't be shared, for obvious reasons, but I mention it because this discovery had a tremendous emotional impact on me—perhaps unreasonably, I felt personally betrayed by this teacher's actions, and fallout from handling my portion of the investigation of this teacher was significant. I got through it, though, by relying on all the strategies I have developed for handling emotional labor.

Strategies I offer other WPAs for handling the emotional labor of assault cases, the strategies I practice myself, are imperfect and incomplete but not ineffective. Meditation is often my go-to solution when I need to take my emotional level from a bursting-head 10 to at least just a finger-tapping 7. I meditate every day with an app called Insight Timer, which offers the prepared and disciplined meditator a simple timer and the less prepared or less disciplined meditator an inexhaustible collection of guided meditations. As I am un/prepared and un/disciplined on different days, I find this blend of options immeasurably helpful. I regularly reach out to other WPAs via text or Facebook messenger—*Has something like* x *ever happened at your school? What do you do about* y*? Is it just me, or is* z *an extremely challenging situation?* The value of these friendships developed throughout my career and especially through the CWPA workshop cannot be overstated when it comes to helping me deal with assault cases in particular. Other strategies are the same for dealing with all stressors: I talk to my husband; I play with my children; I go for long hikes alone in the woods; I distract myself with podcasts and television shows; I swim. And, unsurprisingly for those of us in this particular field, I write.

NOTES

1. The Clery Act, passed in 1990 and brought about through public reaction to campus crime after the dorm room rape and murder of nineteen-year-old Jeanne Clery in 1986, requires universities and colleges who participate in the federal financial aid program to track and report violent crime statistics.
2. Mourning clothes, which became particularly fashionable in Victorian England, were, as Sonia A. Bedikian (2008, 36) explains, "traditionally unflattering," modeled after nun's habits and intended to "denote that the wearer was so overwhelmed with grief she had no concern for sartorial Fashion." The costume for mourning "was created according to cultural rules and was meant to convey a message to the beholder," providing something of an escape from usual conversational and behavioral expectations (36).
3. An excellent national resource is RAINN, an online and telephone resource available 24/7 to victims of sexual violence. The website provides important information, and the hotline may be easier than a counselor for students to access while in crisis. RAINN claims to have helped "more than 2.7 million people since 1994" ("RAINN's Mission" 2020).
4. I write about these incidents now with no names, after significant time has passed since these particular cases and knowing that other similar and also completely different late-term class moves and kinds of assault cases have followed—sometimes with victims moved, sometimes with alleged assailants moved, and sometimes with both parties moved. Given that over 4,000 students a year pass through our main first-year composition course and given the two-year turnaround for our mostly MA-level GTAs, I am not concerned that the identities of any involved victims or alleged assailants will be revealed by this piece being published.
5. In later occurrences, when I called the registrar I was told the Title IX or Student Life representatives were supposed to make such calls. I still don't know if my earlier or later experiences were the norm or whether my university has changed policies or has inconsistent policies about how to process such moves.
6. Another version of the video does include profanity, which is why we are careful to use the *Tea Consent (Clean)* video. The GTA assured me he'd used the clean version.
7. The November 2017 WPA-Listserv threads "We have a Weinstein problem" and "The 'Weinstein problem'" reveal the challenges the field of rhetoric and composition has with sexual assault, harassment, and silence.

REFERENCES

Beal, Daniel J., John P. Trougakos, Howard M. Weiss, and Reeshad S. Dalal. 2013. "Affect Spin and the Emotion Regulation Process at Work." *Journal of Applied Psychology* 98 (4): 593–605. *PsycARTICLES*, EBSCO*host*.

Bedikian, Sonia A. 2008. "The Death of Mourning: From Victorian Crepe to the Little Black Dress." *OMEGA—Journal of Death and Dying* 57 (1): 35–52.

Davidson, Shannon. 2017. *Trauma-Informed Practices for Postsecondary Education: A Guide*. Oregon Student Success Center. Educationnorthwest.org.

Fisher, Bonnie S., Francis T. Cullen, and Michael G. Turner. 2000. "The Sexual Victimization of College Women." Bureau of Justice Statistics. ERIC.

Kingkade, Tyler. 2014. "Colleges Are Reporting More Sexual Assaults, and That's a Good Sign." HuffingtonPost.com.

"RAINN's Mission." 2020. RAINN. https://www.rainn.org/about-rainn.

"Statistics about Sexual Violence." 2015. National Sexual Violence Resource Center. https://www.nsvrc.org/sites/default/files/publications_nsvrc_factsheet_media-packet_statistics-about-sexual-violence_0.pdf.

Stenberg, Shari. 2011. "Teaching and (Re)Learning the Rhetoric of Emotion." *Pedagogy* 11 (2): 349–369.

Tea Consent (Clean). 2015. Blue Seat Studios. https://www.youtube.com/watch?v=fGoWLWS4-kU.

Worsham, Lynn. 1998. "Going Postal: Pedagogic Violence and the Schooling of Emotion." *JAC: Journal of Composition Theory* 18 (2): 213–245.

Yung, Corey Rayburn. 2013. "How to Lie with Rape Statistics." *Iowa Law Review* 99: 1197–1256.

Yung, Corey Rayburn. 2015. "Concealing Sexual Assault: An Empirical Examination." *Psychology, Public Policy, and Law* 21 (1): 1–9.

7
AND SO I RESPOND
The Emotional Labor of Writing Program Administrators in Crisis Response

Kaitlin Clinnin
University of Nevada, Las Vegas

EDUCATION IN A POST-TRAUMATIC AGE

On Monday, October 2, 2017, I wake to a barrage of phone calls, text messages, emails, and social media messages, all asking the same question: Are you safe? Something's wrong, something happened, I think as I search the news headlines. The night before on the Las Vegas Strip, a man with a gun opened fire at the Route 91 music festival, killing fifty-eight people and injuring hundreds in the largest mass shooting in modern US history. The massacre took place 3 miles from the University of Nevada, Las Vegas, where I have been working for three months as an assistant professor and writing program administrator (WPA).

At 5:02 a.m., I read the university's official statement that announces campus will be open and classes will be held as scheduled. The rest of the announcement warns commuters to expect traffic delays due to road closures and parking impacts because authorities are using the campus parking lot as an evacuation location. I drive to work early, compelled to be present for students and instructors. Along my normal commute route, I drive past large digital billboards that normally advertise restaurants and concerts. Now they offer rewards for information about persons of interest and resources to find missing people. The empty streets flash with the blue and red of emergency lights.

I arrive at the silent department office by 6 a.m. The earliest writing class starts at 7 a.m., and I hope the university has sent another email with more information to guide class instruction for the day. No such email arrives. Instead, in my inbox is an email from a new graduate teaching assistant that simply asks, "What do I do in class today?" And so I respond.

Crisis response is an increasingly critical, albeit under-recognized, occupational responsibility of educators. Lynn Worsham (2006, 170) describes the twenty-first century as "an especially catastrophic age characterized by unprecedented historical trauma" that contributes to an individual and cultural "pervasive and generalized mood corresponding to post-traumatic stress disorder." Crises are events such as unexpected deaths, natural disasters, mass gun violence, oppression, wars, genocide, and terrorism that disrupt the expected routine of daily life. People directly and indirectly impacted by such crises may experience trauma, an emotional response to the disruption that manifests in different ways and may continue long after the crisis has ended. The frequency of crisis events suggests that it is no longer a matter of if a crisis will occur but a matter of when. K–12 educators prepare for the possibility of crisis by participating in active shooter drills, training to identify students of concern, working closely with school counselors and resource officers, and developing crisis-response plans (Brock et al. 2016) in addition to their expected educative responsibilities, such as lesson planning and grading. However, as I quickly discovered in my role as a writing program administrator after a mass shooting, WPAs in college settings are rarely prepared to perform the multiple forms of labor—especially emotional labor—that are necessary to safely and effectively respond to crisis.

Writing studies professionals have recognized the impact of crisis in classroom settings, often focusing on the instructor's response to individual students' traumatic life events such as when a student discloses an abusive relationship, a mental health concern, or the potential for violence (Berman 1994; Payne 2000; Thompson 2004). Such pedagogical responses offer writing as a critical tool in the healing process and encourage instructors to create safe environments for students to write about trauma (Anderson and MacCurdy 2000; De La Ysla 2014; Hodges Hamilton 2016; Micciche 2007; Pennebaker 1997). In addition to supporting individual students through traumatic experiences, larger-scale crises may affect the classroom as multiple students and even the instructor may be impacted. Scholars have written about their experiences teaching after large-scale crises such as September 11 (Borrowman 2005; Marback 2005; Murphy, Muckerheide, and Roen 2005), Hurricane Katrina (Johnson, Letter, and Livingston 2009), and campus shootings (see Harris-Moore in DeBacher and Harris-Moore 2016). For example, Patricia Murphy, Ryan Muckerheide, and Duane H. Roen (2005, 70) discuss their classroom responses to 9/11 that involved changing course curriculum to critically analyze, read, and write about the national tragedy. Murphy, Muckerheide, and Roen's post-crisis pedagogical response aligns with studies of other higher education instructors' classroom practices after 9/11. In a post-9/11 survey of instructors at her institution, Michele DiPietro (2003, 25) found that almost 90 percent of the instructors addressed the event in their classrooms by identifying local support resources, facilitating class discussion about the event, and changing deadlines and offering extensions, among other interventions. Although DiPietro's work focused on pedagogical responses to 9/11, instructors in other crisis situations responded in similar ways to their local tragedies, such as adapting course design and lesson plans in the aftermath of Hurricane Katrina (Johnson, Letter, and Livingston 2009) or weaving campus tragedy into the course curriculum as a local case study (Miller 2002). Instructors recognize that crisis at the individual, local, or national level impacts the classroom and often necessitates a pedagogical response, even if instructors do not feel adequately prepared to respond.

In spite of the existing research that addresses the intersections of crisis, trauma, and the classroom, there is little scholarship that addresses the emotional dimension of teaching, learning, and, specifically, administration after a crisis. Writing after their own experiences with campus crises, Sarah DeBacher and Deborah Harris-Moore (2016) find that "there is not much that shines a light on what it means to teach when both teacher and student are traumatized." Their experiences returning to teaching after a hurricane and a campus shooting, respectively, prompt them to consider: "How should we teach in the midst of collective, widespread, and ongoing trauma, when we and all of our students are among the traumatized" (2016). After a crisis event, instructors may experience their own emotional distress while attending to their students' emotional and learning needs. DeBacher writes about feeling paralyzed and struggling to show up in the classroom during the Hurricane Katrina recovery period, and Harris-Moore similarly recounts her difficulty focusing on teaching after a campus shooting. DeBacher and Harris-Moore share their perspectives as writing instructors attempting to return to normalcy after crisis, and their experiences are some of the few narratives that explicitly address the emotional experience of teaching after crisis. Their experiences add to the scholarship on crisis in the writing classroom by providing the instructor perspective to complement the student focus that composes much of the scholarship about writing, trauma, and healing.

As DeBacher and Harris-Moore's (2016) article demonstrates, the professional work of writing studies changes after a crisis impacts students and instructors on campus. Yet there is no similar narrative about the labor of writing program administrators after a large-scale crisis. Building on DeBacher and Harris-Moore's work and my own experience after the Las Vegas shooting, I ask: What is the practical and emotional labor of writing program administrators in crisis response and recovery? How does this labor change after crisis when students, instructors, and administrators are among the traumatized? I suggest that WPAs function as programmatic crisis responders and perform unrecognized emotional labor in this role, often without the necessary training, compensation, and support to ensure their own mental and emotional safety. The lack of preparation and support for emotional labor during crisis response may negatively impact the WPA's physical, mental, and emotional well-being, but these negative impacts can be reduced with preventative, concurrent, and reflective support strategies.

In this chapter, I first describe how WPAs function as programmatic crisis responders who must act before, during, and after a crisis on behalf of the larger institution and the writing program. I then identify the emotional labor WPAs perform during crisis response. Finally, I offer proactive strategies WPAs can implement to effectively respond to crisis while prioritizing their own holistic well-being to prevent mental health consequences and professional burnout.

THE WORK OF WRITING PROGRAM ADMINISTRATORS DURING CRISIS RESPONSE

I write an email to all part-time instructors and graduate teaching assistants, hoping my email can provide some direction when everything feels overwhelming and a return to normalcy seems impossible. I tell instructors that the writing program is primarily concerned with ensuring the safety and well-being of the students and instructors. I inform instructors that anger, fear, anxiety, and grief are normal after a shooting, and they should be attentive to their own feelings as well as their students' feelings. I share national resources about teaching after tragedy and local counseling resources for students and employees. I suggest professional ways to respond to the crisis, such as revising class lessons and relaxing attendance policies for the week. I remind instructors that my door is always open if they need to talk. I end my email with a request that they take care of themselves and each other.

All day, my office and email inbox are full. Graduate students and colleagues in the department come by to share their personal connections to the violence. A friend was at the concert. They were supposed to attend the concert but at the last minute had decided not to go. They can't believe this could happen here. Some just come to my office to take a tissue. Instructors in the writing program contact me about impacted students. A student injured in the shooting. Students who didn't feel safe coming to campus. Students who haven't responded to the instructor's email. What do I do, they ask.

Writing program administrators address occupational crises on a daily basis; the job of a WPA is often to extinguish figurative fires. But sometimes the fires are closer to literal. WPAs may be called to respond on behalf of the writing program to crises that are beyond human control, such as a student or instructor death, a natural disaster, or campus violence. However, there is little disciplinary scholarship on the work of writing program administration during or after crisis. Without a better understanding of writing program crisis response, the various forms of labor WPAs perform to ensure that the writing program functions after a crisis remain unrecognized, unvalued, and unsupported.

In times of crisis, administrators at all levels of education perform critical labor that contributes to safety, security, and recovery. Among their many tasks, administrators establish the tone for crisis response, communicate information to various stakeholders about the crisis and logistics, and ultimately support the transition from crisis to normalcy (Demaria and Schonfeld 2013). Katherine C. Cowan and Eric Rossen (2013) propose that administrators approach crisis as a dynamic process of prevention, preparedness, response, and recovery to more effectively manage crisis situations. Cowan and Rossen's process illustrates the different stages of crisis response and the specific labor of administrators during each crisis stage to act safely and effectively.

Writing program administrators can engage in prevention and preparedness activities to anticipate the needs of various stakeholders during a crisis and develop an appropriate response plan before a crisis ever occurs. Prevention efforts are intended to foster a positive learning environment with resources to support students' and instructors' physical and psychological safety (Cowan and Rossen 2013, 11). Writing program administrators may engage in preventative actions by identifying campus resources and publicizing those resources to students and instructors. Even though it is not possible to completely prevent crises, preventative actions can create a positive writing program environment that is better prepared to support community members during difficult times. In addition to creating a supportive writing program through preventative efforts, writing program administrators can initiate preparedness actions to train instructors and administrators to work with local emergency responders in potential crisis scenarios. Higher education institutions often have emergency management plans that address a wide range of scenarios, including fires, chemical spills, and active shooters; but writing program staff may not be aware of these plans or their role in crisis response. Writing program administrators may collaborate with campus safety offices to inform themselves about institutional emergency procedures and then to offer preparedness training for writing program instructors as part of program orientations or professional development. Engaging in prevention and preparedness efforts may alleviate some of the pressure on WPAs to decide how to respond during high-stress crisis situations.

In addition to prevention and preparedness efforts before a crisis, writing program administrators also perform response and recovery labor during and after a crisis. Response efforts reestablish safety and security during and immediately after a crisis event. Ideally, the response actions should be planned in advance as part of the preparedness stage so the response mode can be activated quickly in the event of a crisis. Response activities for WPAs will vary based on the crisis and local context, but such efforts may include communicating information to instructors and students about institutional operations, changes to program policies or curriculum, or community resources. Finally, recovery activities are the ongoing, often long-term actions that reestablish a sense of normalcy after a crisis event. Recovery may entail establishing new program procedures to support impacted individuals or pedagogical practices to accommodate changing teaching and learning needs.

The prevention, preparedness, response, and recovery process of crisis response is one model that illustrates a WPA's often invisible but critical labor before, during, and after a crisis. These actions should be incorporated into WPA job descriptions to recognize their critical role during crisis response. However, Cowan and Rossen's (2013) process does not address a significant type of labor embedded within each stage: emotional labor.

THE EMOTIONAL LABOR OF CRISIS RESPONSE

All week long, I do my best to hide my shaking hands underneath my desk, the result of adrenaline coursing through my body. My body is in panic mode. I am nauseated. I am experiencing flashbacks to last year during a lockdown on another campus, walking across a deserted campus as everyone huddled in place in locked buildings, eventually finding safety in a building across from the parking garage where SWAT teams searched for explosives. I wonder if I am overreacting. I try to quiet my mind, still my body, and be present for those who come to my office looking for solace, comfort, direction. I am empathetic to their feelings. Las Vegas has been my home for only a few short months, but I feel a similar sense of shattered safety. Again. I have experienced this before. I can offer no solution to erase the loss or ease the hurt. All I can do is ask *"are you okay and what do you need"* and remind others to take care of themselves while neglecting to take care of myself.

After comforting another distraught instructor for an hour, I find myself in the department chair's office. We have a problem, we need to do something, I say. What can we do, he asks. We aren't counselors. I tell him about the instructors in my office, about the undergraduate students who don't feel safe to come to campus. I struggle to keep my voice and hands steady. The university isn't doing enough. Instructors and students are upset and confused by the university's response to the shooting. The instructors keep coming to me because few other resources are available. I can't keep doing this emotional work. My department chair suggests, *"Maybe you should see a counselor. You may have PTSD from your previous experiences with campus violence."* He agrees to ask the campus counseling service to facilitate a workshop on teaching after tragedy later in the week. I return to my office. I go home late. I cry in bed when the lights are off.

I cancel my first-year writing class on Tuesday. I can't focus enough to plan a lesson. I stare at the wall. The thought of standing in front of twenty-four students is unbearable. Most of them are from Las Vegas, several of them work on the Strip. I don't want to search the classroom to see who is absent, to feel that catch in my throat as I wonder why they are absent. I can't bear witness to more suffering. I compulsively update news articles about the victims, looking to confirm my students' safety by their absence on such lists. A UNLV student is among the dead. The institutional response is silence.

I take refuge in the bathroom stall, unable to come out and give any more to anyone. As I walk down the hallway, I meet another new faculty member, one who does not teach in the writing program and therefore someone to whom I do not have to present my mask of professionalism and composed competence. We talk about our numbness and share our grief. We hug as we part to return to work, and she tells me it is the first real human contact she's experienced recently. I silently agree.

Effective programmatic crisis response requires WPAs to take actions to prevent, prepare for, respond to, and recover from disruptive events. But crisis response also requires emotional labor that often goes unrecognized and therefore unsupported. For WPAs, the emotional labor of crisis response is especially invisible because they are not recognized as programmatic crisis responders. Regardless of the job description, WPAs perform multiple forms of emotional labor when responding to crisis that includes eliciting desired emotions from others and managing one's own emotional response in the face of crisis.

At its most fundamental level, emotional labor "requires workers to suppress, exaggerate, or otherwise manipulate their own and/or another's private feelings in order to comply with work-related display rules" (Mastracci, Guy, and Newman 2012, 6). The ability to manage one's own emotions and relate an intended emotion is required for successful job performance, and emotional labor is critical in many service-oriented positions (2012, 4), including WPA positions. WPAs must perform emotional labor on a daily basis to advocate for program policies (Gillam 2003), resolve staffing conflicts (Peters 2003), and take care of the students and instructors in the writing program (Holt, Anderson, and Rouzie 2003). Such tasks require WPAs to understand the needs and emotions of all stakeholders in a given situation so the WPA can effectively negotiate a desired outcome. As Mara Holt, Leon Anderson, and Albert Rouzie (2003, 152) note, such "emotion work is crucially important, often fulfilling, but not officially recognized." The typical emotional labor required of WPAs is under-recognized and unsupported, as evidenced by the other chapters in this collection, but crisis situations further increase the intensity of emotional labor required of administrators (see Imafuji's, Kleinfeld's, Owens's, and Schlachte's respective chapters, this volume).

A crisis further complicates the degree of emotional labor required of service providers, including writing program administrators. Crisis responders like EMTs and police officers often perform intensive emotional labor as they enter emergency situations (Mastracci, Guy, and Newman 2012, 7). To successfully control the emergency situation, crisis responders must perform emotional labor to manage the emotional response of others as well as their own emotions. Crisis responders must quickly analyze the crisis situation to decide what emotions to invoke in bystanders (27). Responders practice emotive sensing, a process in which they identify the emotional state of others in the situation and respond to those emotions appropriately (27). For example, when working with a domestic violence survivor, a social worker practices emotive sensing by recognizing that the survivor feels threatened, so the social worker validates the survivor's feelings and presents a calm demeanor to help the survivor feel safe and secure (29). In addition to analyzing the emotional reactions of those she is trying to help, the crisis responder must also analyze her own emotional reaction. Sharon H. Mastracci, Mary E. Guy, and Meredith A. Newman (2012, 21) find that "suppressing one's own horror while proceeding to perform the job is only one of the many necessities of emotional labor." The responder cannot express personal emotions such as fear, horror, or uncertainty, which if expressed may exacerbate the crisis situation or at the very least prevent a swift and safe resolution. The responder must use compartmentalization techniques to suppress her emotional reaction to effectively perform her job. However, the emotional labor of crisis response does not end with crisis resolution. Responders must later process their emotional responses to prevent ongoing emotional harm, such as post-traumatic stress, vicarious trauma, or burnout (36).

Although writing program administrators are not emergency first responders, crisis situations in educational contexts require that WPAs perform similar emotional labor. My experience as a WPA after the Las Vegas shooting demonstrates how crisis situations that impact the campus intensify the emotional labor associated with typical programmatic work. In the event of a crisis, education administrators act on behalf of the institution as they establish the tone of response and provide guidance about policies, procedures, and resources to support students and staff (Demaria and Schonfeld 2013). In my response after the October 1 shooting, I practiced emotive sensing to anticipate students' and instructors' emotions, including their need for safety and stability. My initial email to all program instructors recognized the tragedy, validated students' and instructors' emotional responses, and offered specific ways to adjust classroom expectations to accommodate student and instructor needs. In the absence of a coordinated university response, I modeled for writing program instructors the response I hoped they would use with their own students: a combination of empathy for students and clear, logical guidance to support the eventual return to routine.

In addition to the labor of expressing appropriate emotions after the shooting, I also labored to suppress the emotions that would have impeded my ability to respond professionally. My personal history with gun violence caused me additional distress in the wake of the Las Vegas shooting. I experienced a school shooting in my hometown of Newtown, Connecticut, and several violent events on campus during my graduate education at Virginia Tech and Ohio State University. School psychologists Franci Crepeau-Hobson and Linda M. Kanan (2013) find that individuals with prior traumatic experiences may have exaggerated reactions to crisis and trauma and that such individuals are particularly at risk for burnout. The personal experiences that made me more prepared to respond to violence in educational settings also made me more susceptible to negative emotional and mental reactions to violence. However, I felt unable to display my emotional distress without compromising my efficacy as the WPA. WPAs simultaneously represent the writing program and the larger institution in their crisis response and must therefore respond clearly. My response was also complicated by my positionality as a young, female WPA who was new to the institution. The shooting represented the first major crisis of my position, and I felt I needed to respond quickly and competently to establish my professional ethos. The professional response necessitated that I express empathy for the instructors and students but suppress my own emotional response that was intensified by my experiences with gun violence and campus violence. I was engaged in constant emotive sensing as I compared my own heightened emotional response to others' emotional responses, which caused me to question and devalue my own emotional distress while being overly sensitive to my colleagues' emotions.

STRATEGIES FOR HANDLING THE EMOTIONAL LABOR OF RESPONSE

At the end of the week, the university counseling center sends two counselors to our meeting about teaching after tragedy. The meeting takes place at the same time as the graduate writing pedagogy and practicum class I teach. The new instructors from my class are all present, as are other part-time instructors, graduate instructors, and department administrators. The counselors present common reactions to trauma, signs instructors should look for in themselves and their students as the city begins to process and heal. The instructors share their feelings about the shooting. I dismiss class after the counseling presentation so that everyone can go home and take care of themselves.

Weeks pass. Instructors continue to contact me about ongoing student concerns. Students who have not been in class since the shooting. Students who have been in and out of surgery. Students grieving their families and friends. I make calls, trying to find resources for these students so they can focus on healing without worrying about navigating the institutional bureaucracy. I am stymied at each turn. There is no central advocacy hub that students can contact for help, so I take it upon myself to advocate for each student. At meetings about student retention, I remind administrators that the shooting is not over, and students still need support.

Months pass. I still hear stories about students and instructors recovering from the shooting, and I still try to help students navigate the system to retroactively withdraw from classes, to complete coursework, to petition a system that didn't anticipate or accommodate their needs. Each subsequent shooting floors me. I am anxious about leaving home. I experience flashbacks that leave me shaking and nauseated. I alternately obsess about shootings and then withdraw from social media and the news after the violence becomes too much. I write a book chapter that leaves me raw, waiting for the healing that apparently comes with writing.

The emotional labor of crisis response is an ongoing process of identifying, understanding, and responding to students' and instructors' needs after a crisis event. Much of the research on educational crisis response focuses on specific actions school administrators and teachers can take to effectively support the students' physical, emotional, and learning needs after a crisis. But students are not the only ones who need support; Crepeau-Hobson and Kanan (2013, 33) argue that "schools must be prepared to support all the adults in the school setting so they can continue to foster the development, learning, and achievement of students." The emotional labor of supporting students under normal circumstances, let alone during a crisis, requires that the teachers and administrators are similarly supported and cared for. For educational administrators like WPAs, emotional labor is intensified because administrators must respond to crisis on behalf of the program and the institution—a complex response that includes managing others' emotional reactions while also managing one's own response and needs. There are preventative, concurrent, and reflective strategies used by emergency first responders that, if implemented in higher education settings, can mitigate the burden of emotional labor. Such strategies would prepare WPAs for emotional labor in advance, provide necessary support during the crisis, and create support structures after the crisis.

First, crisis response must be recognized as one of a WPA's many job responsibilities. Crisis response is not a frequent occupational responsibility, but when crisis does impact the writing program, the typical job responsibilities are preempted to respond to students' and instructors' needs for safety, security, and stability. Subsequently, WPAs must take preventative action to prepare for crisis response. Without adequate crisis preparation, WPAs' emotional labor may be exacerbated by the need to balance competing priorities. Most higher education institutions already have emergency response plans that address common campus safety and security situations. WPAs should identify these resources in advance, familiarize themselves with the campus procedures, and publicize these plans to all writing program faculty. WPAs should also develop writing program crisis plans that align with the existing institutional emergency plans and address program-specific concerns. A writing program crisis-response plan may include communication protocols, classroom logistics, appropriate accommodations, and campus and community support resources. If institutional resources are available, WPAs may collaborate with campus safety and facilities to develop these program crisis plans and to train program staff for crises such as active shooter training. Implementing preventative strategies like writing program crisis-response plans can decrease a WPA's stress during a crisis by establishing clear procedures that address common crisis concerns and preparing all program staff for such situations. Engaging in preventative actions may remove some of the pressure from the WPA to respond quickly and professionally on behalf of the entire program, thereby allowing the WPA to care for her own emotional well-being.

Part of crisis preparation also includes creating preventative practices that help workers recognize their emotional labor and develop proactive strategies to manage their stress and emotions. In their study of emergency first responders, Mastracci, Guy, and Newman found that preventative practices helped first responders manage their complex emotional reactions to their work. Preventative practices such as training and professional discussions about emotional labor before a crisis situation helped workers recognize the emotional dimension of their work and subsequently manage their own emotional responses during and after an emotionally volatile encounter (Mastracci, Guy, and Newman 2012, 141). Training to recognize emotional labor would be beneficial for many aspects of WPA work, but in a crisis context, emotional labor training can prevent burnout and mental health distress. Preparation for emotional labor and honest discussions about the emotional labor of writing program administration could be facilitated in professional settings such as graduate seminars about writing program administration and the annual pre-conference workshop for new and veteran WPAs or in professional documents produced by the Council of Writing Program Administrators.

Preventative self-care plans are another critical tool that may help WPAs manage their emotional labor. Self-care plans allow first responders to set personal non-work goals related to mental and physical wellness so the workers develop coping strategies. The goals become part of the worker's yearly evaluation standards so the first responder's holistic wellness is prioritized as part of their job performance. Again, preventative self-care plans that are part of performance evaluations could be beneficial for WPAs and academics more generally, as these plans could change the academic culture of overwork and burnout (Bodovski 2018) by valuing self-care in its many forms (see Adams Wooten, this volume). Instituting preventative self-care plans can encourage WPA responders to disengage during a crisis situation in order to take the needed time, energy, and space to practice sustaining self-care.

In addition to preventative strategies, support after the crisis response is also necessary to help workers effectively recover from emotional labor without suffering long-term effects. Mastracci, Guy, and Newman (2012, 43) offer critical stress debriefings as one practice that can help first responders process crisis events and their own emotional reactions that occur during and after an event. During critical incident debriefings, involved personnel meet with a counselor to discuss the crisis event in an effort to "resolve lingering images, reactions, and memories" that may contribute to long-term problems like vicarious trauma and burnout (Mastracci, Guy, and Newman 2012, 43). The debriefing process of identifying emotions serves to de-stigmatize emotional responses in work situations and allows workers to discuss professional events in light of their emotional responses. Critical stress debriefings can be useful as part of a WPA's crisis response and ongoing recovery process. WPAs may collaborate with campus mental health professionals to offer critical stress debriefings for writing program instructors after a crisis; these debriefings can create a supported space for instructors to discuss their emotions and identify professional ways to respond to crisis and process their feelings. WPAs may participate themselves in critical stress debriefings with other administrators across campus. If administrator-focused critical stress debriefings are unavailable, individual counseling may help WPAs process their professional response, emotional labor, and emotional reactions. Critical stress debriefings can be included in institutional and writing program crisis-response plans as part of the recovery process. However, it is also important to note that individuals experience crisis and trauma differently. As such, crisis-response plans and critical incident stress management may not completely eradicate the fear, anxiety, and stress that accompany crisis for all individuals, and other interventions may be needed.

CONCLUSION: AN UNEASY RESOLUTION

All writing programs will experience a crisis; it is not a question of if a crisis will occur but a question of when. But in spite of the many crises that have occurred even in the twenty-first century (9/11, campus shootings, unprecedented natural disasters, global pandemics), instructors and administrators experience a continued lack of preparation to act in crisis situation. As Harris-Moore (DeBacher and Harris-Moore 2016) writes, "I was well aware of my lack of training and planning, but also realized the urgency of the situation." We are called to respond, but we do not necessarily know how to respond effectively and safely.

In the event of a crisis, WPAs function as programmatic crisis responders who must manage complex emotions to provide needed support to the writing program constituents, including instructors and students. The role of WPAs as programmatic crisis responders extends from the immediate aftermath of the crisis to ongoing effects. Even though we cannot prevent crisis, what we can alleviate is the burden of emotional labor by recognizing, training, and supporting WPAs to effectively and safely perform this labor. The emotional labor of crisis response can be mitigated by preventative strategies like institutional and programmatic crisis-response plans to prepare WPAs in advance of a crisis and episodic strategies like critical incident stress management to support WPAs after a crisis.

It is almost a year since the October 1 shooting; by the time this is published, more years will have passed. The writing program has established a new normal. We have more conversations about classroom safety and crisis preparations, and our instructor resource site has a section with links to emergency resources, pedagogical responses to crisis, and local counseling and support services. I discuss the emotional dimension of our work with instructors from the beginning of their training, and we create self-care plans as part of our orientation. I facilitate these frank conversations and activities to support instructors' holistic wellness and to prepare them for a future crisis situation that I hope never happens. There is still more work to do, but this is a start.

As I revise this chapter a few days before the anniversary, I still feel fear, anxiety, anger, resentment, and more. The force and frequency of these emotions have diminished over time, but they can be triggered by seemingly innocuous things like a social media post or a reference to gun violence in a conference presentation. I am surprised by how powerfully I react to these triggers, and I wonder if I will feel this way for the rest of my life. I think I will to some degree.

I carefully begin to share my experience with those who will listen. I hesitate to disclose too much lest I be perceived as hysterical or un-scholarly, a balance I struggle with throughout this chapter. Even though every word reopens painful memories and emotions, I write out of the conviction that these are conversations we must have as a profession so that others may not feel so alone or helpless during crisis. I share my experience in the hopes that these strategies can help us recognize our labor, validate our emotional experiences, and care for ourselves as needed so that after a crisis we can move from surviving to flourishing again.

REFERENCES

Anderson, Charles M., and Marian M. MacCurdy, eds. 2000. *Writing and Healing: Toward an Informed Practice.* Urbana, IL: National Council of Teachers of English.

Berman, Jeffrey. 1994. *Diaries to an English Professor: Pain and Growth in the Classroom.* Amherst: University of Massachusetts Press.

Bodovski, Katerina. 2018. "Why I Collapsed on the Job." *Chronicle of Higher Education*, February 15. https://www.chronicle.com/article/Why-I-Collapsed-on-the-Job/242537.

Borrowman, Shane R. 2005. "Introduction." In *Trauma and the Teaching of Writing*, edited by Shane R. Borrowman, 1–10. Albany: State University of New York Press.

Brock, Stephen E., Amanda B. Nickerson, Melissa Louvar Reeves, Christina N. Conolly, Shane R. Jimerson, Rosario C. Pesce, and Brian R. Lazzaro. 2016. *School Crisis Prevention and Intervention: The PREPaRE Model*, 2nd ed. Bethesda, MD: National Association of School Psychologists.

Cowan, Katherine C., and Eric Rossen. 2013. "Responding to the Unthinkable: School Crisis Response and Recovery." *Phi Delta Kappan* 95 (4): 8–12. https://doi.org/10.1177/003172171309500403.

Crepeau-Hobson, Franci, and Linda M. Kanan. 2013. "After the Tragedy: Caring for the Caregivers." *Phi Delta Kappan* 95 (4): 33–37. https://doi.org/10.1177/003172171309500408.

DeBacher, Sarah, and Deborah Harris-Moore. 2016. "First, Do No Harm: Teaching Writing in the Wake of Traumatic Events." *Composition Forum* 34. http://compositionforum.com/issue/34/first-do-no-harm.php.

De La Ysla, Linda S. 2014. "Faculty as First Responders: Willing but Unprepared." In *Generation Vet: Composition, Student Veterans, and the Post-9/11 University*, edited by Sue Doe and Lisa Langstraat, 95–116. Logan: Utah State University Press.

Demaria, Thomas, and David J. Schonfeld. 2013. "Do It Now: Short-Term Responses to Traumatic Events." *Phi Delta Kappan* 95 (4): 13–17. https://doi.org/10.1177/003172171309500404.

DiPietro, Michele. 2003. "The Day After: Faculty Behavior in Post-September 11, 2001, Classes." *To Improve the Academy* 21 (1): 21–39. https://doi.org/10.1002/j.2334-4822.2003.tb00379.x.

Gillam, Alice. 2003. "Collaboration, Ethics, and the Emotional Labor of WPAs." In *A Way to Move: Rhetorics of Emotion and Composition Studies*, edited by Dale Jacobs and Laura Micciche, 113–123. Portsmouth, NH: Boynton/Cook.

Hodges Hamilton, Amy. 2016. "First Responders: A Pedagogy for Writing and Reading Trauma." In *Critical Trauma Studies: Understanding Violence, Conflict, and Memory in Everyday Life*, edited by Monica J. Casper and Eric Wertheimer, 179–204. New York: New York University Press.

Holt, Mara, Leon Anderson, and Albert Rouzie. 2003. "Making Emotion Work Visible in Writing Program Administration." In *A Way to Move: Rhetorics of Emotion and Composition Studies*, edited by Dale Jacobs and Laura Micciche, 147–160. Portsmouth, NH: Boynton/Cook.

Johnson, T. R., Joe Letter, and Judith Kemerait Livingston. 2009. "Floating Foundations: Kairos, Community, and a Composition Program in Post-Katrina New Orleans." *College English* 72 (1): 29–47.

Marback, Richard. 2005. "Here and Now: Remediating National Tragedy and the Purposes for Teaching Writing." In *Trauma and the Teaching of Writing*, edited by Shane R. Borrowman, 53–67. Albany: State University of New York Press.

Mastracci, Sharon H., Mary E. Guy, and Meredith A. Newman. 2012. *Emotional Labor and Crisis Response: Working on the Razor's Edge*. Armonk, NY: M. E. Sharpe. http://www.library.unlv.edu/help/remote.html.

Micciche, Laura. 2007. *Doing Emotion: Rhetoric, Writing, Teaching*. Portsmouth, NH: Heinemann.

Miller, Katherine. 2002. "The Experience of Emotion in the Workplace." *Management Communication Quarterly* 15 (4): 571–600.

Murphy, Patricia, Ryan Muckerheide, and Duane H. Roen. 2005. "Teaching in the Wake of National Tragedy." In *Trauma and the Teaching of Writing*, edited by Shane R. Borrowman, 69–83. Albany: State University of New York Press.

Payne, Michelle. 2000. *Bodily Discourses: When Students Write about Abuse and Eating Disorders.* Portsmouth, NH: Boynton/Cook.

Pennebaker, James W. 1997. "Writing about Emotional Experiences as a Therapeutic Process." *Psychological Science* 8 (3): 162–166. https://doi.org/10.1111/j.1467-9280.1997.tb00403.x.

Peters, Brad. 2003. "An Anatomy of Radical Anger in Writing Program Administration." In *A Way to Move: Rhetorics of Emotion and Composition Studies*, edited by Dale Jacobs and Laura Micciche, 135–146. Portsmouth, NH: Boynton/Cook.

Thompson, Riki. 2004. "Trauma and the Rhetoric of Recovery: A Discourse Analysis of the Virtual Healing Journal of Child Sexual Abuse Survivors." *JAC* 24 (3): 653–677.

Worsham, Lynn. 2006. "Composing (Identity) in a Posttraumatic Age." In *Identity Papers: Literacy and Power in Higher Education*, edited by Bronwyn T. Williams, 170–181. Logan: Utah State University Press.

8
SHELTER IN PLACE
Contingency and Affect in Graduate Teacher Training Courses

Carl Schlachte
Colby College

On the night of October 29, 2012, a Monday, Hurricane Sandy made landfall in New York City. Over the next several hours, we were hit by wind speeds of up to 80 miles per hour, torrential rains, and a storm surge of 14 feet of water, flooding 51 square miles of the city. The storm caused massive power outages for almost 2 million people and $19 billion in damage, and it left forty-three people dead (plaNYC 2013). At noon the next day, the emails started coming in. First, an email from the college, extending the cancellation of classes through Wednesday and promising further updates. An hour later, I emailed my students.

In the fall semester of 2012, I was a novice teacher in my second-ever semester working as an adjunct teaching composition at CUNY Brooklyn College. I didn't know what to do with my students or what to tell them. Our class on Wednesday had been cancelled, so I'd have to deal with that. The students' next essay was also due that day; I'd have to deal with that, too. I had not received any guidance from the college or the writing program administrator (WPA). In the absence of recommendations about how to proceed, I made a judgment and sent an email to my class: "Hopefully you've all made it through the storm alright, and you and your families are all safe." And then I told them that as long as they had power, they should send me their essays by Friday.

Even years later, I feel regret and failure at what I regard as the inadequacy of this response. I knew how bad the situation was: not long after sending the email, I walked to an adjacent neighborhood nearer the water that was particularly hard-hit, to lend whatever aid I could to the cleanup and rescue efforts. Things I saw there—like debris-flecked water lines on street signs halfway through the word "STOP" and cars so waterlogged they were still leaking out, back onto the streets—resonate with me still. But I didn't connect what I experienced to my teaching.

My aim in writing this is not to castigate myself for my failings but to point out how serious the emotional consequences of experiencing a disaster can be and how they can come to bear on pedagogical situations. Perhaps because the impact of Sandy was so broad in New York City and because I was such an inexperienced teacher at the time, the circumstances I encountered after the storm have lingered with me. I wish I'd been better prepared to address the conditions my students and I were facing. I also wish I'd received some guidance on what to do; while emails from the college alerting us to policy changes like the need to make up classes continued to trickle in for the rest of the semester, no official guidance from the Composition Program or the English department ever came.

In 2017, as part of my dissertation research into the ways teachers of college writing respond to disasters that interrupt normal classroom activities, I conducted a series of interviews with teachers at Brooklyn College who had also experienced Hurricane Sandy. Eleven teachers responded to my emailed invitation to participate in interviews, including eight adjuncts or former adjuncts teaching in the Composition Program and three tenure-track faculty members: two in different subfields of literature and the writing program administrator. I asked each of my interviewees about their experiences with the storm, both personal and pedagogical, including what they had done with their classes and how they felt about their responses five years on. I found that I was not alone in wishing there had been more guidance from the program. Ultimately, six of the eight adjuncts I interviewed specifically requested more guidance from the department or institution.[1] I come to this chapter, then, not from the perspective of a writing program administrator but as one of the teachers they supervise. Though my current research engages with issues in writing program administration, that interest arises in part from my frustrations as an adjunct faculty member who felt powerless and unguided in regard to how to respond to such disruptive and emotional circumstances in the classroom.

My aim in this chapter is to offer guidance to WPAs who may face similar situations, in light of these concerns about supporting instructors through a disaster's aftereffects. Earlier in this volume, Kaitlin Clinnin writes about the challenges WPAs face in taking on emotional labor as part of an institutional response to a disaster. While the disaster she addresses—the mass shooting in Las Vegas, Nevada, in October 2017—is a different kind than a hurricane, she similarly notes that in a crisis situation, one role WPAs can play is to offer guidance to the teachers they supervise. Clinnin discusses ways WPAs can sensitively balance the emotional labor of response with the exigency that demands they provide one. I offer an alternative perspective, a cautionary one, about what the effects of a lack of guidance can be. I seek to provide guidance to WPAs who may face the emotional labor of responding to disasters not just in their own courses but in the courses of the teachers they supervise as well, especially when some of the emotional labor they must perform is to direct the work of entire programs suffering the consequences of disaster.

FEELING IN RESPONSE TO HURRICANE SANDY

The experience of disaster is an emotional experience, often causing intense reactions in people affected by it. To this point, much of the scholarship in composition that engages with disaster focuses on responses to specific exigencies, like September 11, 2001 (Borrowman 2005) and Hurricane Katrina (Piano 2014), or offers specific accounts of teaching through disasters and other crises (Adams et al. 2012; DeBacher and Harris-Moore 2016). Another way disaster arises in composition scholarship is—tellingly—in work on emotion. For example, Dale Jacobs and Laura Micciche's (2003) introduction to their collection *A Way to Move* opens by invoking the September 11 attacks; four years later, Richard Miller's (2007, ix) foreword to Micciche's *Doing Emotion* invokes the shootings at Virginia Tech and "America's uniquely awful history of education and violence." Despite the recognition that disaster is increasingly a pressing concern for the discipline of composition, we still lack a more comprehensive approach to teaching through disaster. Addressing this problem is particularly incumbent on WPAs, who are often tasked with managing programmatic responses to disaster, regardless of whether they are prepared to do so. A first step toward preparing WPAs to provide guidance to the teachers they supervise, then, is to build a nuanced depiction of how teachers respond to disaster. By tracing the pedagogical responses teachers offered in the wake of Hurricane Sandy, I provide WPAs with information they can use to shape their own responses, especially as they seek to support the teachers they supervise.

The data for my depiction of disaster response come from a series of retrospective, Institutional Review Board-approved interviews I undertook in 2017 with teachers in the English department at CUNY Brooklyn College.[2] As an institution, CUNY was broadly affected by Sandy; 17,119 CUNY students (undergraduate and graduate) "lived within reach of the storm surge," that is, in areas that were most acutely affected and received, on average, approximately 8 feet of water above the normal sea level (CUNY n.d., 1). Brooklyn College was the most affected four-year school in the system, with 14 percent of its enrollment among this number (CUNY n.d., 2). My interview process began with an email solicitation to the department's entire instructional staff from fall 2012, requesting participants for interviews. Of 129 possible participants, 11 responded. I conducted semi-structured interviews with them, asking questions like "During and immediately after Hurricane Sandy, what would you say were the main challenges you faced as a teacher?" and "Do you think the impact of Hurricane Sandy has changed how you approach your teaching in the years since?" At the end of each interview, participants selected their own pseudonyms, by which they are referred to throughout. All the interviews were audio-recorded, transcribed, and coded following a grounded theory approach (Charmaz 2006). Ultimately, as mentioned, of the 11 interview participants, 8 were adjuncts or former adjuncts teaching various composition courses, 2 were tenured or tenure-track faculty members in literature, and 1 was the writing program administrator, who was tenured and was the most senior faculty member interviewed.

The high number of adjuncts participating reflects the prominence of contingent faculty in the department.[3] These participants' labor status quickly revealed itself to be a salient factor arising from the interviews, as all of the contingent faculty I spoke to made direct reference to their labor status at some point in our conversation.[4] Accordingly, insights from scholarship in areas like work in composition on academic labor, as well as affect theory, can be brought to bear on reactions reported in the interviews. For example, it is not surprising, given the scholarly awareness of the presence of emotion amid disaster, that ten of the eleven interviewees invoked emotion to describe both their own and their students' reactions to the storm. One teacher, Denise, remarked that in experiencing the hurricane, "There were just more . . . feelings, I think, than I was expecting to have." Denise's comment draws our focus to the affective movement of disaster, how it conforms to and defies expectations. As it becomes an increasingly common presence in our lives, disaster is both normal and not normal, an experience Kathleen Stewart (2007, 39) refers to as an "ordinary affect"—found in everyday moments and "permeat[ing] politics of all kinds with the demand that some kind of intimate public of onlookers recognize something in a space of shared impact." The shared impact of disaster represents a loss of normalcy and stability—a particular challenge for teaching, which depends on the regularity of class structures and clearly laid-out schedules, or for administrating writing programs, in which training practicums and policies are used to achieve programmatic consistency. Education scholar Sue Ellen Henry (2013, 15, original emphasis) describes the stability common to both education and identity, writing that "students often see themselves as parts of durable categories (middle class, well educated, well off, smart) rather than seeing themselves as *people* who *have* these qualities." This desire for stability makes them "especially resistant to learning through recognizing their emotions" (16). Disaster punctures this stability, destabilizing all these categories. The resulting uncertainty is extremely challenging for students, teachers, and administrators to face.

As a consequence of the instability resulting from disaster, many of the teachers I interviewed drew distinctions between emotional and logistical responses to Sandy, as Sylvia did in describing her classes: "Most of my students were not really logistically affected. I think everyone was shaken, obviously. But most of them could snap back and still had their books, their work." Sylvia's response suggests an important finding of the interviews: while there was broad recognition of the presence of emotion in the hurricane's aftermath, many interviewees responded on a purely logistical level, reporting adjustments such as schedule shifts, dropped readings and assignments, changing assignments or deadlines, and slowing down the course. Across the interviews, there was consensus that the most significant result of the storm academically was the cancellation of a week of classes. Thus while teachers primarily experienced the storm emotionally, they primarily responded to it logistically. This reaction may also be common because it is somewhat straightforward; Claude noted: "It's hard to know how to respond. So I think in a lot of cases, people just do what they would do anyway." The WPA echoed this to suggest that a particular response to the hurricane was not necessarily merited, saying "if you were hit by a bus and told me you were hit by a bus . . . and you'd be out for two weeks, I would try to accommodate you. So I don't, I don't think that, for me, a hurricane had any dramatic effect on my approach to teaching or my ability to kind of change the rules midstream if we have to." The logic of this response—adjusting for students' needs regardless of the reason for them—makes sense to me. At the same time, it is also notable that the WPA was the only interviewee who did not cite emotion as playing a role in disaster response.[5] Yet even teachers who intend to address emotion often find it challenging to respond to disaster. Ann Cvetkovich's (2007, 460) description of the "divided attention" she and other teachers experienced in the aftermath of Hurricane Katrina, as "a movement back and forth between the everyday business of the semester's beginning and the urgency of the disaster," can explain why teachers often feel vexed with responding—torn between desires for normalcy and for reaction to the atypical situation, both personally and professionally.

The WPA was also the teacher who reported feeling least affected by Hurricane Sandy. This can be explained by experience: in the interview, the WPA connected the hurricane to the prior, much more significant experience of teaching in New York City on September 11, 2001. With 9/11, the WPA said:

> People's lives were changed . . . Radically changed, and changed forever. So maybe Hurricane Sandy changes people's lives forever, but [it's] a much more limited population. And [in] ways that can be fixed. So if your house is flooded, maybe it takes six months and maybe it takes a year, and it's horrible, but it can be fixed. But if your father was at the World Trade Center and is dead, that can't be fixed. So I think that . . . maybe for me . . . a hurricane is not as traumatic. I *know*, not "maybe." It's certainly not as traumatic as something like a terrorist [attack].

This may account for the divergence in responses between the WPA and the other teachers who were interviewed, contingent and tenure track; none of the other respondents were teaching during 9/11. But this comment also suggests that while the effects of Sandy were not equally significant for everyone, prior experiences of disaster are a significant factor in mitigating the burden of emotional response.

The contrast between emotional and logistical responses may demonstrate a hesitancy on the part of these teachers to engage in the emotional labor of responding to highly charged, potentially traumatic classroom feelings. But these reactions were not uncomplicated. Four of the interviewees reported that in retrospect, they regretted not responding more emotionally. Claude, for example, said: "I didn't address—I mean, other than logistically—I didn't address the storm at all in class. I don't think. Um . . . and I sort of wish that I had." Jane, too, argued that an emotional response, which she did not offer, would have been appropriate, concluding: "If you're a good teacher, you probably cared. And you're concerned about your students, you know that this is going to impact their lives, it's going to impact . . . your class. But it seems like nobody really knew what to do or how to respond." Given the prominent role emotion can play in educational contexts even under more normal circumstances, as Micciche (2007), Henry (2013), and others have noted, I want to stress how significantly disaster exacerbates these conditions. A sensitive response to disaster, then, requires a particular emotional response, not just a logistical one. For better or worse, the exigency of disaster necessitates emotional labor.

The question of emotional labor implicates other, more traditionally recognized forms of labor as well. After all, the affective experience of disaster is not distributed equally. The presence of such inequality is heightened in the classroom, which is always marked by power imbalances. Emotion remains tied up in questions of power, particularly in "the tension between personal and institutional power" (Henry 2013, 14). For contingent faculty, the continual pressure of gaining reappointment negatively impacts their identification with their profession. Angela Bilia and her coauthors (2011, 388) noted that "you never fully experience accomplishment as a professional when you are constantly treated as an apprentice who needs supervision and direction from those on top." This kind of wounded identification, which requires directive guidance, may also explain why six of the eight contingent faculty members I interviewed specifically mentioned a desire for more guidance from the writing program, department, or institution. Contrast, for example, the responses described by Sylvia, a tenured professor, and Miriam, an adjunct. Sylvia described advising junior colleagues to make any changes necessary in adapting their classes to the storm, "based on the authority of my personal instinct." Interviewees who were contingent faculty were far more likely to describe a lack of authority, as Miriam did: "As an adjunct . . . I definitely did not feel empowered to, um, 'do anything,' for my students."[6]

Miriam was not the only contingent faculty member whose capacity to respond to the hurricane was limited by her status; even when they are otherwise motivated to address the circumstances, contingent status has a chilling effect on teachers' responses. Contingent faculty members' anxieties about workplace security and efficacy negatively impact their ability to fully respond to disasters, particularly emotionally. Claude noted this directly, saying: "Given in retrospect what a big deal that storm was, I really didn't change that much . . . And maybe if I'd been a more established member of the department, I would've been more comfortable . . . figur[ing] out maybe a more holistic approach to dealing with what the rest of the semester looks like." In light of these concerns about a lack of guidance, I asked the WPA how the Composition Program had responded to instructors' concerns following Sandy. The WPA suggested that the impact the administrative role had on responding to the hurricane was "only in just advising instructors generally to try to be flexible . . . I think that people expect to be able to handle things." When I asked, as a follow up, if many instructors had sought guidance, the answer was "no. Not at all." I asked if *anyone* had, and the answer was "I can't remember. Yeah. I mean, it certainly doesn't stand out. I think we may have sent out some general directive . . . But that's it." These answers reveal a frustrating divide between the alienated experiences of contingent faculty, who strongly desired greater guidance from the program and institution, and the WPA, who did not find it necessary to provide guidance because it was not sought out. Though the WPA reported sending a general directive to teachers, as a person who was teaching at the time, I never received one.

The authority Miriam, Claude, and other contingent faculty sought to legitimize their responses is unfortunately hard to come by, given the proliferation of non-tenure-track faculty positions. In the absence of institutionally supplied authority, a stopgap solution would be for the WPA to use their position of authority—regardless of whether they are a tenure-track faculty member themselves—to supply guidance to their instructors to better equip them to respond to the circumstances they are facing. This need to offer guidance is also where responding to disaster most directly impacts WPA work: while all faculty are tasked with responding to the exigency in their classes, the WPA supervises many instructors who may be grappling with how to respond. Thus a WPA is not only tasked with their own response; they will need to help these instructors manage their reactions as well—leading to increased emotional labor.

LABORING IN RESPONSE TO HURRICANE SANDY

Beyond the ordinary concerns arising from the complex work of coordinating the efforts of many instructors, course sections, and students, disaster forces WPAs to devote extra attention to the already present issues of emotion and labor status in their programs, at a time when these issues are exacerbated by suffering. Certainly, it is incumbent upon WPAs to consider the way labor status impacts their instructors' work, and scholarship in writing program administration has long wrestled with this issue (Lamos 2011; Strickland 2004). Patricia Stephens (2004, 36), for example, has asked how WPAs, already overburdened, can support a staff of part-time instructors, by taking into account both "the emotional impact of long-standing exploitation" on that faculty and "the wide range of expertise and experience" among them. The challenge these issues pose for WPAs is further heightened in the situation of disaster, where strained circumstances exacerbate the emotions and labor concerns of everyone. This is particularly true of WPAs and other faculty—including women and people of color—who because of their identities are already unequally tasked with emotional labor, as Sheila

Carter-Tod notes in this volume. In the aftermath of disaster, much is asked of tenure-track and contingent faculty alike, but WPAs, due to their supervisory roles, are especially burdened with the task of managing both the labor and emotions of a range of instructors.

Unfortunately, as disaster is an abnormally fraught circumstance, the challenges of performing emotional labor in its aftermath are correspondingly more vexed. Several interviewees who discussed attempting a "return to normalcy" as part of their contemporaneous response to Sandy noted that engaging too forcefully or directly with a recent disaster risks re-traumatizing students or teachers themselves. As Sarah DeBacher and Deborah Harris-Moore (2016) point out, it is hard to ask students to explore recent disasters with the "intellectual and critical distance" required to do so; teachers, too, may be "in no position to read those narratives without injury," among other ethical challenges, including allowing opt-outs or grading and commenting on the assignments. Ignoring the events is not recommendable, but neither is forced disclosure. Yet despite the perils posed by offering emotional responses to disaster, many of the contingent faculty members I interviewed reported *wanting* to respond to the circumstances more than they did. A story Denise told, about trying to email her students regarding class cancellations *during* the storm, demonstrates the challenges contingent faculty face in responding. As Denise said, "We're so dedicated to this job that is not very dedicated to us." Though she made a strenuous effort to remain in contact with her students during Sandy, Denise still marked her response in terms of labor status and whether, by its terms, her reaction was appropriate.

One reason labor status makes a difference in response involves guidance. Miriam expressed a desire for an "instructors' rights statement" and explained that if she could have had "an informal discussion with the department or higher-up members of the institution about what my role was," she would have found it both "helpful" and "empower[ing]." When I asked what she meant, Miriam responded that "empowerment can often be, like, the conversation. Or authorization to do or say certain things, you know. Even authorization to get emotional." Miriam believed her response to the storm was limited to logistics precisely because she didn't feel empowered or authorized to be emotional in the classroom. But it is often particularly difficult for contingent faculty to have the kinds of conversations Miriam expressed a desire for because of their status. An analogue for this problem can be found in a comment Harley, a tenure-track faculty member, made about providing his affected students options for adjustments: "they won't necessarily know what they can ask for." The same could be true of contingent faculty, who may feel their options to respond are constrained by their roles; they seek the authorization Miriam desired.

The role for the WPA in this circumstance is to provide the kind of guidance desired by these and other contingent faculty members who were interviewed. I recognize that this requires WPAs to take on another strenuous emotional responsibility, burdened as they already are by numerous emotional demands. But given the acknowledged difficulties surrounding disaster and the stakes of addressing them, it is important to emphasize the positive effects such interventions by WPAs can cause. Nevertheless, we should also be clear about the limitations of these interventions; as the WPA noted in our interview: "I don't ever think it's my role to counsel [students] or to find resources outside the college for them but much more to find resources, to direct them to resources within the college, to people who are trained to deal with such things." This point about training is well taken; counseling is a highly trained skill, and I do not believe that in taking on emotional labor, teachers without that training should seek to fulfill that role for their students. But there is a difference between counseling students and responding to them emotionally, and I do not think being wary of the former precludes us from sensitively attempting the latter.

Moreover, this emotional labor need not be taken up by WPAs alone. Though radically improved working conditions across the academy would do much to rectify the disconnection many contingent faculty interviewees felt with regard to their own authority, a more pragmatic solution would be to recommend that *all* tenured faculty undertake the work of greatly increased personal contact with contingent faculty in challenging teaching situations. WPAs, because of their built-in supervisory relationship with those teaching composition, are well positioned to take on this task; but they should not be the only faculty to bear the burden of emotional response. Instead, WPAs can encourage non-contingent colleagues to reach out to offer the needed guidance. If graduate students are members of the instructional staff, for example, their advisers should be encouraged to speak with them. Ultimately, the goal of these conversations is for less experienced instructors to learn from the teacherly instincts of others and receive validation for the kinds of responses they might offer. This goal is not particular to writing programs, so the WPA should not be the only person addressing it. Even contingent faculty members who have more experience can offer valuable guidance to their colleagues. After all, authority is not only a product of rank; it is also a product of ethos, which can be built over time through confidence in one's role. Beverly, a contingent faculty member, described this bluntly in reflecting years later: "Now [I] would [respond] differently because I have that much more experience as a teacher." This suggests that it would be beneficial to draw on the expertise of any teachers—including contingent faculty—who feel capable of responding to the circumstances. While I am equally hesitant to recommend that contingent faculty take on the additional emotional labor of guiding their colleagues' responses, doing so may also foster their own efficacy. As Jacob Babb and Courtney Adams Wooten (2017) have noted, when instructors of all ranks are collaboratively involved in programmatic concerns, it builds agency for contingent faculty in their own courses. It is appropriate for WPAs to draw on experienced contingent faculty as a resource, distributing the emotional labor each of them must take on.

While increased dialogue between contingent and tenure-track faculty would be a significant step toward addressing the lack of efficacy many contingent interviewees described following the disaster, the channels of communication that enable this dialogue cannot only be established after something happens. Writing programs need to foster ongoing relationships of informal professional development between experienced and inexperienced faculty, regardless of rank. For faculty in secure positions, this means actively seeking to empower contingent colleagues to respond; the interviews suggest that authorization may be what is needed, more than specific tactics of response. For contingent faculty, this means actively seeking authority, practiced through classroom autonomy, within their departments. Many contingent faculty members have autonomy de jure but lack it de facto. This divergence is limiting, and it ought to be corrected before problems arise. Fostering dialogue prior to the irruption of disaster would likely help those who feel disempowered to better understand that they have authority and what responses they can take. As administrators in their departments, WPAs may again be well placed to foster these dialogues, though they should not be the only people with whom these conversations take place.

THE ROLE OF WPAS IN ETHICAL DISASTER RESPONSE

There are two ways to address disasters that disrupt teaching: beforehand, with disaster preparedness, and afterward, with disaster response. Cross-rank conversations, as discussed, can be a key tactic for both disaster preparedness *and* response. In this final section, I offer additional recommendations for both of these modes, given that readers may turn to this chapter and collection in both kinds of circumstances—hoping to prepare for increased emotional labor they know is coming or seeking immediately applicable strategies for situations they suddenly find themselves in. By offering these strategies, I hope to enable WPAs to mitigate and distribute the emotional labor they are asked to perform when disasters arise.

The most readily available space in which WPAs can implement disaster preparedness efforts is in teacher training and development. As part of their supervisory roles, WPAs are frequently tasked with pedagogical development, and WPA scholarship has continued to explore best practices for training new instructors (Reid 2017). WPA scholarship has also attempted to deepen understandings of teacher development as it intersects with key concepts like emotion (Saur and Palmeri 2017) and labor status (Stephens 2004). I recommend that WPAs implement strategies designed to build dispositions of responsive teaching practices—grounded in theories of ethical, experience-based pedagogy—either in teacher training (like practicum courses) or ongoing teacher development efforts (like lectures and workshops). Disaster preparedness and the dispositions it leads to can thus become a regular part of pedagogical development, minimizing, it is hoped, the impact of the emotional labor required of both instructors and WPAs when disaster occurs. Specifically, teacher training interventions should address the same concerns highlighted in my interviews: emotional consequences and questions of authority. While the way a teacher chooses to respond will necessarily depend on the specific circumstances of the disaster, in any instance, preparing for and positioning oneself to respond emotionally and not merely logistically is an important step in adequately addressing the exigency it presents. For example, this may take the form of imagining different types of disasters and possible effective emotional responses to them; as E. Shelley Reid (2017, 137) has argued, teachers should judge their preparedness by "how many variables [they] can identify in a dynamic situation and how many reasonable alternate paths [they] can imagine." Reid (2017, 137) argues that this builds teachers' tolerances for "productive uncertainty," certainly a key factor in confident and effective disaster response that allows teachers to navigate the murky contingency of an aftermath. As my interview with the WPA demonstrated, an important determining factor in feeling equipped to respond to disaster is having experienced one before. WPAs can attempt to simulate this in practicum courses by presenting novice instructors with hypothetical situations and leading them to consider the many aspects—both logistical and emotional—that will influence the responses.

In the realm of disaster response, our options are less well-defined and are limited by the constrained circumstances in which we act. Nevertheless, common questions arise in such instances: How quickly should instructors attempt to reestablish stability, consistency, or a more straightforward model of growth? And if instructors need guidance or authorization in pursuing the response they deem appropriate, how can WPAs supervising them take on this emotional labor without overextending themselves? As I have argued, these questions are inextricably tied up not just in policy minutiae but in questions of emotion; these questions need to be addressed emotionally, at least in part. Because teachers are better able to pursue emotional responses if they feel empowered to do so, in the wake of disaster WPAs should clearly communicate to all instructors that they are authorized to respond as they deem necessary—logistically but also (important) emotionally. When classes resume following a disaster, schedule adjustments will necessarily be made. In such circumstances, teachers may not know what options are available, so the WPA can communicate possible options directly. Alternatively, the WPA can organize an informal forum, either in person or over email, for many instructors to share different modes of response. In either case, because conditions in individual classes may vary extensively, I advise WPAs to allow instructors to determine for themselves how they will respond. Giving instructors guidance provides necessary support, but giving them the freedom to act allows them to better account for both their students' and their own emotional needs. No one should force themselves to respond in a way they are emotionally unprepared for. At the same time, the WPA should caution instructors against *only* seeking a return to normalcy or attempting to make up lost time. As Elizabeth Kleinfeld argues in this volume, addressing tragedy requires us to revise our expectations for what we can accomplish in our work. Simply put: missed class sessions are not recoverable, and the benefits of taking time to address what has occurred can be extremely beneficial.

Certain options may be particularly useful for responding to disaster regardless of the circumstances. WPAs can encourage instructors to write reflectively on the situation they are in, including the ways emotion intersects with their responses. Instructors can ask their students to do the same. This allows people to reflect on their emotional reactions and process them. At the same time, sharing or turning in these reflections should not be necessary; forced disclosure is never desirable. Beyond this, though, keeping reflections personal spares instructors and the WPA from taking on unnecessary additional emotional labor. Some people may still need to share their feelings with others, and if this becomes a significant burden, the WPA should refer them to better-trained and better-equipped campus counseling services. If the disaster is particularly severe, some instructors may wish to allow students to undertake a more sustained reflection on their experience by adapting an existing assignment to meet the exigency. If instructors do this, they should be cautioned to take care with particular challenges arising from students responding to the disaster in a more formal way; instructors may find offering feedback on such pieces challenging.

In all cases, WPAs should prepare instructors to think through the implications of whatever response they offer. WPAs should not be afraid to tell instructors seeking guidance that they don't yet know how to respond and that guidance will come once they've had time to reflect. Instructors may end up telling their students the same thing. A delayed response alleviates the pressure of having the most fitting answer immediately, at a time when people are least prepared to provide one. While I sympathize with the desire to bounce back quickly from disaster, everyone involved in responding—administrators, teachers, and students—can benefit from recognizing that responses emerge and develop over time.

Addressing disaster will always be challenging, a task contingent on outsized factors and subject to intense emotions. Because of their administrative position, WPAs will be put upon to help coordinate the responses the teachers they supervise offer. This is emotional labor, above and beyond the emotional labor they are asked to perform both as teachers and as a regular part of their programmatic work. I admit: it's not fair to ask WPAs to take on so much, especially in extraordinarily difficult circumstances. But despite this burden, I know from my experience with Hurricane Sandy how detrimental, how wounding, the silence of administrators can be to the teachers they supervise. The emotional consequences of not acting linger alongside the disaster. I offer my recommendations in the hope that in future disasters, everyone affected can respond while sensitively addressing and tending to their emotions. WPAs who undertake this work thus undertake to respond ethically and emotionally at extremely trying times, yes; but in doing so, they support the ethical, emotional responses of countless others.

NOTES

1. The other two adjuncts interviewed did not say they felt guidance was sufficient; this issue simply did not arise in their interviews.
2. IRB materials, including the full list of survey questions, email solicitations for participants, and consent forms, are available upon request.

3. I use the term *contingent faculty* to describe employees who are teachers of record but who were appointed on a semester-by-semester basis. Within the context of the interviews, I also refer to these teachers as *adjuncts*, the term used to describe their position in CUNY employment documents. Though some of these teachers were graduate students during Sandy, I do not refer to them as "teaching assistants" or "TAs" because at CUNY, all teaching graduate students were appointed as adjunct faculty. Referring to these teachers as adjuncts and not TAs also more accurately describes their work experience as contingent faculty, not apprentices (Wright 2017). Finally, while nationwide the range of experience and responsibilities among contingent faculty is vast, at Brooklyn College, almost all adjuncts were current or former graduate students at the institution.
4. One tenured faculty member I spoke to made reference to her labor status as well by way of contrast, noting that she was aware of her relative security in the response she offered. She said: "I think I had more freedom, I mean, I don't think I would've done anything differently, but . . . I had the privilege both of being pretty secure in my job and [having tenure]."
5. Denise, as the Composition Program administrator (a staff position), worked closely with the WPA. Denise described their differences in reaction as partly a result of personality, saying that the WPA's personality "is much more, like, stoic than mine. I'm more emotional."
6. Miriam added, "That wasn't a departmental problem for me; that was an institutional problem." To me, Miriam's comment identifies the root cause of the problem of her diminished authority in the classroom as a consequence of institutional hiring practices.

REFERENCES

Adams, Heather, Jeremy Engels, Michael J. Faris, Debra Hawhee, and Mark Hlavacik. 2012. "Deliberation in the Midst of Crisis." *Cultural Studies Critical Methodologies* 12 (4): 342–345. https://doi.org/10.1177/1532708612446435.

Babb, Jacob, and Courtney Adams Wooten. 2017. "Traveling on the Assessment Loop: The Role of Contingent Labor in Curriculum Development." In *Contingency, Exploitation, and Solidarity: Labor and Action in English Composition*, edited by Seth Kahn, William B. Lalicker, and Amy Lynch-Biniek, 169–182. Fort Collins: WAC Clearinghouse and University Press of Colorado. https://wac.colostate.edu/books/perspectives/contingency/.

Bilia, Angela, Christopher Dean, Judith Hebb, Monica F. Jacobe, and Doug Sweet. 2011. "Forum on Identity." Moderated by Sue Doe and Mike Palmquist. *College English* 73 (4): 379–395.

Borrowman, Shane, ed. 2005. *Trauma and the Teaching of Writing*. Albany: State University of New York Press.

Charmaz, Kathy. 2006. *Constructing Grounded Theory: A Practical Guide through Qualitative Analysis*. London: Sage.

CUNY Office of Policy Research. n.d. "In the Eye of the Storm: CUNY Students and Hurricane Sandy." http://www2.cuny.edu/wp-content/uploads/sites/4/page-assets/about/administration/offices/oira/policy/research-briefs/Sandy_Research_Brief_final.pdf.

Cvetkovich, Ann. 2007. "Public Feelings." *South Atlantic Quarterly* 106 (3): 459–468. https://doi.org/10.1215/00382876-2007-004.

DeBacher, Sarah, and Deborah Harris-Moore. 2016. "First, Do No Harm: Teaching Writing in the Wake of Traumatic Events." *Composition Forum* 34. http://compositionforum.com/issue/34/first-do-no-harm.php.

Henry, Sue Ellen. 2013. "Vulnerability and Emotional Risk in an Educational Philosophy." *Emotion, Space, and Society* 8: 11–17.

Jacobs, Dale, and Laura Micciche, eds. 2003. *A Way to Move: Rhetorics of Emotion and Composition Studies*. Portsmouth, NH: Boynton/Cook.

Lamos, Steve. 2011. "Credentialing College Writing Teachers: WPAs and Labor Reform." *WPA: Writing Program Administration* 35 (1): 45–72.

Micciche, Laura. 2007. *Doing Emotion*. Portsmouth, NH: Boynton/Cook.

Miller, Richard E. 2007. Foreword to *Doing Emotion*, by Laura Micciche, ix–x. Portsmouth, NH: Boynton/Cook.

Piano, Doreen. 2014. "Writing in the Cone of Uncertainty: An Argument for Sheltering in Place." *College Composition and Communication* 66 (1): 34–36.

plaNYC. 2013. "Chapter 1: Hurricane Sandy and Its Impacts." In *A Stronger, More Resilient New York*, 9–18. https://www1.nyc.gov/site/sirr/report/report.page.

Reid, E. Shelley. 2017. "On Learning to Teach: Letter to a New TA." *WPA: Writing Program Administration* 40 (2): 129–145.

Saur, Elizabeth, and Jason Palmeri. 2017. "Letter to a New TA: Affect Addendum." *WPA: Writing Program Administration* 40 (2): 146–153.

Stephens, Patricia A. 2004. "A Move toward 'Academic Citizenship': Reading Emotion in the Narrative Structures of Part-Time Faculty." *WPA: Writing Program Administration* 27 (3): 35–51.

Stewart, Kathleen. 2007. *Ordinary Affects*. Durham, NC: Duke University Press.

Strickland, Donna. 2004. "The Managerial Unconscious of Composition Studies." In *Tenured Bosses and Disposable Teachers*, edited by Marc Bousquet, Tony Scott, and Leo Parascondola, 46–56. Carbondale: Southern Illinois University Press.

Wright, Alison Laubach. 2017. "The Rhetoric of Excellence and the Erasure of Graduate Labor." In *Contingency, Exploitation, and Solidarity: Labor and Action in English Composition*, edited by Seth Kahn, William B. Lalicker, and Amy Lynch-Biniek, 271–278. Fort Collins: WAC Clearinghouse and University Press of Colorado. https://wac.colostate.edu/books/perspectives/contingency/.

9
MAKING VISIBLE THE EMOTIONAL LABOR OF WRITING CENTER WORK

Matthew T. Nelson
University of California, San Diego

Sam Deges
University of California, San Diego

Kathleen F. Weaver
Loyola Marymount University

The inciting insight for this volume on the emotional labor of writing administration work came from Arlie Russell Hochschild's foundational research on emotion. Challenging long-held understandings of emotion that had theorized it as a spontaneous, uncontrolled, internal occurrence, Hochschild (1979, 555) revealed emotion instead as "deeply social." Hochschild exposed how the experience of emotion exists not internally and individually but rather with and through other people. A particular feeling will be tailored and internally edited in response to what the individual understands themselves to be expected to feel in that particular situation. "Social factors," such as norms and mores, "guide the microactions of labeling, interpreting, and managing emotion" (555). To say it another way: we manage the expressions of our emotion, both internally and externally, in light of potential social consequences. If we lose out on an opportunity we keenly desired, for instance, the sting of not getting what we want might remain; but we learn that no matter how strongly we might feel, we cannot throw a tantrum because tantrums cause others to treat us in ways that are undesirable. So, over time, the feeling of losing out on what we want changes—the emotion itself changes, becomes more managed and so more manageable.

Hochschild furthered the understandings of the social nature of emotion in *The Managed Heart: Commercialization of Human Feeling* (1983), which focuses on emotion in work environments. Hochschild (and subsequent researchers) explored the ways the workplace requires employees to both respond to others' emotions and manage their own (Steinberg and Figart 1999; Hochschild 1983). From this emerges the notion of emotional work or emotional labor, "the labour involved in dealing with other people's feelings, a core component of which is the regulation of emotions" (James 1989, 21).

Those of us who hold writing program administrator (WPA) (and WPA-adjacent) positions know how much of our jobs are social and emotional, not (solely) intellectual or technical. A more public recognition of this is, of course, the occasion of this current value. In this chapter, we will explore in particular the emotional work involved in writing center administration, where, arguably, "dealing with other people's feelings" and "regulation of emotions" is not just part of the job; it *is* the job.

Part of what we hope to sketch out is the presence of emotional labor at every level in writing center work. From working with writers in one-on-one sessions to negotiating with upper-level administrators on funding priorities (and every point in between), significant emotional work is required for everyone working in a writing center. What are the implications of this? What should it mean for how writing center administrators do their work?

In taking emotional work as our focus, we are animated not just by the theme of the current volume but also by Nicole I. Caswell, Jackie Grutsch McKinney, and Rebecca Jackson (2016, 201), who shed clear light on the predominance of emotional labor in writing center administration. They consider it one of the key findings of their study of the work done by writing center directors new to their roles and call in their conclusion for further examination of emotional labor in writing centers (201). Writing back in 2016, they pointed out that "there are no other writing center studies addressing emotional labor and only a few mentions of emotional labor elsewhere in writing studies" (186). In our work here, we'd like to respond to that call, illuminating at least some of "the particular contours of [emotional] work and its effects" in writing center work (201).

THE EMOTIONAL LABOR OF WRITING CENTER ADMINISTRATORS

Elizabeth Boquet (2002, 7) describes a scene most any writing center administrator (WCA) would recognize: "a stream of students visiting my office . . . to work through, quietly and individually, their concerns about beginning to tutor. One after another, they express their nervousness, their uncertainty about their preparation, their concerns even about the appropriateness of their personalities." Most WCAs would see this kind of work as part of what defines their job at its best (and sometimes most challenging): the one-on-one interaction with student staff. We should also understand it as a clear example of emotional labor. Boquet's volume abounds with situations that would be equally familiar and equally exemplary: having to respond calmly to an emotional faculty member, talking with a "distressed" tutor after a challenging session, and others (18). Typical for writing center scholarship, though, Boquet does not name or draw attention to the emotional labor as such; after all, what could there be to note? The color of the water is a matter of indifference if it's just what you swim in. And more to the point, why bother? For the writing center directors Caswell, McKinney, and Jackson (2016, 187) studied, "emotional labor was a major presence in the participants' work and yet was nearly always the sort of labor that wouldn't be on a job description, in [a] position ad, or easily documented in directors' annual-review materials." This is a large part of what they mean when they conclude that "writing center director labor is largely invisible institutionally" (195).

So it is worth cataloging other instances of writing center emotional work. Roberta D. Kjesrud and Mary A. Wislocki (2011), examining conflict in institutional relationships from a writing center perspective, take as a point of departure those encounters with their respective higher-ups that left them feeling "angered or mystified." In particular, they wanted to investigate "the emotional distress conflict evoked in us" (90). This emotional distress was to them a useful starting point for inquiry precisely because it is so common for WCAs. In other words, to say what would be obvious to anyone who has read this volume up to this chapter: even the managerial and administrative work of running a writing center provokes feelings that must be contended with. While Kjesrud and Wislocki go on to plumb interesting implications of the risks and rewards resulting from the "intense, messy, and often conflict-ridden conversations" necessitated by writing center administrative work, we can step back to again make the simple point illustrated by their study: for WCAs, not only our work with tutors but also our connection to "our professional community . . . features emotion work, often occurring backchannel" (104). Citing Hochschild, they highlight how these conversations are themselves emotional labor—the social manifestation and management of emotion—and suggest that "informal construction of feeling rules"—a crucial part of how emotion is socially managed—is in fact one of the key actions that occurs in the informal community of WCAs (most often on the WCenter Listserv, the widely read email community space of the international community of writing center professionals). Echoing Carrie S. Leverenz from this volume, glossing Laura R. Micciche, we can posit that a certain emotional comportment characterizes a WCA's allegiance to the profession. No surprise, then, that even in "casual" conversations among writing center colleagues, we find emotional labor.

Of course, many jobs require emotional labor; but writing center administration requires a lot of it. "What stood out to us in this study," Caswell, McKinney, and Jackson (2016, 186, emphasis added) conclude in documenting the work lives of new writing center directors, "was the extent of [WCAs'] emotional labor, that relational work they had to do in order to accomplish (smoothly, swiftly, *or at all*) the other tasks on their to-do lists." Kjesrud and Wislocki (2011, 104) flatly declare the takeaway: "Emotion work includes most of what WCAs do to create a successful writing center."

THE EMOTIONAL LABOR OF WRITING CENTER TUTORS

In notable contrast to the job descriptions of WCAs, many manuals/guides written for peer writing tutors list features of emotional labor as key aspects of the job (though never labeled as such). This focus carries into tutor training, where it's common to discuss not only strategies to manage the emotions of tutees but also, and more fundamentally, the kinds of emotions that are appropriate for tutors to display (Agostinelli, Poch, and Santoro 2000; Soven 2005; McAndrew and Reigstad 2001; Barnett and Blumner 2007; Meyer and Smith 1987). While writing center "feeling rules" are rarely discussed explicitly, tutors are made to understand that as writing center employees, they must express only certain kinds of emotion: a generally cheerful demeanor, for example, when greeting students or deliberate patience if a student is rude. They are told to build rapport, to motivate students, and to give helpful feedback—without, however, resorting to any feedback that might make the students feel criticized or judged; likewise, they must avoid instruction that might threaten to make the students feel a loss of ownership over their work (Mackiewicz and Thompson 2013). All through this, tutors must strive to help the students develop their skills as writers. Peer writing tutors are thus burdened with a "complicated responsibility of showing empathy to writers while not allowing them to lose sight of the reason that they [the students] came for help in the first place: to express ideas effectively" (Agostinelli, Poch, and Santoro 2000, 35). The tutor is, in other words, expected to demonstrate specific kinds of politeness, those considered fitted to writing center work. It is a complex mix of peer- and para-professional behavior—empathy on one hand, instruction on the other, all with the intent of producing two specific feeling states in the student: satisfaction and an increased sense of self-efficacy. The complexity of the emotional labor undergirding it all is considerable.

In the context of emotional labor, it is notable in particular that tutors are expected to help students manage stress—stress which, in writing center contexts, comes not only from the challenging (and often less than clear) demands of academic writing and the very personal stakes of revealing one's writing to a stranger but also from external stressors: financial, familial, romantic, roommate, and others. For minoritized students, their position in the institution itself might be a significant source of stress, and this will impact their interactions in the writing center. In a session, a writing tutor may be asked to respond to all or any of these stresses, both those salient to the session's purpose and those not. If the student expresses frustration with, say, the challenge of balancing school and work obligations, the tutor will have to respond. They may be trained to empathize and then move the conversation back to the task at hand, or they may not be trained at all and be forced to find their own way through the moment, but what they almost certainly cannot do is ignore what the student has said—not if they want the session to succeed according to the ethos and practices of writing center work.

Indeed, the philosophy of writing center work, as defined by its lore and core texts, can itself be a source of stress for tutors. Contested but still dominant ideas of writing center work such as those drawn from Stephen M. North (1984) and Jeff Brooks (1991) can, as Jennifer Nicklay (2012) shows, produce guilt in tutors, who compare their own work against these ideals. These writing center "principles" are so often in tension with the reality of sessions—the articulated and unarticulated needs of the student writers, the self-perceived skills of the tutors—that achieving the "standard" writing center session can feel impossible, setting tutors up for feelings of failure (Nicklay 2012; Barnett and Blumner 2007).

It is worth noting, in light of these complex competing demands, that we prize the work of peer tutors precisely because of their ability to, borrowing one definition of empathy, "understand and share in people's experiences" (Miller, Stiff, and Ellis 1988, 254). But we give little consideration to the consequences of this emotional labor. Peer tutors are, of course, themselves students and so subject to the same stresses as the students they work with (such as minoritization, financial pressures). Curious about the effect of writing center work on tutors' psychological well-being, the authors of the current chapter, along with several other coauthors, conducted a cross-institutional empirical study of the interplay between tutors' and tutees' stress/anxiety, exploring in particular whether tutoring sessions in fact caused measurable stress for peer writing tutors. By linking self-reported stress/anxiety survey responses with data from salivary cortisol levels (a physiological measure correlating to stress), the authors found that for tutors who did not have elevated levels of stress/anxiety when they started a tutoring shift, tutoring did not correspond to increased stress levels. (In general, these tutors' salivary cortisol levels decreased during tutoring sessions.) But for those tutors who were feeling stressed/anxious when they began tutoring, salivary cortisol levels remained level or even increased as they tutored.

Our study offers physiological evidence suggesting that the emotional demands we put on tutors impacts them differently, highlighting the need to consider the cost of writing center emotional labor for those who do not share some (or perhaps any) of the characteristics long assumed as the norm for writing tutors (e.g., white, abled, neurotypical, native English speaking, cisgender). Research on emotional labor in other realms tells us that the cost of this work for those in underrepresented groups is higher: "If one has assumed an identity whose normative expectations are contrary to those in the customer-contact role, then emotional labor will have a negative impact on one's well-being" (Ashforth and Humphrey 1993, 100). What we hear testified to by Joseph Janangelo and Sheila Carter-Tod in this volume about the inequitable impact of emotional labor for WPAs from underrepresented groups applies also, in a writing center context, to the (often peer) tutoring staff who perform heroic feats of emotional labor every time they show up to work. Non-white tutors, LGBTQIA+ tutors, tutors of intersectional non-dominant identities of all varieties will bearer greater burdens for the emotional labor they are required to perform as writing tutors. A white tutor working with a student whose writing argues a racist viewpoint will have to perform different, and less, emotional labor than a tutor whose identity is at some level impugned by the student's ideas. Tutors who come from cultures with different politeness norms will need to expend more energy to make their professional comportment fall in line with expected writing center behavior.

The potential consequences for all peer writing tutors of the emotional work we ask them to perform can be extrapolated from the extensive literature on emotional labor, which indicates that the amount of emotional labor required is increased for jobs in which emotions are required to be displayed with significant variety, over a long duration, and without a "script" to mitigate the need for sincerity (Morris and Feldman 1996). These are conditions that certainly describe writing tutoring (as well as writing center administration). In considering the emotional labor necessary for a writing center, we need to take seriously the research showing that people in professions that require emotional work—notably including teachers—can experience high levels of emotional exhaustion, as well as long- and short-term negative health effects (Yanay and Shahar 1998). This theme is repeated by many authors in this volume. WPAs are feeling forced into "complete compliance" (Wenger, this volume), are called to provide support in times of crisis and trauma (Owens, Clinnin, this volume), and are left with worry over their reactions as well as the impact and political correctness (from the university's perspective) of their advice. All of this increases emotional exhaustion and can decrease job satisfaction.

THE IMPLICATIONS OF PERVASIVENESS: WHAT SHOULD A WCA DO?

We have focused here on the emotional labor of both WCAs and tutors to explore (and underscore) Caswell, McKinney, and Jackson's (2016) conclusion that emotional work is "pervasive" in writing centers. What we want to argue now is that if emotional labor is pervasive in our centers, the ways we account for it should be pervasive as well.

Make Emotional Labor Visible

The idea that writing center work is at every level so deeply relational, necessitating significant emotional labor, suggests that we would better honor our work by articulating emotional labor as one of our objects we study. We make conditions worse for ourselves by insisting on a kind of dissociative state in which we only sometimes, in certain situations and with certain audiences, acknowledge our emotional labor. (We think here of Amy Ferdinandt Stolley's call for honesty about the emotional labor of WPA work in this volume and the benefits that can result.) Too often now, we allow it to be erased or obscured in our reporting, our scholarship, even our conversations. It can appear at times that this obfuscation is necessary: "Marcia Bellas (1999), a sociologist interested in academic labor, argues that emotional labor in administration is largely ignored because 'intellectual, technical, and leadership skills are emphasized and highly compensated.' Emotional labor is 'generally not viewed as involving valuable skills and is consequently poorly rewarded'" (cited in Caswell, McKinney, and Jackson 2016, 187). But we are helping to reinforce those norms. If we want our work to be valued, then we must declare its value on its full terms. We must account for emotional work in the writing center formally and explicitly. We must resist the conditions that mean it won't (and can't) "be acknowledged by others and it probably wouldn't appear on annual reports or CVs or in job ads" (Caswell, McKinney, and Jackson 2016, 187).

This is the implicit takeaway in Caswell, McKinney, and Jackson's conclusions about the centrality of emotional labor to writing center directorship and its corresponding institutional invisibility: that invisibility is itself a condition—perhaps *the* condition—that seriously afflicts WCAs, leading to exhaustion and burnout. But again, it is an invisibility we help manufacture. Our scholarship, for example, trends against recognizing the social and emotional aspects of our work, as demonstrated by the near-total absence of research taking it on as a focus. This would be in keeping with the view writing center scholarship often insists on: that of writing center work as fundamentally "intellectual and pedagogical rather than managerial" (Caswell, McKinney, and Jackson 2016, 175). The most heated WCenter Listserv conversations often focus on the professional status of WCAs—on their institutional positioning (do we have tenure-track faculty positions?) and intellectual training (do we have PhDs in rhetoric and composition?). What our community can seem most concerned with is WCAs' capacity for what we'll lightly call here Very Serious Academic Scholarship, scholarship whose boundaries and assumptions best resemble the kinds of research we see taken seriously in other disciplines. (See, for example, the oft-repeated call for RAD research in writing centers.) While writing center–focused research of this kind is important, a single-minded focus on it belies the fact that much of our daily work, though underwritten and backstopped by significant disciplinary expertise, is social and emotional.

Highlight the Emotional Labor of Tutors

Given the work our centers do, an important first step in making our emotional labor show up would be to spotlight the emotional labor of the tutors themselves. We argue, therefore, that WCAs should consider making emotional labor an area of focus in their centers—in training, in their conversations with tutoring staff, and in what they assess and report about their tutors' work.

One practical way this might be accomplished would be to let emotional labor be an ongoing topic for professional development among the tutoring staff. Expanding from Navickas's note on the need to prepare graduate students and early-career WPAs for emotional labor, we would argue that there are good reasons to think this emphasis would have value for writing center tutoring staff as well. Emotional labor, if acknowledged, discussed, and trained for, can aid in the development of emotional intelligence, which is associated with a host of positive work outcomes for both organizations and employees—enough so that it is worth quoting a summary of those benefits at length:

> Researchers have demonstrated that emotional intelligence [EI] is an important personal factor in the success and productivity of organizations (e.g., Newman, Joseph, and MacCann 2010; Zeidner, Matthews, and Roberts 2009). Regulation of the emotions helps employees to maintain "positive affect"—a positive outlook that influences work behaviors favorably (George 1991; Joseph and Newman 2010)—and to restrain "negative affect" (Cheung and Tang 2012). Individuals with high EI experience less stress at work and more control, satisfaction, and commitment to work (Petrides and Furnham 2006; Singh and Woods 2008); they are less prone to experience emotional exhaustion and burnout and more likely to perform their jobs successfully (Huang, Chan, Lam, and Nan 2010). Consequently, high EI employees are less likely to turn to work misbehaviors in the face of injustice or burnout. They have the skills and abilities to regulate their emotions and the tools to cope with such adversities: they can create balance by means of self-control and self-regulation. (Shkoler and Tziner 2017, 159)

Few of our tutors will go on to be writing center professionals, but all will be employees, and all will face challenges in those roles. In light of the direct relationship between emotional skills and success in the workplace, we should invite the student employees we supervise "to recognize and deliberately seek opportunities to practice the range and nuances of emotional displays" (Zalewski and Shaffer 2011, 45). Actionable steps for helping students develop capacities for emotional labor include: (1) explain the value of emotional labor, (2) ask students to be aware of the ways they manage their emotions, (3) help students document the emotional labor they do, (4) identify places and opportunities for students to develop their emotional labor skills, and (5) help students evaluate future career opportunities based on the emotional labor the job demands and the emotional labor the student is comfortable providing (Zalewski and Shaffer 2011, 50–52). These are all actions that would be salient to the daily work in a writing center.

By highlighting the role of emotional labor in the core work of the writing center, we can make that labor visible and meaningful. Arguing for it as a type of professional development for tutors gives us, pragmatically, a reason to report these efforts to our institutions. You might partner with the career center on your campus to demonstrate the need for this preparation. You could set up an empirical research project to track the impacts of these efforts. Through intentional efforts of this kind, writing centers could become recognized sites for knowledge about how to help employees develop the emotional intelligence necessary to thrive in the workplace. In the career-focused environment of contemporary higher education, this could provide a unique and valuable supplement to a writing center's recognized expertise. We do not need to give up our corners—for example, expertise in composition, in peer-to-peer learning, in best feedback practices—to add this to our profiles.

Build Intentionally (and Consensually) around Emotional Labor

If we do take the emotional labor of writing center work seriously—highlighting it, studying it, learning from it—we need also to build an emotionally intelligent culture in our centers. Any efforts taken to build community in the writing center become then not intangibles or add-ons; they are, in fact, integral in two ways: both as a means to allow tutors to vent, normalizing their feelings about their work and sharing strategies for responding to it, but also as a more positive, inclusive version of what Kjesrud and Wislocki (2011) report about the WCenter Listserv for WCAs—a community as a site where communal "feeling rules" can be created, examined, and revised. For tutors, management of their authentic reactions to student behavior is something they often report to WCAs and fellow tutors ("The student came so unprepared"; "They kept looking at their phone"; "They just refused to talk"). We should encourage this kind of sharing among our peer writing staff, recognizing that it requires trust and true community (including between the tutoring and administrative staffs) and a clear, shared commitment to learning from our emotional labor. We would need to make this intention explicit to our staff and invite them to participate openly in the process. Rather than regulating our tutors' emotional labor through unspoken mores and unexamined norms, WCAs can involve them instead in community discussions.

The benefits would include improved inclusiveness. Do tutors from marginalized communities, for example, believe that the "politeness at all costs" implicitly advocated by writing center experts (see, for example, Mackiewicz and Thompson 2013) is an appropriate match for the social justice work so many writing centers want to take up on their campuses? Do these tutors feel that the emotional labor required of them is the same as that of their non-minoritized colleagues? These are questions that currently can't be considered. If we don't make emotional labor explicit and communally examined, we will not be creating just, equitable opportunities for our staff. In a quote we could have deployed in nearly every section of this chapter, Kjesrud and Wislock (2011, 103) frame the stakes of the issue: "Failing to recognize and study emotion as a social construct may lead to unwitting participation in the hegemony of dominant values." To which we say: say it again! While we may in the end ratify the writing center standards and feeling rules as they exist now, by making the work of emotions part of what we talk about, assess, report, and study, we can do so openly and with fuller participation from our communities.

Consider Emotional Labor "Accommodations"

In addition to fostering a writing center space that values the emotional labor of its employees, we might also consider creating options for accommodating any tutor who at times finds themselves unable to do the amount of emotional labor expected of them in tutoring sessions. We suspect that to many WCAs, this will sound tricky. Our commitment to our values might come into tension here with our assumptions about the role of the tutor. But say a tutor is suffering from a major life event and knows that subsuming their own emotions while taking on the students' stress during a session will be harmful to them; or say they suffer from an anxiety disorder that in times of increased stress (such as around exam weeks) makes it similarly draining to do the job of writing tutoring well. Is it so unthinkable to consider making a policy of allowances for these situations, and not by forcing already vulnerable tutors to call in sick and cut themselves off from the pay their writing center work offers?

The implementation of this practice would look different in different writing centers. And considering ways for tutors to "opt out" from the emotional labor of tutoring—perhaps by spending a shift working on an administrative task—is a way for WCAs to meaningfully demonstrate their commitment to the well-being of the tutors who work for them. There is research to suggest that accommodating students' different "psychological, social, and cultural factors will improve the quality and effectiveness of college tutoring programs" (Maxwell 1991, 14). But in a contemporary writing center context, the ability to accommodate the psychological needs of student staff is also pressing, given how many writing centers now intend to be sites for transformative social justice work. Emotional labor is another area in which we must consider equity, diversity, and inclusion—another site in which "we have to carefully create and support spaces for engagement as our staffs bring to the table wide-ranging experiences, values, home lives, and professional goals that will affect how individuals react to transformative efforts" (Blazer 2015, 25). We cannot ask peer tutors to take on the work of exploring emotional labor without acknowledging the varied costs and impacts it can have on them; likewise, we cannot involve them in the challenges of social justice efforts without being honest about, and potentially making accommodations for, the emotional labor these efforts take, especially when implemented in one-on-one tutoring sessions.

Take of Care of Yourself to Take Care of Others

The suggestions we offer here have a somewhat ironic edge. This chapter asks WCAs to do even more emotional labor, to be even more emotionally invested in their centers than they would already be. Promoting emotional labor as a value and a topic of discussion means inviting ourselves, as WCAs, into more conversations that require the management of emotion. To avoid replicating the flaw of tutoring guides that encourage tutors to respond to students' emotional states but without coaching tutors on how to manage their own emotions, we want to emphasize what should be obvious: writing center administrators need to pay attention to "the psychological cost of performing emotional labor," recognizing the reality that "performing emotional labor can be difficult and can contribute to stress and burnout" (Humphrey 2012, 742). The upsides and downsides to this are written all through the current volume, testified to from all directions by our co-contributors. Beyond real concerns over long-term health and well-being—in case that's not sufficiently motivating—we would note the research that indicates the importance of leaders' expressed emotional states to the health of those who work with and for them. "Because leaders' moods are emotionally contagious to followers," Ronald H. Humphrey (2012, 742) notes, "leaders' emotional labor may have significant effects on followers' stress levels as well." As WCAs try to set good professional examples of coping with stress and managing necessary emotional labor, they can reduce the transmission of feelings of stress and work-related pressure onto their tutors. So we urge WCAs to include in their work routines practices and activities that recharge and replenish them.

Now might be the time for us to offer what is perhaps the most straightforward observation: emotional labor takes psychological resources, so we should be training our staff and ourselves in techniques for increasing those reserves—mindfulness and body/breath awareness might be one example. In this volume, for example, Christy I. Wenger argues for mindfulness practices in our daily work, which can help a writing center administrator or WPA "discern how we got to this emotional state in the first place," as well as "help to place a space between our perception of events and our response to them." Students, too, could benefit from these habitual practices as they navigate the stressors of college and of serving as a peer writing tutor. Likewise, Leverenz's advocacy of gratitude practices is something we should mind for both ourselves and those who work with us.

CONCLUSION

In the end, we want to insist on one main point: making emotional labor visible and valued is itself a critically important strategy for responding to the emotional toll our jobs can take on us. Continuing to push our emotional labor and that of our centers into the shadows has significant costs. Research on emotional labor indicates that "what makes regulation of emotional expression more difficult, and thus more labor intensive, are exactly those situations in which there are conflicts between genuinely felt emotions and organizationally desired emotions" (Morris and Feldman 1996, 992). For WCAs, this suggests (in a somewhat meta-way) that failing to acknowledge emotional labor is also itself a kind of emotional labor. The more we attempt to project and perform a kind of professional identity that is solely technical and scholarly—as though our work involved only theories and evidence, not people and power—the more we force ourselves into an inauthentic relationship with our work. We produce in ourselves a form of occupational bad faith. The reality is that our feelings matter, and, returning to Hochschild's insights about the social nature of emotion, not just for us. Our feelings have material and structural effects in our institutions. Micciche (2002, 453) argues this persuasively: "Part of an institutional or departmental tone develops from its members' affective relations to their work. This tone, in turn, communicates a sense of what is possible or impossible, thinkable or unthinkable." Our hope, then, is that as WCAs learn to both see and make visible the emotional labor necessary for their centers' success, they can create space for their emotional labor to be acknowledged and honored.

Our emotional labor is, after all, also the part of our work that brings us the most joy. Caswell, McKinney, and Jackson (2016, 196), for example, note that in the challenging and often overwhelming conditions in which writing center directors work, at least some of the emotional labor can be a source of satisfaction for WCAs—such as, for instance, the connections formed with student staff members. As one review of *The Working Lives of New Writing Center Directors* notes, "Whether we want to define mentorship as emotional labor or not, mentorship seems to be a big reason as to why I, and other writing center directors, stay in the job" (Denny, Paz, and Sicari 2017, 308).

For us, the upshot is that WCAs should consider their centers holistically, allowing emotional labor its due place. We quoted Kjesrud and Wislocki (2011) above as saying "emotion work includes most of what WCAs do to create a successful writing center," but in fact we trimmed one key word. In full, the quote reads: "emotion work includes most of what WCAs do to create a successful writing center *culture*" (104, emphasis added). We omitted the word *culture*, if only to draw closer attention to it here at the end. In our estimation, the successful operation of a writing center means creating and sustaining a healthy writing center *culture*—a system that values the individuals linked to it in as many of the complex dimensions of their personhood as possible.

REFERENCES

Agostinelli, Corinne, Helena Poch, and Elizabeth Santoro. 2000. "Tutoring in Emotionally Charged Sessions." In *A Tutor's Guide: Helping Writers One to One*, edited by Bennett A. Rafoth, 34–40. Portsmouth, NH: Boynton/Cook.

Ashforth, Blake E., and Ronald H. Humphrey. 1993. "Emotional Labor in Service Roles: The Influence of Identity." *Academy of Management Review* 18 (1): 88–115. https://doi.org/10.2307/258824.

Barnett, Robert W., and Jacob S. Blumner. 2007. *The Longman Guide to Writing Center Theory and Practice*. London: Longman.

Bellas, Marcia. 1999. "Emotional Labor in Academia: The Case of Professors." *Annals of the American Academy of Political and Social Science* 561 (1): 96–110.

Blazer, Sarah. 2015. "Twenty-First Century Writing Center Staff Education: Teaching and Learning towards Inclusive and Productive Everyday Practice." *Writing Center Journal* 35 (1): 17–55.

Boquet, Elizabeth. 2002. *Noise from the Writing Center*. Logan: Utah State University Press.

Brooks, Jeff. 1991. "Minimalist Tutoring: Making the Student Do All the Work." *Writing Lab Newsletter* 15 (6): 1–4.

Caswell, Nicole I., Jackie Grutsch McKinney, and Rebecca Jackson. 2016. *The Working Lives of New Writing Center Directors*. Logan: Utah State University Press.

Cheung, Francis Yue-lok, and Catherine Si-kum Tang. 2012. "The Effect of Emotional Dissonance and Emotional Intelligence on Work-Family Interference." *Canadian Journal of Behavioural Science* 44 (1): 50–58.

Denny, Harry, Enrique Paz, and Anna Sicari. 2017. Review of *The Working Lives of New Writing Center Directors*, by Nicole I. Caswell, Jackie Grutsch McKinney, and Rebecca Jackson. *Writing Center Journal* 35 (2): 303–313.

George, Jennifer M. 1991. "State or Trait: Effects of Positive Mood on Prosocial Behaviors at Work." *Journal of Applied Psychology* 76 (2): 299–307.

Hochschild, Arlie Russell. 1979. "Emotion Work, Feeling Rules, and Social Structure." *American Journal of Sociology* 85 (3): 551–575.

Hochschild, Arlie Russell. 1983. *The Managed Heart: Commercialization of Human Feeling.* Berkeley: University of California Press.

Huang, Xu, Simon C.H. Chan, Wing Lam, and Xinsheng Nan. 2010. "The Joint Effect of Leader-Member Exchange and Emotional Intelligence on Burnout and Work Performance in Call Centers in China." *International Journal of Human Resource Management* 21 (7): 1124–1144.

Humphrey, Ronald H. 2012. "How Do Leaders Use Emotional Labor?" *Journal of Organizational Behavior* 33 (5): 740–744.

James, Nicky. 1989. "Emotional Labour: Skill and Work in the Social Regulation of Feelings." *Sociological Review* 37 (1): 15–42. https://doi.org/10.1111/j.1467-954X.1989.tb00019.x.

Joseph, Dana L., and Daniel A. Newman. 2010. "Emotional Intelligence: An Integrative Meta-Analysis and Cascading Model." *Journal of Applied Psychology* 95 (1): 54–78.

Kjesrud, Roberta D., and Mary A. Wislocki. 2011. "Learning and Leading through Conflicted Collaborations." *Writing Center Journal* 31 (2): 89–116.

Mackiewicz, Jo, and Isabelle Thompson. 2013. "Motivational Scaffolding, Politeness, and Writing Center Tutoring." *Writing Center Journal* 33 (1): 38–73.

Maxwell, Martha. 1991. "The Effects of Expectations, Sex, and Ethnicity on Peer Tutoring." *Journal of Developmental Education* 15 (1): 14–18.

McAndrew, Donald A., and Thomas J. Reigstad. 2001. *Tutoring Writing: A Practical Guide for Conferences.* Portsmouth, NH: Heinemann.

Meyer, Emily, and Louise Z. Smith. 1987. *The Practical Tutor.* Oxford: Oxford University Press.

Micciche, Laura R. 2002. "More Than a Feeling: Disappointment and WPA Work." *College English* 64 (4): 432–458.

Miller, Katherine I., James B. Stiff, and Beth Hartman Ellis. 1988. "Communication and Empathy as Precursors to Burnout among Human Service Workers." *Communication Monographs* 55 (3): 250–265.

Morris, J. Andrew, and Daniel C. Feldman. 1996. "The Dimensions, Antecedents, and Consequences of Emotional Labor." *Academy of Management Review* 21 (4): 986–1010. https://doi.org/10.2307/259161.

Newman, Daniel A., Dana L. Joseph, and Carolyn MacCann. 2010. "Emotional Intelligence and Job Performance: The Importance of Emotion Regulation and Emotional Labor Context." *Industrial and Organizational Psychology* 3 (2): 159–164.

Nicklay, Jennifer. 2012. "Got Guilt? Consultant Guilt in the Writing Center Community." *Writing Center Journal* 32 (1): 14–27.

North, Stephen M. 1984. "The Idea of a Writing Center." *College English* 46 (5): 433–446.

Petrides, K. V., and Adrian Furnham. 2006. "The Role of Trait Emotional Intelligence in a Gender-Specific Model of Organizational Variables." *Journal of Applied Social Psychology* 36 (2): 552–569.

Shkoler, Or, and Aharon Tziner. 2017. "The Mediating and Moderating Role of Burnout and Emotional Intelligence in the Relationship between Organizational Justice and Work Misbehavior." *Journal of Work and Organizational Psychology* 33 (2): 157–164.

Singh, Malika, and Stephen A. Woods. 2008. "Predicting General Well-Being from Emotional Intelligence and Three Broad Personality Traits." *Journal of Applied Social Psychology* 38 (3): 635–646.

Soven, Margot Iris. 2005. *What the Writing Tutor Needs to Know.* Belmont, CA: Wadsworth Thomson Learning.

Steinberg, Ronnie J., and Deborah M. Figart. 1999. "Emotional Labor since *The Managed Heart*." *Annals of the American Academy of Political and Social Science* 561 (1): 8–26.

Yanay, Niza, and Golan Shahar. 1998. "Professional Feelings as Emotional Labor." *Journal of Contemporary Ethnography* 27 (3): 346–373.

Zalewski, Jacqueline M., and Leigh S. Shaffer. 2011. "Advising Students to Value and Develop Emotional Labor Skills for the Workplace." *NACADA Journal* 31 (2): 44–54. https://doi.org/10.12930/0271-9517-31.2.44.

Zeidner, Moshe, Gerald Matthews, and Richard D. Roberts. 2009. *What We Know about Emotional Intelligence: How It Affects Learning, Work, Relationships, and Our Mental Health*. Cambridge, MA: MIT Press.

10
EMOTIONAL LABOR AND WRITING PROGRAM ADMINISTRATION AT RELIGIOUSLY AFFILIATED INSTITUTIONS

Elizabeth Imafuji
Anderson University

"I'm not exactly here to talk about turning a paper in late," said Allison,[1] my first-year composition student, a nineteen-year old female who had written in my class about her unstable home life. "There's something going on that might make me miss class sometimes." She paused. "I'm pregnant." Allison seemed nervous, and I thought she was likely to cling to every word I said in response.

I looked Allison right in the eye. I smiled. "Congratulations! A baby is always a blessing." She was visibly relieved at my words, then she grinned and relaxed in her seat. I had said the right thing.

Such a reaction was not natural for me. I don't normally throw around words like "blessing," and because Allison was young and I knew her living situation to be complicated, my gut reaction was to ask: "Are you okay? Are you safe? What are you going to do?" However, I knew from past experiences as a composition instructor and as writing program administrator (WPA) that I was probably one of the first professors she was telling; I have seen many cases when first-year composition (FYC) instructors are often among the first university staff students turn to for sharing their big, personal news, whether exciting or scary or painful. In this case, it must have been quite emotional for Allison to share her news with me. Not only was she young and new to college, but at my institution she may not have seen any other pregnant students in classes or around campus. I needed to consider how my words would affect Allison's emotions. If I seemed worried, how might she feel? I needed to respond in a way that made her feel accepted.

Complicating matters was the institutional setting where Allison and I were student and professor. I teach at a Christian church–affiliated small liberal arts college, a school that has nurtured me as a teacher and scholar and that often supports students in a holistic manner. However, similar to many church-affiliated schools, my institution has developed and enforces a student conduct code that governs many aspects of the students' personal lives. Not all students or faculty find this code to be equitable or fair.

Because Allison was unmarried and pregnant, I was concerned about her possibly facing sanctions for "sex outside of marriage." Would she be required to have a humiliating meeting with the dean's office? Would she be punished in some way? I didn't know. As I did my best to consider Allison's emotions as I spoke with her, I was feeling conflicted about my institution.

"Should I tell my other professors?" Allison asked after she told me about her experiences finding out she was pregnant, calling her parents, and seeing a doctor. As I suspected, I was the first university employee to be informed; I was a trial run for informing other professors and staff. She was scheduled for several doctor appointments; she figured if she told her professors, they would be understanding about the missed classes. Yet, she said, she was very anxious since she didn't know what kind of reaction she might receive.

Again, I carefully weighed my words in responding to this question. Allison was worried about professors shaming her, but I was concerned about reactions from the Student Life Department. If I said she should keep the pregnancy to herself to stall the code of conduct issues for as long as possible, then perhaps she would she feel rejected or scolded. Furthermore, if I suggested waiting to tell and the university administration found out, would I be seen as subversive? Perhaps it would seem I was meddling with the Student Life Department side of the university. I realized I was not certain which offices I could refer Allison to that would be required to keep confidentiality. Was I saying the right thing?

WRITING PROGRAM ADMINISTRATION AND RELIGIOUSLY AFFILIATED INSTITUTIONS

It may seem that concerns with church-related schools' student conduct codes are a niche problem for only a few WPAs. However, in the United States, there were 883 religiously affiliated postsecondary institutions as of fall 2015 (National Center for Education Statistics 2017). These schools cover a range of religions and denominations and represent a variety of institution types, not all of them undergraduate. Yet within just a 60-mile radius of my institution, there are four Christian, undergraduate, liberal arts colleges that have similarly strict student codes.

While "Allison" is a composite character, at these institutions we regularly see students who are facing similar emotionally intense choices that are in conflict with religious schools' codes or missions. These types of church-affiliated schools also may expect that faculty strongly support the institution's mission, and they can require faculty to sign faith statements or even maintain membership in a certain type of church. Thus if faculty disagree with administration about faith-related or church-mandated issues, it can cause tension and require managing emotions for the faculty and for the administrators tasked with upholding institution policies.

This chapter will discuss the needs of WPAs at religiously affiliated schools, especially those with strict student codes. To succeed in such contexts, a WPA should understand rules of student conduct and religious expectations of students and should plan to collaborate with other offices to balance faculty, student, and administration expectations. To reduce their own emotional labor and that of their composition faculty, WPAs should offer training in how to respond to students seeking emotional support, and they should ground that training in the mission and religion of the institution. Helpful self-care practices for WPAs at religious institutions will also be suggested.

SUPPORTING FIRST-YEAR STUDENTS

For both faculty and WPAs, emotional labor often stems from the desire to support first-year students well. Thus the first steps in addressing emotional labor are understanding why students are turning to their composition professors to discuss their emotional distress and mental health issues and learning what these students are seeking when they do so.

Faculty at small residential institutions may be approached by their students for help in personal matters more often than faculty at other types of institutions. In a study of seventy-two schools, Sarah Ketchen Lipson and her coauthors (2015) found that the highest rate of help-seeking for students with mental health issues was at small, private, highly residential campuses and the lowest rate at lower or non-residential, large public universities. At small private colleges, prospective students and their parents are typically marketed the idea that faculty and staff are accessible and relatable; parents are told that if their child has a problem, there will be professors who know them from the small classes and close-knit community, and it will be easy for students to connect and find help.

At Christian schools, students' religious beliefs may be a contributing factor as well, helping to explain why students seek out faculty instead of mental health professionals when they wish to talk about mental or emotional distress. Eric D. Wesselmann and William G. Graziano (2010) and Steve Sullivan and his coauthors (2014) found that some more fundamentalist Christians tend to not believe there are mental health or emotional issues, only spiritual issues; or if they believe mental illness is real, they think it results from a lack of faith and requires a spiritual cure only. While my university and its affiliated denomination do encourage people to seek the mental health care they need, the student population includes Christians from more conservative faith traditions. Some of those students might be avoiding counseling services because they feel it is not spiritual to seek such help. In addition to all the other reasons a student might avoid visiting counseling services, these students may believe that Christians should not seek counseling at all but should seek only spiritual guidance and prayer. Thus they may be coming to their professor instead of to a counselor because initially, they trust the professor more.

Yet at any type of institution, many students need someone to listen. An increasing portion of students need mental health support and do receive it from their counseling center: the Center for Collegiate Mental Health (2017, 4) reports that nationwide during the years 2010–2015, counseling center utilization increased by an average of 30–40 percent, while enrollments only increased by 5 percent. First-year students in particular may be likely to experience distress. Terry L. Gall, David R. Evans, and Satya Bellerose (2000) found that college entry causes stress across three areas of first-year students' life: the domains of academics, living, and dating. During this time of adjustment, students are "faced with a multiplicity of changes and demands within several areas of their life simultaneously at a time when regular sources of support (e.g., family) were less available" (561). Some of the social support to replace what is left behind at home may be coming from first-year writing instructors. These instructors teach small classes and develop relationships through individual conferences, responses to student writing, and in-class interactions. These factors may result in the FYC instructor being the first campus representative who is contacted by a student with emotional or mental health concerns, even students who will eventually receive services from the campus counseling center. Furthermore, the increase in counseling center usage and the need for composition instructors to support distressed students exist even without a recent campus trauma. In this volume, Kaitlin Clinnin's and

Carl Schlachte's chapters discuss the acute increase in students needing support from their instructors and instructors needing support from the WPA in the aftermath of a crisis.

Professors and WPAs are correct if they point out that people in our field are not trained mental health counselors and need to be referring students to licensed professionals. Discussing mental health and emotional distress is not our expertise; teaching writing is. However, as Louise A. Douce and Richard P. Keeling (2014, 1) succinctly point out, "Mental and behavioral health problems are learning problems." As we interact with students, some of them will inevitably be talking to us about their emotional and mental health issues, so instructors and WPAs must keep up with the latest best practices in responding to distressed students. WPAs do not need to figure out this training alone but should develop collaborations with other departments on campus and in the community for referring students and helping connect them with support. Collaborations and training for instructors can not only help students but can also reduce some of the faculty's and the WPA's emotional labor.

UNDERSTANDING THE EMOTIONAL LABOR OF COMPOSITION FACULTY

As I carefully managed my expression of emotions in my conversation with Allison about her pregnancy, I was engaging in emotional labor. Theresa M. Glomb and Michael J. Tews's (2004) model for emotional labor distinguishes among three types of emotional expression in the workplace: genuine, faking, and suppression. In the conversation with Allison, I engaged in faking emotions as I mustered up happiness and enthusiasm for her pregnancy, and I also suppressed my feelings of worry and concern. While it may have been an appropriate way to respond to a situation like Allison's, this manner of managing emotions has been shown to negatively affect workers. Kevin T. Mahoney and his coauthors (2011) studied American college professors' emotional labor and found that faking positive emotions and suppressing negative emotions had adverse effects, including increased emotional exhaustion and decreased job satisfaction. Mahoney and colleagues (2011, 407) point out that professors typically do not receive formal training in relating to students and "may expect to be able to express their felt emotions. When they cannot, and instead fake or suppress emotions, negative outcomes are likely." Responding to students like Allison has always been exhausting for me, and my emotions surrounding such student reactions are not contained to just the hour or so I meet with a student. I replay the student conversation in my mind, questioning whether I hid my worry well enough, whether I responded with just the right expression, whether I said something I should not have said. Each time I see the student in class, some of the emotions arise again as I look for signs of whether they are coping well but know I cannot openly show concern for the student in front of others.

Faculty are likely to be trained in some aspects of responding to students. They learn to follow the Family Educational Rights and Privacy Act and keep confidentiality; they know to follow Title IX federal laws if a student worker reports sexual harassment. Yet faculty are likely to also find themselves in conversations with students discussing nuanced issues that are not easily covered by generalized human resources onboarding trainings, and these conversations can require that the faculty engage in significant amounts of emotional labor. My story about Allison is written from my perspective as instructor and illustrates one type of the many situations that may cause first-year students to approach their FYC professors to discuss very personal information. In seeking the right way to respond to such disclosures, faculty can find themselves bound by rules and attitudes we do not agree with or fully understand as we negotiate student emotions, our own emotions and values, and the institution's codes and administration.

At any institution, faculty may disagree with the administration, but the tensions can be even higher and the expectations even trickier to navigate at religiously affiliated colleges and universities. At my institution, the mission and statement of faith are fairly general, so faculty may assume there will be few causes for conflict with the administration's religious stance. Anderson University is affiliated with the Church of God (Anderson, Indiana), a non-creedal Protestant denomination. The university's mission is "to educate for a life of service in the church and society," and the institutional statement of church affiliation emphasizes that the university is "established and sustained within the free and open traditions of the Church of God." Faculty are generally expected to self-identify as some kind of Christian, but otherwise they do not submit to a list of behavioral expectations or sign a lengthy theological statement. There are two principal parts to the statement of faith faculty sign when they are hired. First, faculty should hold "a belief in and commitment to Jesus Christ and the Christian faith as these are interpreted through the historic witness of the Bible and the contemporary ministry of the Holy Spirit"—a statement designed to be as inclusive of all Christian denominations as possible. Furthermore, faculty should also possess "a vitality of Christian experience which is maturing in insight and application and which is appreciative of differing viewpoints." There is no list of appropriate denominations faculty must attend, and the university has always employed faculty from a variety of Catholic, Protestant, and Orthodox denominations as well as some non-church attenders. With the emphasis on "free and open traditions" and "differing viewpoints" within Christianity, Anderson attracts faculty who would be wary of working at a more fundamentalist institution.

However, students are less likely to feel that the institution is "free and open." Unlike faculty, students are bound by the student handbook and its detailed code of conduct. For example, students are barred from drinking, serving, or being in the presence of alcohol, even when they are of legal age. The student code also governs students' sex lives; all "premarital or extramarital sexual behavior" is against the code. Students are prohibited from cohabitating with a partner. If discovered, these and many other behaviors would result in disciplinary proceedings, including meeting with Student Life staff, fines, letters sent home to parents, or expulsion. Religious education is mandated; students are fined if they do not attend the required number of chapel worship sessions, and they cannot graduate without the two required classes in Christian theology. Based on all these regulations and requirements, some students feel the institution is too insistent and forceful in promoting religious beliefs and regulating behavior.

Once faculty learn about the strict student code and start to hear stories about how students experience my institution's religion, some may begin to feel tension and negative emotions about the interpretation of Christianity that seems to be forced on some students. Insight into how to address these feelings can be found in composition scholarship that has focused on instructor emotions in response to students' religion-centered writing. Juanita M. Smart (2005, 15, 13) recounts how she felt "cornered by the nonnegotiable terms" of a particular evangelical student's rhetoric, which was "a type of religious discourse that was silencing" for Smart during her own youth in evangelical churches. In response, Smart reflects on her own history with religion and on her current religious faith, and she considers how it affects her response to her student's faith-based argument. She encourages instructors to "interrogate" their own religious beliefs (22), to understand why they react to students' religious beliefs in certain ways, and to help students integrate their faith with learning. Douglas Downs discusses a student's homophobic essay and his own "indignant reaction" to that work. Downs (2005, 39) felt "frustrated" that the student engaged in religious dogma as an academic argument; he suggests that instructors reading similar work might feel "impatience, disagreement, and even dejection." Downs then explores useful stances for composition instructors to adopt when there is "discursive conflict," such as guide, translator, mentor, or coach. Both Smart and Downs demonstrate that instructor emotions, even if initially negative, can serve as an impetus for reflection and can lead to a more productive relationship to students' faith-centered discourse. So, too, could instructors' reactions to their institution's religious teachings and restrictions bring up emotions that urge faculty toward beneficial self-reflection and a possible reframing of the conflict. Faculty thus can benefit from writing program training about the religious university's mission and statement of faith.

EMOTIONAL LABOR AND WRITING PROGRAM ADMINISTRATORS AT RELIGIOUSLY AFFILIATED INSTITUTIONS

Instructors untrained in how to respond to conversations with students in distress often turn to their writing program administrator for advice, thus precipitating similar emotional labor for the WPA who must to some extent give the administration's point of view, despite any personal opinions about the student code of conduct. Since the WPA oversees faculty who teach nearly all the university's first-year students, this situation can be frequent and become emotionally draining. In their study of writing center directors, Nicole I. Caswell, Jackie Grutsch McKinney, and Rebecca Jackson (2016, 27) identify emotional labor as "work that invokes care, mentoring, or nurturing of others; work of building and sustaining relationships; work to resolve conflicts; managing our display of emotion." They found that mentoring, relationship building, and gaining trust, among many other tasks, involved emotional labor. These tasks are part of the daily work of writing program directors as well. Not only must they speak for the university, WPAs must also maintain the trust of the faculty member seeking advice and consider the long-term working relationship with that person. In all of these tasks, there is the potential for a WPA to find that their personal commitments conflict with the official university position, and emotional labor can increase in response. Mara Holt, Leon Anderson, and Albert Rouzie (2003, 154) discuss the contradictions WPAs can face when speaking on behalf of the university, against their own beliefs. Emotions they aren't "supposed to" feel are "outlaw emotions," and trying to control them could be a particularly onerous form of emotional labor. These outlaw emotions can stem from "the awkward and ambivalent role that WPAs frequently must play as designated advocates for existing policies that they had no part in creating and with which they don't fully agree" (156). Alice Gillam (2003, 117) describes part of the emotional labor of her WPA position as being compelled to "induce certain feelings and suppress others." When faculty feel they must consult with the WPA for the official university position or the right procedure to follow, the WPA does not have the benefit of the relationship with the student or the feeling of directly helping the student to sustain that work.

Particularly for faculty working at church-affiliated small colleges, these conversations may cause them to feel conflicted about religious-based expectations from administrators. The faculty who serve my writing program have come to me seeking advice for how to respond to students in many situations involving the student code. We have discussed how to respond to a student who wrote about considering an abortion. "There's no way I'm going to get involved in this; surely I'm not expected to?" one instructor implored. In another instance, a composition instructor was upset when a student wrote about their job working in a bar, a job that is explicitly forbidden in the student code because it is antithetical to the church's teetotaling roots. The instructor asked: "Should I explain to the student why they should keep this job a secret? I'll feel subversive if I do. But if the student gets in trouble, I'll feel guilty for not mentioning it. I really wish the student had not written about this." In examples such as these, I do my best to explain the religious reasoning for policies without revealing my own opinions, and then I present faculty with their options. Because I have collaborated with other departments of the university to learn the details of the student code of conduct, the institution's expectations for faculty to uphold that code, and the options for preserving student privacy, I now have the knowledge to offer faculty a variety of ways to respond to students, more so than I did in my early days as WPA.

COLLABORATING WITHOUT COMPROMISING PRIVACY

When Allison, pregnant and living with her boyfriend against school rules, asked me whether she should inform her other professors of her pregnancy, I said it was up to her. She did tell at least one other professor because a few days later a colleague in another department confronted me in my office: "Allison told me she's pregnant. She said she told you first. Are you going to report it?" Report it? To whom and why? My colleague had confused Title IX-based mandatory reporting of sexual harassment—not an issue in this case—with our institution's student code of conduct. As a result of misunderstanding the rules, my colleague told Allison that faculty were required to report her to the dean of students for breaking the rules about extramarital sex and that either that faculty member or someone else would be doing so. "No, we are not supposed report that our student is pregnant." Was I sure? "I'm 100 percent sure. I've talked to the dean about this." My colleague backed down, and I was reminded how tricky it can be for faculty to know where to refer students and what the ramifications might be for referring or reporting. Students are told to reach out if they need help, but faculty are not typically provided with enough training to respond when they do.

Students naturally do not understand the ins and outs of what faculty know and how we can help them. Allison was upset when the faculty member said her pregnancy would be reported: "Why would my professor threaten to tell on me? I felt so judged. This is a Christian university, and everyone should be supporting me." I apologized for my colleague's misunderstanding, confirmed again that Allison was healthy and had support, and listened to how her day was going. Allison was now in the habit of stopping by to chat every week or so, and she seemed to believe me when I said the other faculty member was mistaken and not malicious.

Key to my confidence in declaring that we did not need to report Allison to the dean of students was the fact that I had already been in conversations with various administrators on the Student Affairs side of the university to learn what faculty are expected to do when students are in need of support and how faculty could better collaborate with these offices. Approaching the dean of students for advice about training composition faculty was not something I had considered in my first few years as WPA, immersed as I was in the logistics of composition placement, enrollment, and assessment. However, over time, questions from instructors about what they should do in response to student distress added up. Even just a few intense and unusual situations per term took an emotional toll as I scrambled to figure out how to help in each case. Eventually, I set up a meeting with the dean. I brought a list of a few hypothetical scenarios and talked through each one to find out whether the faculty member would have been expected to report the situation to the administration, whether the reporting would have been confidential, and what kind of help would have been offered to the students.

I was pleasantly surprised at the dean's willingness to talk through all of my questions and training ideas. I learned that the dean of students does not expect or even request that faculty report on students who have violated the code of conduct—as long as no Title IX violation or violence or other egregious situations are involved. Some of my worry over telling faculty that they did not need to report students had been unfounded, as had been some of my angst over whether faculty could be reprimanded for expressing disagreement with the university's religious requirements for students: "As a professor you aren't a counselor, but you can offer your own wise counsel to students." I learned about the ways to refer students while keeping their privacy. Health services can connect students with services for sexual or maternal health while maintaining confidentiality, and counseling services and the campus pastor also maintain confidentiality. If faculty fill out an online "early alert report" about distressed students, though, this method does not maintain total confidentiality free from disciplinary proceedings. However, filling out this "early alert" form can be easier on faculty. A Student Life committee performs the triage for each report, so faculty do not need to decide on our own where to refer students, thus lessening the emotional burden.

I did not leave the meeting with the dean of students any more in agreement with some of the rules or interpretations of Christianity that I had questioned in the first place. I and some of the writing program faculty will still face some dilemmas of conscience about what to say to and do for some students in distress. However, I did leave with new strategies, both for receiving assistance from the staff in the dean's office and for helping distressed students without necessarily contacting that office. Those strategies were then wrapped into writing program training for new instructors.

Because so many first-year composition students are seeking support about mental health issues, I next sought out information from the director of counseling services. She provided me and other campus leaders with resources to train others in how to assist depressed or anxious students, how to respond to students contemplating suicide, and how to handle other all-too-common student issues. I also met and learned the name of the office manager for counseling services intake at my school, so I am now able to mention her by name when I talk to students and instructors, and I can assure everyone that she runs a welcoming office. Rather than being territorial, the dean of student's staff and counseling services staff provided me with information I could use during writing program trainings and were responsive to ideas for helping faculty help students.

REDUCING AND COPING WITH EMOTIONAL LABOR

Training in how to report and refer, along with knowledge about the university's mission, can reduce emotional labor for both composition faculty and the WPA. If instructors already know what they are required to report, where they should refer, and the options for community services, then they will not have to check with the WPA as often. Instead of requiring the WPA to react to an instructor struggling to help a student, training conveys information in a proactive manner so that fewer emotions need to be managed during communication of the information. Certainly, faculty or the WPA may also wish to work for change, to convince administration to alter the student conduct rules that seem the most unfair or that cause the most conflicts of conscience for faculty. Yet by reducing faculty and WPA emotional labor as much as possible within the current policies and rules, more energy and emotional resources would be left to work toward change.

Such training must be tailored to the local community, with plenty of input from licensed mental health professionals. The following concepts should be considered for this training:

- Useful things to say in response to students disclosing painful emotions and trauma
- Discussion of situations that call for referral to the counseling center
- Logistics for the campus counseling center
- Suicide-risk protocol
- May-harm-others protocol
- Situations that call for referral to Student Affairs/dean of students
- Confidentiality and privacy concerns when sharing information
- At religiously affiliated institutions: explanation of the faith-centered regulations, rules, and statements most likely to cause student and faculty distress.

Most of my writing program faculty have undergone this training; new faculty have all been trained in this system and have expressed relief at having the information. Within the writing program, our attitude now seems to be more strategic and less urgent when we discuss helping our distressed students. Personally, the process of collaborating with Student Affairs and then training faculty has decreased some of my own anxiety and concern about students in the writing program because I feel the faculty and I are prepared to respond well when they need support.

Religious information should also be addressed in writing program training at applicable institutions, especially because there will always be conflicts between some instructors' personal religious beliefs and those espoused by the university. Even if the instructor agrees completely with the statement of faith when hired, personal faith may develop over time, or policies or administration may change. In instances of religious disagreement, the university mission and statements of faith and church affiliation can provide a useful framework for continuing to value working at the institution. Kristine Johnson (2014, 87) urges WPAs to focus more on their institution's mission: "When WPAs discuss institutional context, we often focus on internal machinations and politics that must be negotiated . . . Shifting this discussion to mission gives WPAs a fuller way to think about what we and our institutions do in the world." At Anderson University, the "free and open traditions" of the Church of God and the university's "appreciation of different viewpoints" provide me with a foundation for talking to faculty who disagree with particular aspects of the student code. The contradictions are built into the system to an extent, since the university purposefully hires faculty from a variety of Christian faith traditions but then holds students to some traditional Evangelical rules, so there is no need to feel disloyal or hypocritical when disagreeing. Thus I have found it useful to provide this information about church history beliefs to new instructors, especially those without any previous connection to the affiliated denomination. Knowing the rationale and the history behind faith-centered regulations, rules, and statements can help faculty reflect on their place in the institution and their role as educators at a mission-driven institution. When faculty fully understand the religious commitments of the institution and how to work within and around them, they may require less emotional labor from the WPA in the form of conflict resolution, nurturing, and mentoring.

Writing program administrators at religiously affiliated institutions should also allow themselves the time to explore their university's mission, reflect on their own faith, and consider their reasons for working at that institution. This exploration and reflection is valuable work that contributes to a sense of purpose and can lead to job satisfaction; thus it should be considered a type of professional self-care. It can also inspire and motivate writing program research, assessment, and professional development. Lizabeth A. Rand (2001), Michael-John DePalma (2011), and Jeffrey M. Ringer (2013) argue for the importance of taking students' religious beliefs seriously, as such beliefs can constitute an important part of student identity and be valuable resources for their understanding of discourse, rhetoric, and language. In addition, the religious orientation of the faith-based university is also worthy of the WPA's attention. Institutional mission affects discourse, literacy, and education as well, and the time invested in understanding a religious institution's mission and its impact on students and faculty is certainly relevant to the writing program director position. My institution does support the concept of faith development as work. In my annual report, I account for time spent attending university chapel sessions and supporting spiritual activities on campus. I have received professional development funds from the university to participate in meetings and conferences about teaching at religious institutions. My publication in such a conference's proceedings, in which I discussed integrating faith and teaching, counted as a scholarly work for promotion. Furthermore, I give myself permission to feel proud of faith-centered work and to count it as part of my usually eight-hour workday, just as I do other parts of my job. Embracing all or part of an institution's religious mission and serving as program director for others as they negotiate their own relationship to that mission is a significant duty and should be carefully attended to and accounted for when WPAs report on their year's work.

Both faculty and WPAs at any institution who engage in high amounts of emotional labor should consider developing a self-care plan, similar to those commonly used by social workers (see Lee and Miller 2013). For faculty at religiously affiliated institutions, there may be increased emotional labor around religious mission and rules, but at such institutions faculty typically can easily access opportunities for spiritual self-care. Weekly chapel sessions may provide an opportunity to sing as a large group, a practice known to be beneficial for mood and social bonding (Weinstein et al. 2016), and to listen to speakers who are known to be inspiring or encouraging. I take time to visit campus quiet places for meditation and writing; my small campus includes two prayer chapels, a prayer alcove, and a prayer labyrinth—all of which I have used for brief meditation (see Christy I. Wenger's chapter, this volume, for a full discussion of the benefits of mindfulness practices). Religious institutions also offer opportunities to join community reading groups or prayer groups and provide other ways of connecting in community with others. The religiously affiliated institution can demand of faculty an emotional investment, but it also provides opportunities for healthy coping behaviors.

As part of their own coping mechanism, composition instructors can often count on the WPA as a person with whom to debrief after an emotionally charged class session or meeting with a student, but for the WPA, there is no equivalent built-in listener. Not only will WPAs who teach experience their own student-related emotional labor, but they also perform the labor of compassionately helping composition instructors through difficult student situations. Thus a WPA must turn to friends, family members, or a therapist to debrief. I have found it beneficial to talk through such issues with a friend who is the chair of another department on campus because they understand the institutional context and cultivating cross-campus friendships has helped me feel positive, rather than burned out, about my workplace.

CONCLUSION

A writing program administrator cannot save instructors from all of the emotional labor involved in listening to students under distress; nor can they prevent instructors from having conflicts with the religious doctrines or expectations of a religiously affiliated institution. Yet writing program training can help instructors respond confidently to students if it prepares instructors for some of the reasons students will likely be seeking support. Especially when that training addresses the mission and religious history of the institution, it may prevent the WPA from needing to be involved as often when students disclose emotional situations to their instructors. Collaboration with other offices that serve distressed students can further reduce the WPA's work in facilitating student referrals to services and supporting instructors through difficult conversations. Still, the WPA will at times need to fake or suppress emotions in order to represent the administration's or the denomination's point of view on religious requirements for students. Along with healthy self-care practices, reflecting on the institution's mission—asking why we still support what this school aims to do—can help sustain WPAs through these times.

One afternoon as the sun streamed through my office window, Allison approached my office, pushing a baby stroller. "Professor Imafuji, this is Sam," she beamed, introducing me to her tiny, beautiful infant. I had been looking forward to this afternoon for days, ever since Allison emailed to say she would be on campus with her new baby, making arrangements to make up the work she missed while out for maternity leave. As we talked, Allison did not thank me for emotionally supporting her when she chatted with me about her pregnancy worries or her struggles with her professors. She did not say she appreciated how I helped make sure her pregnancy was kept quiet until she chose to officially reveal it to the university administration. She had simply expected that I or any other professor would do those things in response to a nineteen-year-old worried student disclosing her unexpected pregnancy. However, Allison's high level of trust in me was apparent when she visited my office just to show off her child and when she handed baby Sam to me to hold. I did not pray for the baby or say anything overtly religious, as such expressions have never been my habit when chatting with students, but I hoped Allison felt a measure of Christian love in my manner of relating to her as she sought support through times of distress and joy.

NOTE

1. Allison is a composite character drawn from multiple situations I have encountered.

REFERENCES

Caswell, Nicole I., Jackie Grutsch McKinney, and Rebecca Jackson. 2016. *The Working Lives of Writing Center Directors*. Logan: Utah State University Press.

Center for Collegiate Mental Health. 2017. *2017 Annual Report*. University Park: Pennsylvania State University. https://sites.psu.edu/ccmh/files/2018/01/2017_CCMH_Report-1r3iri4.pdf.

DePalma, Michael-John. 2011. "Re-envisioning Religious Discourses as Rhetorical Resources in Composition Teaching: A Pragmatic Response to the Challenge of Belief." *College Composition and Communication* 63 (2): 219–243.

Douce, Louise A., and Richard P. Keeling. 2014. *A Strategic Primer on College Student Mental Health*. Washington, DC: American Council on Education, Student Affairs Administrators in Higher Education, and American Psychological Association. https://www.apa.org/pubs/newsletters/access/2014/10-14/college-mental-health.pdf.

Downs, Douglas. 2005. "True Believers, Real Scholars, and Real True Believing Scholars: Discourses of Inquiry and Affirmation in the Composition Classroom." In *Negotiating Religious Faith in the Composition Classroom*, edited by Elizabeth Vander Lei and bonnie lenore kyburz, 39–55. Portsmouth, NH: Heinemann.

Gall, Terry L., David R. Evans, and Satya Bellerose. 2000. "Transition to First-Year University: Patterns of Change in Adjustment across Life Domains and Time." *Journal of Social and Clinical Psychology* 19 (4): 544–567. doi:10.1521/jscp.2000.19.4.544.

Gillam, Alice. 2003. "Collaboration, Ethics, and the Emotional Labor of WPAs." In *A Way to Move: Rhetorics of Emotion and Composition Studies*, edited by Dale Jacobs and Laura R. Micciche, 113–123. Portsmouth, NH: Boynton/Cook.

Glomb, Theresa M., and Michael J. Tews. 2004. "Emotional Labor: A Conceptualization and Scale Development." *Journal of Vocational Behavior* 64 (1): 1–23. doi:10.1016/S0001-8791(03)00038-1.

Holt, Mara, Leon Anderson, and Albert Rouzie. 2003. "Making Emotion Work Visible in Writing Program Administration." In *A Way to Move: Rhetorics of Emotion and Composition Studies*, edited by Dale Jacobs and Laura R. Micciche, 147–160. Portsmouth, NH: Boynton/Cook.

Johnson, Kristine. 2014. "Writing Program Assessment and the Mission-Driven Institution." *WPA: Writing Program Administration* 37 (2): 68–90.

Lee, Jacquelyn J., and Shari E. Miller. 2013. "A Self-Care Framework for Social Workers: Building a Strong Foundation for Practice." *Families in Society: The Journal of Contemporary Social Services* 94 (2): 96–103.

Lipson, Sarah Ketchen, S. Michael Gaddis, Justin Heinze, Kathryn Beck, and Daniel Eisenberg. 2015. "Variations in Student Mental Health and Treatment Utilization across US Colleges and Universities." *Journal of American College Health* 63 (6): 388–396. doi:10.1080/07448481.2015.1040411.

Mahoney, Kevin T., Walter C. Buboltz Jr., John E. Buckner V, and Dennis Doverspike. 2011. "Emotional Labor in American Professors." *Journal of Occupational Health Psychology* 16 (4): 406–423.

National Center for Education Statistics. 2017. "Fall Enrollment and Number of Degree-Granting Postsecondary Institutions, by Control and Religious Affiliation of Institution: Selected Years, 1980 through 2015." Table 303.90. https://nces.ed.gov/programs/digest/d16/tables/dt16_303.90.asp.

Rand, Lizabeth A. 2001. "Enacting Faith: Evangelical Discourse and the Discipline of Composition Studies." *College Composition and Communication* 52 (3): 349–367.

Ringer, Jeffrey M. 2013. "The Consequences of Integrating Faith into Academic Writing: Casuistic Stretching and Biblical Citation." *College English* 75 (3): 270–297.

Smart, Juanita M. 2005. "Frankenstein or Jesus Christ? When the Voice of Faith Creates a Monster for the Composition Teacher." In *Negotiating Religious Faith in the Composition Classroom*, edited by Elizabeth Vander Lei and bonnie lenore kyburz, 11–23. Portsmouth, NH: Heinemann.

Sullivan, Steve, Jeffrey M. Pyne, Ann M. Cheney, Justin Hunt, Tiffany F. Haynes, and Greer Sullivan. 2014. "The Pew versus the Couch: Relationship between Mental Health and Faith Communities and Lessons Learned from a VA/Clergy Partnership Project." *Journal of Religion and Health* 53 (4): 1267–1282.

Weinstein, Daniel, Jacques Launay, Eiluned Pearce, Robin I.M. Dunbar, and Lauren Stewart. 2016. "Singing and Social Bonding: Changes in Connectivity and Pain Threshold as a Function of Group Size." *Evolution and Human Behavior* 37 (2): 152–158.

Wesselmann, Eric D., and William G. Graziano. 2010. "Sinful and/or Possessed? Religious Beliefs and Mental Illness Stigma." *Journal of Social and Clinical Psychology* 29 (4): 402–437.

SECTION III

Preserving Balance

11
ADMINISTRATING WHILE BLACK
Negotiating the Emotional Labor of an African American Female WPA

Sheila Carter-Tod
Virginia Tech

Sometime early on in my seven years of working as a writing program administrator (WPA), I started to question how my experience may be similar to or different from that of other WPAs. While I found a great deal of general information about being a WPA, I found very little about the experience of being an African American female WPA. Then, after attending the Council of Writing Program Administrators (CWPA) conference for many years and even teaching in the pre-conference workshop, I became acutely aware of how few African American WPAs there were. Collin Lamont Craig and Staci Perryman-Clark (2001, 38) describe this invisibility as follows: "As first-time attendees of one of the CWPA conferences, we noticed the limited representation of people of color, and we were left to wonder why. When and where do we enter this conversation and how might we be more visibly represented in CWPA?"

While I know there may have been African American WPAs who chose not to attend the conference (which is a question for a different piece), I also know that there really are not that many of us. The point that "people of color are underrepresented in the field of Writing Studies" (Garcia de Mueller and Ruiz 2017, 21) has been established and reiterated by numerous scholars and WPAs of color (see Craig and Perryman-Clark 2011; Green 2016; Kynard 2015). This lack of representation, according to Genevieve Garcia de Mueller and Iris Ruiz (2017, 21), has led to a "lack of attention to race in Writing Studies journals, conference spaces, and professional organizational policy." They go on to describe how this absence has a direct influence on the knowledge produced by the field: "While contemporary scholarship often acknowledges race as an important factor to consider in the field, Writing Studies has yet to create a strong body of scholarship that focuses directly on race in WPA work or support systems for WPAs of color. In short, WPAs have yet to embed race as an integral criterion of their work" (23). It is with this recognition that I began to consider ways I could begin to record the stories of we—the few—African American female WPAs. I began the broader project of collecting our stories, struggles, and sustenance by identifying several individuals from very different higher educational institutions and with a range of WPA experience. I then sent out a query asking them if they would be willing to fill out a survey (see appendix to this chapter).

While I initially sent out the survey questions to seven individuals, my larger project goal was to expand that number. Then, based on those who were willing to allow me to do so, I would share the survey answers as base materials for conducting group phone calls to further discuss what had been written. In this chapter, I use my current survey answers (along with outside research) to recognize and analyze the emotional labor of African American female WPAs and to provide some strategies for negotiating the "things we carry."

Following a brief description of the participants in the study, I unpack why I have chosen and fully incorporated as many narratives as possible. Then, using outside research and the narratives, I explain the complexity of emotional labor specifically in respect to the intersectionality of race, gender, and administrative work—specifically in the institution of higher education. Finally, after describing/recognizing the "things we carry" or what emotional labor looks like for African American WPAs, I discuss some possible strategies for negotiation.

For this chapter, I am both researcher and participant. As such, I have woven my own experiences throughout the piece, incorporating my own narratives from my answers to the survey questions. As a result of my work and experiences, I must begin this chapter with the same disclaimer with which I conclude it, which is that strategies for negotiating the emotional labor of any person/people of color (in administration or otherwise) will not alleviate the comprehensive burden imposed by larger, institutionalized systems of racism and oppression. It is in no way my intention to claim that any strategies attempted by those of us within these structures will indeed "change the system"; I am not attempting to do that. What I am trying to do in this chapter is to first recognize the situation through the narratives of lived experiences of African American writing program administrators—expanding on the existing scholarship of the field. While some of our individual struggles connect to larger disciplinary and institutional issues, many have not been recognized, and the connections to the larger disciplinary and institutional issues are often different. This project, and subsequently this chapter, is my attempt to understand how and with whom my experiences did indeed connect and, in doing so, to broaden the larger discussions of emotional labor and explore possible sustainable negotiations for dealing with that labor.

THE PARTICIPANTS

The narratives I include are from five of the participants as well as my own. The participants from whom I gathered these data represent a range of educational environments and work experiences (both in the field of composition and rhetoric and in their work as WPAs). While I know it is important to understand the scope of who the participants are, it is also extremely important to be aware of the fact that there are so very few African American female WPAs, that to be too specific in the participant descriptions would compromise the anonymity of their narratives. With that said, I will give general descriptions to better contextualize both the narratives and my analysis. I will not associate the specifics of the narratives with any specific participant. For the consideration of educational and administrative understanding of the narratives, it is important to note that all of the participants are early- to mid-career professionals. They all have terminal degrees and are all in tenure-track positions. They all have teaching and research experience. They also have all been WPAs for at least two years. Two of the five participants are WPAs at larger, predominantly white institutions (PWIs), one at a mid-sized public PWI, one at a mid-sized private PWI, and one at a minority-serving institution.

THE STRUCTURE

I have focused on weaving together outside research with narrative evidence in order to, as Aja Y. Martinez (2014, 33) argues, "document the persistence of racism and other forms of subordination, [allowing] voices from the margins [to] become the voices of authority in the researching and relating of our own experiences." Martinez goes on to state that it is indeed "crucial to use a narrative methodology that counters other methods that seek to dismiss or decenter racism and those whose lives are affected daily by it" (33). By telling our stories, I am recognizing and documenting "the things we carry." By contextualizing our experiences in terms of larger institutional challenges and more specific disciplinary ones, I develop a foundation for understanding how our emotional labor is both unique and shared. Our narratives provide evidence of our individual stories, thereby testifying to our presence. And our narratives contribute to the growing body of knowledge on what emotional labor "looks like" in a very specific way while allowing for the proposed negotiations to be seen as both personal and at times more broadly universal.

COMPLICATING WHAT EMOTIONAL LABOR MEANS

The emotional labor negotiated by African American WPAs is characterized by the complexities of layered oppression, based on our intersectionality. In other words, while our narratives may indeed overlap with others—with whom we share common identity characteristics—ours are often illustrative of layered points of disadvantage enacted by multiple sources of oppression based on race, gender, institutional space, and academic position. Because of these intersectional layers of oppression and our work as writing program administrators, it is important to identify what I will be exploring as emotional labor. Emotional labor can be described by the sheer amount of uncompensated and unrecognized work associated with being a WPA and the emotional (and at times physical) burden or toll imposed (personally and professionally) for and by that labor. As I discuss later, this definition of emotional labor is further complicated by the intersectionality of our various identities—explored in this chapter as African American and female in institutions of higher education. For African American females and for many other peoples of color, this definition expands to include institutionalized systems of oppression that include barriers and exclusions, condescension and isolation, unacknowledged expertise and reduced validation, implied invisibility and failure to give adequate credit, displacement and denigration, unfair labor expectation and uncompensated labor, and the unclear and unrealistic performative expectations in light of all of these factors.

African American female WPAs function in an institutional space, with layers and layers of powerful institutional infrastructures—both articulated and not—that were specifically designed for the maintenance and advancement of people who are not like us. In other words, there are few, if any, institutional practices and spaces designed for the advancement of African American female administrators. Fredah Mainah and Vernita Perkins (2015, 5) unpack some of the challenges:

> Although female academicians of color are increasingly visible in leadership positions in higher education, the challenges that they contend with in order to achieve this status are not for the faint of heart. Challenges described in the literature include racial and gender bias at work . . . these

women bring a different level of knowing, pose different questions, and share different experiences . . . Unfortunately, [their] experiences do not yet factor into public policies and decision making.

They further describe such barriers and exclusions as "condescension, isolation, dismissal, communication challenges, lack of validation or appreciation, invisibility and failure to receive due credit" (7). Adia Wingfield contextualizes these challenges within predominately white institutions as issues that are similar to those of students of color at similar institutions. Wingfield's (2015, 4–5) study noted:

> Black female faculty were racially stereotyped at work, including being generally expected to entertain and perform for colleagues in ways that were not expected of their counterparts . . . This means that in practice, black faculty routinely face students, coworkers, and administrators who assume that they are not truly qualified for or capable of faculty work—all the while concealing the understandable feelings of frustration and annoyance that result. The overall message is that, like black students, black faculty simply do not belong.

And as stated by Carmen Kynard (2015, 3) when discussing the black female teacher in higher education, "the very theoretical paradigms in which we work often operate from a space that requires the displacement and denigration of black women."

ILLUSTRATIVE NARRATIVES OF THE THINGS WE CARRY

I begin with this point of institutional positionality and the ways it is complicated by race and gender because in the narratives, it constituted the bulk of the emotional labor. While all of the participants had been in higher education for some time, this sense of displacement and denigration was indeed heightened by the WPA position—the overall intersectionality of layered disadvantage of race, gender, and positionality (institutionally and professionally). As an African American WPA, instead of engendering a programmatic belonging, the higher visibility and larger responsibility of this administrative role only serves to exacerbate an existing sense of isolation and denigration. While sharing professional identities with other similarly titled administrators, the study participants expressed over and over again a difference in expectation and treatment, ranging from uncompensated labor to unacknowledged expertise. It is not uncommon to read such descriptions of emotional labor for WPAs; however, when overlapped with race and powerful unspoken attitudes and infrastructures, the emotional labor costs continue to add up—as does the need for strategies for negotiation.

The following narrative describes the emotional labor felt by one participant who was expected to perform uncompensated labor, in ways not expected of her counterparts.

Narrative one: I can distinctly remember when I began as a WPA, I wanted to make sure that I really had a good grip on the overall program and the people. I met with my chair to discuss my ideas and to get a sense of what sort of support I would have both administratively and financially. Luckily, there was a mechanism in place that allowed me to utilize a budget for professional development opportunities, speakers, incentive for instructor special projects, and (almost) anything else I deemed necessary for the program. I worked diligently throughout the summer, making sure that the program was well situated to kick off a comprehensive assessment project in the fall as well as making sure our GTA [graduate teaching assistant] program was established and ready to go. In addition, I conducted job searches to ensure all sections of first-year writing were covered. I was in constant contact with the department head, who relayed the needed undertakings of the program, in order to be prepared for fall.

By the time the summer was over, I had indeed worked the two-and-a-half months that is generally the time I use to conduct research or write. As a nine-month employee, this time was not only my time but also a needed time in order to have any sort of scholarly work while directing such a large program.

In the following fall, I happened to overhear the department head discussing the department budget and the summer stipends that were budgeted for the other program directors. This information came as somewhat of a surprise to me because no such offer or arrangement had been made for me. Upon further research, I found out that previous directors had all been given additional pay for the summer work that they did. When I asked my department head about this matter, the response that I was given was that it hadn't occurred to him to add the budget line item. I was further told that because I had jumped right into the job and seemed so happy with the work . . . the summer had slipped by without a thought as to "such details."

The only difference between the other program directors and the previous WPA and me was race. At the time, I was at such a loss for words that I was unable to formulate what seemed like an obvious question: What would make you decide to delete that line item from the budget if one existed for all other program directors and even the previous WPAs? While I cannot definitively say that the entire reason for the change was race-based, in hindsight, I had little to no other explanation for the obvious discrepancy. When at the end of the following year I did approach the department head about a summer stipend, I was asked to create an hourly estimate of the work that I would be doing. I thought that this must be a generic request, so I asked two of the other program directors for a model of what they used. Neither of them had any idea of what I was talking about. They said that they simply got a set stipend, and it was understood what responsibilities had to be covered during the summer. Again, while I have no proof that this particular practice was not race-based, it did make me questions my place as a director—the value of my work comparatively. I began to wonder why I was not treated as all other directors [were], particularly since my program was the largest in the department. I also began to feel both frustrated and marginalized, as if somehow my work as director was not seen as . . . equivalent to other directors.

Fair compensation as well as a programmatic working budget are often ways to ensure that a writing program and the director of that program are well sustained and productive. Conversely, the choice to deny a program or director adequate funding, by its very nature, implies an undervaluing of the program, the director, or both. Even in difficult budgetary times, departments and programs can advocate for and often secure funding for valued programs and personnel. When these basics are not provided, the assumption is that the WPA is expected to "perform" for "free" for the department. When such expectations are placed on an African American female WPA, the perception of support can easily be interpreted based on the intersectionality of identities of the individual. These perceptions become contributing factors to a devalued sense of the work and the self, as described in the narrative below.

Narrative two: I faced challenges like not having access to the program budget during my term as WPA. The budget was always a bigger deal than [I was]. When [an aspect of] my program was completed, a substantial amount of money dedicated for it was dismantled and placed in another area . . . I was notified that the program was terminated by email, and my salary was reduced tremendously. I never had a formal discussion about the impact the program was making at the university.

While these stories could be analyzed in multiple ways, the difference (and added emotional labor) for an African American female WPA (or any sort of administrator of color) comes from dealing with the sheer volume of such encounters and wrestling with how to read them. Such covert daily micro- and (and often not so covert) macro-aggressions slowly wear away at your professional identity because you begin to doubt yourself instead of the institutionalized constructs from which the people who impose them function. A wealth of information documents budget cuts and other institutional priorities that run contrary to WPAs being able to do their job well. Many of these forces internal and external to the university impact the emotional labor of the WPA; however, that labor is rarely placed at the lived, individual level, as described in narratives one and two. When administrating while black, these struggles feel personal—complicated by representing a (sometimes) marginalized discipline and being from a marginalized people group, explored more later in narrative three. While the emotional labor of working with limited or no programmatic support is real, it is only further complicated by the emotional labor associated with internal struggles with our own interpretation of these situations. In fact, on multiple occasions I have asked myself, Is this decision or behavior related to my race, my gender, or both, and if so, how? While explanations of these decisions exist outside of race or gender bias, the burden comes with finding ways to work in an environment that requires that you solve the needed administrative problem (functioning without sufficient support or funding) while wrestling with the reading of the situation and further having to regulate your reactions, responses, and decisions. Functioning in this environment becomes a constant juggling of emotional negotiations. The challenge to negotiating such burdens enacts an emotional and mental toll of self-doubt, which undermines your ability to lead/direct and function as a productive scholar.

Sorting through the tangled complexities of such situations creates an ever-present inertia of questioning the structural institutional racism not as separate from one's everyday duties but as present in every moment of the job, as described by Carmen Kynard (2015, 3):

> Racism, institutional and structural, is not about some kind of general and generic racially divided world somewhere out there over the rainbow. There is never any moment when racism is subtle or exists as some kind of fine mist that is out there but that I cannot fully see on campus. We need to stop talking about racism and institutions this way in our writing and to our students. Oppression could never work if it were invisible, unarticulated, or unfelt by those it targets.

The abovementioned burdens of negotiation are often further complicated by the fact that many WPAs work in isolation. This sense of isolation is well captured by Sheldon Walcher, Joseph Janangelo, and Duane Roen (2010, 87) when they state that "the day-to-day reality for many writing program administrators is a sense of deep isolation, particularly for those of us at institutions where the work of rhetoric and composition has been historically marginalized and continues to be undervalued." In the case of narrative three, this African American female's WPAs work to showcase the value of her composition program within the larger university led to its own contribution to complicating further individual marginalization.

Narrative three: I had to wonder where the marginalizing ended after our composition program won a prestigious university program award. This award recognized our composition program and faculty for developing and maintaining exemplary teaching and learning environments for students and faculty. The award also came with a program-based monetary honorarium. Because of the scope and reach of our composition program and because of the significantly strong instructional base, it seemed to me like a good fit. I brought the award to our department head's attention.

As plans moved forward for the banquet for accepting this award, our departmental administration moved forward in assembling the "right people" to attend this award reception. Interestingly enough, at no time was there any mention of anyone in our program or even anyone teaching composition being part of those who were to be present for the awards banquet. I mentioned my concern over this oversight to one of our departmental administrators. My institutional memory clearly brought me back to the fact that when another program within the department had won the award some three to four years earlier, that program director had indeed accepted the award at the reception and the money for that program was incorporated into that program's budget. I asked why the department chair planned to accept the award when it was not for the department more generally but more specifically for the composition program within the department. I was told that the department head is the "face" of the department and that this was not personal. I also asked why I was less of a "face for the department" than had been the director of the other program. I was also told that I was possibly being overly sensitive—looking for racial issues where there were none. My white female colleague went on to tell me that this probably says more for the status of the program I represent than it does about my being a black woman. What was I supposed to do when attending the reception? How was I expected to act? How was I to work with my feelings of anger for myself and my program?

Given the broader situated-ness of this experience, it would seem that not factoring in race and gender would be an insufficient way of reading this narrative. Even if the actions were indeed "unintentional," as mentioned before, such situations lead to a host of questions—both personal and professional—which in turn, over time, require a surveillance of behavior deemed appropriate to long-term survival in the department. If we react harshly, clearly pointing out the inconsistencies of the situation, we make others "uncomfortable." If we remain silent and withdraw, we are not active participants in the life of the program and the department. The isolation of the job of WPA coupled with the limited numbers of colleagues with shared experiences means we struggle with the questions and our reactions to the questions while pretending as if all is going well. This behavioral surveillance (regulation of what can and can't be said and how we are or are not allowed to react) leads to a performative normalcy—only further adding to the emotional labor. Marlese Durr and Adia Wingfield (2011) conducted a study that explored the effects of emotional labor on professional women. They first clarified that defining emotional labor should focus on not only the emotional labor but also the relationship of that emotional labor to the performative actions expected in light of it—what they call etiquette: "Etiquette and emotional labor for African American women is defined as performance to describe two levels of personal deportment: (1) a generalized bureaucratic passive aggressive level; and (2) a race-based set of expectations grounded in survival strategies to cope with challenges they face in environments that are unwelcoming" (559).

Durr and Wingfield's expansion of the definition of emotional labor to include the associated performative actions—emotional regulation—is not only illustrated in the above narrative but also helps to more clearly expand the definition of emotional labor. The "generalized bureaucratic passive aggressive level" described in narratives one and two—having to detail work for summer pay or having to function with no budget at all and with programmatic decisions made without consultation—moves beyond general feelings of self-doubt, devaluation, isolation, and marginalization to include the emotional labor of behavioral regulation that is associated with administrating while black and female. Durr and Wingfield (2011, 559, 564) go on to discuss how this emotional labor shapes not only our perceptions but also our reactions: "Working in predominantly white agencies, organizations, and institutions, while living and working as 'black,' may cause part of these women's apprehension and estrangement . . . For professional black women, the performances that they feel compelled to give are shaped by the ways intersections of race and gender isolate them and place them under greater scrutiny."

Narrative four clearly illustrates Durr and Wingfield's expanded consideration of emotional labor by bringing into question situations of behavior regulation. When we attend meetings, the challenge of when and how to speak becomes a complicated negotiation of factors. Ruchika Tulshyan (2015) points out that "regardless of industry, a much lesser proportion of women share their opinions or raise their voices at work when compared to men . . . Add in the complication of speaking as a woman of color, when prevailing stereotypes rear their ugly heads."

Narrative four. Our university was in a stage of expanding their undergraduate student population, which meant we were to expect a significantly larger incoming first-year class. Even with dual enrollment and AP credit, we would still need to be prepared for accommodating more students by opening more sections of composition. Because I had been working with colleagues outside our department who had been giving me the actual numbers of this growing incoming class, I knew that we would need to hire new instructors. I took my information to the department head, who told me the numbers that had been presented to all of the department heads at a meeting with the dean. I repeated the information that I had and requested moving forward with the hire of the needed instructors to accommodate this class. The department head ignored my request.

Later that week, I attended an administrators' meeting in which the department head quoted a higher number of enrollment—a number that he had been given by the dean as a possible [reason] to think about how it might impact the department's need for additional sections of composition. I reiterated that I had been given a much higher number from some colleges in enrollment services and that we would indeed need to hire additional instructors to accommodate numbers that I had been given. The department head ignored me, repeating that he had not been made aware of the numbers that I was presenting him with at the time.

Two months later, the enrollment number reached what I had mentioned to the department head months before; however, I was then expected to frantically hire, in late July, adjunct instructors to cover courses in August. I was so frustrated that the problem could have been avoided if I had been trusted to do my job. At no point did the chair actually say to me that I had been correct with the numbers that I had given to him months before. Nor did he apologize for the situation that his ignoring my information created for me, [for] those being hired at the last minute, [and for] others impacted by his choice to ignore my information.

I often wonder if it is because of the ways in which I present information that makes it such that . . . I am not heard. This situation is not uncommon. In meetings, what I say is often ignored, only to have someone else—often a white male (but sometimes a white female)—say the exact same thing several minutes later and it be[ing] accepted as a good idea. I am fairly plain spoken and do not see a need for high emotion or drama in order to get across my point, yet having this happen so frequently in department, college, and university meetings is frustrating enough for me to feel I need to adopt a different persona. But then who should I be—what behavior makes me someone that those in administration at our university would feel should be listened to. Maybe I need to be more of an angry black woman.

This narrative illustrates that the emotional labor of "etiquette" and performative behavioral modification strategies is particularly powerful because of the nuances of questioning "how" to perform. It is not unreasonable to see how the strain of emotional monitoring of performative behavioral practices can easily lead to what Deidre L. Redmond (2014, 2) calls "going mean":

> We forget that minorities and women, especially minority women, are not granted authority even after earning a doctorate and being hired in a very competitive academic market. It is an uphill battle for authority; they must prove their merit. For women and minorities, it is a frustrating process, and feeling as if they don't have the same status creates distance between them and their colleagues and their students. I believe that helps explain why some minority professors become so overwhelmed that they "go mean." They become cold and, dare I say it, angry . . . It's a symptom of years of devaluation and disrespect . . . It creates a distance that inhibits questioning a professor's authority or devaluing that person.

However, for me and many other African American female WPAs, this "going mean" is not a healthy, sustainable option. It is not a sustainable method of negotiating emotional labor. While tempting (and indeed there were responses that I saw moving in that direction), it was not the most common response or even prevalent enough to see it as an emerging theme. Oddly enough, even the participants who expressed frustrations that were escalating or outrageous did so using carefully chosen, controlled language. In such situations, I wondered if they felt that their responses, even documenting their own lived experiences, needed regulating or that they needed to perform in a certain way even in their responses. Also, several participants mentioned that the behaviors associated with "going mean" went against their perceptions of themselves in their role as WPAs. From what I read of their narratives and for me, creating a persona that responds to one form of emotional labor—"going mean"—can create its own form of emotional labor: performative behaviors in a reactionary way that are unsustainable and personally toxic.

HIGHLIGHTED STRATEGIES FOR NEGOTIATING

What, then, are healthy, sustainable options for negotiating emotional labor as an African American female WPA? Reading through the information shared with me by participants, I found that I was challenged by the concept of "strategies" and weary of proposing reductive overgeneralized ideas that do not reflect the complexity of the situation. In fact, I was forced to set aside the project for a bit because I wasn't sure I wanted to move into the final step of proposing strategies. After discussing my struggle with some other faculty of color, I realized that all I needed to do was utilize the language in the narratives to highlight the proposed strategies of the participants—further allowing me to incorporate more of their experiences. In addition, much like the practices described in the first strategy below, I cross-checked my proposed strategies with my own experiences and personal and professional ethics. Throughout the narratives, the participants utilized strategies based in integrity, integration, and innovation to negotiate the complexity of the emotional labor they experienced administrating while black and female.

Integrity: Establishing and Documenting Personal Systems of Integrity
Establishing and documenting systems of integrity means taking time to concretely document why you are doing what you do based on your own personal, professional, and spiritual ethics. This concept is similar to Elizabeth Imafuji's strategy "to reflect on [your] own faith and consider [your] own reasons for working at that institution" (this volume). It means asking yourself why you became a WPA and what you want to accomplish as a WPA in the next two to three years. In addition, it means taking time to reflect on and revise you own personal boundaries. Document these systems of integrity, externalize your own reality, provide a means of focusing—this may start myopically (with the personal) but can be adjusted more and more panoramically—to encompass the overlapping aspects of our intersectionality. Narratives five and six illustrate this concept of personal and professional systems of integrity.

Narrative five: Several challenges come with the role of a female WPA of color. I am a woman of integrity; I work extremely well with people when they do the right thing. Otherwise, I will not follow the lead. I will not cause friction, but I will speak up when my integrity is on the line. It cost me some heartaches when people profess to be supportive of the needs of the students but do not show it in some decisions that are made.

Narrative six: Since it is hard to understand how I fit into the larger scheme of the department and at times the university, I have decided to focus on what I know is right based on my students and my disciplinary values. For me, it comes back to integrity. There are two ways to think about it. For me, integrity is key to my negotiating the emotional labor of my job because I know that if I am being honest and forthright, holding to a clear sense of principles, then it allows me to avoid the fragmentation that emotional labor can often cause—it allows me to function in a whole, undivided state.

On the surface, this concept of integrity (described in narratives five and six) seems a bit simplistic. However, as I thought about it more, it occurred to me that these systems have been fundamental to my survival as well. Documented systems of integrity establish a foundation on which decisions, behaviors, and practices could be based; because it is a personal response to very specific, localized, personal issues of emotional labor, finding a localized, personal set of standards or values as a solution makes sense. Unlike the performative nature of "going mean," integrity can ultimately be a more sustainable strategy because it provides a lens for negotiating our "overlapping spheres of identity"—personal, professional, spiritual, and others.

For example, a focus on my own systems of integrity meant defining my own boundaries. I had decided to become a writing teacher or a professor of rhetoric and writing because I saw written communication as a means of access to educational opportunities and beyond. It therefore seemed absolutely reasonable for me to consider how my decisions as a rhetoric and writing scholar and a WPA furthered those goals. When it came to being who I was, with all of the complexities of my identities, I had to be reassured that there was a place for me and those like me in any and every professional environment. This meant that my personal questioning could be silenced by acknowledging the rich history of scholars of color who had preceded my time in the academy. It was impossible for me to consider how I could be where I am without them. I also knew how respected and valuable their scholarship is and therefore how my time would continue their legacy. My work and experiences would need to continue to be voiced to shed light on the role of gender and race in writing studies. Even the few surveys I had received back further confirmed the need for attention to be drawn to problems that could easily be overlooked and personally internalized until openly acknowledged and possibly changed.

Professionally, by taking the time early in my WPA career to clearly establish what I saw as my foundational truths (about fundamental disciplinary practices, about labor issues, about students and students' rights, about the role of writing in the department and the university),[1] I was equipped to weather the ever-present daily storms. When it came to professional ethics, I armed myself with research, outcomes statements, and position statements from CWPA, the Conference on College Composition and Communication (CCCC), and the National Council of Teachers of English (NCTE). While it seemed tedious at the time to create my own personal and professional position statements, it provided me with the support I needed to reinforce my functional integrity.

Integration: Creating Communities of Support

One of the more common ways of thinking of integration, particularly as it relates to emotional labor, is to think about effective ways of integrating or aligning your professional scholarly goals with your WPA programmatic goals. While this can be extremely effective, it does not address the earlier-mentioned challenges of isolation described as a key burden of the emotional labor of being an African American female WPA. For the female African American WPA, integration means establishing a network and communities of support. These communities of support can be similar to Courtney Adams Wooten's (this volume) idea of fostering relationships outside of work, where she focuses on personal relationships that sustain us; however, equally important are the outside relationships built by connecting with professional communities. These communities may be found at the university level or professionally at the level of a national organization. These connections provide opportunities to learn from other administrators of color and to collaborate on stories and strategies—thereby breaking down feelings of isolation. Many of the experiences described above are common to a range of administrators from an underrepresented people group, yet the report of feeling isolated is often a key factor in attrition. Finding other women, women of color, and people of color within and outside the discipline reduces the feeling of isolation. Narrative seven describes how integration across campus helped make a difference for one such WPA.

Narrative seven: I had been aware of our university faculty [and] staff black caucus but had never felt that I had time to join. I happened to join shortly after I became WPA and what a difference it made. In meetings and at various functions, I met other administrators of color across campus. While it wasn't really funny, we had to laugh at the commonality of our experiences—how we were treated in our departments. Eventually, we worked collectively on solutions.

Other female WPAs of color have shared how helpful organizational caucuses have been, both professionally and personally. It is also important to note that integration into support units need not only be based on race or gender. Attending CWPA pre-conference workshops has also provided many WPAs of color with opportunities to develop support networks and integrate into ongoing supportive communities. Emotional labor often stems from unacknowledged stresses that go unattended because of issues of time. While it may seem that integration can and will indeed take time (one of the limited commodities for any WPA), it is important to consider prioritizing self-care as an important sustainable ethical value needed to manage the emotional labor faced by any WPA, specifically by African American female WPAs.

Inclusion: Creating Systems for Change

While integrity and integration can indeed assist in negotiating emotional labor at a personal level, inclusion is the one of the best possible methods of negotiating emotional labor at a broader institutional and national level. When I considered the legacy of those in our discipline who have done and continue to do work that intersects race, gender, ethnicity, sexuality, and other intersectionalities of identity, I also noted how instrumental they have been in shaping the discussions and policies of the discipline. In other words, they saw their work not only as scholarship but also as personal and professional activism. Multiple chapters in this volume have dealt with how integration can be key to creating equity (Warnke et al.; Leverenz; and others). This realization is described in narrative eight, when the WPA considered how her work in the governance structure of the NCTE, CCCC, or CWPA could indeed have an impact on how she negotiates her emotional labor.

Narrative eight: It never occurred to me to consider running for office until I began to consider that without my voice and the voice of those like me, things may not change. I kept waiting for someone to "do something" about the issues that we face as black female WPAs. Then it occurred to me that I was contributing to the problem by not doing anything either. Here I have been in the discipline for a very long time and I am constantly exploring issues of race and gender, yet I have not considered that I should be applying what I learn by being included in the governance structure of my field.

While not in great numbers, we are a growing part of the discipline; as such, WPAs of color need to take an active role in the design and governance of organizations. If not at the level of governance, we can also promote inclusion as a way of negotiating emotional labor by creating and supporting initiatives that draw future and current black female WPAs into a pipeline of support through recruitment and mentoring. Earlier in the chapter I quoted Mainah and Perkins (2015) on how African American administrators' experiences often do not play a role in policymaking, yet through inclusion in policymaking and governance bodies, African American female WPAs can change this absence. The process of inclusion in and of itself does have its own emotional labor, yet selective empowering change will not be made without such work.

Inclusion is directly connected to integrity because it allows us to enact our own personal and professional ethics.

I began the project of exploring how African American female WPAs negotiate the emotional labor of administrating while black by establishing a broader definition of emotional labor through both research and narrative; however, this short chapter does not give this subject the time or continued attention it needs. Although I do suggest three negotiating strategies—integrity, integration, and inclusion—that emerged from the narratives in this study, I want to be clear that these are not solutions. Even the concept that we can come up with functional, applicable strategies to address larger institutionalized systems of oppression seems somewhat hollow. Thus as does every piece I have read that explores the complexities of the intersectionality in any scholarly field of study, I, too, call for others to continue to add to the narratives and research. There are indeed patterns across experiences, but before we reduce the narratives to the "common themes," we need the nuances of the stories to be collected and analyzed. As more and more African American women explore the possibility of becoming WPAs, such research provides them with a *real* sense of the problems and possibilities. And as Craig and Perryman-Clark (2011), Garcia de Mueller and Ruiz (2017), Martinez (2013), Kynard (2015), and many others have done, we need to bring attention to—and by doing so ultimately disrupt—the institutionalized practices that create the added emotional labor.

APPENDIX 11.A

1. Do you believe there are indeed challenges to being a female WPA of color, and if so, how would you describe them both generally (professionally) and specifically (your experience)?

2. What is a specific story, situation, or series of stories/situations that you feel best exemplifies the challenges you describe above? Please describe the situation and, as much as possible, expand on the ways your specific positionality as an administrator, as a female, and as a female administrator of color complicated the situation.

3. Do you feel there is a different sort of emotional labor for female WPAs of color, and if so, how would you describe that emotional labor?

4. How do you balance, negotiate, the labor described above, and in doing so, what effect do you feel it has on you both personally and professionally, if any?

5. How has your perspective as a female WPA of color and the negotiation strategies you have developed enhanced your overall academic and scholarly career?

NOTE

1. See the NCTE Position Statements on Writing at http://cccc.ncte.org/positions/writing.

REFERENCES

Craig, Collin Lamont, and Staci Perryman-Clark. 2011. "Troubling the Boundaries: (De)Constructing WPA Identities at the Intersections of Race and Gender." *WPA: Writing Program Administration* 34 (2): 37–58.

Durr, Marlese, and Adia Wingfield. 2011. "Keep Your 'N' in Check: African American Women and the Interactive Effects of Etiquette and Emotional Labor." *Critical Sociology* 37 (5): 557–571. doi:10.1177/0896920510380074.

Garcia de Mueller, Genevieve, and Iris Ruiz. 2017. "Race, Silence, and Writing Program Administration: A Qualitative Study of US College Writing Programs." *WPA: Writing Program Administration* 40 (2): 19–39.

Green, David. 2016. "Expanding the Dialogue on Writing Assessment at HBCUs: Foundational Assessment Concepts and Legacies of Historically Black Colleges and Universities." *Toward Writing Assessment as Social Justice*, special issue of *College English* 79 (2): 152–173.

Kynard, Carmen. 2015. "Teaching While Black: Witnessing and Countering Disciplinary Whiteness, Racial Violence, and University Race-Management." *Literacy in Composition Studies* 3 (1): 1–20.

Mainah, Fredah, and Vernita Perkins. 2015. "Challenges Facing Female Leaders of Color in US Higher Education." *International Journal of African Development* 2 (2): 5–13.

Martinez, Aja Y. 2014. "A Plea for Critical Race Theory Counterstory: Stock Story versus Counterstory Dialogues Concerning Alejandra's 'Fit' in the Academy." *Composition Studies* 42 (2): 33–55.

Redmond, Deidre L. 2014. "A Black Female Professor Struggles with 'Going Mean.'" *Chronicle of Higher Education*, May 27. http://www.chronicle.com/article/A-Black-Female-Professor/146739.

Tulshyan, Ruchika. 2015. "Speaking Up as a Woman of Color at Work." *Forbes Magazine*, October 7. http://www.forbes.com/sites/ruchikatulshyan/2015/02/10/speaking-up-as-a-woman-of-color-at-work/.

Walcher, Sheldon, Joseph Janangelo, and Duane Roen. 2010. "Introducing 'eCWPA Mentoring Project' and Survey Report." *Writing Program Administration* 34 (1): 84–116.

Wingfield, Adia. 2015. "The Plight of the Black Academic." *The Atlantic*, December 15. https://www.theatlantic.com/business/archive/2015/12/the-plight-of-the-black-academic/420237/.

12
IT GETS BITTER
Considering Andy Warhol and Harboring Anger as a Gay WPA

Joseph Janangelo
Loyola University Chicago

That night, when he loved me and sank into me, I thought to myself, It is only with our bodies that we ever really forgive one another; the mind pretends to forgive, but it harbors and reremembers . . .
                        Edna O'Brien, *The Lonely Girl* (1962, 166–167)

I wouldn't take that seriously. You know how bitchy fags can be.
                        Jacqueline Susann *Valley of the Dolls* (1966, 266)

Writer Maurice Blanchot (1981, 18) offers a unilateral injunction against storytelling: "A story? No stories, never again." Perhaps closer to home, writing program administrator (WPA) Diana George (1999, xiv) advises that "a good story does more than hold us in its world as it unfolds. A good story tells us something about ourselves. For WPAs, a good story ought to send us back to the scholarship and the institutional realities with yet another important piece of the puzzle of this work. And that, in the end, is what these stories are meant to do." I could tell some stories, but I doubt they would be good enough to be called edifying, entertaining, or even worth other WPAs' reading. I am not sure that any story tells us something of transfer value about ourselves. That is especially true when those selves are gay WPAs and readers who may seek to understand what drives them.

For me, the WPA "puzzle" remains enigmatic (George 1999, xiv). I find the storyboard of one's working life can be riddled, in the sense of not knowing what some experiences mean and of them feeling diseased and alienating. In other words, its "story" (Blanchot 1981, 18) does not often yield a coherent or enabling understanding (Bruner 2004; Lyotard 1984;

White 1987). In my WPA life, some story points are sharp, shameful, and degrading. They leave me angry at myself for enduring them silently, with little reaction beyond worrying, working harder, and overeating.

Reflecting on the things I have carried and internalized, this chapter examines anger as a self-protective and self-limiting WPA survival strategy. Part I explores what it means to harbor one's anger as "a place of refuge" (*Oxford English Dictionary*). Part II reappraises my commitment to managing my affect as an emotionally temperate gay WPA and colleague. It explores the idea of harboring anger as to "keep (a thought or feeling, typically a negative one) in one's mind, especially secretly," rather than responding immediately and, if need be, officially (*Oxford English Dictionary* 2018). Finally, I offer readers who have felt bullied or harassed some questions for workplace thought and action. Diana George (1999, 64) states that "sexual politics . . . are real and important concerns in the life of WPAs." She offers a "guess . . . that a part of any collection of WPA stories will always address those moments when the WPA must explain to others what it is we do and why" and adds, "that is where the scholarship and the research in this profession come into the workplace" (64). Kelly Ritter (2018, 60) amplifies this idea when she writes that we need "[a] shared understanding within the WPA community at large that no story, or WPA telling a story, is without consequence, and that no documentation of program practice is unimportant to our larger landscape and public presence." Inspired by Blanchot's injunction against storytelling and George's ideas about explaining, I share some working moments that have inspired this gay WPA's anger.

PART ONE: MOMENTS LIKE THIS[1]

One summer, a retired colleague, Martha, died and the Department of English hosted a memorial for her. For years, several department colleagues and staff had characterized Martha as a closeted gay woman. After her memorial, at which our chairperson said Martha's family canceled their attendance, citing a family emergency, I walked behind three senior professors (two of them former English department chairpersons) across campus to the reception. On the way, all three colleagues laughed and joked loudly about Martha and ridiculed her perceived failed life and career, the life secrets she failed to keep, and her alleged alcoholism. As a new WPA, I was too scared to say anything. I found some voice a week or two later, though, when Kat, a textbook representative to the writing program and observant Christian, brought up Martha's demise and added, "She lived the

---

1. All names in this section are pseudonyms.

lonely life of a lesbian." I asked Kat why she thought lesbians lead lonely lives but received no response.

When I directed our department's first composition dissertation, it was on writing center scholarship. The room had guests from Notre Dame as well as Loyola faculty. After congratulating the new graduate, I gave her a book as a present. At that point, the graduate program director (GPD) said from across the room, "What is it Joe, porn?" As committee members and graduate students laughed, I froze. Afterward, I told the GPD that I found it shaming, and she said she thought it was funny. When I asked the chairperson for guidance, he told me faculty complain about everyone.

I took a senior colleague, Mark, to dinner after his wife died. Mark is one of the former department chairpersons who joked about Martha's life right after her memorial. Mark was discussing his teaching scores and said, "I don't want to suck cock for good course evaluations." Mortified, I paid the check. In the work mailroom the next day, another senior colleague mentioned Mark's marriage and told me, "That was a marriage in name only, just like Vivian and Larry's" I withered as he named married colleagues/closeted gay people in other departments for specific reference.

A student wrote on my course evaluation, "I don't approve of his lifestyle." At my yearly performance evaluation, my then chair advised me, "You have to expect that." I then mentioned that a colleague told me, over lunch, "When you first arrived, you were decidedly overweight." That chair advised, "Well, you were."

A colleague, whose family I had hosted several times, invited me to dinner. We were making small talk in his car while driving to his home. Turning his head right, toward me, he smiled and asked, "Do you think Tim is gay?" I said, "I don't know" and attended what was for me an uncomfortable evening.

Last spring, at department meetings, I listened silently while two of my writing program colleagues said, "We have no one in rhetoric and composition." Their words reminded me of our then chair screaming at me the year before: "Your courses don't count" and "You don't fit the grid."

What counts most about these moments was my self-limiting commitment to adopt a temperate affect, to not make a scene or be a hostile "queen" about things. Instead, I assumed a "carry-on" leadership mentality (Kouzes and Posner 2012) that would keep me from being cast as an overly sensitive gay person or give colleagues the satisfaction of letting them see how damaging I found their actions. William P. Banks and Jonathan Alexander (2009, 89) assert that "queer WPAs, of course, invariably see themselves torn in ways that non-queer WPAs may not." I know not of invariability, but my larger response was to file my anger away inward and into perpetuity. My response to workplace shaming has famous queer precedent. I refer to Eve Kosofsky Sedgwick's "Queer Performativity: Warhol's Shyness/Warhol's Whiteness" (1996), which tells and theorizes some of my experience.

Isn't Andy Warhol a perfect paradox? Consider the pale and diminutive "Andy," which is boyish and vulnerable in a "don't hurt me" sort of way. Just the way much of society (including WPA culture?) likes its white gay men. Then, the surname "Warhol" adds queer fame. It references *that* Andy, the notorious gay artist who was enamored of beautiful people but could never be one. Sedgwick (1996, 139) points out that "Warhol's pallor" and "what Warhol allows to be called his 'faggy air'" was an ongoing source of "shame" for him. She shares a diary entry where he writes, "Day after day, I look in the mirror and I still see something—a new pimple" (136). Yet Warhol was also a high achiever, a queer success story, who became terribly famous and wealthy. Perhaps in retaliation for his experience of queer stigma, Warhol made himself weirder and his work more expressive and expensive. Deemed witty and wicked, pathetic and predatory, he can leave us wondering whether he is kidding, angry, or both.

For Sedgwick (1996, 138), Warhol's mixture of self-confidence (predicated on professional achievement) and self-consciousness (based on shame over his pale, pock-marked skin) model "the relation of queer shame/shyness to celebrity." She uses Warhol to suggest that shame occurs early and impactfully to children deemed queer—weird, strange, perhaps gay, and certainly worth less than their peers. Such shaming gets inside you. Its experience and memory are there as a host, disposition, and breeding ground that fuels responsiveness to stimuli. Accordingly, "the shame-delineated place of identity" offers cells "that will crystallize there, developing from this originary affect their particular structures of expression, creativity, pleasure, and struggle" (138). Those cells may eat away at one's self-esteem, yielding a heightened receptivity to shame as well as a strong memory of, and even a taste for, humiliation.

Consonant with Sedgwick's argument, I argue that with some gay WPAs' working lives, shame can fuel a drive toward career success. Yet professional shining never eradicates its drivers. Hence Sedgwick (1996, 135) underscores the importance "of understanding how the dysphoric affect shame functions as a nexus of production: production, that is, of meaning, of personal presence, of politics, of performative and critical efficacy." She writes that "those whose sense of identity is for some reason tuned most to the note of shame" (137) can count revisits that go "from shame to shyness to shining—and, inevitably, back and back again" (135). One truth of internalized shame is that it is on call 24/7, no matter what protective fortification you build or success you achieve: "Thus, one of the things that anyone's character or personality is is a record of the highly individual histories by which the fleeting emotion of shame has instituted far more durable, structural changes in one's relational and interpretive strategies toward both self and others" (141–142).

That (sometimes) broken record, available for strategic and perpetual replay, may include the anger one harbors toward those who sought or seek to shame you.[1] It is small surprise that this porousness/resentment can yield ongoing paydirt for workplace bullies and predators. As Sedgwick (1996, 142) concludes, "To sum up, shame, like other affects, is not a discrete intrapsychic structure but a kind of free radical that (in different people and also in different cultures) attaches to and permanently intensifies or alters the meaning of—of almost anything: a zone of the body, a sensory system, a prohibited or indeed a permitted behavior, another affect such as anger or arousal, a named identity, a script for interpreting other people's behavior toward oneself."

PART II: FEELING(S) LIKE THAT

The named identity that concerns me is *Gay WPA*. Being an effective campus leader with a big job to do is made no easier when you are shame-prone and your saboteurs are contemporary and external as well as historical and internalized. My work here is to offer ideas for how one might perform WPA work effectively and lead a productive career while feeling bullied and vulnerable. What follows are two strategies one could employ. Not surprisingly, they come with costs and complications.

Strategy #1: You could be a Warhol by shining.

By that, I mean you could work hard to become well-known or famous. You could make your detractors jealous by being a spectacular WPA (Conor 2004). Common advice about one way to get over being mistreated when you were young is to become invulnerable by perfecting your body and accumulating wealth. That way your abusers cannot get close enough to hurt you—anymore or any more than they already have. For WPAs with career plans, this can mean perfecting your body of work by outshining your colleagues in terms of publications, grants, high course evaluations, and professional standing. If you channel your suffering into professional achievement, your every career move could become a power move. You inspire your bullies' jealousy by showing them who teaches and publishes "like a boss." Such shining may be akin to queer glaring. You could outshine your colleagues to prove your critics wrong and make it hard for them to un-see how accomplished, respected, and rewarded you are. That way, if your program or programmatic haters, some of whom may be gay, judge your "lifestyle" or resent your reduced teaching load, they cannot deny your professional achievement or prestige. Thus by becoming a Warhol, some blue chip optics are in your favor. That is because you have created a harbor to insulate and protect what may be seen as yours alone.

You might shine so intensely you glare. In addition to becoming terribly successful, you might become a WPA who is terribly difficult to deal with so that people do not cross you out of fear of reprisal and retribution. That could involve performing one version of a gay male stereotype by becoming high maintenance, hypercritical, and fierce. You could engage WPA work as an opportunity to perform "artistic temperament" (Herlihy and Noble 1958, 25) at meetings by being witty and wry, devastating and temperamental. Here your harbor is a threatening citadel of avenging anger. It is there to be seen and feared. If you ever ate dirt, it is time for others to choke on your success.

Claiming *rara avis* status, you could behave accordingly. That means making no apologies and demanding them instead.[2] Most of all, you could become known for shaming others and having a stinging "bye Felicia" at the ready for what you see as inferior work or performance. If Warhol became known for his "faggy air" (Sedgwick 1996, 139), you might, in deliberate turn, become nationally and programmatically known for your ferocious, what some will delight in calling "faggy airs" and attitude.

My bet is that some people will dread and some will applaud the WPA spectacle you create. Moreover, they will recognize your performance of that familiar and rewarding (to them and you) gay male stereotype. By behaving as a volatile source of WPA shade and micro-/macro-aggressions, you can likely preempt any other would-be workplace bullies by seeing to it that they fear you. Note: if you aspire to behaving as a snooty, snotty WPA, follow strategy #1 so you have an impressive curriculum vitae to bolster your performance.

You could also become and remain bitter by letting your anger well up. This can involve maximizing your memories of bullying and indignity and putting them on perpetual or strategic programmatic display. Remembering everything bad that happened to you allows you to archive the indignities you have suffered (recall Sedgwick's "record") and invites you to see your WPA working life in close-up keep because "it"—every program or center problem—is related to you and your suffering. By staying in close contact with your anger (you might begin workplace conversations by saying "remember the times you . . ."), you keep it fresh and alive.

As the writing program's self-appointed gay memory expert, your relationship to passing time is akin to one voiced by T. S. Eliot in *Four Quartets* (1971):

> Time present and time past
> Are both perhaps present in time future,
> And time future contained in time past.

You could engage in what I call palimpsest thinking to blend past and present indignities so that everything is everything. That perspective keeps your anger on tap so that "back then" seems a lot like "right now." That gives you a chance to do your WPA work fueled by righteous anger for those who degraded you and still do. As a memory expert, you could actively resent the privilege of those who have had it easier than you have. You could enact an anger-driven leadership style. You could use your harbor (e.g., rank and scholarship) as a structure that protects and grows your anger. You could use it to exact payback from people who must accommodate your bitterness and attribute your contemporary misdeeds or immaturity to your harrowing backstory. The idea of feeling your anger is expressed by life coach John Schuster (2003, 70), in all caps: "ALWAYS REMEMBER THE SABOTEUR'S NEGATIVE IMPACT ON YOU." He adds, "Never forget the self-doubt and negation, so that you never let yourself feel or think that again" (70). Here, memory fortifies your anger by building another wall around your harbor, as you never, ever forget.

Strategy 2: You could be an Andy by serving selflessly as a gay-lite, gay WPA.
Chris Blankenship (2018, 46, original emphasis) writes that "*there will be unhappy / angry people.*" As a gay WPA, you could profit professionally and socially by appearing to be of a different ilk. On this track, you could demonstrate leadership by becoming known as a high-ethos colleague who puts the needs of others first. *Step one* would be to administrate as though you have forgotten whatever shaming experiences happened. You pretend they did not happen that way or that they did not mean to or hurt you that much. Here your leadership strategy would be to conceal your anger and refuse to present yourself as a predictable and garden-variety drama queen.

Step two: Be discreet about your life. Channel your energy, especially your anger, into helping others while expecting nothing in return. Also, remember to appear enduringly grateful for any kindness shown to you. In this scenario, you become more restrained than emotive in your leadership approach. Instead of being accomplished and quarrelsome enough to evoke your enemies' ire, you are relatable and empathetic in ways that bespeak integrity. That way, some of your judgmental or homophobic colleagues may come to tolerate and even admire you. By appearing to rise above the damage shame has done to your well-being, you may be seen as a gay WPA whose behavior is above reproach. I call that *WPAing as Caesar's domestic partner*. Friendly and approachable, you do not hate or resent anyone. Rather, you love and lead.

Step three: Project a selfless and controlled leadership countenance by being sensible and sensitive to the needs of others. Take your needs off the table by being empathetic, charming, or funny to defuse difficult or degrading situations. This "Let It Go" and "Everything Is Awesome" approach to WPA work may help you be seen as a high-ethos gay person who is neither too angry nor too political. Some colleagues will notice and appreciate this gay-lite performance of WPA leadership. They may find you relatable and admire you for forgetting/hiding/harboring your anger in private. Note: some detractors may characterize your ethos and WPA performance as lacking enough queerness or political engagement. Yet the majority of your programmatic and institutional colleagues may deem you a valued, promotion-worthy "leader." That is because they can see you working effectively (e.g., patiently and selflessly) with others, keeping any drama to and for yourself, and understanding the difference between now and then. As an Andy, there is no discernible *Four Quartets* or workplace trauma for you. This is now and your WPA/WCD (writing center director) go-to question is, How may I help you?

Step four: Exhibit remarkable self-control: know your emotional buttons and give them a workplace timeout. Manage your emotions by remembering that you are there to help others, however privileged, not to be a needy person yourself. Chances are people will appreciate your calm, cheerful affect. It saves them time and makes more space for their needs and drama. Programmatically, it helps things run smoother. If some people are angry that you are not radical or angry enough, your WPA discretion can read as vital for a writing program's secret keeper. As a selfless WPA, you are a minimizer rather than an amplifier of workplace drama. Such conduct can make you look noble and discreet. Colleagues like that because it asks little of them and yields rolling returns. They may feel they can trust you to be discreet about their problems and the confidences they share with you. They may find you to be a palatable version of a gay colleague, *a gay-lite WPA* who offers the team understanding and appreciation.

Step five: Adopt this motto: we are here to work, not to dwell or remember. That comports with mainstream leadership research (Kouzes and Posner 2012) and can help you build your career. If you choose to pretend that you do not notice current indignities and spare others the scene you could make if you did, that you do not get or mind being the joke, some people will appreciate the fact that you do not want to complain or trouble others. That upbeat performance of your emotional labor could be characterized as a worthy model of leadership and self-control. It might get you promoted beyond your program, perhaps under the discreet rubric of "promoting for diversity." If you go this route, you may not have to be as well published as in strategy one. In other words, you may profit by being perceived as more companionable than accomplished.

By being approachably and amusingly gay, you will likely contribute to some of your colleagues' sense of workplace happiness, emotional well-being, and security. At the WPA workplace, a vulnerable Andy's reticence and understatement can be easier for colleagues to work with than a quarrelsome Warhol's perceived flamboyance and demands. For example, some colleagues may enjoy seeing their WPA or WCD self-present as a sweet and appreciative gay person who knows their place at the workplace. By behaving yourself, you could remind your colleagues, who may self-identify as your "allies," of the gay people (e.g., student or teacher) they loved or at least abstained from torturing in school. That could give them some of "the feels" they like feeling.

Your vulnerable affect can yield programmatic rewards. For one thing, it can give your colleagues a/nother chance to enjoy their straight white privilege because they cannot find a logical reason to dislike or discredit you. The kindness they choose to show toward those they see as wounded, damaged WPAs could be cathartic for them. It could help them self-atone for the gay kid(s) and adult(s) they abused (or watched being abused) before they worked with gentle you. A second workplace reward, which again reifies straight white privilege, is that your colleagues and students may find themselves cosseted by the balmy notion that some gay WPAs are rather smart and harmless and not too political for their own and their writing program's own good. Moreover, some of your colleagues and administrators may be relieved to note that some gay WPAs still keep their lives and needs on the relative "low" by contributing valuably to their program or center while modestly asking only for the right to exist. If you WPA with noblesse, you may inspire largesse when some of your colleagues deem you worthy of protection, respect, contract renewal, friendship, and even promotion.

The insidious thing about these strategies and performances is that they often work because they ask so little of your colleagues. You will likely profit in your career by engaging, and engaging in, any of these stereotypes. Yet these strategies work by helping the worst parts of you grow through performing or suppressing your anger. They compromise you because they keep you from being honest about how you feel about the life you have led and the WPA life you are leading now. To some, they are as transparent and tedious as a humble brag. Yet they can garner degrees of workplace currency. I remember an international graduate student saying "my mother told me now is not the time to feel your feelings." That is good workplace advice. ("Manage your affect," my colleague tells me she advises our graduate students.) But I would like to ask things another way, especially for gay WPAs who have been humiliated in life and at work. I am writing to readers of this book who, when they saw Laura R. Micciche's (this volume) words about "self-doubt and self-blame" and Kate Navickas's (this volume) sentence stem "I felt defeated and guilty for . . . ," may have said "gosh, those scholars are writing about me."

When doing the emotional work of WPA work, when it is the time to feel your feelings? Always? Never? Sometimes?[3] In her chapter in this volume, Courtney Adams Wooten wisely reminds us that "it is important to recognize when our emotional interactions are tied to work and when they are free of it and to foster relationships outside of work." One way to enact that idea is for WPAs to access and articulate our feelings in healthy and constructive ways. By that I mean doing more than that which enables you to get the work done, direct your expectations, or earn tenure. Speaking of shame and anger, let us say you decide to "Let It Go." I submit that *it* has to and will go somewhere. Perhaps wild or to pieces. As Sedgwick (1996) argues, even if you can force it to go away, it will not stay away. I do not want you to become embittered or adopt a false career pose. I am very much onboard with Carrie S. Leverenz's ideas in this volume about actively pursuing well-being, although for me, the thought of flourishing seems like a tall and intimidating order, an inaccessible aspiration. Yet in considering your well-being, I offer you these ideas for better enjoying your WPA working life.

Part III: Things to Consider Doing

You might become really real—and realistic—about your anger. Consider its roles and functions in your working life. Your anger may be something you enjoy carrying because it enables certain familiar feelings such as unworthiness, entitlement, or revenge. Yet one of the injustices of anger, a central cruelty, really, is that it hurts the bearer so much. I do not know if it hurts them most of all, but it does hurt them singularly, insidiously, and perhaps indefinitely (Sedgwick 1996). Remember that reward systems can be operative in a toxic sense as well. If you harbor anger, you are likely getting something you like or need out of it. It is likely paying you vital and insidious dividends.

Yet anger can be transformative. For example, Audre Lorde (1981, 8) explains its generative potential: "Anger is loaded with information and energy." She recommends harnessing that energy rather than denying it. She adds that "when we turn from anger we turn from insight, saying we will accept only the designs already known, those deadly and safely familiar" (9). That means learning that "anger is a source of empowerment we must not fear to tap for energy rather than guilt" (9).

Lorde (1981) characterizes guilt, and she is discussing white guilt in particular, as stagnant and self-indulgent. She states "I have no creative use for guilt, yours or my own," and adds that "guilt is only another way of avoiding informed action, of buying time out of the pressing need to make clear choices, out of the approaching storm that can feed the earth as well as bend the trees" (9). With acuity, Lorde describes a better alternative: "But anger expressed and translated into action in the service of our vision and our future is a liberating and strengthening act of clarification, for it is in the painful process of this translation that we identify who are our allies with whom we have grave differences, and who are our genuine enemies" (8).

Consider becoming critically observant of, and relational with, your enemies and saboteurs because they have lessons to offer, even now. Schuster (2003, 71) gives bullies some credit, claiming that "one of the saboteur's skills, you'll remember, is finding and exploiting a weakness." He recommends that we make them objects of study, just as they made us objects of prey: "Learn the methods that saboteurs use in their quest for control" (74). He advises us to "pay special attention to the weakness in your mental or emotional makeup that they play on so you can see how the principles they espouse—innocent and even noble-sounding for the most part, ones you can agree with—disguise the destructive nature of their work" (74). I see this as related to self-care and emotional well-being because it involves trying to understand your workplace bullies not in order to change them or persuade them to respect you (Elder and Davila 2019). Rather, the goal is to study how they operate, to observe and remember their repertoire of strategies, to see them for who they are, and to learn what it is they want to accomplish when they engage with you and your writing program and center. That way, you can be better prepared the next time(s) they hope to strike.

We could ask ourselves why we became and perhaps remain such viable prey. That means becoming attuned to one's own games and needs, however innocuous and inflammatory. Schuster (2003, 74) writes that "we unconsciously recruit many of our saboteurs." He adds that "as long as we stay in denial and refuse to work on ourselves, we attract people into our lives to exploit this weakness" (72). He points to needs that are not necessarily unhealthy or degraded, just real: "We need a foil, an enemy, an external embodiment of the part of us that is limiting our growth on the path. With a raging saboteur in our lives, tromping all over our neediest, limiting parts, we can no longer deny our self-limiting tendencies. With an external force causing the pain, we eventually recognize the work we have to do, the work we have been avoiding" (73).

If we study our receptivity to shame and debasement (Sedgwick), we might notice that "the saboteurs who make your life so difficult, unwittingly invited there by you, teach you what you need to work on" (Schuster 2003, 75). Remembering saboteurs and their influence, we might wonder what our bullies had to offer us that we needed and perhaps still do. We might ask if we ever recruited them or engaged in repeat casting by bringing similar bullies (who go by different names) into our WPA working lives. The suspicion that we may need and recruit our bullies, even by giving them any thought in retrospect, suggests that there can at times be a personal coefficient (Polanyi 1958) to WPA bullying and shame.

"THINKING ABOUT OTHERS"

This section offers questions for thinking about our needs and those of others. It invites us to reflect on what is happening now, the idea that how we processed and archived our past experience may influence our interpretation of current interactions, our wishes for the future, and our fears about could happen or, worse, happen again in life and at work. I am not suggesting that as gay people we have brought bullying on ourselves or that we crave mistreatment. Rather, I wish to expand our repertoire of concepts and strategies, proactive and reactive, for self-protection through self-scrutiny and understanding. To me, that involves considering, at least as a structural possibility, that it is possible to give one's life and workplace bullies and our memories of them increased power and toxicity by internalizing what they say and do. To those ends, I offer some questions for your consideration, reflection, and, perhaps, dismissal.

- How responsive and porous to the words and actions of others are you at work? As a campus leader and to do your work effectively, how porous and responsive do you think you should be and why?
- What are the strengths and limitations of using anger as a workplace survival or success (e.g., motivational or coping) strategy?

"Thinking about Your Self and Others"

While we cannot change other people, we can try to alter our reactions to them. We can strive to re-characterize their negative assessments of our value and work from accurate and definitional to biased and self-interested. These questions invite us to notice patterns of behavior—theirs and ours—that bother us and to consider why they do.

- When colleagues make you angry, at whom are you angry, really? Might the current workplace bully remind you of bullies you have known before in your life? Do you see or recognize any patterns forming? If you have noticed patterns, what makes you such a good host to shaming and bullying? Why do certain feelings or experiences stay with you? Might you be extending a self-limiting hospitality to them?
- John Schuster (2003, 70) writes that "one lesson from an encounter with a saboteur is the realization that you cooperated with the control he or she had over you." If your treatment was all undeserved and you were or are a unilaterally good person, does Schuster's (73) idea that "[we] unconsciously recruit many of our saboteurs" have any truth in your WPA life? For example, have you ever recruited or even mentored your own saboteurs? Here, you might think about your life and workplace bullies. What did or do you want from them? What did or do you want for them?

"Thinking Harder about Your Self and Others"

These questions involve self-scrutiny. They ask us to examine the degraded solace we may derive from workplace victimization. Asking these questions could help us consider the extent to which we participate in our own unhappiness.

- Have you ever sought or found status or solace in being degraded at work? Why? As a WPA or WCD, have you ever acted as though you had dibs on being wounded? Have you ever used your anger as a reason to behave dishonorably or to under-perform?
- Rather than let go, have you ever fed, fueled, groomed, and mentored your anger? Did you have any part in starting, continuing, or

memorializing your anger by remembering people and experiences the way you do?

- Is there anyone who should pay for your mistreatment? If so, what price would you decree? If you ever contemplated or exacted payback or revenge, either from the right or the wrong people, who was hurt most of all?
- Have you ever adopted, or encouraged others in your writing program or writing center to adopt, a "carry-on" response to shaming or bullying? From a leadership perspective, what has that done for or to your students and colleagues?
- How do you know when it is time to manage your feelings or to make them a priority? How have you delineated and weighed the potential consequences and returns? Have you ever considered your anger as an act of narcissism, a "free radical" (Sedgwick 1996, 142) that allows you to feel persecuted and justifies you being less than your best "self" at work, on listservs, at conferences, or at home?

"ESCHEWING IDEATIONS OF PIETY OR INNOCENCE"

This section asks us to imagine that our critics, including our workplace bullies, could be right about a few things. Most gay people know especially well that we cannot be all things to all people.[4] These questions involve considering our own imperfect, occasionally ignoble, impulses and motivations.

- Think of the workplace denigrators and bullies you have known. Are there any things that are accurate or true about their criticisms of your leadership, teaching, collegiality, service, or scholarship? In this volume, Amy Ferdinandt Stolley asks key questions: "What are the outcomes of your emotional labor? Put another way, how does your emotional labor make itself visible (perhaps indirectly) within the program you direct?" Most gay people know that visibility comes with risk. For example, if you were to be seen or characterized as "high maintenance," "oversensitive," or "difficult," what workplace moments and scenes would they point to? Think of the texts (e.g., emails) you wrote or things you said in meetings or conversations that your detractors could use to define you as such. Even if they are wrong about everything else, what one thing might they be right about? I suspect that even the worst people can have a valid point sometimes or about certain things.
- Have you ever been "oversensitive" to perceived injuries and comments of others and less than sensitive or generous in your own actions toward others? Have you been a naive or an unintentional WPA or WCD bully to someone else?
- Does anyone in your WPA working life owe you apologies? To whom do you owe them? Of what uses (Lorde 1981) or value would those

apologies be now? If you are generous and collegial to those who have treated you badly, how well and how badly has your commitment to *bonhomie* or selfless leadership served you, your program, and your writing center?

- Do you ever worry about fulfilling or not fulfilling well enough your colleagues' expectations (aspirational or stereotypical) of a gay WPA or WCD? Do you find that you are letting some people at your school and in your profession down by the stereotypical behaviors you engage in, decline to perform, or fail to perform well enough to pass their inspection and expectations?
- In terms of your WPA life and career, if you were to reap what you have sewn, what would you be reaping? Moving forward, what would you hope to sew?

CONCLUSION

The actor Ingrid Bergman, no stranger to public shaming, is quoted as saying "happiness is good health and a bad memory." *A votre sante*, and let's remember that your mental health is important as well. Let's also remember that harboring painful memories can become a glutting and consuming meal. Think of Ugolino in Dante's *Inferno* and how well that worked out for all concerned. A searing truth is that if you have chosen to be a WPA, you have chosen to be a leader. That means that people depend on you to be and do well. However mistreated you are, you can further damage your life and diminish your students' and colleagues' quality of life by maintaining a fervid "chemistry read" (Liem 2018) with your anger. I do not want you to miss out on the good parts of your life and career or to let others or, worse, yourself cheat you out of feeling valued and valuable. You are valuable. Moreover, think of the most indecent people you have known. They appear to suffer from no lack of self-confidence. Why should you? More important, what good would it do you, your work, and the people who care about you to be someone who "harbors and rerembers" (O'Brien 1961, 167)—someone who takes things "that seriously" (Susann 1966, 266)? As far as I can see, remembering workplace injury and indecency is important so that the same people, and others who use their predatory strategies, cannot sucker you in again. Beyond that, I doubt its value.

I once saw talk show host Wendy Williams offer this description of emotional closure: "You are my friend until you're not." What if you could come to feel that way about your anger? What if you could access your anger when it offers learning points that help you live and work creatively-queerly?[5] Philanthropist Peter Lynch advises us to "know what you own, and know why you own it" (cited in Wei 2015). Lynch refers to your financial holdings. I refer to your emotional holdings. Remember your past, but don't live there. For bullied, insecure, or angry WPAs—bisexual, gay, straight, and collages and composites thereof—working in a complicated present while carrying a freighted past can be a challenge. Yet it is for you to decide if you can define some experiences as "history." It is also for you to determine how much programmatic and public attention you need to have paid to your suffering. To me, it is one thing to host a piety party at home. It is another to cater it at work or online. Speaking of online communication, how many heart-shaped emoticons would sate one's hungers or quell one's pain? To help you move forward so you stand a better chance of enjoying what is ahead for, which is also what is left of, your WPA working life, I offer these suggestions.

You might reappraise your anger and harbor to assess their roles in your working life. We know that anger is a passion. Could you help it transition into a compassion for those who have hurt you? Could you remodel your harbor in ways you have remodeled your thinking? Remember that harbors, like anger, are high-maintenance structures. They keep good things in and out. In addition, while your WPA protective strategies are valuable, there is a paradox that whatever protects you also limits you.

Consider letting it get bitter without remaining bitter yourself. The best idea I can offer is that life and career happiness is a decision, predicated on many decision points along the way. They include achievement, payback, gratitude, and compassion. Some things should not have happened to you because you are a good person, but they did. You are a person, sure. So are your bullies and abusers. Given their cruelty and the damage you sustain(ed), that can be the hardest thing to remember. If some of your bullies ever evolved or gained insight, they might regret how they treated you. Or not. In fact, they might aspire to hurt you again. And again. Next time, "for keeps."

For a quick reminder of how some bullies savor their victories over time, we can consult Grahame Gremore (2018, original emphasis):

> Greg Barrett recently spoke at the Katy Independent School District school board meeting in Texas. He was there to talk about the issue of bullying. Lance Hindt, the superintendent of the Houston-area district, was also in attendance.
>
> Barrett took to the podium to explain that he was often targeted as a kid because of his legal name: Greg Gay.
>
> "I was bullied," he said. "Unbelievably bullied."
>
> "I started out and I had teachers that bullied me, I had kids that bullied me, even the coaches. I had nobody to turn to" . . .

    Then he launched into an emotional story about the time a gang of classmates assaulted him, shoving his head in a urinal and kicking him while he was lying on the ground in the fetal position.
    Barrett was left with a busted lip, covered in urine, and feeling suicidal.
    "Well, I went home and I got the .45 out of my father's drawer and put it in my mouth," he recalled. "Because at this point I had nobody—nobody in the school system—to help me. Is that the way this is going to be?"
    Then he looked directly at Hindt: "Lance, *you* were the one that shoved my head in the urinal."
    To which Hindt responded . . . by laughing.

I share this article to invite you to consider how your bullies may derive enduring pleasure in learning how deeply they have hurt you. One acid truth of being gay is that for some of your saboteurs, bullying was sport and you were prey. Moreover, your bullies may use your recollection of suffering as fodder for laughter and "good times" nostalgia. Facing such truths and studying them without melodrama (a time waster because our life and work clocks keep ticking) is part of what I mean by saying it gets bitter.[6]

If Hindt's reaction disgusts or, worse, surprises you, get ready to read this response to it posted by tnguy222:

> What a little puss. There were two types of people in High School, just as there are two types of people in the world—Sheep and Wolves.
> As a wolf, for sure I was a bully. Often, the bullies go far in life because they are popular enough to marshal people to a Cause (ie bullying in High School). If you are not sitting at the table, you are on the menu.
> My advice, leave the victim mentality behind—it will only hold you back. Become a wolf. Not a lone wolf, but a wolf who works well with others to achieve an objective. Become a Bully. (Gremore 2018)

Whether we frame tnguy222's words as sage advice or embittered strategy, I draw lessons from them: (1) do not expect your WPA predators to change or regret their actions anytime soon or ever, and (2) use your intelligence to remove yourself from their menu, though not in the way tnguy222 suggests. At this point, I do not recommend trying to change, move, understand, or befriend your bullies. Instead, teach yourself not to want that which they cannot or will not give you. Nor do I recommend chasing the vaunted WPA life-work balance (Hesse 2013). If your gay WPA or WCD life lines up into a coherent or inspirational "story" (Blanchot 1981, 18), it may be in part by dint of sentimental editing and compensatory narration.

Lest it get too bitter for these pages, the narrative you compose (Genette 1983) out of your WPA life and career could have something to do with forgiveness. In fall 1999, about a month before his death, the notorious and degraded raconteur and performer Quentin Crisp spoke at the Chicago Leather Archives and Museum. I was there to hear what he had to say. For decades, Crisp had been the recipient of public shame and ostracism for having performed several stereotypes that were deemed to be outdated and toxic. He had also lost some gay admirers and straight allies by publicly criticizing the recently deceased Princess Diana (Barrow 1998). At his talk, Crisp discussed his life of childhood and adult shame and abuse. He mentioned the assaults and indignities he endured by family and strangers, including beatings and rapes on the street. At the age of ninety, Crisp was asked about his survival strategies. My memory records him saying "I told myself I wasn't angry and, in the end, I wasn't." So, on a tactical level, Crisp's words would have you forgive your WPA and life predators.

Remember, though, that WPAs tend to be savvy survivors. As a whole, we would rather thrive than just succeed. So, on an alternate tactical level, you might strive to remember debilitating experiences in ways that are less immersive. By that I mean remembering without reliving or making a toxic return at which some of your detractors would likely roll their eyes or laugh at you.

I have no soothing balm, only more questions. Could you choose to carry some of your WPA experiences more lightly than you have? Could you see yourself recasting some of your bullies and predators as incidental or recurring characters rather than key players in your working life? That would help you ask two questions. So what if they are cavalier or cruel with their discourse and with you? If they do not value you or your talents, why are you valuing them and theirs? One more bit of advice to do your very best to be here and now rather than there and then and to work and live as an autonomous adult. Then get better at it. Be compassionate, from a safe distance, toward your bullies while protecting yourself. They missed out by not knowing, mentoring, or valuing you when you needed them. Now that you do not need them, you can still forgive, remember, and even interact with them at work (but only at work) in less immediate or self-damaging ways.

By off-loading some of your anger, you can negotiate what is—and what is not—yours to carry forward, alone, or for so long that it hurts you and perhaps your family beyond repair. Thinking about what I harbored, carried, and carried on about in these pages has taught me a few things: don't try to change others, don't let them loom large in your life, and don't expect your bullies to understand or even try to be understanding unless they feel some kind of external pressure, say, from a dean or the Office of Human Resources. Here I would like to share a secret about diversity, especially sexual diversity. For many people, their own diversity is meaningful and inviolate. They may feel they deserve some sort of emotional understanding or behavioral latitude because of it. Yet some of those same individuals are quite capable of seeing and characterizing other peoples' diversity as circumspect, a pose, an excuse for underperformance, a racket designed to attract pity, and a bore at the workplace. Long story short: you may be disappointed, enraged, and embittered to see how dull, exploitive, pedestrian, cliché, and unimaginative others see the diversity you deem to be special and sacrosanct. Moreover, harboring one's anger can be a form of narcissism, as we ourselves have likely been someone's bully. Finally, the question Why can't you evolve? is one we should ask ourselves before and much more often than we ask others.

Speaking of others, my guess is that you probably have to be out—what some call "openly gay"—for any of these ideas to stand a chance of working. It is hard to be an impactful writing program administrator or writing center director (or parent, spouse, sibling, or friend) if you are living a life lie. On that note, not quite the "note of shame" Sedgwick (1996, 137) describes but one of complicated gratitude, I dedicate this chapter to the historical and contemporary closet cases of Writing Studies. The secrets you carry cost us something important, including delays in dignity, equity, and self-worth. Have they cost you more?

ACKNOWLEDGMENTS

Many thanks to Courtney Adams Wooten, Jacob Babb, Kristi Murray Costello, Kate Navickas, Yolanda C. Janangelo, Farrell J. Webb, and the manuscript reviewers for sharing their insights and advice. Thank you for letting me learn from you.

NOTES

1. Harriet Malinowitz (1995, 267) articulates the power of that replay when she offers this reflection, "'Pride' is a term I usually tend to shy away from in gay contexts because, unlike its use in certain other contexts—the birth of a child, the achievement of a societally valued goal—the notion of gay 'pride' tends to suggests to me a bittersweet and always ambiguous triumph over shame."
2. Some WPAs and WCDs might choose to perform that stereotype and nuance it with humor. Paul Ranieri and Jackie Grutsch McKinney (2007, 272) discuss using humor as a survival strategy. They advise that "[new] WPAs should exhibit a true rhetorical temperament, one that respects a *logos*-based view of language, developing . . . related attitudes of caution, modesty, and even a sense of humor." Humor is also an understudied LGBT protective mechanism. Jack Babuscio (1993, 27) writes that "humor constitutes the strategy of camp: a means of dealing with a hostile environment and, in the process, of defining a positive identity."

3. This reminds me of Jason Palmeri's (2018) story about being bullied in middle school. Looking back, he writes "athough I now live and teach as an out queer person, I still self-censor quite a bit, still worry that if I act too queer I might find myself back in the trash can" (476).
4. While it is not my project here to offer a detailed review of LGBTQI+ scholarship relating to teaching, writing centers, and writing program administration, I am happy to recommend some important and sensitive work by William P. Banks and Jonathan Alexander (2009), Jonathan Alexander and Jacqueline Rhodes (2015), Harry Denny (2010), Mary Klages (1994), Harriet Malinowitz (1995), Martha Marinara, Jonathan Alexander, William P. Banks, and Samantha Blackmon (2009), Tara Pauliny (2011), Jay D. Sloan (1997), and William J. Spurlin (2000, 2002). The collection *Out in the Center: Public Controversies and Private Struggles* (Denny et al. 2018) also features learned and intriguing discussions of diversity, literacy instruction, and labor.
5. The authors of *GenAdmin: Theorizing WPA Identities in the Twenty-First Century* (Charlton et al. 2011, 83) ask many important questions, including "what do we know about writing program administration and WPA lives" and "what else do we need to know." Tara Pauliny (2011) offers an eloquent response by describing queer and gendered assistant professor administrator (APA) power and vulnerability:

> What I argue here, however, is that while the role of the WPA and the queer theorist may at first seem incompatible, they are actually quite congruent. When the WPA is untenured, or an (APA), she finds herself in an inherently queer position: she is an administrator who is both authorized and de-authorized; she is an integral part of the institution and a potential means of disruption; and she has an ethos that is mobile and shifting as she moves through her daily roles. As a subject who inhabits multiple roles and who exists within various nodes of power, the APA is not merely constrained by this variance but enabled by its possibility. Therefore, instead of seeing such a fraught position as a detriment—which is how the APA has often been conceptualized—this space of instability can be seen as productive and full of potential.

6. To be fair, the alleged perpetrator issued a denial. It was followed by a rebuttal by an alleged witness:

> Afterwards, Hindt released a statement denying the allegations over "a bullying incident [that] occurred more than 35 years ago" and accusing Barrett of trying to "impugn my character and reputation."
>
> But a few days later, another man, Christopher Dolan, came forward to say he witnessed the assault and that Hindt was a known bully throughout middle and high school.
>
> "I do remember, recall, one incident that happened where Lance Hindt took Greg into a bathroom," Dolan tells ABC-13. "He was in the bathroom and put his head, into uh, into a urinal."
>
> "He was a bully and he let people know that he was in charge. Nobody messed with Lance Hindt, not at West Memorial Junior High and not at Taylor High School." (Gremore 2018)

REFERENCES

Alexander, Jonathan, and Jacqueline Rhodes, eds. 2015. *Sexual Rhetorics: Methods, Identities, Publics*. New York: Routledge.

Babuscio, Jack. 1993 "Camp and Gay Sensibility." In *Camp Grounds: Style and Homosexuality*, edited by David Bergman, 19–38. Amherst: University of Massachusetts Press.

Banks, William P., and Jonathan Alexander. 2009. "Queer Eye for the Comp Program: Toward a Queer Critique of WPA Work." In *The Writing Program Interrupted: Making Space for Critical Discourse*, edited by Donna Strickland and Jeanne Gunner, 86–98. Portsmouth, NH: Boynton/Cook.

Barrow, Andrew. 1998. "Quentin Crisp Interview: Old Spice." *Independent* 21. December. https://www.independent.co.uk/arts-entertainment/quentin-crisp-interview-old-spice-1193631.html.

Blanchot, Maurice. 1981. *The Madness of the Day*. Translated by Lydia Davis. Barrytown, NY: Station Hill.

Blankenship, Chris. 2018. "Suddenly WPA: Lessons from an Early and Unexpected Transition." In *WPAs in Transition: Navigating Educational Leadership Positions*, edited by Courtney Adams Wooten, Jacob Babb, and Brian Ray, 37–50. Logan: Utah State University Press.

Bruner, Jerome S. 2004. "Life as Narrative." *Social Research* 71 (3): 691–710.

Charlton, Colin, Jonikka Charlton, Tarez Samra Graban, Kathleen J. Ryan, and Amy Ferdinandt Stolley. 2011. *GenAdmin: Theorizing WPA Identities in the Twenty-First Century*. Anderson, SC: Parlor.

Conor, Liz. 2004. *The Spectacular Modern Woman: Feminine Visibility in the 1920s*. Bloomington: Indiana University Press.

Denny, Harry. 2010. "Queering the Writing Center." *Writing Center Journal* 30 (1): 95–124.

Denny, Harry, Robert Mundy, Liliana M. Naydan, Richard Sévère, and Anna Sicari, eds. 2018. *Out in the Center: Public Controversies and Private Struggles*. Logan: Utah State University Press.

Elder, Cristyn L., and Bethany Davila, eds. 2019. *Defining, Locating, and Addressing Bullying in the WPA Workplace*. Logan: Utah State University Press.

Eliot, T. S. *Four Quartets*. 1971. New York: Harcourt Brace Jovanovich.

Genette, Gerard. 1983. *Narrative Discourse: An Essay in Method*. Translated by Jane E. Lewin. Ithaca, NY: Cornell University Press.

George, Diana. *Kitchen Cooks, Plate Twirlers, and Troubadours: Writing Program Administrators Tell Their Stories*. 1999. Portsmouth, NH: Heinemann.

Gremore, Grahame. 2018. "School Superintendent Laughs in the Face of a Man He Tormented in Middle School." March 26. Queerty.com. https://www.queerty.com/school-superintendent-laughs-face-man-tormented-middle-school-20180326.

Herlihy, James Leo, and William A. Noble. 1958. *Blue Denim*. New York: Random House.

Hesse, Doug. 2013. "What Is a Personal Life?" In *A Rhetoric for Writing Program Administrators*, edited by Rita Malenczyk, 407–414. Anderson, SC: Parlor.

Klages, Mary. 1994. "The Ins and Outs of a Lesbian Academic." In *Tilting the Tower: Lesbians/Teaching/Queer/Subjects*, edited by Linda Garber, 235–242. New York: Routledge.

Kouzes, James M., and Barry Z. Posner. 2012. *The Leadership Challenge: How to Make Extraordinary Things Happen in Organizations*. San Francisco: Jossey-Bass.

Liem, Caroline. 2018. "Everything You Need to Know to Nail a Chemistry Read." *Backstage*. June 10. https://www.backstage.com/advice-for-actors/backstage-experts/everything-you-need-know-nail-chemistry-read/.

Lorde, Audre. 1981. "The Uses of Anger." *Women's Studies Quarterly* 9 (3): 7–10.

Lyotard, Jean-Francois. 1984. *The Postmodern Condition: A Report on Knowledge*. Minneapolis: University of Minnesota Press.

Malinowitz, Harriet. 1995. *Textual Orientations: Lesbian and Gay Students and the Making of Discourse Communities*. Portsmouth, NH: Heinemann.

Marinara, Martha, Jonathan Alexander, William P. Banks, and Samantha Blackmon. 2009. "Cruising Composition Texts: Negotiating Sexual Difference in First-Year Readers." *College Composition and Communication* 61 (2): 269–296.

O'Brien, Edna. 1962. *The Lonely Girl.* New York: Plume.
Palmeri, Jason. 2018. "Disruptive Queer Narratives in Composition and Literacy Studies." Review of *Fashioning Lives: Black Queers and the Politics of Literacy*, by Eric Darnell Pritchard, *Techne: Queer Meditations on Writing the Self*, by Jacqueline Rhodes and Jonathan Alexander, and *Teaching Queer: Radical Possibilities for Writing and Knowing*, by Stacey Waite. *College English* 80 (5): 471–486.
Pauliny, Tara. 2011. "Queering the Institution: Politics and Power in the Assistant Professor Administrator Position" *Enculturation.* March 21. http://enculturation.net/queering-the-institution.
Polanyi, Michael. 1958. *Personal Knowledge: Towards a Post-Critical Philosophy.* Chicago: University of Chicago Press.
Ranieri, Paul, and Jackie Grutsch McKinney. 2007 "Fitness for the Occasion: How Context Matters for jWPAs." In *Untenured Faculty as Writing Program Administrators: Institutional Practices and Policies*, edited by Debra Frank Dew and Alice Horning, 249–278. West Lafayette, IN: Parlor.
Ritter, Kelly. 2018. "Making (Collective) Memory Public: WPA Histories in Dialogue." *Writing Program Administration* 41 (2): 35–64.
Schuster, John. 2003. *Answering Your Call: A Guide to Living Your Deepest Purpose.* San Francisco: Berrett-Koehler.
Sedgwick, Eve Kosofsky. 1996. "Queer Performativity: Warhol's Shyness/Warhol's Whiteness." In *Pop Out: Queer Warhol* (Series Q), edited by Jennifer Doyle, Jonathan Flatley, and Jose Esteban Muñoz, 134–143. Durham, NC: Duke University Press.
Sloan, Jay D. 1997. "Closet Consulting." *Writing Lab Newsletter* 21 (10): 9–10.
Spurlin, William J. 2000. *Lesbian and Gay Studies and the Teaching of English: Positions, Pedagogies, and Cultural Politics.* Urbana, IL: National Council of Teachers.
Spurlin, William J. 2002. "Theorizing Queer Pedagogy in English Studies after the 1990s." *College English* 65 (1): 9–16.
Susann, Jacqueline, 1966. *Valley of the Dolls.* New York: Grove.
Wei, Jessica. 2015. "Peter Lynch—Know What You Own." December 15. https://due.com/blog/peter-lynch-know-what-you-own/.
White, Hayden, and American Council of Learned Societies. 1987. *The Content of the Form: Narrative Discourse and Historical Representation.* Baltimore: Johns Hopkins University Press.

13
FROM GREAT TO GOOD ENOUGH
Recalibrating Expectations as WPA

Elizabeth Kleinfeld
Metropolitan State University of Denver

At the tail end of summer, two weeks before the start of fall semester, a colleague called me. I had my phone on silent, but when the screen lit up to tell me I had missed a call, it caught my attention. Before I could call her back, the voice message transcription popped up on my screen—"I'm so sorry to leave this information in a voice message, but I want to make sure you saw the news about Lucas on Facebook."

Lucas Dembicki was a peer tutor in the writing center I direct, but he was much more than that: my research assistant, my collaborator, close friend to many of the tutors, a mentor and role model to other peer tutors, and more. At thirty-two years old, he had died suddenly of a massive heart attack. I unexpectedly found myself scrambling to convey the news to others, to figure out how to begin a semester on such a sad note, and to negotiate my own loss. One month later, my husband's cousin took his own life. Still reeling from Lucas's death, I had to grapple with a second devastating loss.

It had been my most productive summer professionally; I had multiple research projects under way, had honed a daily writing practice and was actively drafting and revising several articles, and had just accepted a position as associate editor of a journal. I was doing final revisions on sample chapters for a book an editor had shown interest in. In addition, with a new assistant director coming on, I had ambitious plans sketched out for the writing center. With the two sudden deaths, I got a crash course in setting boundaries, modeling self-care, and being vulnerable. But perhaps most significant, I came face to face with readjusting my expectations of what can get done in a semester, an academic year, and a career.

As my chapter title suggests, I will address the sometimes necessary reversal of the idea that we should all be striving to do more all the time and the emotional labor that goes into that recalibration. I had to consider not just what I could reasonably accomplish in the midst of mourning and providing emotional support to my staff but what I wanted to get done and to whom it would matter. After years spent striving to do more and to be more visible in the workplace, which Nicole Caswell, Jackie Grutsch McKinney, and Rebecca Jackson (2016) find is typical for writing center directors, I needed to ratchet down my expectations—and those of others—of what could get done in the writing center and in my own research.

Drawing on my own experience and building on Laura J. Davies's (2017) work applying grief theory to writing program administrator (WPA) transitions, this chapter will focus on strategies for productively engaging with the recalibration of both programmatic and career expectations. In the next section, I provide several snapshots that capture particularly rich moments of me negotiating emotional labor. After discussing some of the themes in those snapshots, I focus on specific strategies I see as fruitful for WPAs (broadly defined) to employ in negotiating emotional labor, both in the wake of tragedy and as a matter of course. The overall effect of the strategies is in line with Laura R. Micciche's (2011) argument for "slow agency": a shifting of energy from the frenzied pace of constant activity toward a more sustainable pace that encourages reflection and collaboration. While I came to these strategies in the aftermath of emotional turmoil, I believe enacting them can help create a more equitable and humane workplace.

SNAPSHOTS

I

I reacted to the news of Lucas's death first not as a writing center director but as a human. My heart ached. I replayed over and over in my mind my last conversation with Lucas (just a few days before he died, he randomly stopped by my office to talk about an idea he had for the research we were collaborating on). I read over and over the last text he sent me, our last email exchange. I read and reread the tributes his friends, family, and colleagues were posting on Facebook. Despite my intense dislike of talking on the phone, I spoke on the phone every day for several days with a tutor Lucas had been very close to, she and I processing our grief and sharing memories together. We shared stories, cried, and commiserated on our loss. The tutor and I texted late into the night. I spoke with Lucas's brother, who I had never met, multiple times on the phone, as he was hungry for details about his little brother's life on campus.

Several days later, when I turned my attention toward reacting as a writing center director, I did what many nerdy introverts might do: I looked at my bookshelves. As wonderful as Christina Murphy and Byron Stay's (2012) *Writing Center Director's Resource Book* is, it has nothing to say about dealing with the death of a tutor. My other go-to books and online resources were similarly silent on the subject. Despite the gendered expectation that as a woman and a mother I would know how to take care of my staff, I had no clue. Finally, I turned to the writing center listserv, WCenter, posting this message:

> Hello, writing center friends. I just learned that one of my peer tutors died suddenly a few days ago. He was well-loved by tutors and clients alike and his death will be heartbreaking to many (including me). Our semester begins on Aug. 21. We have a staff meeting scheduled for Friday, Aug. 18. I am going to arrange for someone from the counseling center to be available before, during, and after the staff meeting. What else should I do? What advice do you have for notifying clients? Should I continue with the planned agenda for the Friday meeting or ditch it? And how do I maintain some semblance of composure when I am as wrecked by this news as my tutors? Any and all advice appreciated and needed. Elizabeth

My post generated an outpouring of support, both on the listserv and off. I received dozens of responses, some with specific pieces of advice—for example, to have someone from the counseling center at the staff meeting, to ask staff how they want to remember Lucas, and to hold a writing center–only memorial event—and many more that simply conveyed heartfelt condolences. Every one meant something to me and helped me feel connected to other directors across time and space. Some shared stories of losing their own tutors, others suggested coping strategies. One day I received a beautiful handwritten condolence note from a writing center director I had never met. At both conferences I attended that semester, people approached me to say they had seen my post on the listserv and wondered how I and my staff were doing. These exchanges were important, in part because they confirmed that my grief was normal.

II

Four weeks after Lucas's death, my husband's cousin took his own life. Will was thirty-one years old, an avid motorcycle rider and outdoorsman. My husband described him as more of a little brother than a cousin, and Will often accompanied us on motorcycle rides, camping, and rafting trips. A couple of years earlier, the three of us had done an epic motorcycle ride from Denver to Oregon's west coast, camping along the way.

I went to campus the day after learning of Will's death but made myself scarce by closing my door for part of the day and hiding out in the library later. I told my assistant and chair about Will's death but no one else; I just couldn't bear to say the words. The next day, I left for a conference. I was relieved to have the excuse to not be on campus, and the intensity of the conference kept me busy. When I got home Sunday night, I emailed my assistant and chair, letting them know I would work from home Monday, be on campus minimally Tuesday, be gone for memorial events Wednesday and Thursday, and be on campus minimally again on Friday. I ended the email with "I will create an out-of-office message letting folks know that I am largely unavailable this week. Thanks for understanding."

That Tuesday, after spending a few hours on campus holed up in my office with the door closed, I sent an email to the entire writing center staff:

> Writing Center friends and colleagues, Thank you for giving me plenty of space today. My family has suffered a sudden and tragic loss and we are all reeling. I will not be on campus on Wednesday and only for a bit on Thursday and Friday. Thank you for your understanding and patience with me this week. I love and appreciate all of you.

For the next two weeks, I minimized my time on campus, arranging to participate in several meetings by phone and canceling others altogether. I kept myself obsessively busy to keep from falling apart, helping to write Will's obituary and collecting and editing friends' and family members' memories of Will into a book.

Having spent much of my career haunted by the words of an early supervisor—"you are much too emotional at work"—I was proud of the somewhat stoic figure I had become. As I communicated with people that I would miss meetings, many of my emails relied on my busyness:

> Jennifer, I will miss our call this week. Unfortunately, a dear cousin died suddenly last week and there are multiple memorial events this week that I am involved with.

The busyness was not the real reason I couldn't attend meetings, however; the fact is, I was nearly paralyzed with grief.

III

When I returned to work the following Tuesday, I found a bundle of fresh herbs on my desk with a handwritten note that said "Parsley, Sage, Rosemary, and Thyme (according to tradition/folklore, these are healing herbs). Parsley = Comfort, Sage = Strength, Rosemary = Love and Remembrance, Thyme = Courage." Although the note was unsigned, I recognized the handwriting as that of a professional tutor who had worked in the writing center since before I came on as director. The thought of her putting time and energy during her weekend into finding a unique way to comfort me was moving and set the tone for how I would deal with the tutoring staff. I still did not know exactly how I was going to present myself and my grief—a different grief from the grief about Lucas because no one at the writing center knew Will—to the staff, but the bundle of herbs indicated that at least some of the staff wanted to be let in.

Later that day, a peer tutor who was also in the class I taught that night popped into my office. "I'm so sorry to hear about your loss," she said. "I'm a good listener if you need to talk to someone." Her offer caught me off guard, and I quickly and defensively told her I was fine and closed my door. As I walked to class an hour later, I played over in my mind how unhappy I was with that reaction. I recognized that my response hinged on the authority and age differential between us—and my discomfort with sharing my emotions at work. When I got to class, I asked the peer tutor to come out in the hall. "I am unhappy with how I handled your kind offer earlier. Can I have a do-over?" She said yes and I told her, "I don't need to talk, but I would love a hug."

IV

Two weeks into the semester, my chair asked all faculty in the department to serve on two department committees, with the expectation that most of us would also serve on committees at higher levels. I told her I'd be doing the bare minimum for service that year, at both the department and higher levels. I did not ask permission or promise to do more in the future to make up for my light service load. I simply told her, "This is what I will do." To my surprise, she immediately agreed.

V

There's a white board leaning against a bookcase in my office outlining research projects. It is in the way constantly, blocking two shelves of the bookcase. I move it around as I need access to the bookcase, always putting it right back, leaning against the bookcase—in the way—when I am done. It is a reminder of the vision Lucas and I had of what the writing center would be, had he lived. Possibly the writing center will fulfill that vision at some point, or perhaps it won't. I still don't have the stomach to imagine pursuing the plan without Lucas.

I dropped the ball on so many things that I stopped keeping track of them. Even now, I sometimes come across an archived email or am reminded by a random encounter of something I let drop. Three research protocols approved by the Institutional Review Board collecting dust. A tutor training project I was collaborating on with colleagues from other institutions put on indefinite hold. Data collected last spring sitting in an unopened email.

At some point after Will's death, when I hadn't been on campus regularly for a week or so, one of the tutors who had presented me with many ideas for making our website more robust suggested I hand the website over to her. I would normally have said no, concerned that I didn't have the time and energy to train her, but exhausted by grief, I agreed and referred her to IT for training. When another tutor asked if she could take over the planning for an online tutoring pilot, I agreed. I told both that I would have little energy to support them. We instituted weekly fifteen-minute progress meetings (Hicks and Foster 2010), but otherwise I left them to their own devices.

DISCUSSION

These snapshots indicate a clear tension between my expectation that being productive as a WPA means crossing tasks off a list and the reality that simply being present was both work for me, as evidenced by the amount of sheer energy and determination it sometimes took to be on campus, and productive, as demonstrated by how my mere presence helped build trust and made staff feel supported. These snapshots illustrate that much WPA work is accomplished simply through being physically present in the workplace. The days I was on campus but checked out emotionally were valuable to both staff and clients. The signal my open door sent—even when it was not fully open but only cracked—was that the WPA was there, on the job, part of the collectively experienced trauma of Lucas's death and later, concerned about the well-being of staff and clients even in the wake of her own personal tragedy. Jackson, McKinney, and Caswell (2016) found that much of the work of writing center directors involves emotional labor, including "mentoring, advising, making small talk, putting on a friendly face, resolving conflicts, and making connections; it also included delegating tasks and following up on progress, working in teams, disciplining or redirecting employees, gaining trust, and creating a positive workplace." Simply being in my office, making even very rudimentary conversation, saying "sounds good" when staff ran an idea past me, or saying "I can't deal with that right now, but thank you for bringing it to my attention" enabled me to do many of the tasks Jackson, McKinney, and Caswell (2016) list, such as making small talk and connections, gaining trust, and creating a positive workplace.

Although being present is important, it wasn't always clear to me how to behave when I was present. At the two memorial events for Lucas, my "job" was to mourn, remember, hug, and cry; but at the August staff meeting, I lacked that level of clarity. At most beginning-of-the-academic-year meetings, I aim to present and engage tutors in a vision for the upcoming year, but that felt completely inappropriate after Lucas's death. I decided instead to provide a safe space for processing grief. Unlike the two memorial services, the staff meeting was awkward and quiet. The new staff who never knew Lucas probably felt awkward because they didn't know him, and returning staff might have felt self-conscious about their emotional responses in front of new staff. I think my open crying at both events—not by choice but by temperament—helped returning staff members feel it was okay to display emotion, and as awkward as it was for new staff to see their boss crying, I believe my show of vulnerability helped create the sense of an open and accepting workplace.

My initial dismissive response to the peer tutor's offer to listen grew in part out of a sense that leaders don't burden their employees with their own emotional baggage; however, I realize now that when I asked that tutor for a "do-over," I was performing the important emotional labor of acknowledging her offer and building trust. In the past, I have shown compassion for others while denying my need for compassion, but I am no longer comfortable with the double standard I enacted. By demonstrating my need for compassion and delegating work to others, I built trust and rapport.

STRATEGIES

As I write this, I realize that I was not just grieving the loss of Lucas and Will—I was also grieving the loss of my vision of what the writing center would do and be as well as progress on my scholarly projects. Here I find it helpful to bring in Davies's work understanding writing program transitions through the lens of grief theory. Davies (2017, 44) suggests adopting William Worden's theory of grief, which focuses not on what mourners feel but on what they do: they process pain and loss, they make changes to their routines to accommodate what is missing, and they learn to live in their new reality without denying the importance of what used to be. As with any personal crisis, the death of a loved one requires juggling responsibilities in the immediate aftermath and also longer-term recalibration of expectations. Neo-liberal ideas about faculty and WPA workloads can make both the immediate juggling and the longer-term recalibration feel like failures, but I argue that we should understand these adjustments as empowering moves that resist academia's patriarchal culture. Moreover, I urge us to focus on acknowledging the actions and labor inherent in these adjustments.

Drawing upon my own missteps, insights, and experiences, I offer the following strategies for WPAs who need to recalibrate expectations downward in the wake of a crisis.

1. Shore up support before you need it.

As a nerdy introvert, I am generally more comfortable finding the support I need in a book than by interacting with others, but the outpouring of care I received from colleagues was incredibly helpful, both in terms of helping me figure out how to support my staff and myself as we grieved and also in making me feel connected to a world outside my personal tragedies. I was grateful that I had established networks for professional support, including a small group I had become part of through the National Center for Faculty Development and Diversity (see Adsit and Doe, this volume, for more on the NCFDD), a writing group, and access to the WCenter Listserv. I was particularly grateful that I had taken the advice of Kerry Ann Rockquemore (2011): "Stop asking people: 'Will you be my mentor?' Start asking people for what you need." The local writing group I belong to, for example, was already used to me asking directly for what I need, so when I told them I was lowering my expectations for the year and needed them to support me in that, they did. My NCFDD small group helped me resist the urge to self-isolate out of embarrassment over my emotions.

2. Resist notions that grieving or struggling with a crisis is unprofessional.

Mary Anne Hazen (2008, 78), who studies grief in the workplace, points out that because "working people tend to spend as much time or even more time at work and with their colleagues than at home with family," understanding grief in the workplace matters. One of the writing center directors studied by Jackson, McKinney, and Caswell (2016) shared the common belief that he had to hide his emotions at work, "performing a particular, socially acceptable, and valued emotional stance." Hazen acknowledges that displaying grief in the workplace can be considered "unprofessional" but finds that the stress of "hidden grief" contributes to decreased work engagement and quality. Citing this research in meeting with my chair, I articulated as a goal to create a workplace where staff, myself included, could feel safe expressing grief.

I did my best to model self-care for staff (for more on self-care, see the chapters by Clinnin and Imafuji, this volume). There were many days following the deaths of Lucas and Will when merely being in my office with the door open was challenging. Recognizing my presence in the writing center as itself a form of work helped me articulate it as such to myself and others. It's a form of work that can't be checked off a to-do list, but my being in my office, visible to staff and faculty—or even in my office with my door closed, with only my "do not disturb" sign on the door visible—was work. It contributed to creating a safe environment for grieving, and it allowed staff to see that they could trust me when I told them it was safe to grieve at work.

Another key step I took to push back against the idea that struggling with a personal crisis at work is unprofessional is that I tried to offer thanks instead of apologies when I pulled out of a project or was unprepared for a meeting. Apologizing would have implied that I *should* have been able to perform as if nothing had happened on top of doing my grief work. Instead, I thanked people for their patience, understanding, or flexibility.

3. Prioritize based on institutional, college, and department goals.

In the days before the staff meeting, I spent my few clear-headed hours reviewing the writing center's five-year strategic plan and the university's strategic plan. Anything that didn't clearly align with the university's strategic plan I assigned a lower priority to. I reviewed my department's planning documents and did the same thing. By reviewing the institutional and departmental goals, I was able to examine all the projects I wanted to get done and zero in on the ones that would be most visible and valuable to those who would evaluate me. This gave me a big-picture framework for the year. Once I had a clear sense of the things I could do that were in line with the goals of the institution, college, and department, I was able to frame what I did in terms that were recognizable to those around me. For example, one of my institution's goals is for "MSU Denver faculty, staff and students [to] feel valued and engaged in an environment of empowerment, trust, inclusion and fairness." I articulated my hosting a memorial for Lucas as a way to build trust with my staff, connecting it to the goal.

For shorter-term planning, I prioritized by asking three questions about any task I considered doing: Does this need to be done? Does it need to be done now? Does it need to be done now by me? The first question helped me pare down tasks to the things that really mattered. The second question helped me defer some tasks to the future. The third question helped me delegate tasks. These three questions gave me clarity on a daily basis. As I considered whether to do tutor observations, it was clear that yes, observations had to be done, but they did not need to be done by me, so it was easy to delegate to the assistant director. I had been working with two writing center directors from other institutions on a project to create materials to train our tutors in mind-set theory. Although I could certainly see benefits to doing the mind-set training for tutors, when I asked the first question, "does this training need to be done," I realized the answer was no. A climate survey I had developed did need to be done and did need to be done by me, but for weeks, my answer to "does this need to be done now" was no, which helped me defer it for a month without guilt.

Yes, there were consequences for not getting things done or for getting them done weeks or months after I had planned. I was not as well-prepared for a conference presentation as I would have liked, for example, but I trust that most members of the audience will not judge the entirety of my work on that one presentation.

These two prioritizing activities made it possible for me to accept that I would not be able to "do all the things" and that the truly important things would get done. They also helped me recognize and let go of busyness. Maggie Berg and Barbara Seeber (2016, 21) acknowledge that "academic culture celebrates overwork, but it is imperative that we question the value of busyness. We need to interrogate what we are modelling for each other and for our students." When I had the emotional energy only to do what absolutely had to be done, it became possible to respond to emails at a slower pace—and also to not be bothered when others responded to emails at a slower pace.

4. Under-promise and over-deliver.

Economists and psychologists theorize that we consider the potential for being disappointed by an outcome when we make decisions (Bell 1982, 1985; Loomes and Sugden 1982, 1986; Van Dijk, Zeelenberg, and Van der Pligt 2003). According to these theories, lowering expectations to bring them in line with probable outcomes is one way people avoid disappointment. As WPAs, we can do this strategically to help ourselves and those we report to feel less disappointment in our lowered expectations and instead recognize what was accomplished. Many WPAs have high expectations of themselves; Carrie Shivley Leverenz (2010, 4) notes that "for feminist administrators, the urge to 'do more' includes not just the goal of improving the programs for which we are responsible, but also the goal of changing the institution." On the surface, my urge to do more was put on hold when Lucas died, but in retrospect, I see that what I did in terms of lowering expectations for myself, my staff, and my supervisors was very much in line with feminist principles and "the goal of changing the institution." I now understand the magnitude of what I was doing—bringing expectations and goals in line with available resources, including emotional resources, and how to articulate that to people around me. In August, I told my chair I would be doing the bare minimum, so when I discuss building trust with my staff through hosting the memorial for Lucas in my annual report, it will exceed her expectations.

This strategy has been more challenging for me to apply to the trajectory of my career. Like the writing center directors studied by Jackson, McKinney, and Caswell (2016), I enjoy seeing myself as leaving a legacy for my students, the students who come to the writing center, the students who work as peer tutors, and the faculty who consult with me on teaching writing. Putting the book project and others on hold brought me to a sobering reality: my legacy may not be what I had hoped. While Micciche (2002) reminds me that disappointment seems to come with the territory of WPA work, I am working to connect the work I am able to do to my own big-picture life goals; I may not end up making a difference in the ways I had hoped, but I am able to see that, for example, the two tutors who took on revamping the website and piloting the online tutoring program felt empowered by me. That's me making a difference.

5. Reframe changed expectations as proactive, deliberate, and purposeful.

This foregrounds the dynamic nature of goal setting, acknowledging that realistic and responsible goal setting is contingent on resources, institutional needs, and local needs. In this light, recalibration is normal and responsible rather than a sign of failure. This is a way to highlight the emotional labor, the *doing of things*. When we put aside some goals to focus on others—in this context, me putting aside the goal of developing a mind-set training to focus instead on the goal of helping my staff work through their grief—we are by definition doing what leaders do.

These recalibrations should be highlighted in annual reports, progress reports, and other genres in which our activities and accomplishments are recorded; this is in line with the suggestions in Stolley's chapter in this collection. For example, rather than saying that I am not moving forward on three research protocols in my annual report, I will say that I deliberately moved those research protocols to the back burner to put my energy into supporting my staff through a shared trauma.

Identifying the supporting of my staff as an accomplishment in official documents frames it as labor and valuable; further, it articulates emotion "as active rather than reactive," a key understanding Micciche (2016) argues for. Rather than articulating Lucas's death and the aftermath as a reason some things did not get done, I frame the deliberate decisions I made after his death as work. Instead of apologizing for my inability to conduct tutor observations after Will's death, I count my delegation of tutor observations to the assistant director as a responsible use of resources; similarly, I count delegating projects to tutors as providing them with leadership opportunities.

6. Reconsider ideas of legacy.

The two premature deaths focused my attention on the question of how I and my career would be judged if I died suddenly. My productive summer had encouraged me to think about my research seeing a wider audience, but the deaths of Lucas and Will introduced into my thinking the possibility that I would never see my projects through. My grieving then further derailed my progress on those projects.

There is another way for me to think about my legacy, disconnected from my scholarship, as I alluded to above: as helping to create a more humane environment for others. When we recalibrate expectations in the face of tragedy, we can see what we are doing as advocating for others to be able to do the same thing. When we resist the culture of not acknowledging emotional labor as work, we are paving the way for our future colleagues to not be held to these patriarchal, unhealthy, and often discriminatory standards. If we adhere to the conventional notions of grieving at work as unprofessional or work attending to emotion as somehow "less than" other work, we legitimize and normalize the status quo. This is comparatively easy for me to say, as someone with the privileges of whiteness, tenure, and the status of full professor; people of color, members of the LBGTQIA community, those without tenure, and others may be much more vulnerable to negative judgment for resisting the status quo. That puts more responsibility on those of us with privilege to create more humane conditions for our junior and future colleagues. When we serve on tenure and promotion committees, when we move into roles in upper administration, we have a responsibility to not replicate patriarchal conditions.

CONCLUSION

My chapter title relies on conventional, patriarchal notions of "great" and "good enough." E. Shelley Reid (2010, 128) explores what it means to be a "'good enough' feminist WPA," focusing on the tensions that complicate any attempts to enact feminist principles and concerns about "not measuring up" and not "being properly feminist." Reid's point is that many of us feminist WPAs worry and feel conflict about whether we are "good enough" in enacting feminist principles when we are representatives of the institution. This understanding of "good enough" is about aspiring to be better. I want us to understand "good enough" as success. The "good enough" I have played with in this chapter is about recognizing that "good enough" is really all there is and that aiming to be more than that is an illusion. In arguing for a more deliberative academic practice, Berg and Seeber (2016) highlight how hyperbolic the neo-liberal language around performance has become, citing a job ad for an administrator to take an institution "beyond greatness."

There is some acknowledgment in our field that speed is not always a good thing and that, in fact, slowness in research (Lindquist 2012; Berg and Seeber 2016), in teaching (Berg and Seeber 2016), and in administrating (Micciche 2011) allows us to engage in nuanced ways with the complexity of what we do. Micciche (2011) suggests using the concept of hypermiling, in which drivers try to get as far as they can with minimal fuel, as a metaphor for WPA work. This approach emphasizes energy conservation and carefully analyzing energy use to account for "the consequences of missteps" (78). She notes that "despite my first impression, hypermiling does not compromise one's ability to get anywhere; it merely slows the pace of arrival" (78). The strategies I have outlined can be used on an everyday basis to move toward a hypermiling approach to WPA work.

The strategies I've offered are not simply ones that can help when dealing with a crisis—it took back-to-back tragedies to clue me in, but I believe these are things we should be doing *anyway*. Recognizing our emotional labor as valuable work that makes a difference and bringing that attitude to everything we do at our institutions will change academia for the better—for us, for our colleagues, and for our students.

REFERENCES

Bell, David E. 1982. "Regret in Decision Making under Uncertainty." *Operations Research* 30 (5): 961–981.
Bell, David E. 1985. "Disappointment in Decision Making under Uncertainty." *Operations Research* 33 (1): 1–27.
Berg, Maggie, and Barbara Seeber. 2016. *The Slow Professor: Challenging the Culture of Speed in the Academy*. Toronto: University of Toronto Press.
Davies, Laura J. 2017. "Grief and the New WPA." *WPA: Writing Program Administration* 40 (2): 40–51.
Hazen, Mary Ann. 2008. "Grief and the Workplace." *Academy of Management Perspectives* 22 (3): 78–86.
Hicks, Michael, and Jeffrey S. Foster. 2010. *Adapting Scrum to Managing a Research Group*. https://www.cs.umd.edu/~mwh/papers/score.pdf.
Jackson, Rebecca, Jackie Grutsch McKinney, and Nicole I. Caswell. 2016. "Writing Center Administration and/as Emotional Labor." *Composition Forum* 34. http://compositionforum.com/issue/34/writing-center.php.
Leverenz, Carrie Shively. 2010. "What's Ethics Got to Do with It? Feminist Ethics and Administrative Work in Rhetoric and Composition." In *Performing Feminism and Administration in Rhetoric and Composition Studies*, edited by Krista Ratcliffe and Rebecca Rickly, 3–18. Cresskill, NJ: Hampton.
Lindquist, Julie. 2012. "Time to Grow Them: Practicing Slow Research in a Fast Field." *JAC* 32 (3–4): 645–666.
Loomes, Graham, and Robert Sugden. 1982. "Regret Theory: An Alternative Theory of Rational Choice under Uncertainty." *Economic Journal* 92 (368): 805–824.
Loomes, Graham, and Robert Sugden. 1986. "Disappointment and Dynamic Consistency in Choice under Uncertainty." *Review of Economic Studies* 53 (2): 271–282.
Micciche, Laura R. 2002. "More Than a Feeling: Disappointment and WPA Work." *College English* 64 (4): 432–458.
Micciche, Laura R. 2011. "For Slow Agency." *WPA: Writing Program Administration* 35 (1): 73–90.
Micciche, Laura R. 2016. "Staying with Emotion." *Composition Forum* 34. https://compositionforum.com/issue/34/micciche-retrospective.php.
Murphy, Christina, and Byron Stay, eds. 2012. *The Writing Center Director's Resource Book*. New York: Routledge.
Reid, E. Shelley. 2010. "Managed Care: All-Terrain Mentoring and the 'Good Enough' Feminist WPA." In *Performing Feminism and Administration in Rhetoric and Composition Studies*, edited by Krista Ratcliffe and Rebecca Rickly, 128–141. Cresskill, NJ: Hampton.
Rockquemore, Kerry Ann. 2011. "Will You Be My Mentor?" *Inside Higher Education*. November 14. https://www.insidehighered.com/advice/2011/11/14/essay-mentoring-and-minority-faculty-members.
Van Dijk, Wilco W., Marcel Zeelenberg, and Joop Van der Pligt. 2003. "Blessed Are Those Who Expect Nothing: Lowering Expectations as a Way of Avoiding Disappointment." *Journal of Economic Psychology* 24 (4): 505–516.

14
NAVIGATING WPA EMOTIONAL LABOR WITH MINDFULNESS
Practical Strategies for Well-Being

Christy I. Wenger
  Shepherd University

> As leaders, we are called to take care of the people within our program by attending to both their professional and emotional needs. We have theorized the role of affect, emotion, and empathy in the writing classroom . . . we also need to consider how the emotions that arise from human relationships—grief, joy, love, shame, worry, hope, and so on—affect our workplaces and writing programs. (Davies 2017, 49)

The interminable writing program administrator (WPA) is always available. If you can't find her teaching or observing a writing class, she is in her office meeting with teachers to mentor and support them. She spends as much time as possible working with these teachers to make sure they feel cared for and listened to, which she hopes will increase their longevity in her program and ensure that her well-researched and up-to-date curriculum is carried out successfully. Because she advocates for writing across campus, she is involved in so many committees that she often forgets their official names; when writing is a concern, she finds herself unable to say no. In addition to meeting with students, her office hours are filled with administrative tasks such as hiring new teachers and finding classroom space for an increasing number of first-year writing sections. As for the classes she teaches, she lesson plans when she gets her kids to bed at 8 p.m., after making dinner and collapsing at her desk. She learned these work habits as a graduate student WPA studying for her comprehensive exams—days marked by pages read and written, days measured by writing workshops held and classroom observations conducted for fellow teaching assistants, all to give her a fighting chance in the job market.

It's hard to write a description of the interminable WPA without feeling guilty. The reality is, she's who I once was and who I still catch myself trying to be: everywhere at once and everything to everyone. While I know I can't sustain such an unbalanced and unhealthy commitment to my work, I worry that this WPA shows my weaknesses. With two children of my own, I might not be on campus as much as I could be, as much as I was before I had children with evening dance classes and daycare pickup times. I know that as the primary advocate of writing on my campus—where I direct the writing program and am the sole "writing expert" as my colleagues like to call me—the more committees I sit on, the better I can keep writing a central campus focus. But I don't want to live on campus; I want a balanced life where my family and my self-care are not edged out by around-the-clock work. Balance is elusive and difficult to maintain, and the interminable WPA lurks in the background, normalizing excessive work habits and laying the blame on me, the individual who cannot carry them out. I'm not alone in my guilt. The un-shakeability of such interminable standards is why E. Shelly Reid (2010) calls herself a "good-enough" WPA when she seeks to question the sustainability of her work habits; it is why in my epigraph Laura J. Davies (2017) passionately calls for us to locate the emotion work in our programs so we can better care for the people who staff them but stops short of listing the WPA herself as in need of emotional consideration. As Laura R. Micciche (2002) has suggested, we are ambivalent about the emotionally charged space the WPA tends to occupy.

I consider the WPA in this chapter, examining how she is socialized into performing emotional labor, often at the expense of her own self-care; while that labor is a systemic and corporate issue, one that cannot be reduced to the individual emotor, I argue that it must also always account for the individual. After outlining theories of emotional labor in the next section and highlighting how these theories are implicated in Western binaristic thinking about emotion as private "inside" work, I turn to the practical and theoretical lens of secular mindfulness, of paying full, open attention, to find alternative heuristics of emotions as agentive and inter-relational. Through the lens of secular mindfulness, which is indebted to Eastern contemplative theories of the interconnectedness of life, bodies, and feelings, emotional labor becomes worthy of collaborative discussion, opening a space for generative talk about ecological agency and communal well-being.

In what follows, I approach emotional labor rhetorically from my point of view as a newly tenured WPA at a public, liberal arts university. I explore how mindfulness, an attentional present-oriented practice cultivated through contemplative activities such as meditation, allows WPAs a tangible and practical means of approaching emotion as an embodied rhetorical action within communicative networks, as felt simultaneously "inside" and "outside." Mindfulness is a powerful theory and practice for WPAs because it literally remaps the emotional geographies of WPA work. It responds to why interminable work habits should not be our goal and why our emotional health as administrators is an integral part of the discussion regarding the sustainability of our work. I end this chapter by offering specific mindfulness practices that can provide WPAs with ways of dealing productively with the emotional economies of university workspaces and bringing emotion work within the parameters of our job descriptions and public discussions of our daily labor. While these are practices that employ mindfulness, they do not require all WPAs to become yogis or Zen meditators; mindfulness can be enacted through the daily tasks of WPA work.

MAPPING EMOTIONAL LABOR THROUGH MINDFULNESS

Among planning a curriculum for my writing program, writing grants, designing and performing assessments, and staying abreast of scholarship, my job as a WPA is intellectually demanding. The intellectual labor of my job lends well to categorization in my annual report, which makes it visible to others, but most days I come home emotionally burned out before I am intellectually fatigued. As Amy Ferdinandt Stolley argues in this volume, we lack strategies that "tie emotional labor to more quantifiable and universally valued outcomes a range of audiences would understand and appreciate when evaluating our faculty activity" (106). Though my heavy load of emotional labor often goes uncategorized—and therefore largely unrecognized—on any given day, I must negotiate conflicts between writing students and the teachers they feel have treated them unjustly, navigate grade appeals and plagiarism cases, validate the feelings of contingent instructors who haven't been given the teaching schedules they requested and therefore feel betrayed, and manage my own feelings when yet another round of budget cuts disproportionately impacts my writing program while less vulnerable programs stay afloat.

The enormity of emotion work within administration is a reason why Micciche (2016; 2002, 432) tells us to "stay with emotion" more than a decade after she examines the culture of disappointment within writing studies in general and WPA work in particular. To make this work visible, we might start with Micciche by looking to Arlie Hochschild's (1983) concept of emotional labor as the management of emotions in the workplace. Hochschild's theory of emotion recognizes that emotions are shaped by our social, cultural, and, therefore, workplace environments and that emotional labor is particularly acute in service fields where the creation and maintenance of feeling becomes objectified: "service with a smile" quite literally becomes a good provided. Of such service, Hochschild (1983, 8) notes, "the workers I talked to often spoke of their smiles being on them but not of them" so that emotional labor is always a matter of performance, of acting, that alienates the self from herself, unknowingly or knowingly: emotional management occurs as we attempt to accommodate emotion norms and align "what we feel" with how we are "supposed" to feel. Hochschild's perspective considers well the interiority of emotional labor and largely accounts for this labor through individual action; her analysis rests on the ideal of self-actualization, here contrasted to the less desirable consequence of self-alienation. While Hochschild's theories are touchstones for any serious discussion of emotional labor, below I problematize these theories with concepts and practices drawn from mindfulness, for two primary reasons:

1. Like many Western conceptions of emotion work, the collaborative nuances of cooperative emotion within social-emotional environments remain largely unexamined. The relationality and intersubjectivity of administrative work are well-known. Theories of emotion based primarily on the individual performance of emotion and understandings of the fundamental interiority of emotion are too bound within the individual to be of the greatest use to WPAs.

2. Hochschild's perspective analyzes a particular kind of blue-collar service, which, while sharing certain characteristics with WPA work, can also vastly differ from the white-collar service expectations of jobs like writing program administrators that routinely produce knowledge and relationships as primary "goods" within a knowledge economy. The differences in the services provided invite a level of conflict and require a degree of agency on the level of the individual unexamined by Hochschild.

So while Hochschild's theories make emotion work visible, they do not easily capture the nuances of WPA work, nor do they particularly invite WPA agency. Certainly, there are many times WPAs must provide such "service with a smile" despite our lived emotional experience. There are instances when my complete compliance is expected, such as when I collaborate with outside, public partners like local high schools to organize our co-enrollment programs. A university open house for visiting seniors and their parents is an occasion when I must often subsume my frustration with my university as it onboards more high school students than ever before while denying me needed resources such as teaching staff, classroom space, and necessary technology. To do my job effectively, I must smile and be accommodating to these students in this moment. And no matter how terrible my day has been, when meeting with a teacher who has a concern, I put aside my own emotional needs to bolster the teacher's confidence, perhaps by working with her to develop course materials until her anxiety over teaching a new assignment or theme in her course has eased. But I see more space for resistance and agency in the emotional labor of WPAs than Micciche outlines and Hochschild's theories allow.

While there are certainly populations of WPAs who risk losing tenure and job security if they do not plaster on a permanent smile, some others have, at times, more freedom to express disappointment and to challenge the emotion rules of our workplaces and university cultures—more freedom than, say, waitresses or flight attendants who work in social environments where such challenges might be seen less as intellectual prowess or expertise and more as insubordination. I'm not in a particularly powerful position within my university, where I am the sole (and first) WPA, with a very small program operating budget and little visibility within a literature department, but I do find myself able to leverage my workplace culture's value of critical inquiry and expertise and corporate expectations that I am a knowledge worker (and my recent tenure) to my advantage when navigating attendant emotion work. In the case of dual enrollment, even if at open houses with parents and interested students I am expected to be agreeable above all else, I can later raise concerns to my dean and provost over hiring enough instructors to staff additional co-enrollment sections or question the expectation that I will advise these students and counsel them as they transition to university culture without additional programmatic resources.

In my department, I have also resisted my role as sole mentor of our writing instructors by creating a mentoring program that pairs tenured colleagues with contingent ones for observations and teaching support. So while it is true that emotional labor often exposes how WPA work is codified as "women's work" that "reinscribes women as nurturers whose job involves the unpaid labor of nurturing others" (Micciche 2002, 441), I have been able to expose the inequities of this unpaid labor, if only by refusing to take it all on without complaint. If before I put my mentoring program in place I was the only one to hear grievances, moderate teaching anxieties, and offer teaching evaluations—all tasks heavily vested in emotion work—I am now the point person in a larger mentoring network that pairs contingent instructors with tenure-track faculty who can offer additional guidance. And while it's an imperfect system because I carry a heavier load of emotional labor than many of my departmental colleagues, the program still works against gendered double standards that would otherwise have me shoulder alone the emotional labor of mentoring while at the same time it addresses the material limitations of the WPA, who is but one member of a larger program and department.

As I approach the emotional labor of my job, I am wary of discussions that do not underscore the sociality of emotion and the ways our emotional labor as WPAs is shaped by the emotion rules of our workplace environments and enforced by the individuals with whom we share and shape those environments. In other words, I want a more agentive understanding of emotional labor, one where there is space for choice and conflict as well as connection to others. To find a new approach, I go to the contemplative practice and philosophy of mindfulness, or moment-to-moment awareness.

I'm interested in a relational understanding of emotional labor approached through mindfulness, one that keeps the WPA in focus but also understands her emotions ecologically as sources of agency, as actionable tools, and not only a means of control or workplace oppression. This view of emotional labor leverages a "rhetorical ecological feminist agency [that] is socially constructed, ecologically located and enacted, ethically responsible, rhetorically directed, and pragmatically oriented. It values experiential alongside disciplinary knowledge and recognizes that place and situation constitute knowledge" (Ryan 2012, 80). The notion of a rhetorical ecological feminist agency is harmonious with mindfulness, which poses a fundamental interconnectedness of life and validates situated knowledge and ethical responsibility (Siegel 2007, 295–296). For over a decade, I have practiced mindfulness through meditation and yoga and have taken these practices into my classrooms and workspaces as I have witnessed their positive impact on my thinking, learning, and feeling and seen popular and academic interest in them explode. More than any other tool I've applied to my work as a WPA, mindfulness has helped me productively navigate the emotional labor of my job and helped me reframe discussion of emotions as connective, public, and integral to my program's flourishing as well as my own. A mindfulness practice rooted in any one of a number of contemplative arts, ranging from meditation to yoga or tai chi, which requires formal practice on the centering and directing of attention, is useful for the WPA; mindfulness can also be practiced through any of our daily actions, including our administrative ones. Indeed, the application of mindfulness to the whole of life is the point: we step on the yoga mat so we can thrive off of it.

The contemporary discussion of mindfulness is a valuable one for WPAs because it is incredibly accessible and already part of a normative cultural narrative. It's almost impossible today to read a magazine or listen to a podcast without being exposed to ways to become "more mindful," "less stressed," and "more Zen." Public speaker Deepak Chopra, media mogul Oprah Winfrey, and ABC News correspondent-turned-mindfulness-journalist Dan Harris are all celebrities who have taken advantage of this growing cultural narrative. As a result, I focus my analysis of mindfulness on popular representations of contemporary practice and theory, though, of course, mindfulness has a long history in the contemplative arts of yoga and in religions such as Buddhism and Quakerism.[1] Jon Kabat-Zinn (1994, 4), the founding director of the Center for Mindfulness in Medicine, Health Care and Society and a founding father of contemporary, secular mindfulness, defines mindfulness as moment-to-moment, nonjudgmental attention. It is the process and result of attending to the present moment and temporarily releasing ruminations of the past or the future so that all attentional facilities can focus on the present. Kabat-Zinn notes, "It is neither shutting things out or off. It is seeing things clearly, and deliberately positioning yourself differently in relationship to them" (30).

My own mindfulness practice consists of daily meditation and weekly yoga practice. Some days, my meditation might be twenty minutes in the relative peace and quiet of my home, and others it might be only three minutes of "stolen" time on campus, consisting of me sitting in my office chair after I've taught two classes and before I conduct a colleague's teaching observation. While there are many varieties of meditation—guided and unguided, silent or with sound, walking, mantra-based—rooted in goals of spreading loving-kindness or compassion, my cornerstone practice is one where I focus on my breathing. In a relaxed position, I close my eyes and tune into my breath, following the natural in-breaths and out-breaths without trying to change them. My intention is to focus primarily on my breath. While I've gotten better at this single-pointed focus with experience, I have also advanced simply because I've become kinder to myself so that when I notice my thoughts wandering or I become distracted, I recognize the wandering or distraction as part of the meditation, label it, and gently reattempt to focus on my breath. Self-compassion is, not surprisingly, a recognized benefit of mindfulness (Jacobs 2015), one most administrators have a hard time practicing.

My personal experience with meditation is backed by science. With the increased neuroimaging and brain scanning capabilities of modern science, contemporary understandings of mindfulness have been tested by neuroscience, which has proven that mindfulness is indeed two-pronged as my experience suggests: it is practiced to "strength[en] the brain's ability to focus on one thing [like the breath] and ignore distractions," according to scientific journalist and emotion theorist Daniel Goleman and behavioral neurologist Richard Davidson's collaborative research (Goleman and Davidson 2017, 131). Mindfulness practice results in a kind of trained selective attention, according to clinical psychologists, where we to learn to approach "thoughts and feelings as events in the mind, without over-identifying with them and without reacting to them in an automatic, habitual pattern of reactivity" (Bishop et al. 2004, 232). Because it is a process of shaping anew our responses and reactions, mindfulness is therefore intimately bound up with the project of understanding and mapping our feelings, making it a logical lens from which to view emotional labor. Instead of simply *having* feelings, mindfulness teaches us to *discern* them, to explore why, how, and when we feel, and to acknowledge the choices we have in responding to our own and others' feelings.

In the case of the WPA, mindfulness may allow her to respect, identify, and label her feelings rather than immediately acting on them. Mindfulness shifts her way of being in the world, giving her a new script to follow. As the sole WPA on my campus and the only compositionist in my department, I find myself habitually taking on a defensive position when my colleagues do not include the writing curriculum in departmental program reviews and revisions. For instance, in a recent department meeting, my colleagues presented a refashioned English education major. However, there was no mention of including any of the writing courses under my purview in the new curriculum map; an unrelated departmental discussion of assessment a few weeks earlier had also left out our writing classes. After seven years in my department, I expect more. I get frustrated when I feel writing is purposefully left out of the conversation, which can quickly lead me into a spiral of doubt about my position and the sustainability of being the only writing specialist. Applying mindfulness to these instances allows me to recognize my feelings of insecurity, frustration, and anger as such without necessarily reacting to them, which would present as immediate defensiveness during these meetings.

Mindfulness allows me to introduce a space between my perception of events and my response to them. Instead of reacting, I can respond; with mindfulness, I am able to respond intentionally to these omissions as opposed to unconsciously and reflexively, thereby disrupting a pattern of automatic reactivity to thoughts and feelings. For instance, in the case of the revised English education major, I listened first to the proposal, which was concerned about giving students more course choice. When I eventually responded, I intentionally laid aside my frustration and my diatribe about the inherent importance of writing for our graduates, especially future educators, and framed my desire to include upper-level writing courses alongside literature classes as a means of providing genuine choice for our students, who could then choose among all our offerings. Had I not mindfully paused and listened first so I could respond and not react, I may not have been able to convince my colleagues to include upper-level writing courses in the major, as I was eventually able to do. I was able to pause mindfully during this discussion in part because I've attempted to bring the intention of mindfulness to my workspaces, consciously inviting the practice into my interactions with colleagues, much like I do when I unroll my yoga mat and step onto it. Years of practicing mindfulness both within and beyond my workspaces has made it easier for me to call upon mindfulness as an intention as I step into these spaces where conflict may occur because emotional investments run high. However, even beginners can set an intention of mindfulness, an intention to which we can be habituated over time; as with other habits of mind, mindfulness is cultivated with practice.

I don't mean to suggest that mindfulness is a cure-all. My mindful responses to emotional trials as a WPA does not mean that I still don't face difficult emotions or that I don't feel them in my body as they arise; indeed, with mindfulness, my experience of these emotions is keen. But instead of habitual reaction, when I bring awareness to the frustration I feel welling up, it is like a boulder of emotion I can see but not pick up:

> A teacher walking with his students points to a very large boulder and says, "Students, do you see that boulder?" The students respond, "Yes, teacher, we see the boulder." The teacher asks, "Is the boulder heavy?" The students respond, "Oh, yes, very heavy." And the teacher replies, "Not if you don't pick it up." (Shapiro and Carlson 2009, 6)

Mindfulness psychologists Shauna L. Shapiro and Linda E. Carlson provide this koan-like tale to expose how mindfulness promotes expanding our perspective to find a third way, not a way out. As applied to my own example of departmental conflict, I remind myself that my colleagues' entrenchment in their own fields does not necessarily mean they do not respect what I do or that I need to start looking for another job. While not quite the off-loading strategy Joseph Janangelo suggests in his chapter in this volume, as the mindfulness adage insists, we may choose not to pick up the boulder of certain emotions when they don't serve us; but the process of mindfulness is valuable in that where we once saw no choice, we now see more options. More choice leads to smarter action and more opportunities for connection, according to Kabat-Zinn (1994, 50): "When we have to push, we push. When we have to pull, we pull. But [with mindfulness] we know when not to push too, and when not to pull." We might productively see all of WPA work as learning when to push, when to pull, and when to let go.

Mindfulness is both an inter- and an intra-personal tool that can open our discussions of emotional labor to include the more agentive subtleties of emotional understanding. Emotional understanding is the intersubjective experience of sharing emotion and building connection by attempting to understand another's emotional standpoint (Hargreaves 2001, 1059). WPAs engage in emotional understanding when they "reach down into their past emotional experiences and 'read' the emotional responses of those around them" (Hargreaves 2000, 815). Of course, understanding is labor, too, but it is a nuanced concept that highlights conflict, misunderstanding, and, importantly, relationality. Emotional understanding requires that we consider the individual WPA who is constantly reading her environment and interacting with others to determine appropriate displays of emotion. Emotional understanding isn't just about showing compassion or feeling empathy for others; rather, it is consciousness of the ways emotions reside within us and around us, dynamically connecting us to others and situating us ecologically in our environments. It is therefore a means of mindful, ecological agency for the WPA who can leverage this understanding at the level of her own body and resultant connections to others to achieve her goals while remaining committed to her own emotional well-being.

For instance, my program recently underwent a shift from teaching Stretch model writing to a co-requisite model of basic writing instruction. For many reasons beyond the scope of this chapter, this shift has been a generally positive one, as it has consolidated my efforts as a WPA and brought the university writing curriculum and instructors under the same "roof" (physically was well as metaphorically). Because it has erased the need to negotiate labor divisions between the writing program and the learning center where the Stretch classes were held, it has been a positive change for me as a WPA. However, the movement of several teachers from the learning support center to my program and the dissolution of previous chains of command has understandably been emotionally challenging for everyone involved. While I am excited about the new possibilities for an updated curriculum and a unified program and it would be easy to translate this excitement into a flurry of new initiatives, I am taking this time to be slow and mindful, to pause, waiting for my instructors to tell me when it is again time to "push." My emotional investment in this programmatic change is not simply vested in my own emotional life as a WPA as a matter of my own commitments and values but is also shaped by social and political consequences that influence how my administrative work is organized and structured and the possibilities university structures provide me with to lead.

What I am suggesting is that approaching emotional understanding through mindfulness provides more options for harnessing a WPA's ecological agency than do other social views of emotion. For instance, Sara Ahmed's (2015, 10) theories of emotion are popular in our field for the ways they suggest a social view of emotion as not existing within a body but rather moving between bodies: "emotions are not 'in' either the individual or the social, but produce the very surfaces and boundaries that allow the individual and the social to be delineated." If emotion is not found in either social or individual bodies alone, it is best to see emotion in terms of circulation, a "transference of affect" where objects such as bodies become "sticky," according to Ahmed (2015, 91). While it seems that Ahmed captures relationality much better than Hochschild because of the ecological nature of her networked conception of emotion, Ahmed does not allow emotion to rest inside. We are therefore right back to viewing emotion ambivalently as it rests within the WPA. Both Hochschild and Ahmed fall victim to Western conceptions of space that tend to see the body as bounded, either because it contains socially constructed emotion "inside," as Hochschild's analysis leads us to believe, or it is viewed as a border that needs crossing, a barrier between understanding and shared experience, as Ahmed's circulation metaphors invoke.

If we instead rethink the labor of emotional understanding through the rhetoric of mindfulness, we can see both the sticky effects of emotions within our workplaces and writing programs and how emotions can be a site of individual agency for the individual WPA, a way to claim her presence and to act with intention to increase her own well-being. Daniel J Siegel (2007, 132) studies how mindfulness "creates a state of neural integration and flexible self-regulation" that results in attunement to both ourselves and others that allows receptive awareness of emotions, which results in better "harness[ing of] the social circuits of mirroring and empathy." The ecological interconnectedness of mindfulness remains sensitive to the structural ways my writing program is shaped by the collective emotions of the instructors but also validates the personal investments of me as a WPA and my own well-being. If our jobs will always require us to engage in emotional understanding, then we are better suited to performing that task while respecting our own self-care by employing mindfulness.

SITTING WITH EMOTIONS: STRATEGIES FOR RESILIENT WPAS

To juggle the demands of emotional understanding as a WPA with self-care requires resilience. "Resilience suggests attention to choices made in the face of difficult and even impossible challenges," note Elizabeth A. Flynn, Patricia Sotirin, and Ann Brady (2012, 1) in their study of resilience for feminist writing scholars. Flynn, Sotirin, and Brady stress resilience as a process rather than as solely a property of the individual: "not a state of being but a process of rhetorically engaging with material circumstances and situational exigencies . . . not as a quality of the heroic individual but as always relational" (7). Resilience is a powerful feminist action because it transforms the "way a life is lived," if not the material circumstances of that life. What results is not a fairytale ending but instead "ongoing responsiveness" (7). Resilience changes the ways we respond to our environments and the people within them; it is itself a product of relationality in the same way emotional understanding is. Recent scientific research shows that mindfulness results in resilience because it encourages compassion for oneself and others and the prioritization of well-being (Jacobs 2015). Mindfulness helps develop resilience because it emphasizes agency; we practice mindfulness to cultivate resilience as a rhetorical choice and action in collective and communal networks.

There are several strategies I suggest WPAs use to remake the emotional geographies of their workplaces and work identities to mindfully navigate the heavy toll of emotional understanding and to promote resilience that will lead to increased well-being: (1) practice mindfulness, both informally and formally; (2) actively promote well-being through healthy work cultures; and (3) cultivate safe spaces by "sitting" with emotions. I overview these below.

1. WPAs should practice formal (where the main activity is practicing mindfulness for its own end) and informal mindfulness (where another activity is completed through the frame and application of mindfulness).

If mindfulness can help WPAs approach everyday experiences like mentoring, committee work, and collaborations with other faculty differently, with an eye toward emotional understanding and the goal of developing resilience, then it makes sense for WPAs to practice regularly. Current research on mindfulness capitalizes on the brain's neuroplasticity, or its ability to rewire in response to training, and science suggests the sustained practice of mindfulness results in altered traits such as a weakening of the circuitry for attachment to initial perceptions and ruminations and an increase in compassion (Goleman and Davidson

2017, 274). Mindfulness, in short, helps us to imagine new ways of compassionately interacting with colleagues and to use self-reflection to the end of treating ourselves more generously. As my earlier examples illustrate, mindfulness has a direct and positive impact on emotional labor because it makes us better at attuning to our own feelings and developing emotional understanding of others' feelings so we can build connection while respecting the integrity of our emotional states.

Mindfulness thus presents itself as a powerful tool for navigating our emotions and actively taking charge of our well-being. As Kabat-Zinn (1994, 4–5) notes, mindfulness practices like breathing or walking mediations or simply giving full attention to daily activities can provide a "powerful route for getting ourselves unstuck, back in touch with our own wisdom and vitality." For these reasons, I teach my students to use mindfulness practices as they write, and we experiment with yoga, meditation, and mindful movement so each can find a passion (e.g., yoga, tai chi, prayer, meditation) that makes such practice feel meaningful. I often ask my students to watch Dan Harris's short animated video on how to meditate[2] to provide a general overview of how to begin mindfulness practice; this video can be a helpful starting place for WPAs, too. For interested beginners to mindfulness, I suggest starting a practice of meditation, potentially the most accessible practice because it requires no special equipment or training. Beginners might start by setting a timer for five minutes, sitting comfortably, and closing their eyes. Spend this time observing the breath and perhaps locating the physical sensation of the breath on either the nose or in the lungs or belly. The approach should be one of observation and not judgment, assessment of the process, or rumination on other thoughts. The goal of meditation is not to erase outside thoughts but simply to recognize them as such; success is not found in an empty mind but in one that can create some distance between the perception and focus on the breath and the awareness of everything else.[3] Formal practice is important because it becomes a training ground for awareness.

We can also experiment with charging automatic, habitual parts of our day—like brushing our teeth, walking to class, taking a daily run, or enjoying a morning cup of coffee or tea—with purposeful mindfulness, taking sage advice from Thich Naht Hanh (1976, 4–5) who suggests that mindfulness should be practiced informally by attending fully to whatever activity we are doing in the moment: "While washing dishes one should only be washing the dishes, which means that while washing the dishes one should be completely aware of the fact that one is washing the dishes." To fully and mindfully experience a routine chore like dishwashing, we might start by slowing down to better focus on the opportunity presented by the chore instead of rushing through it so we can move on to something better or multitasking our way through it by chatting on the phone, for instance. As we focus on dishwashing, we might feel the slick, soapy water and the rough texture of the scrubby sponge between our fingers, feel the rush of the clean water from the faucet as we rinse, and hear the loud click of the dish as it clacks and clatters on the drying rack. We might also note any attendant feelings dishwashing brings forward, such as feelings of comfort and the familiar, clean smell of the kitchen, as these feelings bring forth memories from our youth when our parents cleaned while we did homework at the kitchen table.

WPAs can similarly use daily experiences, such as the walk to a meeting or the moments before checking email, to practice mindfulness throughout the day. A simple walking meditation can be executed during your next walk to a committee meeting if you slow your pace, put away your phone or notebook and feel the ground underneath your feet, and attend to the sounds of students passing classes, the birds chirping outside, the feel of the sun on your skin as you walk to the adjacent building on campus. Or we might take a moment for silence and focus on our breath every time we open our email. I encourage all WPAs to do what my students do: find a formal practice that "sticks" and regular moments in their days that they can inject with mindfulness, moments that would otherwise be given to mindless routine. Such small practices can make a huge impact: a present orientation has been linked to a higher state of perceived well-being, suggesting that the way mindfulness shifts our orientation in time and space is healthy for our physical and emotional states (Seema and Sircova 2013, 5).

2. Actively promote well-being of individuals and cultures through healthy workspaces by approaching them as connected.
In her study of the recent uptick in interest in positive emotions within writing studies, Jill Belli (2016) warns of the dangers of conceiving of well-being as an individual quality. She critiques positive psychology and the educational reforms built on this movement for focusing on how the individual responds to external challenges and ignoring the corporate and systemic issues that threaten well-being. In this closed loop, responsibility rests on the individual to "be well" so external conditions like under-funded programs and a culture of overwork remain unquestioned: "Not surprisingly, in a time when budgets, resources, and

academic freedom are increasingly eroded, this emphasis on personal responsibility and success via individual emotions has gained considerable traction" (2016). Belli even warns that contemplative practice might usher in such a problematic focus on individual well-being unintentionally through the "back door."

Yet the exclusive focus on the individual is not consistent with the theory and practice of secular mindfulness. Contemplative practice is actually a means of attending to emotion while not collapsing well-being only to the individual. As an abiding presence of awareness, mindfulness is a way of being not only with oneself but with others, as we live socially and connected. Mindful attention to emotions counteracts this narrow focus on the individual while still attending to the individual's presence, allowing us to talk about her resilience as both an embodied property and a process. The geography of mindfulness is such that both the presence of the individual and our connection to others is non-dualistically appreciated. For instance, WPAs can facilitate mindfulness through the breath, according to Kabat-Zinn (1994, 24), because it is "the current connecting body and mind, connecting us with our parents and our children, connecting our body with the outer world's body." The breath illustrates how we are flowing and changing from moment to moment so that while we have a center, it is not stable; what we find there now is impermanent. If we've previously understood emotions, like writing, using a "border mentality" (Reynolds 2004, 6), we've focused our attention more on crossing boundaries than on the places and spaces constructed by those boundaries in which we might dwell. As WPAs dwell within those spaces through mindfulness, they understand that these spaces are not fixed; they are constantly made and remade. Mindfulness can therefore promote both individual and corporate shifts toward well-being as it asks us to consider the present moment, to find presence and joy in slowing down, and to see resilience not as only a personal trait but also as a product of social relationships. When we approach resilience as a process and a rhetorical response, we can begin to ask questions about how we might create resilient programs and resilient programmatic structures that are flexible and adaptive and, above all, mindful.

The benefits of mindfulness can be understood as helping us remap the emotional geographies of our workplaces and our own emotional territories, promoting the well-being of both. Ahmed (2014) declares on her blog that self-care is warfare. Her statement resounds for WPAs who, like other academic administrators, link work stress to time poverty and the boundlessness of our jobs (Berg and Seeber 2016, 7). WPAs can start by replacing a culture of overwork and speed with one that promotes "habits of conducting our work and our lives in ways that promote both our own and others' well-being" (12–13). This can simply mean mindfully slowing down our pace: mindfulness literally lengthens the space of the "now" for the WPA by inserting space between the perceiving of an event or the recognition of a feeling and the acting on that event or feeling. One such method of promoting mindfulness in our workspaces is to enact Micciche's (2011) "slow agency," by being purposeful and taking care and time to allow decisions and actions to slowly develop; another is to take Maggie Berg and Barbara K. Seeber's (2016, 11) advice to act with purpose, "taking the time for deliberation, reflection and dialogue, cultivating emotional and intellectual resilience." What slowing down and acting with purpose has meant for me is that when I am given a complicated task and a short deadline, I ask for more time. For instance, when approached by my university to revise our basic writing curriculum two fall semesters ago, I refused the spring deadline I was originally given on the grounds that a semester turnaround was much too short. I didn't dismiss the deadline out of hand but instead explained the research I would need to complete to develop a new curriculum and outlined the training I would need to offer our writing instructors to enact the updated curriculum. It felt both strange and liberating to refuse a too short deadline—strange because my university has a habit of making these kinds of "change the world in a day" requests; liberating because after lengthy discussion about why I was taking the time purposefully to engage in reflection and dialogue, I was granted a longer deadline. And while sometimes more time is simply about more time, the positive results for me have grown: my request led to funded time to research and develop a new curriculum, which itself helped me write a request for additional writing instructors that was granted and resulted in new hires.

3. Cultivate safe spaces by "sitting" with emotions.

In addition to approaching tasks in a more measured and deliberate way to manage negative emotions and increase well-being, we can also reclaim emotional spaces through the mindfulness practice of compassionate listening. As a mindfulness practice, compassionate listening is meant to attune us to the present moment, to our feelings as they arise within it, and to the experience of another's feelings without taking those feelings on as our own. A compassionate listening practice WPAs might apply to their workplaces is **RAIN**, an acronym for **r**ecognize, **a**llow, **i**nvestigate, **n**on-identify. In the first step, we suspend judgment and follow the present moment to **recognize** the emotional geography of the situation, our place within it, and how connected or removed we are from others. As we consciously attune to our feelings, we also pay attention to how our body feels. Next, we **allow**, or pause judgment to let whatever we are thinking, feeling, or sensing simply be. This is a radical shift from what we tend to do, which is jump to judgment or rumination. Allowing moves to **investigating**, which requires that we become mindful scientists of our emotional experience, working to identify the source of our feelings and what choices we have in our response to the situation, rewriting the habitual patterns of reaction we might otherwise follow. Tara Brach (2013), mindfulness expert and clinical psychologist, adds that in this stage we might ask questions like: "What most wants attention? How am I experiencing this in my body? Or What am I believing? What does this feeling want from me?" Investigating does not mean we must accept the situation as it is; that is why the last step is **non-identification**. The final aim is discernment of how we got to this emotional space in the first place so we might be better able to prioritize self-care and compassion for ourselves and others. "Compassion arises naturally when we mindfully contact our suffering and respond with care," notes Brach (2013).[4]

RAIN is a form of compassionate listening as "holding space" for others *and* ourselves. Holding space is offering nonjudgmental support; it requires presence and a learned practice of sitting with emotions. It recognizes the fundamental interconnectedness of all of life. Renowned contemplative teacher Hanh (2010) has discussed contemplative listening as learning to "recognize the existence of wrong perceptions in the other person and wrong perceptions in us. The other person has wrong perceptions about himself and about us. And we have wrong perceptions about ourselves and the other person. And that is the foundation for violence and conflict." Through RAIN, we can move past automatic behaviors and well-worn ways of thinking to see situations and people as if for the first time, which can help us mitigate conflict through the intention and execution presence of "intentionally remembering to be fully present with whatever comes up so that you are not always on automatic pilot or acting mechanically" (Kabat-Zinn and Kabat-Zinn 1997, 108). RAIN illustrates how mindfulness provides an "ethics of inquiry" that asks, "What is conducive to my own and others' well-being" (Shapiro and Carlson 2009, 6). This is a query that can and should drive us as WPAs.

When we consider Megan Boler's (1999, 16–17) description of emotions as "inscribed habits of inattention," the relevance of mindfulness to navigating emotional understanding becomes clear. If emotions are culturally shaped by the routines and rules we internally imbibe based on the social rules of our environments and interactions, then we will process certain emotions about our experiences and ignore others based on the feeling rules we maintain. Mindfulness, with its focus on intentional and sustained attention, therefore has the ability to intervene in our emotional processing to the ends of making us more aware of not only the full range of what we feel but also why we are feeling those emotions, cultivating meta-awareness of our emotions and emotion work. Mindfulness can help us see emotions as habits and provide us with a different script to follow, especially in the "hot moments" of our jobs, one that prioritizes well-being. Mindfulness productively opens our discussions of well-being to include simultaneously the personal, the pedagogical, and the programmatic.

NOTES

1. For a primer on mindfulness and historical context, texts such as Elizabeth DeMichelis's *A History of Modern Yoga* (2004), Jon Kabat-Zinn's *Wherever You Go, There You Are* (1994), and Bhante Gunaratana's *Mindfulness in Plain English* (2015) are good starting places.
2. https://vimeo.com/131682712.
3. If the process of beginning a meditation practice sounds daunting to my readers, I suggest starting with guided mediations available through smartphone apps like Meditation for Fidgety Skeptics by 10% Happier or my favorite, the Insight Timer, a very popular resource of thousands of meditations, including those by renowned teachers like Sharon Salzberg and Jon Kabat-Zinn. There is also a virtual treasure trove of guided meditations by teachers like Kabat-Zinn on YouTube.
4. For those who would like to practice, **RAIN**, Tara Brach's guided meditation can be found online here: https://www.youtube.com/watch?v=wm1t5FyK5Ek&t=80s.

REFERENCES

Ahmed, Sara. 2014. "Selfcare as Warfare." https://feministkilljoys.com/2014/08/25/self care-as-warfare/.
Ahmed, Sara. 2015. *The Cultural Politics of Emotion*. New York: Routledge.
Belli, Jill. 2016. "Why Well-Being, Why Now? Tracing an Alternate Genealogy of Emotion in Composition." *Composition Forum* 34. https://compositionforum.com/issue/34/why -well-being.php.
Berg, Maggie, and Barbara K. Seeber. 2016. *The Slow Professor: Challenging the Culture of Speed in the Academy*. Toronto: University of Toronto Press.
Bishop, Scott, Mark Lau, Shauna Shapiro, Linda Carlson, Nicole D. Anderson, James Carmody, Zindel V. Segal, Susan Abbey, Michael Specca, Drew Velting, and Gerald Devins. 2004. "Mindfulness: A Proposed Operational Definition." *Clinical Psychology: Science and Practice* 11 (3): 230–241.
Boler, Megan. 1999. *Feeling Power: Emotions and Education*. New York: Routledge.
Brach, Tara. 2013. "Working with Difficulties: The Blessings of RAIN." https://www.tara brach.com/articles-interviews/rain-workingwithdifficulties/.

Davies, Laura J. 2017. "Grief and the New WPA." *WPA: Writing Program Administration* 40 (2): 40–51.

DeMichelis, Elizabeth. 2004. *A History of Modern Yoga*. New York: Continuum.

Flynn, Elizabeth A., Patricia Sotirin, and Ann Brady. 2012. "Introduction: Feminist Rhetorical Resilience—Possibilities and Impossibilities." In *Feminist Rhetorical Resilience*, edited by Elizabeth A. Flynn, Patricia Sotirin, and Ann Brady, 1–29. Logan: Utah State University Press.

Goleman, Daniel, and Richard J. Davidson. 2017. *Altered Traits: Science Reveals How Meditation Changes Your Mind, Brain, and Body*. New York: Random House.

Gunaratana, Bhante. 2015. *Mindfulness in Plain English*. Somerville: Wisdom Publications.

Hanh, Thich Nhat. 1976. *Miracle of Mindfulness: An Introduction to the Practice of Meditation*. Boston: Beacon.

Hanh, Thich Nhat. 2010. "Oprah Talks to Thich Nhat Hanh." http://www.oprah.com/spirit/oprah-talks-to-thich-nhat-hanh/all#ixzz57OxunuFN.

Hargreaves, Andy. 2000. "Mixed Emotions: Teachers' Perceptions of Their Interactions with Students." *Teaching and Teacher Education* 16: 811–826.

Hargreaves, Andy. 2001. "The Emotional Geographies of Teaching." *Teachers College Record* 103 (6): 1056–1080.

Hochschild, Arlie. 1983. *The Managed Heart: Commercialization of Human Feeling*. Berkeley: University of California Press.

Jacobs, Tom. 2015. "Evidence Mounts That Mindfulness Breeds Resilience." https://greatergood.berkeley.edu/article/item/evidence_mounts_that_mindfulness_breeds_resilience.

Kabat-Zinn, Jon. 1994. *Wherever You Go, There You Are: Mindfulness Meditation in Everyday Life*. New York: Hyperion.

Kabat-Zinn, Myla, and Jon Kabat-Zinn. 1997. *Everyday Blessings: The Inner Work of Mindful Parenting*. New York: Hyperion.

Micciche, Laura R. 2002. "More Than a Feeling: Disappointment and WPA Work." *College English* 64 (4): 432–458.

Micciche, Laura R. 2007. *Doing Emotion: Rhetoric, Writing, Teaching*. Portsmouth, NH: Boynton/Cook.

Micciche, Laura R. 2011. "For Slow Agency." *WPA: Writing Program Administration* 35 (1): 73–90.

Micciche, Laura R. 2016. "Staying with Emotion." *Composition Forum* 34. https://compositionforum.com/issue/34/micciche-retrospective.php.

Reid, E. Shelley. 2010. "Managed Care: All-Terrain Mentoring and the 'Good Enough' Feminist WPA." In *Performing Feminism and Administration in Rhetoric and Composition Studies*, edited by Krista Ratcliffe and Rebecca Rickly, 77–92. Cresskill, NJ: Hampton.

Reynolds, Nedra. 2004. *Geographies of Writing: Inhabiting Places and Encountering Difference*. Carbondale: Southern Illinois University Press.

Ryan, Kathleen. 2012. "Thinking Ecologically: Rhetorical Ecological Feminist Agency and Writing Program Administration." *WPA: Writing Program Administration* 36 (1): 74–94.

Seema, Riin, and Anna Sircova. 2013. "Mindfulness: A Time Perspective? Estonian Study." *Baltic Journal of Psychology* 14 (1–2): 4–21.

Shapiro, Shauna L., and Linda E. Carlson. 2009. *The Art and Science of Mindfulness: Integrating Mindfulness into Psychology and the Helping Professions*. Washington, DC: American Psychiatric Association.

Siegel, Daniel J. 2007. *The Mindful Brain: Reflection and Attunement in the Cultivation of Well-Being*. New York: W. W. Norton.

15
HOW TO BE A BAD WPA

Courtney Adams Wooten
George Mason University

Neo-liberal discourses about how much work can be squeezed out of employees has drawn attention to the assumptions people make about faculty's lives, especially in terms of the work they do and when. Often citing the "time off" faculty receive—particularly summers—critics point to these times as inefficiencies that reflect on faculty as lazy and unproductive and their lives as easy. *Forbes*'s inclusion of "tenured university professor" as number five in its list of "The 10 Least Stressful Jobs in 2017" is just one of the many examples of how this narrative is passed on.

In response, academics have spoken out about the many hours of work they do, not only during their contracted time but also during "breaks." One of the most recent responses is Anastasia Salter (2018); citing a Twitter debate about faculty workloads in February 2018, she explores conversations that have happened about faculty workload and how she and others have responded to them. Some of these conversations occurred when John Ziker, Matthew Genuchi, Kathryn Demps, and David Nolan's research at Boise State University about faculty workloads emerged in 2014. Colleen Flaherty's (2014) report on their preliminary research explained that "on average, faculty participants reported working 61 hours per week—more than 50 percent over the traditional 40-hour work week. They worked 10 hours per day Monday to Friday and about that much on Saturday and Sunday combined." Unlike commonly held views that tenured professors slack off, their study also found that "full professors reported working slightly longer hours both during the week and on weekends than associate and assistant professors, as well as chairs." Of this time, Ziker, Genuchi, Demps, and Nolan concluded that "faculty participants spent 17 percent of their work week in meetings—including those with students—and 13 percent of the day on email (both for research and with students)" (Flaherty 2014). Their research also found that meetings and email comprise "30 percent of faculty time [that] 'was spent on activities that are not traditionally thought of as part of the life of an academic'" (Flaherty 2014). Of course, such claims are complicated by other reports, including those occurring informally on Twitter in 2018, that faculty do not work this many hours per week and that the amount of time spent on their work varies widely.

Debates about faculty work time overlap with increasing research into the negative effects of overworked and stressed-out employees. This includes research showing that those who work more than forty hours per week don't actually end up being very productive once they have passed the forty-hour mark (Robinson 2012) and that the costs of having overworked employees can outweigh the benefits (American Institute of Stress 2017). While the Twitter debate about faculty workloads shows that faculty themselves do not have consensus about workload, writing program administrators (WPAs) are particularly prone to the real-life effects of overworking, especially because we experience the additional layer of administrative work on top of the typical research, teaching, and service trifecta. While the existing research about overwork considers quantifiable data such as hours worked, it does not account for emotional labor and how that can affect faculty lives outside of work. Because so much of WPA work is emotional labor, overworking often means taking on additional emotional labor that extends into our personal lives in pernicious but often overlooked ways.

This chapter builds on Sara Ahmed's (2010) theory of happiness scripts and Lauren Berlant's (2011) theory of cruel optimism to argue that a central component of WPAs' work is determining how to handle the emotional labor inherent in their workloads. In part, this must occur by considering the happiness scripts set out for WPAs and how one's actual work fits into or contests these scripts, identifying the cruel optimism inherent in WPA work, and determining how to prioritize those parts of our jobs that are truly valuable for ourselves and our writing programs. Finally, publicizing how WPAs can find a work-life balance and avoid undertaking too much emotional labor is a necessary part of reconstructing WPA happiness scripts and countering the overwork WPAs often experience.

EMOTIONAL LABOR, HAPPINESS SCRIPTS, AND CRUEL OPTIMISM

WPAs frequently perform emotional labor because we view part of our identities as tied to doing this work; it is seen as part of the job that we embrace. Feminist theorist Ahmed's (2010) theory of happiness scripts and affect theorist Berlant's (2011) theory of cruel optimism provide useful lenses in thinking about the work WPAs do and why. This section provides a brief explanation of each of these theories and how they help WPAs understand our labor, including our emotional labor. Before exploring strategies for embracing or resisting an (un)reasonable workload, it is necessary for WPAs to consider how we have constructed our everyday work lives and the identities we view as integral to them.

Happiness is a central tenet by which many people determine whether they should or should not do something, including what kind of career they want to have and why. Ahmed (2010) theorizes how happiness delineates the way we view our own and others' lives. She claims that happiness, rather than a state of being, is society's way of reinforcing norms as good and goods (11). People further associate particular objects—what Ahmed calls "happy objects" (22)—and choices with happiness because they directly relate to our society's ideas about who someone should want to be or become. According to Ahmed, happiness thus helps us determine why we desire what we do (203). She contends, "The science of happiness could be described as performative: by finding happiness in certain places, it generates those places as being good, as being what should be promoted *as* goods . . . The science of happiness hence reinscribes what is already evaluated as being good as good. If we have a duty to promote what causes happiness, then happiness itself becomes a duty" (6–7, original emphasis). For WPAs, this means we locate happiness in our work because it is seen as good in itself as a way to help students, instructors, and so on, and because it is a good that allows institutions to function smoothly. However, happiness can become a duty when WPAs are told they must be happy because they can often find jobs in higher education when people in other fields cannot and because those working in their programs are in much more precarious positions; therefore, pressure is put on WPAs to embrace whatever our careers require of us, even if it is not positive, because we are the few who are fortunate enough to have secure jobs.

As the WPA identity is formed, what Ahmed (2010) calls "happiness scripts" are created for WPAs. Happiness scripts are dependent on socio-cultural ideas of what is "natural or good" (59). They help WPAs identify what it means to be happy in their positions at particular institutions and in particular departments through an identification of what that location needs or desires. One of the happiness scripts I intuited as a graduate student was that WPAs must constantly perform emotional labor—by mentoring inexperienced instructors and TAs, meeting with people in the department and around campus, talking with concerned students and parents—to be perceived as adequately creating and sustaining community. As might be imagined from this scenario, happiness scripts do not always create good feelings; instead, they can serve as "straightening devices, ways of aligning bodies with what is already lined up" (91). Happiness scripts, in other words, do not allow WPAs much leeway in determining what makes *them* happy and how they can best serve as WPAs in a particular place. Instead, we are supposed to identify happiness in largely predetermined scripts that reinforce our value in the academic community, even if such value is not personally fulfilling. Happiness scripts can be more complicated for women, people of color, members of the LGBTQIA+ community, among others, who often face additional challenges in appropriately conforming to these scripts and being viewed as "capable of being happy 'in the right way'" (13). A male WPA might more easily be excused than a female WPA for not constantly performing emotional labor because men are not expected to have the same responsibilities for doing this work that women are. For jWPAs, the effects of this emotional labor can be especially malicious. Irene Ward (2002, 58) alludes to this when she describes the particular difficulty a young, new WPA can experience, especially if they do not have the built-in support system of a partner or children to buffer the work they will do on the job. While the conflicted position of jWPAs (and now liminal WPAs; see Phillips, Shovlin, and Titus 2014) has been debated (see Dew and Horning 2007; Charlton et al. 2011), there seems little doubt that new WPAs, especially those who are young and occupy vulnerable subject positions, experience more emotional labor than older and less vulnerable WPAs. In addition to the challenges already described, they face additional moments of trying to convince others that they have authority and to earn respect in a variety of situations, both positive and negative. A WPA's happiness, therefore, springs from their ability to conform to predetermined ideas of what should make a WPA happy even as they negotiate expectations particular to their own subjectivities.

Berlant's (2011) concept of "cruel optimism" serves well to flesh out Ahmed's theory of happiness by identifying fault lines in these scripts. She claims, "A relation of cruel optimism exists when something you desire is actually an obstacle to your flourishing," citing examples of food, a political project, or a new habit that could bring "an improved way of being" (1). People can form attachments to all of these that ultimately fail to make a transformation possible and instead bind them to something that is "a situation of profound threat" and also "profoundly confirming" (2). Not all WPA work exists in a state of cruel optimism;

however, there are quite a few aspects of typical happiness scripts that do. These are points that can hinder our ability to do sustainable work as WPAs and also as individuals. Although performing emotional labor can seem like a necessary and even enjoyable part of WPA work, a relation of cruel optimism can develop when we fail to identify how such labor can lead to our own burnout and sometimes to problems in our programs if not properly identified and addressed (as other chapters in this collection discuss). Identifying how happiness scripts can embody objects of desire that actually harm WPAs is a necessary aspect of thinking through the emotional labor WPAs do and how we can mitigate some of the negative effects of performing too much emotional labor.

WPA HAPPINESS SCRIPTS AND EMOTIONAL LABOR

Because Ahmed's (2010) concept of happiness scripts relies on a group's formulation of what is "natural or good," in thinking about WPA happiness scripts and how they interact with emotional labor, we must go to some texts about WPA lives to examine the ways they present the identity of WPAs. These can range from books and articles about writing program administration to mentoring panels at the Council of Writing Program Administrators (CWPA) conference that communicate happiness scripts to new generations of WPAs. Ironically, these happiness scripts often encapsulate unhappiness because some aspects of working as WPAs are viewed as naturally negative (such as firing underperforming teachers or dealing with university administrators). I argue, however, that these parts of the work service happiness scripts because they fit into the jobs WPAs are told we will and must do to "express happiness in proximity to the right things" (Ahmed 2010, 59). Although these individual things may make WPAs unhappy, they are part of a job that we have chosen, in part because it aligns us with things we and others value. In other words, happiness scripts spring out of a communal understanding of a WPA's identity that links to values WPAs are assumed to uphold and are generally believed to be true. Moments of cruel optimism occur when those things WPAs think make them happy—often tied to emotional labor—actually keep them from thriving professionally or personally because they bury WPAs in an endless cycle of labor with no clear end point or goal.[1] In our field's accounts of WPAs' emotional labor, some of the happiness scripts that simultaneously exist as objects of cruel optimism include high workload, negotiating political relationships on campus, and sacrificing personal relationships off campus for the job, which I discuss in further detail.

High workload is a common part of WPA work, one most WPAs simultaneously embrace and decry, naturalizing sacrifice of our selves to the greater cause of the writing program as a part of our happiness scripts that is obviously potentially destructive. Ward (2002) is one of the most thorough explorations of the emotional labor WPAs experience that centers around high workload. She describes many aspects of the emotional labor WPAs experience on the job, explaining how burnout can happen and strategies for avoiding it. One pertinent aspect of burnout as she describes it is "emotional exhaustion" that relates to "compassion fatigue" or the inability to continually provide emotional support for others (50); a symptom of emotional exhaustion is "dread of going to work" because WPAs perceive the constant drain on ourselves that we will experience at work, which impacts our personal lives (51). Such emotional exhaustion can easily occur in WPAs because of the many relationships we have to maintain—sometimes simultaneously—with students, instructors, TAs, departmental colleagues, and administrators. Juggling these many types of relationships and their individual needs can be very difficult, especially when, as often happens to me, WPAs are expected to quickly change hats. Going from one meeting with upper administrators in which I am an advocate for the writing program to another meeting in which I am a mentor to TAs to another meeting in which I am serving instructors in my program creates a powerful drain on emotional resources that can be difficult to counter. Ward also discusses how role conflict, ambiguity, and overload, which also involve a lot of emotional labor, contribute to feelings of burnout. Although Ward presents this information as a vehicle to offer strategies to avoid burnout, part of this work is in trying to help potential WPAs assess whether they are able and willing to take on everything involved in WPA happiness scripts, good and bad. In other words, the many facets of emotional labor are viewed as simply parts of the job that are not going away and that are inherent to this work without recognition of the cruel optimism—and endless laboring—this script creates.

Negotiating political relationships at an institution is another facet of a WPA's work involving emotional labor that our field naturalizes as good, even as it can be difficult and sometimes harmful. Several chapters in Linda Myers-Breslin collection *Administrative Problem-Solving for Writing Program and Writing Centers* (1999) present how WPAs handle their own and others' emotions as a necessary part of being effective—and happy—WPAs. In particular, the section "Professional Issues of Departmental Authority and Professional Development" offers several common scenarios in thinking about the emotional labor WPAs often perform, many of which will seem familiar to readers. For example, in one scenario in which a new WPA is working to change curricula, contributor Ben W. McClelland (1999, 177) argues that "a good administrator gets to know the people in an organization, working from those within the closest circle of associates outward . . . In the early days take the time to talk face-to-face with colleagues and staff members, whenever practicable." Although this is certainly good advice, the phrase "a good administrator" reinforces the high amounts of emotional labor WPAs, especially those new to their positions, are expected to exert if they are to be seen as doing their jobs well and therefore be labeled as happy.

Successfully navigating difficult political situations, especially if as an untenured WPA, is also readily identified as the mark of a good WPA by our field, as reflected in Barry M. Maid's (1999) explanation of his attempts to eliminate an exit exam for first-year writing courses. Much of his work in this case involved recognizing where power lay in the department—between the chair and faculty—and a power struggle occurring between senior and junior faculty. In this process, he zeroed in on two things that he needed to gain support for changes to the curriculum and exit exam: first, "a departmental vote (a majority was all that was needed) could change any curricular issues," and second, "even if I, or any junior faculty, managed to get enough votes to change departmental policy on any particular issue, we had to lobby those votes in such a way that we did not offend or threaten senior faculty who might later oppose granting us tenure" (206). Although Maid frames his experience in terms of power, it seems clear that he performed much emotional labor in determining how power existed in his department and then in using personal interactions and connections to marshal that power for the good of the writing program, a change that is viewed as good or happy. Such emotional labor forms a clear part of the happiness scripts circulated and reified in our field through such scholarship and stories told to each other about similar events even as it contributes to the burnout that Ward (2002) describes and that recent attention to faculty workload only exacerbates.

Such burnout results not only from emotional labor performed while on campus but also from bleed-over to our lives off campus, even as the field's happiness scripts revolve around such labor. Despite the belief that faculty lives are cushy, allowing faculty to work flexible, minimal hours and to spend a lot of time at home, the pressures for WPAs to constantly be available to others on campus form an integral part of WPA happiness scripts; a good WPA is always available to students, instructors, administrators, and others. This, of course, means that their personal lives suffer. Douglas Hesse's early piece "The WPA as Father, Husband, Ex" (1995) is a notable essay that explores these ideas; here, I turn to his later text "What Is a Personal Life?" (2013) to explore the personal costs of the emotional labor WPAs take on. Speaking to the very context I recount at the beginning of this chapter, Hesse (2013, 408) claims that "the particular distinction for professors [as separate from other professionals], however, is that beyond a point, their worktime is self-inflicted—and boundlessly so." He recounts the ways professors internalize calls for them to do more work as a justification for their desire to do that work, pointing to the fact that "WPAs, like people in every profession these days, are never completely out of the office" (409). And even though we could put limitations on the time we spend working, WPAs' desires—born partially out of WPA happiness scripts being built around high workloads involving emotional labor—to do this work often mean that we push ourselves to constantly work and to be open to work all the time. Hesse here points out the personal problems that can develop from this mind-set, including lack of attention to physical and mental health, as well as his belief that "a healthy [personal life] helps you not only deal with your job, it helps you do your job better" (411). Like Ward, Hesse offers advice about how to counteract this desire to work all the time and how to make time for a personal life. However, what remains unchanged is the revolution of WPA happiness scripts around an amount of emotional labor that cannot help but impact our personal lives. Even as WPAs recognize that high workload and high amounts of emotional labor can hurt us, the perceived benefits we and our programs get from such labor often place us into an endless cycle of emotional laboring. Then, WPAs experience cruel optimism by embracing the emotional labor that ultimately can harm rather than help our careers, programs, and lives outside of academia.

The ways these texts and others present happiness scripts naturalize the high amount of emotional labor that is required of WPAs, particularly in terms of embracing workload, negotiating institutional relationships, and maintaining personal relationships. Even though some of the scholarship in our field presents strategies for countering the amount of work WPAs are asked to take on, they do not contest the idea of the "good WPA." This idealized person, whom many WPAs strive to embody, willingly performs an inhuman amount of emotional labor without concern for their personal well-being. Instead, they constantly put the health of the program, instructors, and students above themselves as a willing sacrifice to the writing program and the WPA field. Particularly since the position of the jWPA is unlikely to disappear, it is imperative that the field reconsider the happiness scripts we pass on to each other, especially to gWPAs and jWPAs, about the ways WPAs are expected to take on and handle emotional labor. I next call on WPAs to find ways to achieve a work-life balance and to publicize such strategies. I view these as potentially disruptive, calling for more WPAs to embody a "bad WPA" identity that allows them to experience personal well-being and that potentially disrupts current WPA happiness scripts.

PUBLICLY BEING A BAD WPA AT WORK AND HOME

This section asks WPAs to embrace measures that will help us avoid overwork, especially in terms of the emotional labor we do, and then to publicize our strategies for doing so. Because of the neo-liberal forces at work in faculty lives, any WPA who has achieved work-life balance can feel secretive about this because they do not want other WPAs, their own departments, or the public at large to feel as if they are not working hard enough. At a previous institution, for me that meant being cautious about how much I publicized my ability to do research even as I juggled administrative, teaching, and service work. I felt that if others saw that I was able to do all of these things without overworking, I would be penalized for not having enough to do. However, it matters a great deal how WPAs support and pass on happiness scripts to other WPAs, especially to graduate students anticipating becoming WPAs. I call on those who have figured out how to be "bad" WPAs by securing a work-life balance to join me in sharing strategies about how to do so and to do so in public venues such as the CWPA conference, in journal articles or other book chapters, and in conversations with other WPAs and graduate students. Participating in changing the happiness scripts about WPA roles, including emotional labor, is a vital part of our mission if we are invested in the long-term health of individual WPAs and our field. Since other chapters in this collection explain a few ways to create sustainable emotional workloads (see Kleinfeld; Leverenz; Wenger), I offer here a few strategies that I have used as a bad WPA by refusing to take on a lifestyle of overwork—especially in terms of often-invisible emotional labor—that is detrimental to my overall health. These include deliberately collaborating with others on campus, setting aside time for non-WPA work, limiting time spent on email, journaling, exercising, and establishing relationships outside of work.

One of the most important ways to embody a bad WPA identity is **to take some of the collaborative work other scholars have called on us to do and make it more deliberate** (see Adler-Kassner 2008; Miller

1996; Ratcliffe and Rickly 2010; Micciche and Strickland 2013). I suggest that we must seek connections outside of the writing program that can beneficially serve us and our programs. For example, at my previous institution I worked closely with the graduate director to communicate about particular teaching assistants and to brainstorm ways to approach any issues they might be having. We also tag-teamed difficult conversations with teaching assistants so that neither of us had to handle the emotional labor of such discussions alone. Although this does not completely remove emotional burdens from WPAs, it allows for more support when doing emotional work that can diffuse the feeling that we are the only ones invested in it.

Because emotional work can often derail an entire day, WPAs need **to actively set aside time to focus on other work**. As a new WPA or when first going into a new WPA position, it can be useful to use a time-tracking app such as Toggl (https://www.toggl.com) to figure out how much time is actually spent on WPA activities. Such apps typically allow users to set up categories that they then use to "clock in" and "clock out" with throughout the day; then, they can generate reports showing them how much time is spent on what types of activities in a day, a week, a month, or longer. Keeping track of how much time is spent on administration, research, teaching, and service is a useful way to visualize where time is going and perhaps where changes should be made in time use. I used Toggl the first two years I was in my first WPA position to grasp how much time I was spending on different aspects of my job and to make adjustments. As might be expected, I discovered that I had some days where I worked ten or more hours per day, and I learned to adjust other days in the week so they were shorter to account for these. This didn't mean I wasn't exhausted on those long days, but it did mean I set limits for myself and provided other time to relax guilt-free.

Perhaps one of the most ubiquitous interruptions in a WPA's day that can cause emotional stress is email. Most WPAs know the feeling of seeing emails pop up from instructors or students in their program and feeing anxious about what situation they will encounter. In years past, I made it a priority to answer emails quickly and efficiently, almost always having my email open while working because I thought good WPAs are available to others most of the time, even electronically. I also allowed my phone to push email notifications to me on a regular basis so that I was routinely interrupted in my personal life with the knowledge that I had emails waiting for me (and that, as a Type A person, I struggled to ignore). More recently, however, I have begun strategically turning my email on and off—and, most important, setting my phone so I have to choose when to check my email—so I can have uninterrupted time to focus on grading, research, putting together teaching materials, and living a personal life without the stress of wondering what the next email will say or ask me to do. One of the most important boundaries to set up as a bad WPA is that **emails will not be checked—or will be checked very infrequently—at night, on weekends, or whatever parts of the day/week make most sense to an individual**. Without some time that is designated as email free, emotional labor from the WPA job can easily creep into our personal lives and affect our ability to truly relax.

Since work can often become part of home life, WPAs need to find additional strategies to handle emotional labor as it creeps into the personal. Although self-care has been criticized as an inadequate response to neo-liberal forces that particularly affect women and people of color (see Mahdawi 2017; Yahm 2018), this does not mean WPAs should not create habits that will foster their emotional well-being even as they fight against systemic forces that operate on all workers. As other chapters in this collection detail (see Wenger in particular), reflective activities such as meditation and journaling can be ongoing habits that protect WPAs' emotional health. These strategies serve as an emotional clearing ground through which we can think about what is happening in our lives without judgment and try to focus on what is most important to us. One way to spend a minimal amount of time on this activity is **to keep a five-year line-a-day journal that provides a few lines on which to record what happens each day**.[2] The most useful part of this activity is that each page of the journal is dedicated to a day of the year, allowing the writer to see what has happened on that particular date each year the journal is kept. This has allowed me to track milestones and setbacks, remembering and tracing how I have pushed forward from struggles and built on successes. Such moments of reflection provide emotional space in which to grow as a WPA and a person by thinking about events over many years instead of just considering one day, month, or year at a time.

Another priority for WPAs must be **to care for their physical bodies as well as their mental and emotional selves**. Because of ties between the physical and the emotional (see Penedo and Dahn 2005 for a review of this research), physical health should be seen as a necessary component of caring for ourselves. Although academics can particularly fall prey to the idea that our intellectual life is more important than our physical bodies, the benefits of exercising extend beyond prolonging life to "improv[ing] mood and reduc[ing] symptoms of depression and anxiety" (Penedo and Dahn 2005, 191). Despite the prevalence of research that proves such a wide range of benefits, WPAs, like other American adults, often struggle to exercise an adequate amount. A 2013 study by the Centers for Disease Control and Prevention (CDC) found that only 20.6 percent of adults met *both* aerobic and muscle-strengthening guidelines.[3] In general, US adults struggle to adequately exercise according to the CDC guidelines, and WPAs, who spend much time at our desks and sitting in meetings, are particularly prone to the negative effects of inactivity. About a year after starting my first WPA position, I realized that no one was going to prioritize my health for me; I had to make time myself. I started working out four to five times each week and spending more time cooking healthy foods at home. While this isn't a space in which to proselytize about either of these, it can be easy for WPAs to sacrifice their own health in the name of their jobs. I urge us as a field to make personal health a priority above and beyond being a good WPA.[4]

One central aspect of mental health in particular is having a social support system. Research shows that feeling lonely can have negative results on a person's overall health and that social support can increase mental health (see Cacioppo et al. 2002; Thoits 2011). WPAs can often view time spent with those in our writing programs as social support, especially if meetings happen around lunch or over a beer. However, it is important to recognize when our emotional interactions are tied to work and when they are free of it and **to foster relationships outside of work**. For me, this has meant maintaining relationships not just with colleagues but with my siblings, whom I am very close to, as well as professional relationships that extend beyond work into deep friendship. It has also meant finding friends who are outside of academia with whom I can relax without ties to my professional life. Although maintaining such relationships takes time, it is time WPAs especially need to prioritize as a way to balance out the high amount of stressful emotional labor we perform at our jobs.

EMBRACING THE BAD WPA IDENTITY

As this chapter shows, debates about faculty workload are ongoing, but emotional labor has remained a largely invisible aspect of that workload that WPAs in particular struggle to make visible for ourselves and others (see Stolley's chapter, this volume, about how to accomplish such visibility). While my tactics do not necessarily address such visibility, they do ask WPAs to be more reflective about the amount of emotional labor we perform and to develop concrete strategies for ameliorating this labor. In particular, we have to learn to value our personal lives and health as much as our work so we prioritize ourselves without feeling guilty or ashamed, as if we are no longer good WPAs. While some of us may be able to handle a high workload for some time, this is not typically sustainable over the course of a career that lasts decades. Hence, I believe we should embrace the identity of bad WPAs by refusing to sacrifice ourselves to a system that offers few life-sustaining rewards in return. We cannot continue to use students and faculty in our programs as excuses for ignoring our own well-being, especially as we participate in the co-construction of WPA happiness scripts. Ideally, we can become part of a new movement to redefine what it means to be a happy or good WPA that does not include overworking and performing endless emotional labor.

What would happen if more of us—or all of us—decided to be bad WPAs *and to tell others about it?* What if, when we found strategies that worked, we told others about them as a service to the profession and a service to ourselves? We may not remake the world, but we could remake what WPA happiness scripts look like and create more justifiable, reasonable expectations for future generations of WPAs who will have a lot on their plates already. We could be bad WPAs as a way to resist neo-liberalism and its misunderstanding of faculty workload, even if we aren't known as the best WPAs. And we could be bad WPAs because doing so will make our emotional lives sustainable, which would allow us to continue to serve as WPAs for a long time. Ultimately, I urge WPAs to analyze and support themselves with the same level of rigor and sensitivity we have been taught to reserve for our programs, colleagues, and students in the creation of new WPA happiness scripts that are sustainable and life-affirming.

NOTES

1. Here, I borrow from Hannah Arendt's (1958) theory of labor as mechanical work that maintains life but is ultimately futile and therefore never-ending.
2. Many thanks to my friend and colleague Summar Sparks for telling me about line-a-day journals years ago in graduate school.
3. To meet both these guidelines, "respondents had to report engaging in at least 150 minutes per week of moderate-intensity aerobic physical activity or 75 minutes of vigorous-intensity aerobic physical activity per week, or an equivalent combination of moderate- and vigorous-intensity aerobic physical activity, and participating in muscle-strengthening physical activity at least two times per week" (Centers for Disease Control 2013).
4. Here, I must acknowledge the need to focus on health rather than weight; equating weight with health is a pernicious myth our society perpetuates to wage a war on people viewed as "overweight" instead of focusing on actual health (see Hobbes 2018 for a detailed analysis of this myth).

REFERENCES

Adler-Kassner, Linda. 2008. *The Activist WPA: Changing Stories about Writers and Writing.* Logan: Utah State University Press.

Ahmed, Sara. 2010. *The Promise of Happiness.* Durham, NC: Duke University Press.

American Institute of Stress. 2017. "Workplace Stress." https://www.stress.org/workplace-stress/.

Arendt, Hannah. 1958. *The Human Condition.* Chicago: University of Chicago Press.

Berlant, Lauren. 2011. *Cruel Optimism.* Durham, NC: Duke University Press.

Cacciopo, John T., Louise C. Hawkley, L. Elizabeth Crawford, John M. Ernst, Mary H. Burleson, Ray B. Kowalewski, William B. Malarkey, Eve Van Cauter, and Gary G. Berntson. 2002. "Loneliness and Health: Potential Mechanisms." *Psychosomatic Medicine* 64 (3): 407–417.

Centers for Disease Control and Prevention. 2013. "Adult Participation in Aerobic and Muscle-Strengthening Physical Activities—United States, 2011." *Morbidity and Mortality Weekly Report* 62 (17): 326–330. https://www.cdc.gov/mmwr/pdf/wk/mm6217.pdf.

Charlton, Colin, Jonikka Charlton, Tarez Samra Graban, Kathleen J. Ryan, and Amy Ferdinandt Stolley. 2011. *GenAdmin: Theorizing WPA Identities in the Twenty-First Century.* Anderson, SC: Parlor.

Dew, Debra Frank, and Alice Horning. 2007. *Untenured Faculty as Writing Program Administrators: Institutional Practices and Politics.* West Lafayette, IN: Parlor.

Flaherty, Colleen. 2014. "So Much to Do, So Little Time." *Inside Higher Ed,* April 9. http://www.insidehighered.com/news/2014/04/09/research-shows-professors-work-long-hours-and-spend-much-day-meetings.

Hesse, Douglas. 1999. "The WPA as Father, Husband, Ex." In *Kitchen Cooks, Plate Twirlers, and Troubadours: Writing Program Administrators Tell Their Stories,* edited by Diana George, 44–55. Portsmouth, NH: Boynton.

Hesse, Douglas. 2013. "What Is a Personal Life?" In *A Rhetoric for Writing Program Administrators,* edited by Rita Malenczyk, 407–414. Anderson, SC: Parlor.

Hobbes, Michael. 2018. "Everything You Know about Obesity Is Wrong." *Huffington Post,* September 19. https://highline.huffingtonpost.com/articles/en/everything-you-know-about-obesity-is-wrong/.

Mahdawi, Arwa. 2017. "Generation Treat Yo' Self: The Problem with 'Self-Care.'" *The Guardian,* January 12. https://www.theguardian.com/lifeandstyle/2017/jan/12/self-care-problems-solange-knowles.

Maid, Barry M. 1999. "How WPAs Can Learn to Use Power to Their Own Advantage." In *Administrative Problem-Solving for Writing Programs and Writing Centers: Scenarios in Effective Program Management,* edited by Linda Myers Breslin, 199–211. Urbana, IL: National Council of Teachers of English.

McClelland, Ben W. 1999. "A New Millennium for the Writing Program: Introducing Authority and Change to Traditional Folks Who Employ Time-Worn Practices." In *Administrative Problem-Solving for Writing Programs and Writing Centers: Scenarios in Effective Program Management,* edited by Linda Myers Breslin, 167–179. Urbana, IL: National Council of Teachers of English.

Micciche, Laura R., and Donna Strickland. 2013. "Feminist WPA Work: Beyond Oxymorons." *WPA: Writing Program Administration* 36 (2): 169–176.

Miller, Hildy. 1996. "Postmasculinist Directions in Writing Program Administration Work." *WPA: Writing Program Administration* 20 (1–2): 49–61.

Myers-Breslin, Linda, ed. 1999. *Administrative Problem-Solving for Writing Programs and Writing Centers: Scenarios in Effective Program Management.* Urbana, IL: National Council of Teachers of English.

Penedo, Frank, and Jason R. Dahn. 2005. "Exercise and Well-Being: A Review of Mental and Physical Health Benefits Associated with Physical Activity." *Current Opinion in Psychiatry* 18 (2): 189–193.

Phillips, Talinn, Paul Shovlin, and Megan Titus. 2014. "Thinking Liminally: Exploring the (com)Promising Positions of the Liminal WPA." *WPA: Writing Program Administration* 38 (1): 42–64.

Ratcliffe, Krista, and Rebecca Rickly. 2010. *Performing Feminism and Administration in Rhetoric and Composition*. Mahwah, NJ: Hampton.

Robinson, Sara. 2012. "Bring Back the 40-Hour Work Week." *Salon*, March 14. https://www.salon.com/2012/03/14/bring_back_the_40_hour_work_week/.

Salter, Anastasia. 2018. "Weekend Reading: Academic Workload Edition." *Chronicle of Higher Education*, February 16. https://www.chronicle.com/blogs/profhacker/weekend-reading-academic-workload-edition/65046.

"The 10 Least Stressful Jobs in 2017." 2017. *Forbes*, January 18. https://www.forbes.com/pictures/587e8d2a4bbe6f1f20eb169c/5-tenured-university-prof/#37ef017f64a7.

Thoits, Peggy A. 2011. "Mechanisms Linking Social Ties and Support to Physical and Mental Health." *Journal of Health and Social Behavior* 5 (2): 145–161.

Ward, Irene. 2002. "Developing Healthy Management and Leadership Styles: Surviving the WPAs' 'Inside Game.'" In *The Allyn and Bacon Sourcebook for Writing Program Administrators*, edited by Irene Ward and William J. Carpenter, 49–67. New York: Longman.

Yahm, Sarah. 2018. "Prescribing Mindfulness Allows Doctors to Ignore Legitimate Female Pain." *Slate*, February 5. https://slate.com/technology/2018/02/doctors-are-increasingly-pushing-mindfulness-on-chronic-pain-patients.html.

Conclusion

WHAT NOW AND WHAT NEXT?
Strategy Sheets for Negotiating Emotional Labor

Courtney Adams Wooten, Jacob Babb,
Kristi Murray Costello, and Kate Navickas

Despite the diversity of approaches to emotional labor represented here, all the authors in this collection call on WPAs to be reflective and deliberate about the emotional labor we perform and how we handle it. Following suit then, instead of offering a typical conclusion to this collection, we asked the authors to provide a one-page strategy sheet based on each chapter. These strategy sheets consolidate some of the specific tactics offered in this collection to help WPAs consider particular types of emotional labor and how they can work with, around, and through the emotions they experience. These are meant to be quick and easy references when WPAs encounter particular situations and heuristics for considering additional strategies. In addition to consulting, enacting, and sharing these strategies and heuristics, we ask WPAs to continue to add to them in conversations, presentations, and publications about the emotional labor we all do.

These strategy sheets provide a wide range of ideas for negotiating the emotional labor of administration. Several of them offer concrete methods for making emotional labor visible in different institutional locations, like Amy Ferdinandt Stolley's strategies for recognizing emotional labor in professional documents and Nelson and coauthors' strategies for supporting such labor in writing centers. Many offer WPAs specific resources, ways of responding, and ideas for processing emotions during times of crisis and tragedy (Hensley Owens—sexual assaults, Clinnin—campus shootings and crises, Schlachte—natural disasters, Kleinfeld—loss), while others offer advice from specific fields (Leverenz—positive psychology and Wenger—mindfulness) or meaningful reminders, tips, and ways of reframing for preserving the self (Carter-Tod, Janangelo, Adams Wooten). Further, there are strategies for studying emotional labor (Navickas), for negotiating the emotional labor of religiously affiliated schools (Imafuji), for negotiating emotional labor in two-year colleges (Warnke et al.), and for creating a more complex and better representative model of professional development that includes emotional labor (Adsit and Doe).

In Stolley's chapter on making the emotional labor of professional documents more visible, she tells the story of using posters and phrases of motivation hung on the back of her office door as a way of talking honestly about her pedagogy and emotional labor during a job interview. We hope these concluding strategy sheets can function much like the posters and motivational quotes Stolly references. That is, that they can serve as quick, easy to consume, and visible touchstones of advice, support, or tips for what to do now to help us get through the day or a difficult situation, to remind us to care for ourselves, or to encourage us while we care for others. It bears repeating that while we can all benefit from such advice and strategies, these strategies are not intended to eliminate emotional labor but to help us negotiate that labor in ways that preserve and sustain. We end with a note of hope—first, that these strategies are useful and motivational to fellow WPAs through whatever emotional labor and situations we find ourselves in; and second, we hope that as a field, we will continue to add to these strategies and to make our emotional labor visible, viable, and valued.

Strategy Sheets

Strategy Sheet
HOW TO FLOURISH AS A WPA
Strategies from Positive Psychology

Carrie S. Leverenz

WPAs who find themselves struggling to flourish in their administrative positions may benefit from applying therapeutic interventions of positive psychology, popularized by Martin E.P. Seligman and his Authentic Happiness Program at the University of Pennsylvania (https://www.authentichappiness.sas.upenn.edu/).

According to Seligman (2011), "flourishing" depends not on the absence of negative emotion but on the strengthening of positive emotions. Positive psychology works to increase clients' sense of well-being by focusing on five elements: positive emotion, engagement, meaning, positive relationships, and accomplishment. Increased attention to these elements can contribute to resilience.

Positive psychology contends that we are happiest when doing what we are good at. Seligman thus recommends that we identify our signature strengths and create opportunities to use them more. Using widely validated surveys, Seligman (2011, 243–265) has identified twenty-four signature strengths, organized into six broad categories: Wisdom and Knowledge, Courage, Humanity and Love, Justice, Temperance, and Transcendence. Take the VIA Signature Strength questionnaire here: https://www.authentichappiness.sas.upenn.edu/testcenter. Then look for opportunities as WPA to use your strengths toward increasing your well-being in the following areas (with the acronym PERMA):

Positive emotion (what most people think of as happiness). We can increase our store of positive emotion by (1) consciously expressing gratitude and (2) identifying and savoring positive experiences to counter the outsized effect negative experiences have on us psychologically.

Engagement, what Mihaly Csikzentmihaly (2004) calls "flow": a mental state characterized by "(1) Complete involvement with the task (2) A sense of being outside everyday reality (3) Great inner clarity (4) Knowing that the activity is doable (5) A sense of serenity—no worries about oneself (6) Timelessness—totally focused on the present and (7) Intrinsic motivation—whatever produces flow becomes its own reward." Do more of the parts of WPA work that lead to flow.

Relationships. Build more positive relationships; limit the effects of negative relationships. We can't take care of everybody. We can't make everyone like us or even respect us. In relationships, we can only control ourselves.

Meaning. Remind ourselves and others of what's meaningful about supporting writing. Make WPA work more meaningful by connecting with other projects and programs on our campuses, in our communities, and beyond.

Achievement. Invest in getting better at WPA work that you like and are good at. Do boring or routine tasks quickly to make time for the things that require higher-order thinking.

REFERENCES

Csikzentmihaly, Mihaly. 2004. "Flow: The Secret to Happiness." TED Ideas Worth Spreading. https://www.ted.com/talks/mihaly_csikszentmihalyi_on_flow#t-1119503.

Seligman, Martin E.P. 2011. *Flourish: A Visionary New Understanding of Happiness and Well-Being*. New York: Free Press.

Strategy Sheet

YOU LOST ME AT "ADMINISTRATOR"
Vulnerability and Transformation in WPA Work at the Two-Year College

Anthony Warnke, Kirsten Higgins,
Marcie Sims, and Ian Sherman

TACTICS, STRATEGIES, AND HABITS OF MIND FOR GRAPPLING WITH EMOTIONAL LABOR

- **Remember that change is inherently, not lamentably, emotional.** Vulnerability and even some contention are essential for change and progress. Listen and move forward in positive ways. See emotion as generative for progress.
- **Center your calls for change on repurposing (Stenberg 2015) the shared vision and preexisting structures.** If possible, articulate the ways your ethos and your work as WPA align with or extend the already existing values and structures of your department. You're not remaking the department out of whole cloth; you're making a quilt from existing pieces.
- **Defensiveness is not always personal.** Community colleges are contested territories that often devalue the professional identities of faculty. WPAs should read defensiveness as representative of tensions within a larger context.
- **The epistemologies that drive reform exalt what is empirical and data-driven.** However, faculty narratives are valuable, and it's in narrative where the emotions attach and circulate. Faculty stories of success can valuably add nuance to generalized, quantitative data.
- **Community colleges often value more horizontal and autonomous structures.** Introducing structures at a community college can feel like surveillance or intrusion. See Carolyn Calhoon-Dillahunt (2011) regarding how to do WPA work without the formal WPA role.
- **Make negotiating a new position within a history possible without obliterating that history.** Rather than clinging to old stories or completely detaching from hard situations, stay close to difficulty with mindful presence. The battles of the past are not eclipsed by innovation; they are fundamental to it.

- **Gain strength from the scholarly community.** Immerse yourself in the rich subset of WPA scholarship concerning the two-year college as well as WPA and assessment scholarship more generally. Study the published work of Klausman, Ostman, Calhoon-Dillahunt, Raines, Hassel and Giordano, Adler-Kassner, Gallagher, Stenberg, Toth, and others. When you see a CFP that promises you an opportunity to further explore and reflect on your narrative, seize that opportunity and join the scholarly dialogue.
- **Work on multiple dimensions of equity.** The WPA must not accept that they are managing an unjust labor system that is out of their control but must recognize that they can be advocates for more equitable labor systems through WPA work.

We reflect on the fact that this edited collection has given space for own storymaking as WPAs (Adler-Kassner) to develop and further galvanize our work. By guiding us through a process of reflection and narrative construction, as well as an additional process of synthesis, writing this chapter has allowed us to more deeply collaborate as we engage with scholarly work. This opportunity has helped us to reconcile—and to productively leave open—key aspects of our interactions with our emotional landscape and local context. By collaborating and invoking the form of autoethnography, we have attempted a feminist repurposing of the existing resources (Stenberg), in terms of both the narrative ecology and the affective landscape.

REFERENCES

Calhoon-Dillahunt, Carolyn. 2011. "Writing Programs without Administrators: Frameworks for Successful Writing Programs in the Two-Year College." *WPA: Writing Program Administration* 31 (1): 118–134.

Stenberg, Shari J. 2015. "Introduction." In *Repurposing Composition: Feminist Interventions for a Neoliberal Age*, 1–14. Logan: Utah State University Press.

Strategy Sheet
EMOTIONAL LABOR INTERVIEW

Kate Navickas

STRATEGY FOR NEGOTIATING THE EMOTIONAL LABOR OF BECOMING

Conducting an interview that focuses on emotional labor, ideally with an administrative predecessor.

RATIONALE

The purpose of this strategy is to better negotiate the *emotional labor of becoming* within a new administrative and institutional position. The act of becoming is emotional labor because becoming is always a negotiation between who you understand yourself to be (often understood in terms of the values we hold) and the realities we come in contact with (e.g., a new professional position and institutional context). Emotional labor comes into play when we must make decisions based on values that might conflict with our sense of identity.

CAVEAT

The act of interviewing a superior or new colleague about emotional labor as a new administrator is risky and will involve varying layers of power based on institutional context, individual personalities and prior relations, individual identities and disciplinary alliances, and others. As a strategy, interviews that focus on emotional labor are an ideal strategy and should only be used when the circumstances and contexts make this an appropriate option.

CONSIDERATIONS TO START WITH

- Who might I interview? What is their institutional role?
- What is my sense of the emotional labor of this position so far?

- What did I previously hope this administrative position would involve?
- What are the risks of interviewing this person about emotional labor?
- What do I hope to gain from an interview focused on emotional labor?

POTENTIAL INTERVIEW QUESTIONS

1. When you first came to this position, how did you understand the work? What were your initial emotions in response to getting hired and starting the position? Did you have any internal struggles regarding the job?
2. What were some of your early struggles or accomplishments in this position?
3. What are some of the emotional components of your work? Could you map out different emotions you attached to different parts of the work?
4. As you've transitioned to your new role, what emotions have you experienced? How would you describe transitioning in terms of emotional labor?
5. What do you think you're most proud of having done in this position? What would you want your legacy to be? And what emotions do you attach to that work?
6. In what ways has the emotional labor of the job changed for you?
7. How have you negotiated the emotional labor of your work?
8. What advice do you have for me, especially in terms of negotiating emotional labor?
9. What does it mean to acknowledge emotional labor for you? What does it mean to share the emotional labor of your work with me? With others publicly?

Strategy Sheet

WHAT WE TAKE AND WHAT WE MODIFY FROM NCFDD

Janelle Adsit and Sue Doe

WPAs can and often already do subscribe to a fuller model of professional development and faculty support than the one pledged by NCFDD, but WPAs, as campus leaders, can also take the best parts of the NCFDD model and improve on them. NCFDD is instructive in terms of what it does and what it does not do, helping WPAs articulate key objectives for themselves.

1. WPAs should go beyond NCFDD definitions of productivity.

    Work to redefine productivity through enlarged definitions of "what counts" in faculty work.

    Work to restore the full range of work engaged in by faculty, including teaching, service, the administration of programs, and engagement in the community, rather than a de-bundling of faculty roles that divide the faculty and create tiers of opportunity.

    Educate institutional leadership about varied forms of scholarship other than the traditional publication of the journal article or monograph to include such scholarly production as multimodal composing, coding, curricular design on new media platforms, policy writing, and public translation of academic research, which are all legitimate forms of scholarship that need to be more fully recognized.

    Strive to construct faculty who are contributing citizens whose work both inside and outside the university extends public understanding of how faculty have value to the culture.

2. WPAs should strive to deliver forms of affective support.

    Consistent with the social justice commitments of most WPAs, successful faculty development should include resistance to structures in higher education that devalue faculty work and motivate through derision and shaming. WPAs should ever more fully frame faculty development and support as a belief in faculty capability.

    WPAs should use their leadership positions to identify damaging cultural practices such as micro-aggression and use their positions and communication skills to identify problems and solutions.

3. WPAs should educate themselves and faculty about the ways privilege and bias function in classrooms and workspaces.

   In ways that go well beyond those imagined by NCFDD, WPAs should consciously seek redress to racist, classist, ableist, ageist, and sexist attitudes that pervade higher education. While tenured WPAs will have more protections for undertaking this work and full professors even more than associates, the WPA leader and those who teach writing under WPA leadership, across all ranks, must be educated about intersectional oppression and seek to understand ever more fully writing programs' often unconscious participation in discriminatory attitudes and behaviors, including their effect on students.

4. WPAs can, should, and do address structural labor problems as a matter of equity.

   WPAs should use the existing work in rhetoric and composition, combined with their leadership positions, to argue against the de-bundling of the faculty role and its dissection into specialization. Where de-bundling has become the norm, WPAs should work to address equity challenges that privilege star researchers over star teachers.

   The WPA should work strenuously to improve the status, compensation, and working conditions of those teaching off the tenure track.

   The WPA should work to reverse the trend in higher education that posits contingency as a money-saving, flexibility-saving, broad-based strategy rather than a short-term solution. Contingency does not serve faculty or student needs; it supports management's desire to maximize flexibility and save money.

5. WPAs should engage in self-care and the protection of faculty time.

   Protecting faculty time for writing, as NCFDD does, is just one part of the equation. The WPA should also extend notions of care to areas beyond NCFDD's single-minded focus on writing and publication.

   WPAs, if untenured or seeking promotion to full professor, must guard time for those things that are valued for promotion.

   WPAs, if full professors, should use their position to argue for expanded notions of what counts as productivity and survey what faculty really need by way of support.

   WPAs, regardless of rank, should actively protect non-working hours as free from email and job taskers, for themselves and for those who work with and for them.

   WPAs should be supported and support others in the jealous guarding of restorative non-work time that includes meals, exercise, sleep, time with friends and family, and enjoyment in whatever way faculty define it.

Strategy Sheet
STRATEGIES FOR DISCUSSING EMOTIONAL LABOR IN YOUR PROFESSIONAL WPA DOCUMENTS

Amy Ferdinandt Stolley

To describe your emotional WPA labor in your professional documents (such as job application materials, administrative philosophies, annual activity reports, or tenure and promotion materials), the following heuristic can help you think through both what to say and how to say it so your document(s)—and your emotional labor—are more visible.

STEP ONE: IDENTIFY EMOTION-DRIVEN ACTIVITIES

- What activities do you do that qualify as emotional labor?
- What do you do when you are attentive to others' emotions in the workplace?
- What do you do when you are attentive to your own emotions in the workplace?

STEP TWO: COUNT THE HOURS

Log the time you spend on the emotional labor activities you identified in Step One. Keep track of these hours for several weeks or even a full semester.

- How many hours each week do you spend on emotional labor?
- Would your audience like to know this figure (i.e., is your intended audience numbers-oriented)?
- What patterns do you see in the time you spent on emotional labor?
- Is your emotional labor tied to recurring semester events (midterms, finals)?
- Is your emotional labor the result of out-of-the-ordinary events?

STEP THREE: IDENTIFY OUTCOMES

- What results do you see from your emotional labor?
- How does your emotional labor make itself visible in your program?
- What policy, curricular, or personnel changes have been made in the program as a result of your emotional labor?

STEP FOUR: ALIGN OUTCOMES

- How do your emotional labor outcomes you identified in Step Three align with department-, college-, or university-wide initiatives or projects?
- How do your emotional labor outcomes align with the university's mission and strategic plan?
- How do your emotional labor outcomes align with disciplinary theories or principles about writing pedagogy, student development, and faculty development?

Strategy Sheet
PREPARING FOR AND MANAGING THE EMOTIONAL LABOR OF SEXUAL ASSAULT REPORTS

Kim Hensley Owens

RESOURCES TO HAVE ON HAND

- Kleenex
- Contact information for counseling services on campus—and know what the intake procedures and costs are. Develop a contact in counseling services you can call directly.
- Contact information for the Title IX office, Student Life/dean of students, and registrar
- Bookmarked access to sections of student and employee handbooks that deal with assault
- Bookmarked access to your school's Safe Working and Learning Environment Policies
- RAINN website https://www.rainn.org/
- National Sexual Assault Hotline: 800.656.HOPE
- Information about any victim-witness programs in your community

WHAT TO SAY AND DO IN THE MOMENT

To help a reporting victim in the moment, be ready to follow this advice from the Nova Network of Victim Assistance (https://www.novabucks.org/otherinformation/rape/#):

- Listen without judging.
- Let them know the assault(s) was not their fault.
- Let them know they did what was necessary to prevent further harm.
- Reassure the survivor that he or she is cared for and loved.
- Encourage the sexual assault victim to seek medical attention.
- Encourage the survivor to talk about the assault(s) with an advocate, mental health professional, or someone they trust.
- Let them know they do not have to manage this crisis alone.

STRATEGIES FOR MANAGING THE EMOTIONAL LABOR OF SEXUAL ASSAULT REPORTS

- Let yourself feel the emotions you need to, even if that sometimes means letting down your guard and crying with a teacher or administrator in your office.
- Handle required actions based on the assault as efficiently as possible by having a set of resources (see above) at the ready.
- Meditate, either with an app like Insight Timer or on your own.
- Reach out to/vent with other teachers/WPAs via email, text, or Facebook Messenger.
- Talk in real life with partners or friends (ideally non-work friends).
- Play with children and escape with exercise or entertainment.
- Write—journal entries or for publication or both.

Strategy Sheet
STRATEGIES FOR MANAGING THE EMOTIONAL LABOR OF CRISIS RESPONSE

Kaitlin Clinnin

Writing program administrators often function as programmatic crisis responders. When a crisis situation occurs, WPAs must perform practical labor to support students and instructors during and after the crisis. Such labor may include communicating critical information, suggesting appropriate classroom responses, identifying local support resources, and advocating for impacted individuals. However, crisis response also requires a significant amount of emotional labor that often goes unrecognized.

In a crisis situation, WPAs must manage their own emotional response while also attending to the emotional needs of program stakeholders. WPAs may need to suppress emotions such as fear, anxiety, and grief to perform their administrative duties. WPAs must also care for the emotions of students and instructors by practicing emotive sensing, a process of recognizing the emotions of others and presenting appropriate emotions that can help the WPA act to resolve the crisis situation. As part of the professional response, WPAs may need to hide their emotions or express emotions they are not actually feeling.

WPAs perform emotional labor as part of the typical job responsibilities, but a crisis situation increases the emotional labor required of WPAs because the emotions are strong and the stakes are high. The burden of unrecognized and unsupported emotional labor can cause physical, cognitive, and mental distress for crisis responders like WPAs. The emotional labor associated with crisis response cannot be avoided, but WPAs can engage in preventative, concurrent, and reflective strategies to mitigate the potential negative effects of emotional labor.

PREVENTATIVE STRATEGIES (BEFORE A CRISIS)

- Prepare for crisis situations in advance by learning campus emergency procedures and identifying critical offices and resources.

- Develop and publicize a writing program crisis plan that addresses program-specific concerns such as communications protocols, classroom logistics, and campus and community support resources.
- Collaborate with campus safety and counseling offices to facilitate emergency situation and emotional labor training for writing program faculty.
- Create a personal self-care plan to identify mental and physical wellness goals.

CONCURRENT STRATEGIES (DURING A CRISIS)

- Recognize the emotional dimension of crisis response by naming and validating emotions.
- Practice self-care according to the personal self-care plan; try to get adequate food, water, physical activity, and sleep.

REFLECTIVE STRATEGIES (AFTER A CRISIS)

- Collaborate with campus mental health professionals to facilitate critical stress debriefings for impacted faculty and administrators.
- Practice continued self-care and seek additional resources as needed.
- Revise the writing program crisis-response plan and resource list as needed.

Strategy Sheet

A HEURISTIC FOR WPAS IN DISASTER RESPONSE

Carl Schlachte

PROVIDING GUIDANCE TO INSTRUCTORS

Many teachers in writing programs, if they are junior or contingent in their departments, may need explicit authorization from the WPA to address the circumstances in the way they see fit.

This means WPAs should provide the following:

- Practical guidance on issues like schedule and assignment changes.
- Dispositional guidance, like an "authorization to get emotional" with students.

The WPA can distribute this emotional labor by *encouraging conversations* between more senior and experienced teachers and more junior and less experienced faculty throughout their departments.

- These conversations are not about writing pedagogy per se, so they need not come from within the writing program. Faculty across specializations and positions should have these conversations.
    - For example, if instructors are graduate students, the WPA might suggest having conversations with their advisers.
- These conversations have two goals:
    - To learn from teachers' instincts.
    - To get validation for the kinds of responses they might wish to offer.
- Optionally, the WPA could explicitly organize these conversations by providing an informal meeting place and time (like a brown-bag lunch) or digital space (like an email thread) where they could take place.

IF CLASSES ARE CANCELLED FOR A PERIOD OF TIME

Lengthy class cancellations obviously necessitate schedule changes. In instances like this, teachers may feel rushed to try to cover whatever they can in a shortened period of time.

The WPA can do the following:

- Encourage teachers to go against the impulse to rush and to "return to normal."
  - There's no getting back the time that's lost, and slowing down to allow students to address their experiences can have real benefits.
- Offer teachers a range of options for response so they know what some possibilities might be.
  - Optionally, the WPA could organize a method for sharing different instructors' plans to provide a wider range of potential responses.
  - The WPA should let instructors decide for themselves which of the many numerous kinds of response they would like to offer.

OPTIONS FOR RESPONDING TO DISASTER IN WRITING CLASSES

- Providing students with structured reflection time, the results of which need not be shared if students don't want to do so.
- Allowing students to use an existing assignment to optionally reflect some more could be useful, though it can be difficult to offer feedback on such pieces—unless perhaps the instructor framed it as only intended to help the students express their experience more clearly and precisely.

In all cases, the WPA should *remind instructors to consider the emotional needs of not just their students but themselves as well.* Investigating disaster may lead to negative emotional consequences for all involved, so instructors should also take care. This goes for WPAs as well: *do not neglect your own emotional needs* in the aftermath of disaster.

Strategy Sheet
STRATEGIES FOR MAKING WRITING CENTER EMOTIONAL LABOR VISIBLE

Matthew T. Nelson, Sam Deges, and Kathleen F. Weaver

Emotional labor predominates in the responsibilities of nearly all positions in a writing center. If embraced with care, the centrality of emotional labor in writing center work affords an opportunity for writing center administrators to improve both their work and their work lives and to make their centers rich, rewarding, and humane environments for tutors.

1. **Make emotional labor part of your center's culture and conversations.** Involve writing tutors in discussions about the emotional labor and feeling rules that govern their work in the writing center. Invite them to interrogate, question, and learn from those aspects of their work.

2. **Cultivate a positive community and healthy culture in the writing center.** Understand that making space for the intentional development of expertise and fluency related to emotional labor will require trust and the capacity for honest communication. Look for ways to foster community, both within the tutoring staff and across the different levels of the organization.

3. **Recognize that different forms of emotional labor are required of different individuals and with different costs.** Efforts to create an equitable and inclusive work environment should include consideration of emotional labor. Normative expectations should be examined to avoid exploitation, domination, and prejudice.

4. **Make emotional labor part of your staff's professional development.** Let tutor training be informed by findings from research on emotional labor and emotional intelligence in the workplace. Create reflective and dynamic activities for tutoring staff to develop skills related to emotional labor and workplace emotional intelligence.

5. **Research emotional labor in your center and your institution.** Partner with units, departments, and courses to explore the impact of training and education related to emotional labor.

6. **Include emotional intelligence training and resilience strategies in your staff training.** Train staff on techniques for increasing emotional resilience, for reacting to workplace challenges with poise and intelligence, and for handling emotional labor in real time.
7. **Accommodate the diverse needs of tutoring staff with regard to emotional labor.** Create procedures for allowing tutors to occasionally opt out of tutoring when doing so is necessary for their psychological well-being.

Strategy Sheet

COPING WITH THE EMOTIONAL LABOR OF WRITING PROGRAM ADMINISTRATION AT RELIGIOUSLY AFFILIATED INSTITUTIONS

Elizabeth Imafuji

Train faculty to respond to students in distress. If instructors already know what they are required to report, where they should refer, and the options for community services, they should not need to involve the WPA as often in the emotionally draining task of supporting students in distress. Training can include protocols for dealing with students with depression and anxiety, protocols for accessing immediate help for suicidal students or students in danger, logistics for how to refer, and details on how to maintain privacy and confidentiality when students disclose their involvement in situations in violation of the student code of conduct.

Collaborate. At religiously affiliated institutions with strict codes of conduct for students, some faculty may wish to help distressed students without triggering disciplinary proceedings. By collaborating with other offices, including but not limited to Student Affairs/Student Life and the counseling center, WPAs can learn how faculty can best support students without losing students' trust and without betraying their own values or conscience.

Teach instructors about mission. Knowing the rationale and the history behind faith-centered regulations, rules, and statements can help faculty reflect on their place in the institution and their role as educators at a mission-driven institution.

Make time for spiritual self-care. For faculty at religiously affiliated institutions, there may be increased emotional labor around religious mission and faith-centered rules and regulations, but at such institutions faculty typically can easily access opportunities for spiritual self-care. Singing as a large group, listening to encouraging speakers, visiting campus quiet places for meditation, or joining small groups in the community can be helpful practices.

Record and count faith-based service and professional development. In annual reports, I account for time spent supporting campus spiritual life, including participation in chapels, service projects, and denominational responsibilities. I record my attendance at conferences about teaching at religious institutions and list faith-based publications.

Reflect. Writing program administrators at religiously affiliated institutions should allow themselves the time to explore their university mission, reflect on their own faith, and consider their own reasons for working at that institution.

Strategy Sheet
ADMINISTRATING WHILE BLACK
Negotiating the Emotional Labor of an African American Female WPA

Sheila Carter-Tod

INTEGRITY: ESTABLISH AND DOCUMENT PERSONAL SYSTEMS OF INTEGRITY

Creating systems of integrity, either established or reestablished, means concretely documenting why you are doing what you do based on your own personal, professional, and spiritual ethics.

Ask yourself why you became a WPA and what you want to accomplish asا WPA in the next two to three years. In addition, this means taking time to establish, reflect on, and revise your own personal boundaries.

Integrity provides a means of focusing that may start myopically (with the personal) but can, when explored more closely, be focused more and more panoramically—to encompass the overlapping aspects of our intersectionality.

INTEGRATION: CREATING COMMUNITIES OF SUPPORT

Integration for the female African American WPA means establishing networks and communities of support. These communities may be found at the university level or professionally at the level of a national organization. These connections provide opportunities to learn from other administrators of color and to collaborate on stories and strategies, thereby breaking down feeling of isolation.

INCLUSION: CREATING SYSTEMS FOR CHANGE

While integrity and integration can indeed assist in negotiating emotional labor at a personal level, inclusion is the one of the best possible methods of negotiating emotional labor at a broader institutional and national level. When I considered the legacy of those in our discipline who have done and continue to do work that intersects race, gender, ethnicity, sexuality, and other intersectionality of identity, I also noted how instrumental they have been in shaping the discussions and policies of the discipline. In other words, they saw their work not only as scholarship but also as personal and professional activism. This realization was described by one survey respondent when she considered how her work in the governance structure of NCTE, CCC, or WPA could indeed have an impact on how she negotiates her emotional labor.

While not in great numbers, we are a growing part of the discipline; as such, WPAs of color need to take an active role in the design and governance of organizations. If not at the level of governance, we can also promote inclusion as a way of negotiating emotional labor by creating and supporting initiatives that draw future and current black female WPAs into a pipeline of support through recruitment and mentoring.

Strategy Sheet

THINGS TO DO AND REMEMBER
"It Gets Bitter: Considering Andy Warhol and Harboring Anger as a Gay WPA"

Joseph Janangelo

THINGS TO DO

- Become real—and realistic—about your anger. Consider its roles and functions in your working life. Your anger may be something you enjoy carrying because it enables familiar feelings of unworthiness, entitlement, or revenge.
- Become newly observant of and relational with your saboteurs because they have lessons to offer, even now.
- Ask yourself why you became and perhaps remained such viable prey. What payoff do you get out of being bullied or mistreated?
- Ask yourself if you recruited your saboteurs or engaged in repeat casting by bringing similar bullies, who go by different names, into your WPA working life.
- Consider how responsive and porous to the words and actions of others you are at work. As a campus leader, how porous and responsive do you think you should be?
- Think about why certain feelings or experiences of shaming and bullying stay with you. How are you extending self-limiting hospitality to them?
- Consider if, as a WPA, you have ever acted as though you had dibs on being wounded or used your anger as a pose or excuse to behave badly or under-perform.

THINGS TO REMEMBER

- Avoid piety by understanding that harboring one's anger can be a form of narcissism and that we ourselves have likely been someone's bully.
- Reappraise your anger and harbor to learn how they contribute to your workplace performance and happiness.

- Career happiness is a decision, predicated on many decision points. They may include professional achievement, payback, gratitude, and compassion toward those who seek to degrade you.
- Don't try to change your bullies. Teach yourself not to want that which they cannot or will not give you.
- Be compassionate toward your bullies, but do so in ways that are safe for you.
- Try to remember debilitating experiences without reliving or repeating them.
- Do your very best to be here and now instead of there and then and to live and work as an autonomous adult. Then get better at it.

Strategy Sheet
STRATEGIES FOR A SUSTAINABLE, EQUITABLE, AND HUMANE WPA PRACTICE

Elizabeth Kleinfeld

1. **Shore up support before you need it.**

   Reach out to people to establish networks of professional support beginning in graduate school. Create or join a writing group, join a WPA professional organization, attend conferences and meet other WPAs, and join a WPA-oriented listserv. The people you meet in these ways can offer valuable emotional support and humane advice when you need it.

2. **Resist notions that grieving or struggling with a crisis is unprofessional.**

   Instead of putting energy into hiding normal emotional responses to tragedy, practice compassion toward yourself and others. Model self-care and setting healthy boundaries, which will help create a safe environment for grieving. Offering thanks for the patience or flexibility others extend to you rather than apologizing for feeling emotions helps disrupt the idea that grieving should not occur in the workplace.

3. **Prioritize based on institutional, college, and department goals.**

   When you realize you can't "do it all," prioritize projects that align with institutional, college, and department goals. Frame the projects you do tackle in terms that echo the language of those goals, which will help those above you recognize them as aligned with larger outcomes. In terms of day-to-day tasks, prioritize based on what must get done by you now. Anything else can be done tomorrow or by someone else—or perhaps it doesn't actually have to get done at all.

4. **Under-promise and over-deliver.**

   Using the strategy described above to prioritize, commit to doing the bare minimum. If you do even one more thing than you committed to or progress just a little farther on a project than you promised to, everyone will be pleasantly surprised. Recognize that by committing to do only the bare minimum, you are actually setting healthy boundaries, in accordance with the second strategy discussed above, and then claim setting healthy boundaries as another goal met.

5. **Reframe changed expectations as proactive, deliberate, and purposeful.**

   Highlight in annual reports and other program documents the adjustments you make to goals to demonstrate that your leadership responds to a dynamic workplace. Identify your decisions to not pursue a particular project or to delegate work to others as proactive decisions.

6. **Reconsider ideas of legacy.**

   Instead of thinking of your legacy as defined by projects—scholarship or initiatives—reframe it as defined by creating a workplace that is more just, healthy, and supportive for junior and future colleagues.

Strategy Sheet
MINDFULNESS
A Valuable Emotion Practice for WPAs

Christy I. Wenger

What is mindfulness?

Mindfulness means paying attention in a particular way: on purpose, in the present moment, and nonjudgmentally (Kabat-Zinn 1994, 4).

- Mindfulness is a specific method of paying attention that helps us learn to focus on thoughts and feelings without over-identifying with them.
- Mindfulness can be developed through formal, contemplative practices like meditation, yoga, tai chi, and many martial arts, among others.
- Mindfulness can also be developed through informal practice where we use a daily task like brushing our teeth, washing the dishes, or walking the dog—charging the task with the intention of mindfulness and thereby changing how we execute it.

Why should WPAs try it?

Mindfulness does not involve trying to change your thinking by thinking some more. It involves watching thought itself . . . By watching your thoughts without being drawn into them, you can learn something profoundly liberating about thinking itself, which may help you to be less of a prisoner of those thought patterns—often so strong in us—which are narrow, inaccurate, self-involved, habitual to the point of being imprisoning, and also just plain wrong (Kabat-Zinn 1994, 94).

- The selective attention that results from mindfulness allows us to watch our thoughts and feelings without reacting to them, to see them at a distance, and therefore to break automatic reactions and allow us space to reshape our responses.
- It can help us remap our feelings and give us concrete strategies for handling the intense emotional labor of our jobs. Instead of simply *having* feelings, mindfulness teaches us to *discern* them, to explore why, how, and when we feel, and to acknowledge the choices we have in responding to our own and others' feelings. This provides us with greater control over our emotional well-being.

Okay, I'm ready to try mindfulness. What should I do?

- Try meditating. Set a timer for a few minutes. In a relaxed position, close your eyes and tune in to your breath. Follow the natural in-breaths and out-breaths without trying to change them. When other thoughts pull your attention from the breath, gently redirect your focus. Find additional guided meditations here: https://insighttimer.com/.
- Apply **RAIN** to difficult emotions, an acronym for **r**ecognize (recognize your emotional environment and your emotions), **a**llow (pause judgment to let your feelings simply be), **in**vestigate (identify the source of your feelings), **n**on-identify (recognize that you are not your feelings). Find a guided RAIN practice here: https://www.youtube.com/watch?v=wm1t5FyK5Ek&t=80s.
- Learn more about mindfulness and find other practices:
    - Association for the Contemplative Mind in Higher Education: http://www.contemplativemind.org/programs/acmhe.
    - Mind and Life Institute: https://www.mindandlife.org/.
    - Mindful: https://www.mindful.org/.

REFERENCE

Kabat-Zinn, Jon. 1994. *Wherever You Go, There You Are: Mindfulness Meditation in Everyday Life.* New York: Hyperion.

Strategy Sheet
HOW TO BE A BAD WPA

Courtney Adams Wooten

DEVELOPING A NEW MIND-SET ABOUT WORK

Overall, resist WPA happiness scripts predicated on high workload, constant navigation of political relationships on campus, and the sacrifice of personal relationships off campus.

CONCRETE STRATEGIES TO ADDRESS EMOTIONAL LABOR

1. **Develop strategies for creating a sustainable workload, especially in terms of emotional labor**, including those mentioned here (see below) and elsewhere in this collection (see Kleinfeld; Leverenz; Wenger in particular, although all chapters include such strategies).
2. **Take some of the collaborative work other scholars have called on us to do and work to make it more deliberate** (see Adler-Kassner 2008; Miller 1996; Ratcliffe and Rickly 2010; Micciche and Strickland 2013).
3. **Actively set aside time to focus on other work.** Time trackers such as https://www.toggl.com can be useful to track and manage time.
4. **Create the expectation that emails will not be checked—or will be checked very infrequently—at night, on weekends, or during whatever parts of the day/week make the most sense to an individual.** Turn off automatic email checks on phones and any other electronic devices to avoid the constant barrage of emails.
5. **Keep a five-year line-a-day journal that provides a few lines on which to record what happens each day to track successes and failures.** This is an easy way to journal and reflect without using up a lot of time (unless that is something you enjoy doing and prioritize daily).
6. **Care for your physical body as well as your mental and emotional self.** Academics generally prioritize the mind over the body, but they are interconnected and need to be equally valued (see Penedo and Dahn 2005).
7. **Foster relationships outside of work.** These can be maintaining relationships with partners or spouses, children, family, and friends, but they need routine check-ins and quality time.

FOSTERING A NEW MIND-SET ABOUT WORK IN THE FIELD

Create new happiness scripts in our field that address these questions: What would happen if more of us—or all of us—decided to be bad WPAs *and to tell others about it?* What if, when we found strategies that worked, we told others about them as a service to both the profession and ourselves?

REFERENCES

Adler-Kassner, Linda. 2008. *The Activist WPA: Changing Stories about Writers and Writing.* Logan: Utah State University Press.

Micciche, Laura R., and Donna Strickland. 2013. "Feminist WPA Work: Beyond Oxymorons." *WPA: Writing Program Administration* 36 (2): 169–176.

Miller, Hildy. 1996. "Postmasculinist Directions in Writing Program Administration Work." *WPA: Writing Program Administration* 20 (1–2): 49–61.

Penedo, Frank, and Jason R. Dahn. 2005. "Exercise and Well-Being: A Review of Mental and Physical Health Benefits Associated with Physical Activity." *Current Opinion in Psychiatry* 18 (2): 189–193.

Ratcliffe, Krista, and Rebecca Rickly. 2010. *Performing Feminism and Administration in Rhetoric and Composition.* Mahwah, NJ: Hampton.

INDEX

academic communities: caring in, 23; socialization in, 99
academic discourse: emotional constructs in, 91–92
academic rank, 105–6
academics: ideal, 78; work and responsibilities of, 97, 270–71. *See also* administrators; faculty
Accelerated Learning Program, equity-centered, 42
accountability models, 40
achievement, 32–33, 290
Achieving the Dream, 38
acting, surface and deep, 22–23
activities: attention to, 263–64; emotion-driven, 106–7; low-value, 86
Adams Wooten, Courtney, 59, 155
adjunct faculty. *See* contingent faculty
Adler-Kassner, Linda, 51
Administrative Problem-Solving for Writing Program and Writing Centers (Myers-Breslin), 275–76
administrators, administration, 50, 97–98, 108; African American, 309–10; agency of, 69–70; availability of, 251; crisis response by, 132–34, 141–42; culture of, 48–49; feminist, 247; reflection, 106–7; support and advocacy for, 139; valuing, 20–21
advice, peer, 239
advocacy: for students, 138; for teachers and administrators, 139; for WPA positions, 41
affect: expressing, 122–23; managing, 219–24; theory of, 82–83
African Americans, 13, 200, 309–10; etiquette and performance behavior, 206–8; female WPAs, 197, 198, 199; inclusion, 212–13; marginalization, 203–5; self-care, 211–12; uncompensated labor, 202–3
agency: administrative, 69–70, 71; emotion and, 255; slow, 238
Ahmed, Sara, 7, 20, 34, 59, 64, 82, 98, 261, 265; happiness scripts, 271–73
Alexander, Jonathan, 217; "Frameworks for Failure," 34
ambivalence, 27

American Psychologist, 33
Anderson, Leon, 21, 98, 136, 184
anger, 216, 311–12; bitterness, 220–21; and helpfulness, 221–22; learning from, 229–30; offloading, 232–33; realistic, 224–26
apologies, 228–29
approachability, 223
arousal, as flow experience, 29
assailants, 119, 120–21, 127(n4)
assessment. *See* evaluation
attendance policy, 108
attention: divided, 149–50; mindful, 263–64, 265, 317
Authentic Happiness Program, 289
authority, 23, 208; of contingent faculty, 154–55
autonomy, classroom, 39
availability, 251; and work-life balance, 276–77

Babb, Jacob, 155
Bad Ideas about Writing (Ball and Loewe), 9
balance: personal-professional, 13; work-life, xiv, 4–5, 19, 79, 84–85, 93(table)
Ball, Cheryl E., *Bad Ideas about Writing,* 9
Banks, William P., 217
Barrett, Greg, 230–31
barriers, 44; racial and gender, 201–2
Beal, Daniel J., 122
becoming, emotional labor of, 58–62, 72, 293–94
behavior, 227; performative, 207–8
being present, 243
Bellerose, Satya, 180
Bellas, Marcia, 167
Belli, Jill, 264
"Be of Use, To" (Piercy), 97
Berg, Maggie, 246, 266
Bergman, Ingrid, 229
Berlant, Lauren, 7, 82; theory of cruel optimism, 271, 273–74
bias, racial and gender, 200–201
Bilia, Angela, 151
binge writing, 85
Black Lives Matter, xiv–xv
Blacks. *See* African Americans
Blanchot, Maurice, 215

319

Blankenship, Chris, 221
Bloom's Taxonomy, 47
Boler, Megan, on emotions, 267–68
Boler, Michalinos, 43
Boice, Robert, 83
Boquet, Elizabeth, 162–63
Borrowman, Shane, *The Promise and Perils of Writing Program Administration,* 27
boundaries: healthy, 313; in writing, 265
Boyer Commission, 85
Brach, Tara, 267
Brady, Ann, 262
Brescoll, Victoria L., 99
Bright-Sided (Ehrenreich), 33
Brooks, Jeff, 165
Brotheridge, Celeste M., 22
Buddhism, 257
budget, and uncompensated labor, 202–3
bullying, bullies, 312; critical observation of, 225, 226; performance, 219; pre-empting, 220; responses of, 230–31, 234(n6); responses to, 232–33; vulnerabilities, 228
burnout, 5, 253, 275, 276
busyness, and grieving, 240

Calhoon-Dillahunt, Carolyn, 53, 291
campus police/safety officers, 120, 134
Canagarajah, Suresh, 41
career coaching, 79
career opportunities, 169
Carey, Tamika, *Rhetorical Healing,* 81
caring for others, 22, 26
Carlson, Linda E., 259
Carrick, Tracy Hamler, 57, 58; on conflict negotiation, 69–70; on Cornell writing program, 68–69; as WPA, 63–67; on writing centers, 67–68
Carter-Tod, Sheila, 166
Caswell, Nicole I., 8, 21, 57, 58, 65, 162, 163, 164, 168, 238, 242, 243, 244, 247; on emotional labor, 59–60, 173–74, 184; on WCD identity, 61–62, 68
Center for Collegiate Mental Health, 180
Center for Mindfulness in Medicine, Health Care and Society, 257
Centers for Disease Control and Prevention (CDC), 281
change: structural, 291, 309–10; in TYC writing programs, 43–47; and vulnerability, 52–53
Charlton, Jonikka, "Twenty More Years in the WPA's Progress," 100–101
child refugees, 3–4
Chopra, Deepak, 257
Christians, mental health issues, 180

church-affiliated schools. *See* religiously affiliated institutions
classes: cancellations of, 145–46, 147, 303–4; changes in, 119–20
classrooms: autonomy, 39; as safe space, 118–19
Claude, on disaster response, 149, 150, 151
Clery Act, 116, 127(n1)
Clinton, Hillary Rodham, 96
coaching, shaming as, 88
collaboration, 191, 254, 262, 278–79, 307, 317; sexual assault issues, 118–19, 121
college culture, sexual assault and, 125
committee work, 262
communication(s), 46, 133; NCFDD, 78, 80–81
communities, 12–13; support, 211, 309; WCA, 163–64
community colleges, 48, 53, 291–92. *See also* two-year institutions
community reading groups, 190
compartmentalization techniques, 137
compassion, 230; toward bullies, 232, 312
compassion fatigue, 275
compensation, fair, 202–3
composition: as feminized, 23; at two-year institutions, 42
Condition on the Academic Workforce, 78
Conference on College Composition and Communication (CCCC), 210, 212
confidentiality, 178, 182, 187
conflict, mediation/negotiation, 47, 69–70, 253
conscience, and code of conduct reporting, 187
consciousness, of emotions, 260
consent, 12; sexual, 123–24
contemplative practice/arts, 256, 265
contingent faculty, 45, 159(n3): disaster response, 151–52, 153, 159(n3); and Hurricane Sandy, 148–49; working conditions, 154–55
control, flow experience, 29
conversations, as emotional labor, 163
coping behaviors, 190
corporatism, language of, 48, 49
cortisol levels, 166
Costello, Kristi, 10
Council of Writing Program Administrators (CWPA), 100, 110, 140, 197, 210, 211, 212, 274
counseling, 19, 135, 138, 180, 239, 307
courage, 25
course placement, 40
course preparation, 107

COVID-19 pandemic, xiii
Cowan, Katherine C., 133
Craig, Collin Lamont, 197
Crepeau-Hobson, Franci, 137
crime, student-perpetrated, 118
crisis response, xiv, 12, 129–30, 132, 142, 285, 313; emergency management plans, 133–34; programmatic, 135–38; strategies for, 139–41, 301–2; support and advocacy in, 138–39
Crisp, Quentin, 232
critical observation, of saboteurs and enemies, 225–26
critical stress debriefings, 141
cruel optimism, theory of, 271, 272–73
crying, 122, 243
Csikzentmihaly, Mihaly, 289; on flow, 28–29
culture, administrative and faculty, 48
curriculum development, 47
Cvetkovich, Ann, 149
CWPA. *See* Council of Writing Program Administrators

daily writing practice, 83
Dalal, Reeshad S., 122
damage, from Hurricane Sandy, 145, 146
date-rape drugs, 120
Davidson, Richard, 258
Davies, Laura J., 8, 10, 57, 238, 243, 252
deaths: grief and processing, 243–44; reactions to, 10, 237, 238–39; suicide, 239–40
DeBacher, Sarah, 131–32, 147, 153
debriefings, critical stress, 141
dedication, of contingent faculty, 153
deep acting, 22–23
defensiveness, 53, 291
Dembicki, Lucas, 237, 238, 239; remembrance, 241–42
Demps, Kathryn, 270
Denny, Harry, 65, 67
DePalma, Michael-John, 189
deportment, personal, 206
destabilization, 149
development, NCFDD, 76–77
dialogue, contingent and tenure-track faculty, 155
disappointment, culture of, 253
disasters: instructor responses to, 156–57; preparedness and response, 155–56; responses to, xiv, 145–46, 149–50, 303–4; support and guidance for, 146–47; WPA and faculty responses, 152–53
discretion, and personal lives, 221–22
discrimination, against gays, 216–17

distress, student, 179, 180, 184
diversity, 233
division of labor, WCDs, 61
documents, 12; on emotional labor, 103–4; professional, 285, 286, 297–98
Doing Emotion: Rhetoric, Writing, Teaching (Micciche), 8–9, 105, 147
domestic violence survivors, emotive sensing work with, 136
Douce, Louise A., 181
Downs, Douglas, 183, 184
Durr, Marlese, 206

Education Northwest, 125
effortful regulation, 123
Ehrenreich, Barbara, 34; *Bright-Sided*, 33
Elbow, Peter, 26
Eliot, T. S., *Four Quartets*, 221
email, 279–80, 317
emergency management plans, 133–34
emergency resources, 142
emotional geography, recognizing, 267
emotional harbors, 230
emotional intelligence, 169, 170, 306
emotional labor, xiii; acknowledgment of, 167–68; interiority of, 254; scholarship on, 6–8
"Emotional Labor: Why and How to Teach It" (Mastracci, Newman, and Guy), 6–7
emotion rules, workplace, 255–56
emotions, 136, 265; behavioral rules and, 164–65; as choice, 259–60; controlling, 3–4; expressing, 122–23, 137–38, 181–82, 243; feminine, 96; nonresidence of, 66–67; outlaw, 184–85; positive, 24, 26, 28, 289; processing, 285; sharing, 241; social construct of, 161, 171; as sticky, 71; suppression of, 46; surface and deep acting, 22–23; in workplace, 98–99, 244–45, 253–56
emotive sensing, of crisis responders, 136–37
empathy, 23, 71; expressing, 164, 165
empowerment, of instructors, 153–54
enemies, critical observation of, 225–26
energy: conservation of, 249; grief and, 242; positive, 26
engagement, 30, 289–90; as flow, 28–29
enjoyment, of writing life, 83
Enos, Theresa, *The Promise and Perils of Writing Program Administration*, 27
equity, 53, 78, 93–94(table), 292, 296; NCFDD on, 86–88
ethical responsibility, 256
etiquette, and performative behavior, 206, 207–8

"Evaluating the Intellectual Work of Writing Administration" (CWPA), 110
evaluation, faculty, 20–21, 48
Evans, David R., 180
exclusion, racial and gender, 200–201
exercise, 281, 282(n3)
expectations, 317; lowering, 246–47; readjusting/reframing, 237–38, 314; after tragedies, 157, 242–43

faculty, 10, 45, 46, 48, 78, 80, 87, 155, 189; development, 76–77; emotion expression, 181–82; evaluation/assessment by, 20–21; mindfulness, 262–63; narratives of, 53, 291; power of, 49–50; productivity, 84–86; redefining work, 85, 88; at religiously affiliated institutions, 182–85; reporting and referral training, 187–88; responses to disaster, 151–53; and student codes of conduct, 185–87; student help-seeking and, 179–81; success, 75–76; support of, 295–96; workloads, 270–71
Faculty Fellows program, 84
faculty of color, negotiation by, 208–9
faith-centered work, 190
Family Educational Rights and Privacy Act, 182
family members, as coping mechanisms, 190
fatigue, surface acting and, 122
Fedukovich, Casie, 85
feeling rules, 170; in writing centers, 164–65
feelings, 228, 253, 266, 315. *See also* emotions
femininity, 96
feminism, and political resistance, 115
feminist methodology, in interviews, 62–63
first-year composition (FYC), 12, 23; sexual assault issues, 117–18; students, 177, 179–81
Flaherty, Colleen, 270
flourishing, 19, 289
flow, engagement on, 28–29
Flynn, Elizabeth A., 262
forgiveness, 231–32
Four Quartets (Eliot), 221
"Frameworks for Failure" (Gross and Alexander), 34
Frank, Adam, 8
Frederickson, Barbara, 33
friends, and coping mechanisms, 190–91
fundamentalist Christians, 180

Gall, Terry L., 180
Garcia de Mueller, Genevieve, 197
Garfield, Charles, 50
Gates Foundation, Bill and Melinda Gates, Achieving the Dream, 38
gay, gays, gayness, 13; anger, 232–33, 311–12; internalized shame, 218–19; mistreatment and discrimination, 216–17; needs of self and others, 226–28; personal lives, 221–22; professional achievement, 219–20; realistic anger, 224–26; self-control, 222–23; self-critiques, 228–29. *See also* LGBTQIA+; queers, queerness
Geertz, Clifford, 63
Geller, Anne Ellen, 65, 67
gender, 201; double standards, 255–56; marginalization, 203–5
gender bias, 200–201
gender confirmation surgery, 22
Genuchi, Matthew, 270
George, Diana, 215, 216; *Kitchen Cooks, Plate Twirlers, and Troubadours,* 7
Gillam, Alice, 185
Glomb, Theresa M., 181
goals, recalibration of, 247–48
"Going Postal: Pedagogic Violence and the Schooling of Emotion" (Worsham), 8
Goleman, Daniel, 258
grading, contract vs. weighted, 59
graduate instructors, training, 30. *See also* tutors
Grandey, Alicia A., 22
Gratitude Letter, 28
Graziano, William G., 180
Gremore, Grahame, on bullies, 230–31
grief, grieving, 10, 13, 313, 242; after deaths, 237, 238, 239; self-care in, 240–41; theories of, 243–44; in workplace, 244–45, 249–50
Gross, Daniel M., "Frameworks for Failure," 34
growth, departmental, 46–47
Grutsch McKinney, Jackie, 21, 57, 58, 59, 65, 162, 163, 164, 168, 173–74, 184, 238, 242, 243, 244, 247; on identity, 61–62; on writing center models, 67–68
guilt, 165, 225
Guy, Mary E., 45, 136, 140, 141; "Emotional Labor," 6–7

habits of inattention, 267–68
habits of mind, 291–92
Hall, Donald, 97, 109
Hall, Megan, 85

Hanh, Thich Naht, 263
happiness, 35, 223, 272; academic, 20–21; as decision, 230, 312
happiness scripts, 276; and workload, 277–78; WPA, 271–73, 274
Harley, on student support, 153–54
Harris, Dan, 257, 263
Harris-Moore, Deborah, 131–32, 147, 153
Hawisher, Gail, 62
Hazen, Mary Anne, on grief in workplace, 244, 245
healing process: after deaths, 240–41; writing as, 130, 138
health, 22, 79, 93(table), 282(n4); physical and mental, 280–81, 317
health services, conduct code reporting, 187
helpfulness, channeling anger, 221–22
help-seeking, student, 179–81
Henry, Sue Ellen, 149
Hertog, James, 51
Hesse, Douglas: "What Is a Personal Life?," 277; "The WPA as Father, Husband, Ex," 277
higher education, xiii, 48–49
high school students, university open houses, 254–55
Hindt, Lance, 230–31
Hochschild, Arlie Russell, 22, 163; *The Managed Heart: Commercialization of Human Feeling*, 6, 161–62; on management of emotions, 253, 254
Holt, Mara, 21, 98, 136, 184
Horner, Bruce, 41
humanity, 25
Humphrey, Ronald H., 172
Hurricane Katrina, 130, 131; responses to, 147, 149–50
Hurricane Sandy, 12–13; impacts of, 147–48; responses to, 145–46, 151–52, 158; shared impacts of, 148–49

identity, identities, 57, 59, 166; bad WPA, 278–82; internalized shame, 218–19; professional, 10, 71, 201, 291; TYC instructors, 37–38; work, 11–12; writing center directors, 56, 60–61
illness, 107
Imafuji, Elizabeth, on integrity, 209
inattention, inscribed habits of, 267–68
inclusion, inclusiveness: of people of color, 212–13; in writing centers, 170–71
independent writing program, 63; status in, 64–65
individuals, personal responsibility, 264–65

institutional positionality, 201
institutions: changes in, 291; goals of, 245–46; hierarchies of, 26–27; histories of, 71; political relationships, 275–76
instructor, 253; empowerment of, 153–54; disaster responses, 145–46, 151–52, 156–57, 303–4
integration, 211
integrity, 212, 309; professional systems of, 209–10
intellectual labor, 253
International Writing Centers Association membership, 65
intervention(s), 89–90, 156
interviews, 72; on emotional labor of becoming, 58–62, 293–94; emotional, 56–57; feminist methodology, 62–63; on Hurricane Sandy impacts, 148–49; job, 97; self-reflective, 71
investigation, in RAIN process, 267
invisibility, institutional, 168
Isaacs, Emily, 65
isolation: of people of color, 211; of WPAs, 205–6
Ivtzan, Itai, 34
Ivy League, 57, 64

Jackson, Rebecca, 21, 57, 58, 65, 163, 164, 168, 238, 242, 243, 244, 247; on emotional labor, 59–60, 173–74, 184; WCD identity, 61–62
Jacobs, Dale, *A Way to Move*, 8, 147
Jaggar, Alison M., 82
Janangelo, Joseph, 38, 166, 204
job market, 9, 97
Johnson, Kristine, 189
Johnson, Sara Z., 42
journaling, 106–7, 280, 317
judgment, and compassionate listening, 266–67
junior faculty, power of, 50. *See also* contingent faculty; tutors
justice. *See* social justice work

Kabat-Zinn, Jon, 257, 260, 263
Kanan, Linda M., 137
Keeling, Richard P., 181
Kerr, Tom, 98, 104
Kirsch, Gesa, 63
Kitchen Cooks, Plate Twirlers, and Troubadours (George), 7
Kjesrud, Roberta D., 163, 174
Klausman, Jeffrey, 38, 52
Knight, Melinda, 65
knowledge, 24, 62, 256
Kynard, Carmen, 201, 204

labor, structural, 296
Langdon, Lance, *Composition Forum* 2016, 9
Langstraat, Lisa, 82
language barriers, 44
Las Vegas strip shooting, 12; UNLV response to, 129, 134–35, 137
leadership, 87, 229; as gay WPA, 221–23; listening and translating in, 47–51; vulnerability in, 223–24
learning: from anger, 229–30; problems in, 181; resistance to, 149
legacy, 247, 248–49, 314
Leverenz, Carrie Shivley, 247
LGBTQIA+ community, happiness scripts, 273. *See also* gays; queers, queerness
Lipson, Sarah Ketchen, 179
listening: compassionate, 266–67; as leadership, 47–51
literacy laborers, 37
lockdowns, 134
Loewe, Drew M., *Bad Ideas about Writing*, 9
Lomas, Tim, 34
Losada, Marcial, 33
Lu, Min-Zhan, 41
Lumina Foundation grants, 38
Lutz, Catherine, 122
Lynch, Peter, 229–30

Maddow, Rachel, on child refugees, 3–4
Mahoney, Kevin T., 181
Maid, Barry M., 276
Mainah, Fredah, on racial and gender bias, 200–201
Managed Heart: Commercialization of Human Feeling, The (Hochschild), 6, 161–62
management discourse, 48–49
marginalization, of people of color, 203–5
Martinez, Aja Y., 199
Massumi, Brian, 7
Mastracci, Sharon H., 45, 136, 140, 141; "Emotional Labor," 6–7
maternal health, 187
maternity leave, 191
McClelland, Ben W., 276
McLeod, Douglas, 51
meaning, 31–32, 290
mediation, 47, 257–58
meditation, 126–27, 190, 256, 263, 264, 268(n3), 316
meetings, 270, 272–73
memorial services, 243
memory, memories, 221; maintaining, 241–42
men, emotional expression, 99
mental health, 229, 281, 317, 140; student help-seeking, 179, 180, 181

mentoring, 101, 110, 184, 255–56, 262, 272
"Mentoring WPAs for the Long Term: The Promise of Mindfulness" (Moore), 10
messaging, institutional, 90
metalabor, 60
#MeToo movement, 116
Micciche, Laura, 7, 23, 27, 34, 71, 164, 238, 249, 252, 266; *Doing Emotion*, 8–9, 105, 147; *A Way to Move*, 8, 147
micro/macro-aggressions, 220
mid-career slump, 96–97
Miller, Richard, 26, 147
Miller-Cochran, Susan, 42
mindfulness, xiv, 13, 173, 252, 253, 256, 268, 315–16; attention, 263–64; emotional choices, 259–60; in interacting with faculty, 262–63; meditation, 257–58; in program changes, 260–61; RAIN practice, 266–67; responding with, 258–59; workload and, 265–66
minorities, and authority, 208
mistreatment, 226, 228; of gays, 216–17
Monday Motivator emails, 80, 89; on commitment to writing, 87–88; theory of affect in, 82–83; on work-life balance, 84–85
Moore, Cindy, "Mentoring WPAs for the Long Term," 10
mourning, 37, 238; clothes, 117, 118, 127(n2)
Muckerheide, Ryan, 9/11 responses, 130–31
multiculturalism, 49
Murphy, Christina, *Writing Center Director's Resource Book*, 239
Murphy, Patricia, 9/11 responses, 130–31
Myers-Breslin, Linda, *Administrative Problem-Solving for Writing Program and Writing Centers*, 275–76

narcissism, 233, 311
narratives, 68, 153, 199–200, 291
National Center for Faculty Development and Diversity (NCFDD), 12, 244; on academic success, 92 (table); communications, 78, 80–81; equity project, 86–88; faculty development, 76–77; on faculty productivity, 84–86; on faculty success, 75–76; on intervention, 89–90; on resistance to writing, 83–84; rhetorical moves, 92–94(table); self-help discourse, 79, 81–82; theory of affect in, 82–83; and WPA priorities, 91–92, 295–96
National Council of Teachers of English (NCTE), 210, 212

National Survey of Student Engagement, 110
NCFDD. *See* National Center for Faculty Development and Diversity
negativity, 28; memory and, 221
negotiation, 53, 60, 291; conflict, 69–70, 253; of emotional labor, 64, 198, 200; by people of color, 208–9
neo-liberalism, 49; on work-life balance, 270, 278
networking, networks, 211, 309, 313; mentoring, 255–56
neuroscience, meditation, 257–58
Newfield, Christopher, 49
new knowledge, 115
Newman, Meredith A., 45, 136, 140, 141; "Emotional Labor," 6–7
Newton, Connecticut school shooting, 137
New York City, disasters in, 12, 145–46, 150
Nicklay, Jennifer, 165
noblesse, in leadership, 223–24
Noddings, Nel, 22
Nolan, David, 270
non-identification, in RAIN process, 267
North, Stephen M., 165
Nova Network of Victim Assistance, 299

O'Brien, Tim, *The Things They Carried,* 5
Office of Human Resources, 232
open houses, university, 254–55
oppression, institutionalized, 198, 200
organizations, design and governance of, 212
outcomes: aligning, 109–11; identifying, 108–9
outcomes assessment, 47
overwork, 46; WPAs, 271, 278

Palmeri, Jason, 8
Palmieri, Jennifer, 96, 111, 234(n3)
pandemic, xiv, xv
Papp, James, 48–49
pedagogic violence, 8
peer review groups, safety of, 118–19
peer writing tutors, 164; emotional accommodation, 171–72; emotional work, 166–67; professional development, 168–69; psychological well-being, 165–66
people of color, xv, 273; marginalization of, 203–4; negotiation by, 208–9; self-care, 211–12; underrepresentation, 197–98
performance, 206, 219, 220, 249, 254
Perkins, Vernita, on racial and gender bias, 200–201
Perryman-Clark, Staci, 197

persistence, 32
personal life: of gay professionals, 221–22; WPA workload and, 276–77, 280
Phillips, Talinn, 10
physical health, 280–81, 282(n3), 317
Piercy, Marge, "To Be of Use," 97
place, in emotional geography, 267
planning, short- and long-term, 246
politeness, as writing center standard, 170–71
political correctness, 49
politics, institutional, 9, 275–76
positions: negotiating, 53; non-tenure and tenure track, 65–67
positive emotions, 264
positive psychology, 19, 21–22, 33–35, 289–90
Post-Tenure Pathways series, 80
post-traumatic stress disorder, 130
power, 5, 234(n5); departmental, 276; personal and institutional, 151; senior and junior faculty, 49–50, 155
prayer groups, 190
predominantly white institutions (PWI), 90, 199
pregnancies, 22; at church-affiliated schools, 177–78, 185–86, 191
prestige, professional, 220
preventive strategies, 133, 140, 301–2
private colleges, student help-seeking, 179–81
privilege, 20, 90; white, 223, 225; workplace grieving and, 248–49
problem solving, 26, 34, 101
productivity, 169, 219, 242, 295; and well-being, 84–86
professional achievement, shining in, 219–21
professional development, 202, 295–96, 308; tutors, 168–70
programmatic crisis responders, 132
projects, prioritizing, 313
Promise and Perils of Writing Program Administration, The (Enos and Borrowman), 27
psychological resources, 172–73
PTSD, 135
public education, de-funding, 49
public service, 7
pursuit of happiness, 20
PWIs. *See* predominantly white institutions

Quakerism, 257
Quality Matters, 47
"Queer Performativity: Warhol's Shyness/Warhol's Whiteness" (Sedgwick), 218

queers, queerness, 234(n3); workplace shaming, 217–18

race: marginalization, 203–5; scholarship on, 197–98; and uncompensated labor, 202–3
racial bias, 200–201
racism, xiv–xv, 5; systemic/structural, 198, 204
RAINN, 127(n3), 299
RAIN practice, 266–67, 316
Rand, Erin, 8
Rand, Lizabeth A., 189
rape, 120. *See also* sexual assaults
reading groups, community, 190
reading instructors, 41
reality, constructing, 51
Redmond, Deidre L., 208
reflection, reflective processes, 102, 308; in administrative work, 106–7
registrars, and class changes, 119
Reid, E. Shelley, 156, 249, 252
relational work, 60–61, 261
relationships, 26, 85, 211, 290; building and maintaining, 109–10, 184; managing, 21, 30–31; outside work, 281, 317
religious beliefs: faculty and, 188–89; and student writings, 183–84
religiously affiliated institutions, 13, 186, 308; mission/orientation at, 189–90; statement of faith, 182–83; student conduct code, 177–79, 184–85, 307; student help-seeking, 179–81; writing programs at, 188–89
remembrance, 241–42
representation, of people of color, 197–98
research, vs. administration, 20–21
resilience, 19–20, 262, 306
resistance, 115, 255; dancing with, 77, 78; to writing, 83–84
responses: to disasters, 149–50, 303–4; to hurricanes, after, 145–47, 151–52, 158; mindful, 258–59; to sexual assault, 10, 12, 117–21; to shootings, 134–35, 137; to trauma, 10, 125–26, 129–31
responsibilities, 19, 97, 154; personal, 264–65
responsibility models, 40
responsiveness, ongoing, 262
reward systems, toxic, 225
Rhetorical Healing (Carey), 81
Ringer, Jeffrey M., 189
risk: professional, 104; and visibility, 228
Ritter, Kelly, 8, 216
Rockquemore, Kerry Ann, 75, 90, 244; Monday Motivators, 83, 84–85, 89

Rodrigo, Rochelle, 42
Roen, Duane H., 204; 9/11 response, 130–31
Roozen, Kevin, 61
Rose, Shirley K., "Twenty More Years in the WPA's Progress," 100–101
Rossen, Eric, 133
Rouzie, Albert, 21, 98, 136, 184
Royster, Jacqueline Jones, 63
Ruiz, Iris, 197

saboteurs, critical observation of, 225–26
safe spaces, 130, 243; classroom as, 118–19; compassionate listening, 266–67
safety, 132, 135, 142; sexual assault issues and, 118–19
Saldana, Johnny, 81
Salter, Anastasia, 270
sanctions, student codes of conduct, 178
satisfaction, personal and professional, 108–9
Saur, Elizabeth, 8
scholars, marginalized, 87
scholarship, 53, 168, 292; productivity, 79; on race, 197–98
school shootings, 130, 131, 137
Schuster, John, 221, 227
Second Wave Positive Psychology, 34
secret keepers, gays as, 222–23
Sedgwick, Eve Kosofsky, 8; "Queer Performativity," 218
Seeber, Barbara K., 246, 266
self, 12, 98; needs of, 226–28
self-actualization, 254
self-advocacy, 80; NCFDD recommendations for, 82–84
self-alienation, 254
self-atonement, white privilege and, 223
self-care, 140, 172–73, 190, 211–12, 240, 252, 262, 296, 307, 313; politics of, 86–87; as warfare, 265–66
self-compassion, 257
self-confidence, 218
self-consciousness, 218
self-control, 222–23
self-critiques, 228–29
self-discipline, 32
Selfe, Cynthia, 62
self-help, NCFDD discourse, 79, 81–82, 89
self-isolation, in grieving, 244
self-regulation, 87, 261
self-scrutiny, 227–28
Seligman, Martin E.P., 19, 28, 289; achievement, 32–33; on signature strengths, 24–25
senior faculty, power, 50

sensitivity, 71
September 11, 2001 (9/11) terrorist attacks, 8; responses to, 130–31, 147, 150
service with a smile, 254–55
service work, 241, 308
sexual assaults, 5, 182; emotional responses to, 121–22; prevention and reporting, 123–25; reporting, 115–17, 299–300; reports and response, 12, 126; responses to, 10, 117–21
sexual consent, 123–24
shaming, shame, 88, 221, 228, 232, 233(n1); internalized, 218–19; workplace, 216–18
Shanti Project, 50
Shapiro, Shauna L., 259
shining, professional achievement, 219–21
shootings, 5, 10, 147; campus, 130, 131, 137; Las Vegas strip, 12, 129, 134–35
Shovlin, Paul, 10
Siegel, Daniel J., 261
signature strengths, identifying and deploying, 24–25
slow agency, 238, 266
Smart, Juanita M., 183, 184
social factors, in emotion, 161, 171
social goods, and happiness, 20
socialization, 34, 252
social justice work: emotional accommodation, 171–72; in writing centers, 170–71, 295
social norms, 20
social stratification, 89
social support systems, 180, 281
social workers, 136, 137
Sotirin, Patricia, 262
spiritual issues, 180
staff, 65, 248; crisis training, 139–40. *See also* faculty; instructors; tutors
stakeholders, in crisis response, 133
statement of faith, as faculty requirement, 182–83
status, 99; writing center/writing program, 64–67
Stay, Byron, *Writing Center Director's Resource Book*, 239
Stenberg, Shari J., 43, 115, 122
Stephens, Patricia, 152
stereotypes: gay male, 220, 224, 229; performative behavior, 206–7
Stewart, Kathleen, 148
stoicism, 240
Stolley, Amy Ferdinandt, 71, 167, 228
stories, storytelling, 5, 51–52, 215–16, 291

strengths, signature, 24–26
stress/anxiety, peer tutors, 165–66
Strickland, Donna, 45
student conduct code, 189; faculty responsibilities, 185–87; faculty training, 187–88; at religiously affiliated schools, 178–79, 183, 307
Student Life Department, and code of conduct, 178, 183, 187
students, 13, 23, 30, 108, 110, 122, 127(n4), 130, 131, 138, 169, 170, 177, 263, 307; adjustments to disaster, 153–54; codes of conduct, 185–87; help-seeking for, 179–81; impacts of trauma on, 124, 125–26; multilingual, 41–42; open houses, 254–55; and peer tutors, 165–66; religious beliefs, 183–84; responses to disaster, 149–50; safety of, 118–19; sexual assault cases, 116–17, 119–20
success: academic, 79, 92(table); faculty, 75–76; WPA priorities for, 91–94
suicide, reactions to, 239–40
Sullivan, Steve, 180
support, 309, 313; in sexual assault cases, 116–17
surface acting, 22, 122
surgery, 22
surveillance, behavioral, 206
surveys, 213; African American WPAs, 198, 199; on WPA emotional labor, 100–101, 102–3
survival, focus on, 24
Sylvia, disaster response, 151

Taggart, Amy Rupiper, 10
teachers, 126, 131, 139, 153, 156, 255; class changes, 119–21; disaster response, 146, 149–50
teaching, 13, 21, 107, 110, 138, 156; on-line, xiii–xiv; philosophy, 102–3
Tea Consent (Clean), use of, 123–25, 127(n6)
temperance, 25
tenure, 80, 105–6; and administrative work, 20–21, 22
tenure-track, 86, 87
Tetreault, Molly, 66, 67
Tews, Michael J., 181
therapeutic interventions, 19
therapy, 190–91
Things They Carried, The (O'Brien), 5
Three Blessings Exercise, 28
time, 290, 296; management, 266, 278, 317
time tracking, 279, 297, 317

328   INDEX

Title IX, and sexual assault cases, 117, 127(n5), 182, 185, 186
Titus, Megan, 10
Toggl, 279
tragedies, 285; expectations after, 157, 242–43
training, 9, 30, 156, 186, 305; in reporting and referring, 187–88; staff, 139–40
transcendence, 25
translation, in academic leadership, 47–48
translingual theories, 41
trauma, traumatic events, 5, 79, 117; responses to, 10, 124, 125–26, 129–31, 137
Trauma-Informed Practices for Postsecondary Education (Davidson), 125–26
triage training, xiii–xiv
Trougakos, John P., 122
Trump administration, 3
trust, 184, 222–23
Tulshyan, Ruchika, 206
tutors, 306; emotional accommodation, 171–72; feeling rules, 164–65; inclusiveness, 170–71; professional development, 168–70; psychological well-being, 165–66; self-care, 172–73
"Twenty More Years in the WPA's Progress" (Charlton and Rose), 100–101
two-year institutions (TYCs), 52, 291–92; change at, 43–47; creation and evolution at, 11–12; instructor identity, 37–38; WPA positions at, 39, 40–43
"TYCA Guidelines for Preparing Teachers of English in the Two-Year College," 42

Uhlmann, Eric Luis, 99
underpromising, 313
underrepresentation, people of color, 197–98
understanding, emotional, 260
universities, 89; student help-seeking, 179–81

victims, sexual assault, 118–21, 127(n4)
violence, 8, 135, 137
visibility, 228; of emotional labor, 173, 305–6
vulnerability, 43, 219, 223, 223, 234(n5); change in, 52–53

Walcher, Sheldon, 204
Warhol, Andy, 218
Way to Move: Rhetorics of Emotion and Composition Studies, A (Jacobs and Micciche), 8, 147

WCAs. *See* writing center administrators
WCDs. *See* writing center directors
WCenter Listserv, 163–64, 168, 170, 239, 244
Weiss, Howard M., 122
well-being, 79, 93(table), 132, 266; and personal responsibility, 264–65; and productivity, 84–85; psychological, 165–66
Wesselmann, Eric D., 180
"What Is a Personal Life?" (Hesse), 277
White, Geoffrey M., 81
white privilege, 223, 225
Williams, Wendy, 229
Winfrey, Oprah, 257
Wingfield, Adia, 201, 206
Wislocki, Mary A., 163, 174
women, 34, 255, 273; performative behavior, 206–8
Worden, William, on grief, 243
work, 27, 252, 318; administrative habits, 251; and identity, 11–12; meaningful, 31–32
working conditions, 108–9; contingent faculty, 154–55
work-life balance, xiv, 4–5, 19, 79, 252, 276–77, 278; NCFDD on, 84–85, 93(table)
workloads, 317; changing, 243–44; faculty, 270–71; and happiness scripts, 277–78; managing, 313–14; mindfulness and, 265–66; WPA, 272, 275
workplace, 223; emotion in, 98–99; emotional expression in, 181–82, 240, 255–56; grief in, 244–45, 248–49; managing emotions in, 253–54; shaming in, 216–18
Worsham, Lynn, 121, 122; on crisis response, 129–30; "Going Postal," 8
"WPA as Father, Husband, Ex, The" (Hesse), 277
"WPA Outcomes Statement," 38
WPAs. *See* writing program administrators
writing, 9, 85, 130, 138, 190, 210, 263, 265, 304; commitment to, 87–88; religious dogma in, 183–84; resistance to, 83–84
writing center administrators (WCAs), 167–68; as informal community of, 163–64
writing center directors (WCDs), 5, 56, 72; interviews, 60–61; Ivy League, 57–58, 65
Writing Center Director's Resource Book (Murphy and Stay), 239
writing centers (WCs), 10, 56, 65, 285; at Cornell, 68–69; as cozy homes, 67–68; emotional accommodation, 171–72;

emotional labor, 167–68, 305–6; feeling rules, 164–65; inclusiveness, 170–71
writing program administrators (WPAs), 132, 238, 249, 271, 275; bad identity, 278–82, 317–18; and emotional labor, 101–2; emotional expression, 254–56; emotional labor surveys, 100–101; happiness scripts, 272–73, 274; and institutional missions, 189–90; isolation of, 205–6; priorities for success, 91–94

writing programs, 203; changes in, 260–61; crisis plans, 139–40; at religiously affiliated institutions, 188–89
writing studies, 253, 264; on race, 197–98
Writing Walk-In Services, 58, 72

yoga, 257

Zembylas, Michalinos, 40
Ziker, John, 270
Zoom, xiv

www.ingramcontent.com/pod-product-compliance
Lightning Source LLC
Chambersburg PA
CBHW060513080526
44586CB00012B/470